The Invention of Private Life

D1478403

for Anita and Purnendu
with my very best wishes
— Sudipta

The Invention of Private Life

Literature and Ideas

SUDIPTA KAVIRAJ

COLUMBIA UNIVERSITY PRESS

NEW YORK

Columbia University Press
Publishers Since 1893
New York Chichester, West Sussex
cup.columbia.edu
Copyright © 2015 Sudipta Kaviraj

Published simultaneously in India with Permanent Black

ISBN 978-0-231-17438-1 (cloth : alk. paper)
ISBN 978-0-231-17439-8 (pbk: alk. paper)
ISBN 978-0-231-53954-8 (e-book)

Library of Congress Control Number : 2014956816

Columbia University Press books are printed on permanent
and durable acid-free paper.
This book is printed on paper with recycled content.
Printed in United States

c 10 9 8 7 6 5 4 3 2 1
p 10 9 8 7 6 5 4 3 2 1

Cover design and art by Anuradha Roy
Illustration inspired by a drawing by Jamini Roy

References to websites (URLs) were accurate at the time of writing.
Neither the author nor Columbia University Press is responsible for URLs
that may have expired or changed since the manuscript was prepared.

for
SHASHWATI

Contents

The Invention of Private Life

Introduction

Literature as the Mirror of Modernity

The essays collected in this volume analyse literature but their concerns lie at the intersection of three different academic disciplines: the study of literature, social theory, and intellectual history. Literary criticism approaches literature primarily from the point of view of its internal aesthetic values; sociology of literature, on the other hand, seeks to understand the relation between literature and society. Some approaches to literary texts tend to reduce them to history, or historical raw material. It is interesting to see that this particular form of reduction—of literature to history—is not only a problem in modern culture. Dhananjaya, the author of *Dasarupaka*, a major text on literary and dramatic theory in medieval India, remarked in his invitation to literary texts:

Ānandaniṣyandiṣu rūpakeṣu vyutpattimātraṃ phalam alpabuddhiḥ |
Yo 'pītihāsādivad āha sādhus tasmai namaḥ svādaparāṅmukhāya ||1.6||

[those who have only an elementary proficiency in understanding literary representations, and consequently have a rather limited comprehension of this field, those who maintain that literature is like history, I bow to them too, who are averse to the pleasure-secreting qualities of literary texts]

In a sense, Dhananjaya could be accused of a philosophical indiscretion. It is possible to claim that the only valid response to literature is a deferential silence. Literature is to be enjoyed, not taken apart by analysis. A possible defence of literary analysis in the face of this criticism would be that analysis is itself enjoyment of a different variety which does not interfere with the process of enjoying literature; and since great literature also helps us think about its own worlds in

interesting and unprecedented ways, it is important to reflect on the
way the text sees the world, and, as far as possible, the way the world
saw the text. Particularly because I am not a scholar of literature, I
should explain what draws me into it, and what I was trying to do
when I wrote these essays.

I have an interest in two fields of study—modern Bengali literature,
and social and political theory. Initially, I believed these two fields of
intellectual curiosity were entirely separate and had nothing to do
with each other: that their co-presence in my mind was simply an
accident of taste, that it just so happened I had an intellectual liking
for literature and political theory. For a long time in my academic life,
I did not try to bring these two interests together. Then, two things
broke this wall of separation decisively. I started to ask a question
about the global nature—or if you like, claims—of Western political
theory. This was not an illegitimate question in view of the amount
of intellectual effort we had invested studying and trying to master
it in our education. It is not irrelevant to ask what, if anything, the
entire tradition of Western social theory is trying to achieve. It is of
course true that social and political theory is a vast field of unusual
diversity and creativity in Western thought, and it might be hard to
find a single identifiable purpose in this body of thought. Yet it is not
implausible to ask such a question.

From this point of view, what we call Western political theory
appears to be a kind of self-reflection of European modernity. This
is the primary form in which European modern societies asked the
central questions about the deep historical change that was affecting
them since the time of the renaissance. Modern social theorists in
the West collectively invented a form of reflection on their own fast-
moving history which sought to understand the 'meaning' of historical
change. Though the idea of a 'meaning in history' is often derided by
philosophers pursuing strong ideals of conceptual clarity, the basic
sense of this phrase is not hard to grasp: it refers to the direction of
historical processes, detection of patterns, and evaluative judgements
on events and processes that constitute historical change.

Underlying this vast field of enquiry is the implied sense that
modernity is a historical stage of deeply paradoxical quality. It intensifies
the impulse towards clarification, understanding, even transparency
of history—on the grounds that the historical field is increasingly

marked by vast attempts at collective, concerted action, revolutions, movements, the creation and destruction of states, and the deliberate transformation of economic and social structures. The demand for transparency is linked to the idea and ideal of self-consciousness: the idea that since human beings collectively and individually undertake such actions, they should be clear about their purposes, if not their consequences. But many modern Western thinkers also suggest that the question of 'transparency' in history has to be complex, as there are forces and patterns in modernity which make this history unusually cognitively untransparent. Although thinkers like Hegel, Adam Smith, Marx, and others advanced similar intuitions, I would like to illustrate this by taking a theme from de Tocqueville.

In the last chapter of *Democracy in America*, after his magisterial survey of the history of democracy in the West, de Tocqueville evinces a paradoxical sense of cognitive bafflement: 'I go back from age to age up to the remotest antiquity; but I find no parallel to what is occurring before my eyes: as the past has ceased to throw its light upon the future, the mind of man wanders in obscurity.'[1] I do not think the phrase, 'the past has ceased to throw light upon the future', is mere rhetoric: it seems to gesture towards a deeper obscurity at the heart of the making of modern history. Modernity is a stage of history in which, as Marx noted in another famously Shakespearian rhetorical phrase, 'all that is solid melts into air'. There is a shared sense in all these writers that the time we call modernity produces social structures of an unprecedented, paradoxical kind. Such structures possess all the Durkheimian qualities of imposing constraints upon actions, but they also undergo frequent restructuring—not because modern society is replaced by another form, but because the self-transformation of structures is in the nature of modernity itself. Modernity is cognitively intractable in a special sense, because of this reason. Social theory is the cognitive pursuit of this elusive fugitive structure of the present.

If this is true of European modernity and social theory, it raises an interesting question for Indian history. If modernity was cognitively challenging to Western intellectuals, it must have been equally baffling for their Indian counterparts, because Indian modernity is inextricably linked to European colonialism. As the changes associated

---

[1] de Tocqueville 2000: vol. II, book 4, ch. VIII: 331.

with modernity are introduced, at least partially, by external power, it must have constituted a more intractable cognitive problem for Indian intellectuals. Where does the serious reflection on modernity's predicaments and bafflements lie?

Much of the serious reflection on the surprise of modernity, I came to realize, is contained in literature. Modernity introduced new literary forms to Indian creative writers—such as the novel and the autobiography; but literature also served as the great field of reflection on the nature of modernity, and its cognitive and ethical exploration. It is in Indian literature that much of the interrogation of modernity happens. It is not surprising therefore that some of the questions that were central to modern European social theory also constituted significant themes in Indian literary reflection. What was the nature of the self— did modernity alter this nature? What was the character of power under conditions of modern history? How is the power of the modern state felt by individuals? How does the modern political movement, so central to politics in modern times, affect the nature of the personality of a sensitive individual who responds to a revolutionary call? Is love possible between intensely self-conscious individuals? Is even something as fundamental and universal as love itself redefined? How do individuals cope with the transience of affections, the fragility of social ties?

Questions like these are not secondary to modern Indian literature: they are woven into its primary reflective fabric. The essays in this collection are primarily concerned with questions of this kind: they are not conventional literary questions, but I believe they are central to the modern Indian literary tradition. These essays view modern Indian literature as a primary field of theoretical-philosophic reflection on the nature of modern times, and particularly the experiential interior of it. Literature is so essential for the understanding of modernity precisely because it deals with experience. History, or standard social theory, explores these themes from the outside, as it were, through large aggregate processes; literary works explore them from the inside. They do not merely try to show what happens in history, they also try to capture how it feels to live when modern history happens. Accordingly, these essays are situated at the boundary of literature and social theory: they ask questions, taken from social theory, of literary texts.

There is a second way in which literature bears a crucial connection to the modern. It is generally acknowledged that the autobiography, along with the novel, is one of the major genres of modern literature. Biography is not modern, autobiography is. Biography is based on a radical separation between character and author. Premodern literature is full of biographies of the most varied forms—biographies of saints, of warriors, of heroes of action, contemplation, renunciation. Autobiography is by comparison unheroic, though there is always an underlying temptation towards a surreptitious exaggeration in narratives of the self. But autobiography, particularly the early modern versions of it like the one by Sibnath Sastri (analysed in one of these essays), serves an essential function in the ethical persuasion in favour of modernity. Sastri's autobiography is centred on two relations of intimacy—with his two wives, and with his father. Sastri's father should be taken as a figure, not an individual. The characteristics to be found in him are not the entirely contingent, accidental features of a Sanskrit scholar with a high premodern education: he constitutes a type, a figure that can stand in for a whole generation of premodern intellectuals troubled by a world being restructured with baffling rapidity and finality in which they are both inhabitants and outcasts.

The exchange between Sastri and his father captures a central theme of intellectual life in the early modern period. His father evidently regarded the Brahmo ideas his son absorbed in Calcutta as a monstrous and degrading fashion, something which ought to be historically transient but is not. To his father, Brahmo ideas are alien suggestions, external to his embedded ethics, and should seem abhorrent to a highly educated Brahmin youth of good character. When Sibnath refuses to renounce his modernist ideas about family and social life, his father rejects him completely, refusing to speak to him for the rest of his life, till the last tragic, emotionally wrenching reunion before his death. This rupture of intimacy signals a central moral conflict of the early modern epoch, a fascinating spectacle of a battle of ethicality between two cultures, the premodern and the modern. To play on Sheldon Pollock's wonderfully evocative phrase, it shows the final end of the 'ends of man' at the end of premodernity, a process by which a conceptual world of ethics, based on Hindu dharmic ideals of *chāturvarnya* and *purusārthas*, loses its moral adequacy for a new generation of intellectuals (like Sastri) placed electively between the two conceptual worlds. We do not grasp the dignity and the tragic quality of the confrontation if we do not understand that it is a battle of two ethical worlds. Sastri faces an immense challenge: he has to convince his father that his conduct is not driven by fashion, or, even worse, by the modern pursuit of unrestrained selfish inclination, but an opposite, equally demanding moral vision of the good life. What modernity offered were not fashionable, meretricious, ethically suspect ideas, but alternative ethical ideals. They demanded equal rectitude, an equally attentive cultivation of a moral personality, an even more elaborately self-critical reflexiveness. The deep tragedy of the encounter was that although the moderns saw the premoderns as following an ideal of moral life, though a degenerate and indefensible one, traditional persons rarely saw their sons following a moral ideal at all. The story of Sibnath Sastri's autobiography is so historically significant precisely because this morally excruciating tragic drama was played out in innumerable families' internal lives. It was the norm in those modernizing times, not the exception.

Although this collection contains only one reading of a single autobiographic text, the autobiographic form plays an indispensable role in the moral transformation towards modernity.

The essay titled 'Literature and the Moral Imaginations of Modernity' adds a supplement to this argument. Narratives of elective affection, celebrated in modern novels, perform a function complementary to that of the autobiography—in persuading individuals to own a modern life-ideal, and to live by its rules. Probably the most significant function of modern literature was a supplementary one to the ethical discourse of philosophic writings and autobiographic narratives. Autobiographic narratives too centred on solemn ethical questions: but gave them a narrative form. Ethical principles could be stated assertorically: like the injunction that an individual must always speak the truth, or that one should take decisions autonomously about one's own life. Philosophical writings provided compelling arguments in favour of such ethical principles. Autobiographic narratives brought an experiential dimension to ethical imperatives: these showed how real individuals tried to live by such ethical principles in real lives— the hardness of choices, the emotional sacrifices involved, and the satisfaction of successful ethical conduct. The narrative form helped readers understand the difficulties of leading an ethical life in the face of the surprising complexities that life throws in people's paths, and the nobility of this pursuit in a way that mere assertoric statements never could. That is why, although modern people knew the principles of autonomy, they avidly read stories about selves.

Still, it is hard to believe that the conversion of large numbers of people to the modern ideals of life could be driven only by abstract philosophical ideals, however high-minded. In other words, people did not decide that it would be a good idea to lead a modern life primarily by reading Kant or Mill, or autobiographies which showed the epic struggles of individuals with a surrounding oppressive society. Sanskrit literary theory suggests that statements can be classed in three categories: the tone of the master/*prabhusammita* (like a master), in which the sastras speak to us; the tone of the friend/*suhrdsammita* (like a friend), like the *puranas* or the *itihasas*; and the tone of enchantment/love/*kantasammita* (like a lover), a manner of utterance which convinces by charming us. All three impart what is considered knowledge, but by speaking in different tones, and to different effects. The charm of the literary, poetic voice persuades us to make principles our own: not by making us submit in awe, or by persuading us by good advice, but by charming us and finding a way to our heart, so that the decisions and desires become our own. This is the deepest way of persuasion. To put my argument in their terms, the literary work charms us into modernity—by placing fictive models in front of our imagination. People decide to act in modern ways because they think it is good to live like that; and some of the great impulse towards this emulation comes from literature: it happens through the combined effect of novelistic narration, lyric poetry's exploration and painting of emotions and interiority, and the introspective grandeur of the autobiographic story.

Novels, in particular, and their translation into moving pictures of emotional seduction produced the most powerful incentives for the moral persuasion of modernity. It is true that characters in the novels were fictions, phantasms in one sense, but these phantoms—like Gora, Devdas, Sucharita, Lavanya—had the most insidious ways of penetrating into the real lives of individuals, acting like shadow individuals who populated the world of readers, walking noiselessly with them, showing constantly how they could lead their lives. They produced a shadow world of romantic love which affected actual lives of intimacy in an immensely powerful fashion, providing to real people a powerful sentimental education, breaching the immovable authority of traditional conventions. These characters were impossible to invigilate, keep away, or police; they broke down the fortresses of orthodoxy by infiltrating the minds of young girls, and populating their minds with ineradicable dreams.

Literature and Re-enchantment

Also, it is quite evident, in reading modern Bengali literature, that one of its primary tasks was to repaint with colour a world which was bleached of beauty by excessive rationalism and the advance of disenchantment. By the language of his songs and poetry, Tagore seeks to re-enchant the world; others, like Sukumar Ray, try to do the same thing with humour, and Abanindranath Tagore with a narrative language which can paint the world with words. This particular aspect of the role of literature in modernity is not explored in the essays that follow.

In order to explore the complex ethical and historical associations of literary texts, these essays are, as I said, methodologically placed at the interesting and uncertain frontier of literary criticism, sociology of literature, and social theory. Despite my interest in answering historical and theoretical questions, I believe it is always essential to respect the integrity of literary texts when studying them, and never to reduce them entirely into an archive for historical enquiry. It is true that texts always tell us about the world, but this 'aboutness' is a complex matter; texts never tell us about their world simply and straightforwardly. Texts always have a way of seeing their worlds, and it is hopeless to try to extricate a picture of that world unaffected by that way of seeing. I have tried not to forget the literariness of my texts, and not to suppress a sense of textual pleasure in pursuing drier historical problems. Because, eventually, it is essential to remember what makes the literary text what it is: it is *niyatikṛtaniyamarahita*, it is *hladaikamayi*, it is *ananyaparatantra*, and it is above all *navarasarucira*. This is a world in which the laws instituted by nature are in suspension;

it consists solely of pleasure; it is unconditioned by anything else, such as history, and above all it is made resplendent by the nine rasas. Despite our attempts to bring it close to the mundane world of history, I still wish to follow the spirit of ancient criticism and want the poetic word to be victorious.

Niyatikrtaniyamarahitam hladaikamayim ananyaparatantram
Navarasaruciram nirmitiam adadhati bharati kaver jayati.

Precisely because it is outside my field of academic research, I have a more acute sense of the help I have received from many friends and teachers. I learnt to think about literature from my teachers at different stages—Amar Dutta, Gauriprasad Basu; and in Sanskrit poetry from Madhusudan Goswami. I benefited immensely from years of long conversations, often involving most instructive and enjoyable disagreements, with Asok Sen on modern Bengali literature, especially Tagore and the modern poets, and with Namvar Singh about Bengali, Sanskrit, and to a lesser extent Hindi poetry and criticism. I have always learnt from conversations on literary themes with Rajeev Bhargava and Sunil Khilnani, though I could not directly share Bengali texts with them. My greatest debt in the historical study of literature is to Sheldon Pollock. I thank him for his friendship and the intense vitality of his intellectual interaction. Participation in two of his projects, on Literary Cultures in History and on Sanskrit Knowledge Systems, were unusually intellectually stimulating and instructive. Presentations at these meetings gave me more clear and complex understanding of both methodological and substantive questions of literary studies. Conversation with colleagues who participated in those projects, and who read and kindly commented on my drafts, was intellectually invaluable. On Bengali literature, I have had greatly productive exchanges of ideas with Partha Chatterjee, Dipesh Chakrabarty, and Arindam Chakrabarti. I am indebted to Ranajit Guha, Pranab Bardhan, and Kalpana Bardhan for discussions that were always enjoyable and deeply instructive. I have learnt a great deal not only about Sanskrit and vernacular literature, but about literariness from Charles Hallisey and Lawrence McCrea.

Copyright over the essays reproduced herein vests with me. Some have been slightly revised for publication in the present collection. Whenever necessary, the first unnumbered footnote gives the source of first appearance.

References

de Tocqueville, Alexis. 2000. *Democracy in America*. Chicago: The University of Chicago Press.

1

On the Advantages of Being a Barbarian

Ideally, I would like to be taken as a Barbarian (in the Greek sense of a person whose language is unintelligible) but a cosmopolitan one. This is not simply being provocative. The first hope is that it will be seen that I have a different natural and conceptual language from my academic interlocutor, and a different cultural apparatus. However, the second hope qualifies the first. People like us should not, even for temptations of nationalism, exaggerate our difference with intellectuals of the West, since we are formed, in one very significant part of our intellectual deliberative life, precisely by intellectual influence from the West. We thus have much higher levels of ordinary curiosity than can be expected in any modern person in the spectacle of the West; we are formed and shaped by those influences, and by that history. But cosmopolitanism means at least two things: first the acceptance in advance of the possibility that your own culture can be inadequate, or fallible. Or, it may not have developed a particular skill of human creativity in a certain way. In that case, we should be easily prepared to draw upon the other cultures we know to give us a more satisfactory intellectual life. I try to emphasize these two things by teaching not merely Indian politics, but also Western political theory. Yet this cosmopolitanism is of a very complicated kind.

One of the most interesting features of intellectual inhabitancy in the modern world is that the West can be indifferent towards the rest of the world's cultures; but they can't similarly neglect the West. I wish to argue that this is grounded in the partly unfounded assumption of progress and Western superiority in everything, a strangely unsustainable intellectual stance. Though, equally strangely, it is held as a general framework of belief by an astonishingly large number of Western academics. This does not mean that, if asked, they would assent to this view; but their entirely comfortable ignorance about how the rest of the world thinks—though they primarily think about thinking—can be made intelligible only by this unstated, unreflective belief. I wish to argue further that this is considerably to our advantage, for the rather uncomplex reason that access to two cultures is, in some ways, better than one. Our presence as academics in the Western academy should, ideally, contribute to a dialogue. I think it is rash to be too hopeful about this in the short run: in the present state of the constitution of knowledge and the rewards that go to its various forms, it is likely that we will continue in the present state in which we know too much about the West, while the West knows too little about us.

My academic interest has been in three different areas: political theory, the study of the Indian state, and the study of Indian literary culture—apparently subjects without much connection. I have, however, felt over time that there are serious and subtle interconnections which actually drove me from one field to the next. I shall try to explain what each of these means to me, because in each case I think I have been forced to take an intellectual position which is rather different from the mainstream academic thinking on these subjects. I would therefore like to give a justification of how I see these subjects, and second, whether these have any seriously defensible connection except my purely adventitious liking for them.

The Present State of Knowledge about India— Orientalism and Political Correctness/The Composition of Internal and External Knowledge

My impression about Western knowledge about knowledge of India is that it has made immense strides in one respect at the cost of falling back strikingly in another. It does not have to be seriously argued now that a great part of the earlier forms of Western knowledges about India were Orientalist in Said's sense of the term. There were, that means, at least three things wrong about it. First, it was quite often cognitively misleading or absent-minded. Either it was so absorbed about its images about itself that it emphasized and usually exaggerated the difference between the West and the Orient, casually translating every bit of difference into inferiority. Second, it admitted the existence of internal knowledges in those societies only if these found a place in a knowledge organization produced by Western Orientalists. The pandits's views about Hindu scriptures were considered trivially arcane, but their information, reorganized by Western scholars, was acceptable. Thus there was a strong prejudice in favour of Westerners knowing these societies better than their inhabitants. Finally, these cognitive inadequacies were never detected because this knowledge had another non-cognitive purpose connected to the power of colonialism. We can add to these a fourth bias: the tendency to neglect contemporary events in Oriental societies and the tendency to concentrate on its rich cultural history.

Compared to that kind of Orientalist knowledge, the present state of Western knowledge about India is certainly less tainted by Orientalism. However, I am deeply struck by a kind of double standard I come across quite often, at times in surprisingly clever people. There is a tendency among Indianists to treat Indians' work as nationalist and politically tendentious, while adopting a crass and unreflexively nationalist, or Western-dominant attitude in their own, and seeing their lingering pride in the British empire as the legitimate afterglow of a glorious past. I am surprised by the sensitivity of British academics when we speak about racial attitudes in British rule in India; surprisingly, even now imperialism is not seen retrospectively as a totally indefensible business. There is little understanding that just as in the West there is a kind of moral consensus against the holocaust, in India there is, understandably, a similar consensus against colonialism. Some academic work in India in recent years has sought to be self-conscious about that and tried to get out of that bias. Subaltern Studies history creates such outrage precisely because it has sometimes attempted to read history against the grain of nationalist thinking.

I have tried to stress the need to step out of what I call 'the nationalist history of nationalism'. But two points should be made about this as well. The first is that because nationalism of a certain kind forms a kind of 'cultural habitus' for most of us, simply to say we should step out of the nationalist history of nationalism is not necessarily to be able to do it. I am sure, despite our conscious or declared intention, our actual historical practice must constantly fall short of it. It is the task of our European colleagues to point that out to us without the pleasant and defensible dishonesty produced by politeness; and when it is done, we should not, on our side, react viscerally to that as the rebirth of colonialism.

Second, the resolve to relate to nationalist assumptions critically does not necessarily mean that we reject every one of them. I feel surprisingly unapologetic about Indians wanting to be politically independent; I find the general business of colonialism rather unattractive. And to prove our credentials as people liberated from nationalist parochialism, we need not adopt the Cambridge history resolve to show that Indian nationalism was inspired entirely by slovenly self-interest of the lowest possible kind. I can be critical and supportive of some nationalist ideas: I feel moderately pleased that we became independent of Britain, though I am not beside myself in joy with what Indian politicians have done with that freedom. I do not find the crass Namierite premises of Cambridge history attractive or acceptable. But I think today it is difficult to find advocates of that kind of post-imperial history among people in Western universities. It has become generally politically incorrect to be a supporter of colonialism, even retrospectively, which, to imitate a famous book on British history, 'is a good thing'.

Third, the two great spectacles of Indian contemporary life, the one of poverty and the other of democracy, and the rather more complex wonder about how the two can stay alive together, have drawn a lot of attention in Western scholarship. This has, understandably, led to a huge shift in the Western academic output and curiosity about India. Instead of the earlier interest primarily in India's past, and what were conventionally known as Orientalist/Orientological studies consisting of philology, religious philosophy, linguistics, classical Sanskrit literature, and drama, academic interest has been enormously redistributed and the main emphasis has shifted towards social sciences: history, sociology, economics, cultural studies, and politics, etc. This is a huge advance in some ways. It is true in some cases—mainly among lower levels of academic work—that, occasionally, traditional colonial attitudes express themselves, but that is generally a negligible problem: and such uninformed or unsympathetic writing should be answered by ignoring them rather than answering them.

But I feel this advance has been at the cost of something else which is quite vital. Although earlier Orientalist studies often treated the difference as inferiorized, they took the difference and some aspects of it quite seriously. One of the most serious, I personally feel, is the ordinary cognitive courtesy of registering that Indians have their own languages—Sanskrit, Arabic-Persian, and the vernaculars—apart from the ubiquitous existence and convenience of English. The first step of taking someone culturally seriously is to accept the seriousness of his language. Sadly, this is slowly slipping in the new studies of social sciences. This can be for several reasons, three of which can be specified clearly. First, often social scientists simply take on unconsciously the unheedingly universalistic assumptions of positivistic social sciences, and assume that the state either is or is not; democracy exists or does not; there is no sense in asking complicated and delay-causing questions like 'is it quite a state?' Second, more often, they simply find enough people with English producing enough writing in English to maintain the illusion that, given that they are reliably bilingual, scholars do not have to know the vernacular. And finally, in some cases, scholars engage in painstaking fieldwork—not merely once, but over long years, nursing their identical field; thus, even if they do not speak the language, the recurrent opportunity of checking the statements of politicians against others, and checking statements against behaviour, gives them ample opportunity to test what they say. Anthropologists are the only branch of social scientists who—usually because their fieldwork is in relatively remote areas, and among people who usually speak only a vernacular, and because they mistrust mediated reports—usually learn languages. But this I think causes an enormous problem.

Accessibility is not necessarily an antidote to intellectual prejudice. It is a truism that people in the West now know much more about the rest of world, if knowing means primarily viewing. But the increased traffic of images also means a repetitive opportunity for re-confirming prejudices—in which the Western media, including the liberal segment, plays an intensely active role. The task of academic knowledge, I would think, is to slowly criticize and counteract this ritual of self-congratulation.

Study of the History of Political Theory

Since Marxist theory is interrelated on all sides with other forms of European social thought, even to assert its incontrovertible superiority over other 'ideologies' we had to acquire some understanding of other theoretical arguments.

More systematic study of social theory tended to show me that instead of what Marxists claimed about Marx—that his work was separated by an unbridgeable gulf from ideological theories before and around him—his thought was actually a part of a process of thinking about European modernity. It seemed that despite their enormous theoretical differences, most modern European theorists acknowledged that for some reasons modernity as a historical period was particularly difficult to grasp cognitively. Each one of them suggested a way of finding a process that was centrally causal to modernity. Each offered a theory of that particular process, which, because of the assumption of causal primacy, thus became a theory of modernity in general. I still retain my belief that Marxism is a most powerful theory in this group, but I have been forced to abandon the more orthodox certainty that it can simply, entirely unassisted, provide us with an understanding of the sociology of the modern West. It has to be complemented, in proper contexts by theoretical arguments from Hegel, Weber, Tocqueville, Durkheim, and others. However, this kind of enquiry forced me into another question which forms the basis of much I have written in the last decade.

In the case of people like me, the reading of these theories happened always in the inescapable context of an everyday life in modern urban India. Reading these theories gave rise to an irrepressible sense of both their familiarity and their distance: it appeared that things in my historical experience were both similar and different: it was essential to separate them. Schematically, I concluded that modernity comprised processes like industrialization, secularization, étatization, and individuation, which were universal: but this did not imply that the actual events or end-states would be similar to those in the West. This made Western social theory indispensable and inadequate at the same time: that corpus showed us what modernity was as well as what was involved in making theoretical sense of it, but it was idle to expect it to produce a theory of our experience as well. I lost my faith in a transitionist theory of modernity: the belief that the European past showed us the image of our future.

But this naturally leads to another question: did not Indian culture produce some form of self-reflection on our experience of modernity? If it did, where was it? I felt we have traditionally looked at the wrong place. Theory is a form of reflection, just as poetry and drama are.

For complex historical reasons, this form was not highly developed in Indian culture; literature, by contrast, was. It was hardly surprising that when Indian intellectuals reflected upon these questions, particularly the nature of our modernity, they did it through literary forms. I have accordingly tried to read literature, at least literary texts, with questions of social theory in mind.

Begriffsgeschichte

In doing Begriffsgeschichte I have tried to combine the careful, historical, contextual study of texts with the method of focusing on concepts that are central to the prosecution of a particular type of social practice, inclining probably a bit towards the latter. I tried this, with a slightly Bengali frivolousness, in a study of the idea of 'filth' and public space by looking at the history of a particular park in Calcutta.[1] Personally, I have felt that the intellectual discourses we ought to study with particular care are the vernacular, since that is the theatre of greater intellectual and artistic originality. Often, the English discourse is produced by the same figures, but they are a pale shadow of the passion, argumentative force and eloquence they show in their own language. Evidently, when they wrote to other interlocutors in other regions, or about more general questions, they often wrote in English, and those texts and discourses have to be taken with the utmost seriousness. But we should not slip into the easy supposition that what comes out in vernaculars is inferior in quality. Happily, the idea that when Indians write in vernaculars they are more original than in English has got wider support, and young scholars have turned to vernacular material, often producing compelling studies of intellectual history. But other scholars find it impossible to admit of this possibility. Oddly enough, Indian education is increasingly becoming more monolingual than before, with the unfortunate result that academics trained in modern methodological skills often lack the more basic skills of a confident use of vernaculars. But in some ways the line of argument about enumeration of communities has had a great deal of support—both within India and outside—among scholars working primarily in history and anthropology. This in part

---

[1] Reproduced in Kaviraj 2011: ch. 7.

is a consequence of the wide interest in Subaltern Studies, where this argument first appeared.

Study of the State in India

My second substantial interest in a longer-term historical sociology of power stemmed from the realization that in the Indian context, unlike in the European, modernity had been introduced by the power of the state—first colonial, then nationalist. The meaning of the phrase 'primacy of the political' appeared to me in a much stronger and altered light. But the study of the state became infinitely tangled and deferred by a mass of problems. I became convinced that to understand both the effectiveness of the state—what it has been able to do in modern India and its failures, what we expect it to do but which it cannot—it is essential to see it as part of a historical sociology over the long term. To understand the vexed question of how much the national state has taken over from the colonial state it is essential to understand the state of colonial power. After all, all this is a study of modernity in India, and I became convinced that in India, if not in the Third World, the forces of modernity have entered primarily by the expedient of the state and its initiatives rather than by the unassisted causal powers of capital—however impressive it may have been in Europe. Even capitalism in India requires the crucial support of the state. We have to understand the state because it occupies such a large part of the story of modernity in India.

However, the major problem is to work out a way of communicating between the disciplinary languages of political scientists and historians. By academic convention, political scientists did not look at the problems of political life historically; historians, by contrast, did not always ask the question about the global nature of political authority and its place in society, though they generated a highly detailed picture of political processes in society. I have tried to argue in works over the last decade or so that the major change in Indian modernity was not even the extension of the capitalist mode of production as much as the state mode of power, i.e. the primary change in India's modernity is the conversion of a society in which order was produced primarily by religious authority to one in which it is mainly produced by the state. The entire story of India's modernity is how this society has become centred on the state.

The Study of Literature and its Links with Social Theory

I also have serious differences with people practising history of ideas in relation to the study of literature. I cannot deny that my interest in literary texts is driven at least in part by my sense of enjoyment of literary texts; but I can now see a deeper connection between literature and my general interest in theoretical ideas. Modernity brings in a general instability of the most fundamental conditions of social existence, and in no society can it pass without causing the greatest and deepest intellectual disquiet. Some of the most important European thinkers put this disquiet quite directly at the heart of their theories: nearly all of them imply that modernity, because of the instability at its heart, because it is so difficult to equate it with any single social arrangement or state of affairs, is particularly hard to grasp and encompass cognitively. Although modernity, out of all social systems of human existence, is the one created as a result of the deliberate designs and acts of human groups, it is also the most difficult to understand. It would have been utterly surprising if modernity did not cause a similar disquiet in India, or if Indian intellectuals did not try to understand its nature. However, every society applies to its great and most complex tasks those skills it has developed for a long time, in which it is intellectually adept and confident. Indian culture did not have a pre-existing tradition of social theory; but it did have a long and distinguished literary tradition. It is hardly surprising therefore that the self-reflection of modernity that happens in Europe in the form of social theory does so in India in the form of literary writing. It is necessary to modify the hardness of this distinction, however. I think, in Europe theoretical reflection in the more abstract conceptual form was always followed by a commentary in an artistic-literary form. It is hardly surprising that those contemporary historians of ideas who have sought to understand the peculiar constellation of ideas Europe has lived with for the last three centuries have often supplemented the chronicle of theory with a history of literary reflection, particularly in relation to the novel.[2] It is also noticeable that a number of theorists

---

[2] The list is too distinguished and long to really require mention, but it stretches from Gramsci, Lukács, Bakhtin, Lucien Goldmann, and René Girard, to Charles Taylor and others today.

and social philosophers who are dissatisfied with modern liberal social thought have turned to the intellectual resources of the European past, a large part of which consists in philosophical reflection on literature. Again, in nineteenth-century India intellectuals facing philosophical questioning from the modern West similarly used the resources of their own tradition—mostly literature—to find reasonings, arguments, values, attitudes which they could recover and reinterpret. To study literature is not to move away from theoretical questions, but to find a way of moving into them in a serious manner. In the Western universities, there is not yet a great deal of work of this type on India—for understandable reasons. As I pointed out before, technical linguistic skills have gone through a decline; and there is a tendency, which I deplore, to study Indian writers in English as representative Indian authors rather than vernacular figures. But in a different sense, this in fact moves parallel to trends in Western writings on social theory, though, again for understandable reasons, Western writers writing this kind of work are usually not familiar with earlier trends in other cultures.

Theory: What is Post-colonial Theory?

But because of my primary interest in social theory, I would like to return briefly to the problem of theory—of, about, and from the Third World. Theory from non-European sources has been associated rather too tightly with what is now known as post-colonial theory. I do not respond warmly to it not because I do not agree with what this theory does, but because I am sceptical about its claim to being theory at all. There is hardly any doubt that those associated with this trend are extremely proficient with strands of contemporary theoretical thinking in the West, and write fluently in these idioms. But that was not the claim which launched this 'theory': that was to be different from Western theory. Now it is ironic, to say the least, to argue that the sign of breaking away from Western theory is to show great proficiency in it. It is undeniably true that their thinking or enterprise is theoretical; but they do not constitute a different body of theory. On one side it represents a desire for a theory which is distinctive—which I am prepared to respect, provided that this desire is not confused with the production of the theory itself. In some cases the trouble is that, in the case of cultural criticism, the analyses are not so much of non-Western texts of value but of Western texts dealing with the West. Thus, critics might produce scintillating analyses of sixteen unmindful paragraphs in Jane Austen or Wilkie Collins or Dickens where they write about India. Unfortunately, and quite simply, that is not equivalent to a study of six volumes of Tagore. I feel that serious and more worthwhile theory might be produced by that kind of engagement rather than of the kind produced by Said, which was essential, therapeutic, cathartic, but eventually not very central. It is a catalogue of how Westerners failed to get something right, not of how non-Westerners thought about anything at all. Paradoxically, I believe we can produce more serious non-Western theory if we think somewhat less of what the West has done right or done wrong in the past, or even what the West at present thinks about what we do.

References

Kaviraj, Sudipta. 2011. Filth and the Public Sphere: Concepts and Practices about Space in Calcutta. In Sudipta Kaviraj, *The Enchantment of Democracy and India*. Ranikhet: Permanent Black.

2

Literature and the Moral Imaginations of Modernity

Although modernity is currently a widely discussed theme, its moral dimension is relatively neglected. This is surprising, because the moral dimension is quite crucial to the historical triumph of modern culture. Modernity's challenge to traditional societies never succeeds historically until it is able to advance a moral argument for its superiority.

I want to exaggerate Weber's claim in the *Protestant Ethic and the Spirit of Capitalism*. The standard reading of Weber's work is that he demonstrates that Protestantism fashioned an ethical doctrine that provided the activity of capitalist accumulation with a new moral legitimacy. In traditional moral systems, the activity of amassing wealth was associated with the lowly dispositions of greed, selfishness, and a pitiless passion for money. It required a fundamental transvaluation to view diverse forms of self-regarding activity as intrinsically valuable. I read Weber as saying that until Protestantism advanced a powerful moral argument in its favour, the civilizational project of modernity was fatally incomplete.

As nineteenth-century Bengali discussions saw it, modernity as a new civilization could be justified by three different arguments. The first is the argument of comfort or—'commodious living' in Hobbes's lapidary phrase—the idea that capitalist modernity leads to a revolutionary expansion of productivity which makes a more satisfactory and comfortable material life possible for all. It is wrong to underestimate the power of the enchantment of material prosperity.

This essay was first published in *The Moral Fabric in Contemporary Societies*, edited by Grazyna Skapska and Annamaria Orla-Bukowska, Brill, Leiden, 2003.

This was usually supplemented and framed by a wider rationalist argument that the modern world is based on the expansion of scientific reasoning and social rationalization in Weber's sense. It is also an immensely powerful ideal, particularly for intellectual tastes. But it must be recognized that, in the moral context of traditional societies, neither of these two arguments is incontrovertible.

In the Hindu and Buddhist traditions of India, it is possible to make the counterargument that it is not a life of acquisitive excess but one of restraint of desire that is truly morally worthy. These religious traditions had well-rehearsed arguments which stressed that the desire for material goods was eventually illimitable; the constant movement towards prosperity produced discontent. Material things also gave diminishing pleasure.

The expansion of knowledge can similarly be seen as a morally neutral or indifferent achievement. Being knowledgeable is not the same as being good or being happy. Traditional religious beliefs also warned against the tendency of knowledge to produce unjustified arrogance. What traditional cultures find far more unsettling is the idea that modernity is not a proposal for living without morals, but by more stringent ethical rules, and that living by rationalistic rules gives human beings greater dignity that living by religious ones.[1] This deeply Kantian theme constantly reappears in the religious and ethical debates in early Indian modernity and is very clear in the discourses of early modern Bengal from the late nineteenth century.

To understand moral change, at least in the Indian context, we require a historical phenomenology of morals. The question of explaining or even making sense of moral change is exceedingly difficult, and the present studies appear to miss some crucial questions. It is widely recognized that moral systems are different between societies, and between historical periods in the same society. Durkheimian sociology would treat these distinct moral systems as self-contained wholes, so we see clearly that the moral system of traditional Hindu society is fundamentally different from that of the modern West or even modern India. But precisely because these are systems of 'conscience collective'—collective consciousness about

---

[1] The classic statement of this position is, of course, Kant's *Groundwork for the Metaphysics of Morals* (Kant 1785).

matters of conscience—the question is how they ever change at all. What are the processes, the mechanisms that effect this baffling transformation of those rules of conduct in a society that are not merely universally respected, but taken for granted?

In Indian social science there has been much discussion about the historical transition to modernity, and in trying to understand this change historians have paid increasing attention to the peculiar persuasiveness of literature rather than the standard analysis of philosophical and theological disputation.[2] In the first stages of the transition, modernity is typically supported by arguments of scientific rationality and commercial prosperity. Yet as greater self-confidence is gained, its advocates are able to claim that modernity is not just rationally and economically superior to traditional forms, but that it offers, crucially, a superior ideal of the ethical life.

In studying the moral transition to modernity, why should we study literature of all things—why not philosophy? Answers to this question must be given twice: one specific to India, and another more general. A puzzling feature of Indian intellectual history is that although India has a great philosophical tradition dating back to classical antiquity, historically this tradition evinced little interest in questions of the justifiability of social relations.

At this moment I can only report this fact, not explain it. Contesting schools of classical Indian philosophy developed and carried on long disputes in the fields of ontology, epistemology, logic, and aesthetics, in addition to producing powerful theological doctrines interpreting the religious significance of Hindu beliefs. Strangely, Indian thinking did not develop a specialized field of social philosophy. Consequently, classical philosophic schools debated question like whether the world really exists or not: whether in their mundane existence human beings can really be happy; whether reliable knowledge is at all possible; or whether inferential knowledge is trustworthy; but not questions like whether the caste system is justified. This peculiarity of the classical tradition lends a peculiar twist to the modes of reflection on modernity in India. Literary reflections rather than social theory

---

[2] Two most interesting works in this direction are Chatterjee 1994 and Chakrabarty 2000. These themes are however also explored in works by Arjun Appadurai, Homi Bhabha, Gyan Prakash, and many others.

settle civilizational judgements about whether modernity offers an overall better way of existence than earlier forms, about what Hans Blumenberg called 'the legitimacy of the modern age'.

Questions—about the rationalization of society; the alterations in fundamental religious beliefs; the decline of traditional authority of the king in the political world, of Brahmins in social life, and of the father inside the family; the immense changes in habits of intimacy between the sexes—asked and answered by social theory in the West, are all analysed and answered through literary writing. They are found in the discourses internal to literary forms like the novelistic narrative, lyrical poetry, and autobiographic writing.

Charles Taylor has suggested that in the modern world human beings have no recourse but to live theoretically. I take this to mean that social theories provide modern people with large-scale moral and cognitive maps in living their social lives. Equally, in their small-scale but individually-taken decisions about their personal lives, these theoretical structures enable them to ground their decisions and ways of acting in the world. If that is true, in the case of modern Indians this ineluctable theoretical function is performed by texts of modern vernacular literature rather than by reading the texts of Kant and Mill.

A widespread supposition is that modernity implies an unprecedented transformation of society's moral imagination. This way of being morally in the world needs to be outlined in its main principles, filled out in detail, ethically justified by close reasoning, and finally disseminated across society. Philosophical and theoretical debates of great intensity—which also happen in modern India—are normally restricted to circles of intellectuals, and cannot spread very far to re-constitute the moral 'common sense' of society. Literature, I wish to suggest, plays a fundamental role as the primary vehicle for the dis-semination, popularization, and eventually the normalization of these ideas about moral conduct.

The triumph of modern life requires the conversion of ordinary people to modernity's moral imagination, and turning these new moral precepts into the constituents of a Gramscian 'common sense'. This is what literature accomplishes historically. In the nineteenth century some ordinary Indians began an immense transformation of their moral universe. They began to conceive of God in a new way, they fell in love and related to women in their lives in a new manner, they became thoughtful about their own moral life in an unprecedented fashion, and they subjected themselves to new and stringently exacting moral standards. The cumulative effect of this led to a new conception of the moral life.

God is conceived not as unpredictable, vengeful, or manifesting himself in all objects of the external world; instead, God sits subtly inside the individual's heart and whispers his moral promptings in a distinctly Rousseauian way. People are persuaded to do this, to introduce such incalculable changes in their moral lives, I suggest, not by directly reading Rousseau and Kant, whom few could understand at that time.[3] Rather, this process is executed through reading the literary works of writers like Bankimchandra Chatterjee and Rabindranath Tagore, who persuaded their audience through the work of literary enchantment. Something as large and as fundamental as conversion to a different morality can happen only through a discourse that is constant, not intermittent—a discourse that is insistent, intimate, subtle, ubiquitous, intertwined with people's very existence. This is a discourse which speaks to us through the splendour and insidious persuasion of our own language and its indefinable wonders.

To understand the intellectual history of Indian modernity, it seems essential to move beyond a conventional sociology of literature which specializes in examining how literature reflected social change. I wish to suggest that we need to widen the scope of this sociology of literature and turn the explanatory point in the reverse direction: to view how literary discourse forms the directions and contours of our emotions, structures moral intentionality, and shapes the moral personality of ordinary individuals by celebrating the modern way of being in the world as both intellectually admirable and socially possible. Ethics and emotions are in any case closely, inextricably linked, as I shall try to show by analysing the socially radical consequences of narratives of romantic love.[4]

---

[3] This is due to two separate difficulties. First, Indians would have to overcome the difficulty of reading intricate theoretical arguments in a foreign language; and second, both the form and the content of such arguments were vastly different from conventional traditional ideas and ideals of life in India.

[4] I have tried to show this in greater detail in the case of Tagore's poetry in 'Tagore and the Ideals of Love', in Orsini ed. 2006.

I shall now use some examples from standard modern forms of literature to show how literature first suggests and then justifies a modern conception of the self, around which eventually a whole structure of modern moral sensibility takes shape. First, let us turn to the modern novel. Like all great civilizations, the Indian was rich in narrative conventions. And there is a long and powerful cultural tradition which argued that moral life—what it means to act well in situations of moral complexity or puzzlement—can be examined through narrative devices.[5] The Hindu epics, like the *Mahabharata*, do not offer their readers a simplistic sense of moral order and security by telling a tale of the final eradication of evil. Rather, they constantly place narrative figures in situations that are morally puzzling or transgressive, and prove that in actual human lives it is difficult to follow ethical rules—because although the rules are clear, human lives are not. Moral excellence—living a good life—is a matter of improvisation and adventure.[6]

In traditional Hindu society the greatest ethical challenge is breaking the moulds of typical life-patterns determined by caste laws. Traditional narrative conventions, unsurprisingly, reflected and reinforced the moral sensibility of caste by the narrative depiction and celebration of these types. In conventional stories, Ksatriya princes led lives of bravery, the Brahmins lives of intellectual excitement.[7] Comparably, in Buddhist tales, merchants often showed their own caste virtues.[8] In terms of literary theory and narratology, these

[5] In the Hindu religious tradition, narratives are given pride of place in moral instruction. This is because of an implicit theory that the simple stating of moral principles is not always helpful in assisting individuals through situations of moral conflict in real life. Precepts stand splendidly alone, and unilluminated; in real life, moral situations are often difficult to judge precisely because individuals have to decide between moral principles. Narratives, by placing characters in complex situations, offer us guidance about real moral choice.

[6] I have suggested that this kind of narrative reflection on morals is continued by the modern narrativistic traditions with great success—for example, in the novels of Bankimchandra Chattopadhyay. See Kaviraj 1995: ch. 1.

[7] Ksatriya was the second caste in the *varna* hierarchy to which rulers and warriors belonged.

[8] Not surprisingly, in the epics but also in classical stories, the heroic characters usually come from the two upper castes—the Brahmins and the

traditional characters fall generally into the pattern described by Bakhtin in his illuminating essay on the difference between the formation of characters in the epic and the novel.[9] As Bakhtin suggests in his essay about European classical literature, the characters in the Indian epics also come narratively fully formed.

Usually the events of the narrative arrange severe tests for the attributes of the heroic character, but the figure is already entirely formed when the narrative begins, even if this is in his childhood. He already has inside him those qualities which make him both typical and extraordinary. A character is 'typical' in the sense that he can have only those dispositions which are peculiar and distinctive to his occupation or social class—moral courage, sharp intelligence, independence of spirit, defiance of earthly powers if he is a Brahmin, and correspondingly, bravery, military skills, an irrepressible sense of justice, strength of character, and fortitude if he is a Ksatriya. But heroic characters of traditional stories would have to possess these 'typical', i.e. caste-specific, virtues to an extraordinary extent in order to qualify as the subject of celebration through a narrative. In ordinary circumstances, he is a Durkheimian hero in the sense that he demonstrates in an exemplarily intensified way the caste ethic of a particular social group. He is extraordinary not because his behaviour is idiosyncratic or deviant, or because his thinking is distinctively individual, unlike that of any other person; in fact, it is an emphatic lack of 'distinctiveness' in the modern sense which makes him a hero.

Since the society's sociological structure requires a finite number of social types, and each of these groups has a clearly determined trajectory through life, the narrative economy of the society is also correspondingly limited. It is, in fact, interesting to see not merely the restriction of types of characters, but also how traditional societies make do with a relatively small number of foundational stories and read them repetitively. The hunger for the narratives of a modern society is satisfied by writing ever new stories; in traditional societies,

---

Ksatriyas. Interestingly, while the female figures conform to types, they are much less determined by caste roles. In Buddhist stories a striking difference is the use of *sresthis* (big merchants) in crucial and celebratory roles—something conspicuously absent from the Hindu narrative traditions.

[9] Bakhtin 1998.

by telling the same stories over and over again. In the case of the stories of the epics or even the *puranas* in India, readers do not come to the narrative with the question typical of the modern reader—'what happens next?' Most readers hear the basic outline of the story early in their childhood; and thus, when they read the story or hear it repeatedly later, the central question among the readership is not 'what happens next?' but 'what is the meaning of things happening this way?'

Such a narrative economy is radically transformed by the coming of the novel. First, the aesthetic idea of the novel itself is shatteringly new in the context of caste society and its ordering of individual lives. The novel, in contrast with the epics, is always a celebration of *ordinariness*, Ordinariness, however, means several things in the aesthetics of the modern novel. Different aspects of this modern aesthetic of ordinariness have to be distinguished and explored because the meaning of ordinariness and its counterpoint to traditional narrative ideals vary in specific cultural contexts. In terms of traditional narrative aesthetics, the very idea of a narrative celebration of an ordinary, unexemplary individual's life, or a passage of experience in the life of an otherwise undistinuished person is almost a contradiction in terms. How can a person deserve to be a hero, deserve to be the subject of narrative celebration because he is ordinary, because his life is *not* spectacular?

In Indian society, the ideals of caste provide an added piquancy to the idea of the ordinariness of narratable lives. To conceive of an individual life as 'ordinary', in the sense that it could happen to any man irrespective of caste, is itself a radical departure from the segmented trajectories and routines of lives. Second, as is well known, there is a deep connection between the ordinariness of the hero of modern narratives and the central theme of character development in the *bildungsroman*—which becomes the dominant genre in Bengali and later Indian novel writing. Over a period of about fifty years, the accepted structure of narratological conventions is completely re-cast in favour of the modern novel. By the middle of the nineteenth century, writing in the epic or the *puranic* style becomes formalistically impossible.

There is a second, associated meaning to ordinariness in the aesthetics of the novel. From the point of view of the older combination of ethics and aesthetics, a most unsettling thing about the novel is the celebration of moral ordinariness that lies at its heart. This goes against the logic of the traditional caste order in several interconnected ways. First, the novelistic story of the slow, experiential 'making' of a human character simply assumes as its setting the modern world in which human fate is indeterminate, not a trajectory predetermined by birth into a particular occupational caste. In traditional Hindu social order, individuals could be ordinary representatives of a particular caste which fixed their occupation, aspirations, and range of possible trials they would face in their social lives. Despite its settledness, a Ksatriya's life is not entirely free from surprises; the life of a warrior is necessarily beset with risks. But these surprises themselves were segmentary—risks of a particular type specific to a life of that kind.

By contrast, the modern novel decided to tell the stories of lives which were ordinary by a new definition. Because the plots of the novels routinely followed the fates of modern individuals in the quintessentially modern spaces of the city, they tracked the experiences of not an ordinary Brahmin or Ksatriya, but of a human being without any exemplary instantiation of brahminical or heroic virtuous in caste terms, and who thus lived a more open-ended and confusing life. Often these people were not virtuous in a more straightforward sense: the novel form showed a distinct partiality for depicting lives of individuals who were often confused, usually imperfect, unable to live up to the principles they believed in, morally flawed and vulnerable. The response they elicited was not a distanciating admiration, but of identifying pity. Readers were not meant to deify these characters, and consider the exploits of heroes to be beyond the capacities of people like themselves. Rather, the imperfection and fallibility of these heroes made them similar to ordinary people, and their internal monologues on moral problems could directly throw light on an average person's own daily mundane struggle with the demands of goodness.

By conventional aesthetics, the literary celebration of the morally imperfect character was impossible. This was a travesty or literary values and of aesthetic principles. For modern writers, this was precisely the point of literary reflection on the place of the moral in human life—to depict human beings in their imperfection and vulnerability, in their difficult but unavoidable search for their own selves—a self that was not given to them by caste, but fashioned by experience and self-reflection. The novelistic character constantly reflects and assesses the whole of the life he has already lived. He extracts principles, and modifies, or at least attempts to modify the rest of his life, and give it more deliberate shape. Thus, the novel form was the primary vehicle for familiarizing people with living life in a casteless way. The narrative celebration of the ordinary itself signalled a declaration of moral change.

Gradually, modern writers perfected a more complete moral argument for the new kind of narrative they were writing. The function of older narratives, it was claimed, was not merely to demonstrate the virtue of a particular kind of life—usually of the prince and the warrior—but clearly, by showing the adventures of their lives and the inevitable fact that, at times, even these exemplary characters failed to rise to the ideals of their vocation. Literary narratives taught its ordinary readers/listeners lessons of kindness (*karuna*). In response to this, modern novelists began to assert that—precisely by showing the incompleteness of the realization of moral ideals and the vulnerability of characters in a world in which life trajectories were no longer predetermined and where individuals are constantly surprised by the changeability of conditions —the novel also trained its reader, the ordinary individual, to treat others with understanding, if not kindness. It is for this reason that the novel has to follow its strangely paradoxical principle of a fictional truthfulness, in place of traditional literature which often entertained by presenting the fantastic.[10] The characters in these novels were of course imaginary and fictive, but their life trajectories, the events which constituted their narrative, and, most fundamentally, the social world through which they picked their way, had to be entirely credible. Otherwise, the moral pedagogy of the novel would fail.

In early modern India, as indeed in the West, the two literary forms of the novel and lyric poetry discursively complemented each other. They contributed in distinctive and mutually supportive ways to the great transformative shaping of emotions that the historical

[10] Indeed, according to one of the most important classical texts of Indian literary aesthetics, the first distinguishing feature of *kavya* (litera-ture) is said to be that it is a field in which the laws of nature are suspended (*niyatikrtaniyamarahitam*—in the very first verse of Mammata's *Kavyapra-kasa*).

transition to modernity required. At the centre of modern narrative conventions lay the moral normalization of romantic love—the narrative development of an elective relation of affection between two individuals.

In an abstract, general sense, elective love was not a new idea: in the traditional literatures of India there were famous figures like the divine couple, Radha and Krishna, who transcended all social restrictions to realize their transgressive love for each other. It was a resplendent ideal of romantic attachment, much admired for obvious reasons by modern writers; but it was generally assumed that this ideal of love, between two socially unaccredited lovers, was not a socially practicable ideal in actual human lives. At times, this ideal was interpreted in an entirely metaphysical, metaphorical key. The shatteringly radical characteristic of the new kind of romantic love was its social availability and normalcy in ordinary daily life.

The novel bore a double relation with social reality: it partly reflected social practice, partly presented an ideal for social practice to follow. While the novel pretended, in the face of social facts, that this kind of elective affection was both morally preferable and sociologically common (which in nineteenth-century Bengal it definitely was not), the task of exploring the subtle states of mind that accompanied this kind of romantic longing was left to romantic poetry. Again, this represented a great departure in the aesthetic conventions that governed poetry. Conventionally, poetry was primarily devoted to two master subjects—narrative (telling epic or historical tales) or devotional. With modernity, poetry slowly but decisively moved away from these traditional themes. The subject of new poetry was rarely devotional, and almost never narrative in the classic sense, since the primary vehicle of the narrative, which had much greater analytical aspiration, had become a new kind of literary prose. The narratives of modern novels aspired to provide to their readers something close to an enjoyable epistemology of social relations. This was increasingly difficult to accomplish in the restrictive structures of verse making. In fact, the telling of tales in prose instead of verse is itself a radical literary transformation.

As the task of literature became more analysis than celebration of the lives of protagonists, prose became the proper vehicle of such analytical and reflexive storytelling. Prose narratives did not merely describe the social world, they also analysed and criticized it. They focused often on the sufferings of an individual maladjusted to his social world in various ways.[11] Analysis and criticism could not be properly executed in the charged, highly emotional, declamatory styles of traditional verse. Prose was the natural language of calculation, sobriety, and rational analysis, and therefore best suited to the predominantly cognitive purposes of the modern novel.

With modernity, the displacements in poetics were no less startling. In conventional love poetry in Sanskrit, and in early vernaculars (for instance, in Bengali and neighbouring Hindi) from the twelfth century, there existed a rich tradition of writing on love, but its endlessly repetitive and luxuriating subject was feminine beauty. Consequently, it is poetry dedicated overwhelmingly to the figure of the extraordinarily beautiful woman. Correspondingly, the aesthetics of this love is one of physical eroticism conceptually crystallized into the aesthetic category of *srngara*.

In nineteenth-century Bengali poetry a startling transformation of this poetic aesthetics, centred on the concept of *srngara*, takes place. In the modern reflection on love that romantic poetry slowly develops, beauty of that entirely physical nature is increasingly viewed with deep suspicion. The resplendent beauty of traditional heroines is seen, in one type of modern novel, as destructive of the intimate, emotional companionate relationship between the sexes, a new context in which the woman at the centre of the narrative is not the object of universal desire, but an individual who only falls in love with another specific person. All her qualities, including her physical beauty, are meant for that intimate special relationship, not an object of indiscriminate, universal adoration. Lovers choose this individuated feminine heroine, not because of a beauty which would be desired by everyone, but for an emotional singularity which can be understood only by another individual.[12] Thus the individuals are perfectly ordinary, but irreplaceably special only to themselves. And

[11] This line of argument is classically developed in the works of Georg Luckas. See especially Lukacs 1978.

[12] In modern Bengali literature this transformation in the ideal of love is clearly discernible in the novels or Bankimchandra Chattopadhyay and Rabindranath Tagore.

clearly such aesthetic ideals bear a strong connection with the sphere of modern ethics, as such relationships produce the ideal family of companionate marriage.

I wish to make two rather general points about this kind of poetic elaboration of subjectivity. First, the displacement of attention from physical beauty leads slowly to the elaboration of a new conception of the beauty of emotions, an idea deeply informed by the new moral ideals of restraint, innerness, and refinement of sensitivity; the primary vehicle of this form of ideal is a new figure of the individualized woman. In Tagore's novels, for instance, the writer often explicitly comments on the women's physical ordinariness.[13] Women are emotionally individuated through the events of the narratives, leading to a new ideal of refinement and sensitivity which makes a woman noticeable in real life and narratively interesting in the novel. Against this under-emphasis of their beauty—sometimes simple under-determination of their physical appearance—stands the constant emphasis and elaboration of their emotional and increasingly ethical character: their perceptions, feelings, states of mind, their development into a distinct personhood through the staple of the *bildungsroman*—meetings, misunderstandings, and final resolution or reconciliation. They are formed into individuals who cannot be mistaken for anyone else, or interchangeable with others, unlike the repetitive splendour of physically beautiful feminine figures. Nothing is more unevolving than physical beauty, and thus more unsuitable for narratives of the search for self.

The moral relation between genders is intriguingly affected by this transformation. In traditional literature, the refinement or idealization of the two genders differed significantly. Sexual ideals were divided between the literary and social ones of a courageous and upright male and a beautiful and playful woman. The transactions between these two types were often narratively arresting, but men and women did not aspire to a common pattern of emotional cultivation. In the romantic ideal, these patterns were equalized—patterns of refinement were identical for men and women, with suitable adaptation to their socially designated roles. A common refinement contributes to an ideal of moral equality.

---

[13] In the famous novel *Gora*, for example, the first time the heroine makes an entry the narrator makes a comment about her pleasing but ordinary looks.

Besides novels and poetry, autobiography can be seen as a form that epitomizes the reflexivity of the modern self by a constant recursive moral revaluation of lives. Autobiographies and other para-autobiographic forms—like letters or diaries related to real lives, or imaginary autobiographical novels—help individuals find new and periodic moral totalizations of their life experience. Assessing the moral meaning of a life is not done collectively, measuring each individual life against an ideal of fulfilment common to all those that belong to a caste. It is done individually—each person opening himself to unrepeatable experiences and finding moral fulfilment in his own personal way. Also, finding the moral meaning of one's life is not done once and forever; it is constantly renewed because, despite one's efforts, the realization of moral ideals in real lives always remains imperfect. Unlike narratives which elaborated and stated the moral ideals of the past, in which there was a constant expounding and elaboration but no real surprise, the new moral narrative is full of surprises because individuals are weak, sinful, irresolute, and tragic, ennobled only by their often failing search for the ideal.

In Bengali culture, as elsewhere, there was a strong connection between this emerging literary aesthetics and a new ethics of individuality and domesticity. Here I can only offer a very brief sketch. In nineteenth-century Bengal, something like a vernacular version of the discussion between Kant and Hegel on the nature of ethics is played out on a large scale. This new ethics is, of course, initially read in Western texts, then imagined, and then adventurously practised in actual personal conduct by a minority within the modern elite. However, these examples of unconventional, personal conduct remained, initially at least, heroic examples of individual experimentation in a society which looked with sullen disapproval at these 'outlandish' ways of a privileged and imitative minority.

We must remember that in the colonial context, with the early traces of nationalist resentfulness against Western ways, it was easy to condemn such behaviour as an apish flattery of the Englishman. Often such behaviour was condemned by both traditionalists and nationalists as being driven by a desire to gain the approval of the British, ungrounded in any serious independent moral reflection. As long as such conduct was confined to a tiny minority among the elite, and the majority of people calmly carried on arranged marriages, this mode was merely individual and extraordinary. It could be said to have deserved honour due to its moral heroism—the main point in Hegel's critique of Kant—but it could not be called an 'ethical life' because it simply did not bear the effortless, taken-for-granted quality of real, embedded ethical rules.

The literary idealization of this model of conduct in fact contributed to its becoming *sittlich* in several ways. First, it produced a powerful intellectual argument through the narratives themselves, not merely allegedly reporting events of love, but in doing so also exhibiting how fulfilling such ways of behaving and experiencing emotions could be. Second, they tended to create an impression of a commonplaceness of such actions and behaviour, lending them a misleading aura of ordinariness. Such things happened all the time in the novels, within a society in which they could (in principle) happen only rarely. Fictional characters became, in a sense, shadow people in this social universe, performing, despite their 'irreality', the immensely imaginatively powerful function of setting examples, making arguments, and providing advice to real individuals on the point of falling in love. It is hardly surprising that these novels have an intrinsically discursive quality: characters do not merely fall in love: they appear more intent on an intellectual elaboration of what falling in love means.

All this produces a new sensibility in which romantic love becomes a highly influential literary, aesthetic, and idealized norm. Couples actually married by solid familial negotiations would go devotedly to watch romantic films, and would either exult in the fulfilment such love gave to marriages, or condole its tragic failure and the unfulfilled lives of cinematic heroes. But through this aesthetic experience their own relationships would be transformed in small, imperfect, and partial ways. Often, couples who did not enjoy sufficient sovereignty over their own lives and so could not enter into romantic marriages would try, retrospectively, to transmute their mundane relationships with love's miraculous touch. Tagore's work in particular shows the definite emergence of a new ideal of love in Bengali society—an ideal in this dual sense. It is both an aesthetic ideal replacing the *srngara* ideals of the past as much as an ideal of the ethical life.

The three forms of modern literary composition—the novel, lyric poetry, and autobiography—all contribute towards two crucial imaginative processes in a modern culture. They present an aesthetic representation of what a modern life is, usually in an idealized form. And they help constitute a moral ideal, contributing to people's conversion to that ideal almost surreptitiously through the silent persuasion of aesthetic enjoyment. It is possible to argue for the moral significance of these narratives for another reason. Familiarity with Western modernity introduces new modern ethical ideals to Indian social groups. But their actual pursuit in real lives requires a crucial element of 'translation' or 'transfer'. The abstract elaboration of moral ideals through philosophical discourse tends to treat the ideals singly, and in a decontextualized form. People face their moral dilemmas in real life in complex and untidy contexts. Narratives situate fictive individuals in situations of great complexity, particularly through the complex opposition of locally valid moral orders. The principle of the moral autonomy of individuals might be elaborated to great lengths in an abstract form in discussions of Kantian ethics. Yet, when individuals actually propose following a course of individuality in their real lives, they have to deal with the specific principle of filial duty to parents, articulated in the peculiar Hindu caste doctrines. In narratives, this dilemma is worked out in a vernacular context of moral life. In the moral persuasion of people towards a modern ethics, literature plays a crucial role, supplementing more abstract philosophical discourse. This kind of narrative contextualization of ethical principles leads to processes of cultural adaptation which link up our arguments with theories of multiple modernities.[14]

Finally, the coming of modernity in all societies has two moments—the disruptive and the constructive. Some older practices cease working and new ones are installed in their place. It is at the constructive moment that modernity in non-European societies starts becoming different from European precedents. There is a very simple reason for this. The processes of modernity initially involve only small cities that are strategically placed in the social structure. But as modernity gathers strength, it affects wider sections of the population until it comes to affect all through its economic, political, and cultural transformations.

European precedents and European ideals dominated the cultural formation of the early modern elites in colonial Bengal. These elites were fluent in English, erudite in European history, and revered

---

[14] For a number of papers collectively arguing in favour of a perspective of multiple modernities, see Eisenstadt, ed. 2000.

European modernity—or at least its idealized pedagogic versions. With the expansion of the modernist project to other areas of society, the availability of Europe as an imaginative structure becomes progressively weaker. Neither their education nor their life experience gave common Indians a rich sense of Europe's modern past. Less educated people, drawn from the poorer classes, always have to improvise when inserted into modern structures and its imaginative compulsions.

We, as intellectuals, while reporting on modernity, tend to exaggerate the imaginative availability of Europe—the constant presence of the modern West as the universal ideal of modern civilization. This has been an image created by modern Europe about itself which is selective and deeply misleading. In this picture, modernity is a one-dimensionally positive achievement without alienation, without wars, without the looming presence of the state which often crosses over from discipline into totalitarianism. This ideological image of Europe offers individualism without loneliness, power without destruction, discipline without domination. But this imaginary Europe—which the real Europe needed in order to pursue its historical purposes—is, in fact, much less available to people who live in the universe of vernaculars. Ordinary people, when helped by democracy and social change to exercise greater sovereignty over their collective history, do not replicate the intellectual's tendency to repeat Europe's mistakes in order to repeat its triumphs. In the modernity being shaped in the multiple universes of vernaculars, and in the experience of the dispossessed, the imaginative power of the European precedent is greatly reduced. When these groups engage in the business of creating a new world, they are more likely than are the elites to create a world which is more deeply original.

References

Bakhtin, M. 1998. Epic and Novel. In *The Dialogical Imagination*. Austin: The University of Texas Press.

Chakrabarty, Dipesh. 2000. *Provincializing Europe*. Princeton: Princeton University Press.

Chatterjee, Partha. 1994. *The Nation and Its Fragments*. Princeton: Princeton University Press.

Eisenstadt, S.N. Ed. 2000. Multiple Modernities. *Daedalus*, Winter.

Kant, Immanuel. 1785/1948. *Groundwork for the Metaphysics of Morals*. Trans. H.J. Paton, Routledge, London.

Kaviraj, Sudipta. 1995. *The Unhappy Consciousness: Bankimchandra Chattopadhyay and the Formation of Indian Nationalist Discourse in India.* Delhi: Oxford University Press.

Luckas, Georg. 1978. *Theory of the Novel.* London: Merlin Press.

Orsini, Francesca. Ed. 2006. *Love in South Asia: A Cultural History.* Cambridge: Cambridge University Press.

3

The Two Histories of
Literary Culture in Bengal

Introduction

A general reading of the history of a particular literature requires, first of all, a principle of organization. Histories of Bangla literature usually offer a narrative of continuity: they seek to show, quite legitimately, how the literary culture develops through successive stages—how the literary works of one period become the stock on which later stages carry out their productive operations. These studies are less interested in asking how literary mentalities come to be transformed or how a continuing tradition can be interrupted, or in speculating on the possible reasons behind these significant literary turns. In an attempt to move away from these conventional histories, which record unproblematically the sequential narrative of the production of texts and their authors, this essay gives attention primarily to two questions. The first is: What were the major historical 'literary cultures', that is, the sensibilities or mentalities constructed around a common core of tastes, methods of textual production, paratextual activities (like performance, recitation, or other use in religious, non-literary contexts), reception, and the social composition of audiences? The second question, closely related to the first, is: How

This essay first appeared in *Literary Cultures in History: Reconstructions from South Asia*, edited by Sheldon Pollock (Berkeley: University of California Press, 2003). I thank Sheldon Pollock for detailed comments at different stages of its preparation. I have benefited greatly from discussions with Alok Rai, Francesca Orsini, and Dipesh Chakrabarty on various themes that have gone into its writing.

do literary cultures, especially deeply entrenched literary cultures, change?

The treatment of Bangla literary history in this essay, therefore, focuses more on textualities or text types than on individual texts, and it offers hardly any literary-critical analysis of major canonical works. A figure like Rabindranath Tagore is treated with relative neglect, since he does not represent a phase of serious interpretative contention or rupture in literary production or taste, although his work dominates the modern Bangla literary sensibility. The struggles of the generation immediately following Tagore to challenge and replace his aesthetics—with a more modern one that tried to come to grips with the problem of evil—are given greater attention.

This essay looks at two types of questions about literary transformation: the first concerns chronological changes in sensibilities or styles of literary production; the second, which cannot be ignored in any history of Bangla literature, is the problem of inclusion and exclusion of different social groups within this literary culture. The literature each group produces, receives, and enjoys contains internal structures of language, mythical content, imagery, or iconic systems that tend to include some Bangla readers and exclude others. It is important to note at the outset that even the question 'What is Bangla literature?' is not an innocent or non-contentious one. Writing the history of Bangla literature was part of the project of literary modernity, and since this was entirely dominated by a Hindu upper stratum of society, the initial historical accounts tended to ignore Islamic elements by suggesting either that they belonged to a separate cultural strand (called Musalmani Bangla), or that these texts were not of sufficient literary quality to find a place in an exalted history of literary art. This is the central question of the complex 'place' of Islamic culture in Bangla literature.[1] Comparisons with literary cultures from neighbouring regions of northern India, especially the Hindi, Urdu, and Gujarati regions, might yield interesting themes for further understanding of

[1] There has been a good deal of writing and analysis on the exclusion of Muslims from modern Bangla literature. We must, however, maintain a distinction between a large 'political' point that asserts the fact of this exclusion and deplores it for moral and political reasons, and a more textual and literary question about exactly how this exclusion works in the body of the literary texts. See, for example, Bandyopadhyay 1986.

the relation between the Islamic and the Sanskritic in Indian literary tradition as a whole.

Two Approaches to the Past: Tradition and History

The history of Bangla literature has two beginnings, and some of the most significant problems of its historiography stem from the problematic relations between these two separate historical stages. For the history of Bangla literature can have two equally plausible narratives, each with its own internal coherence and problems. In conventional critical discussions on the history of Bangla literature, its origin is placed in the tenth century, when Buddhist religious compositions known as *caryapadas* were being written in a language recognizable as the first ancestor of modern Bangla.[2] This narrative of Bangla literature is parallel and comparable to those of other North Indian languages, many of which emerged in a typical evolutionary pattern from Sanskrit. Classical Sanskrit developed several distinctive literary styles of composition.[3] The Apabhramsha form diversified into various styles and eventually created the distinctive individual vernaculars. Gradually, the Bangla vernacular crystallized into its particular linguistic shape and came to have an identifiably distinct literature.[4] Even after its linguistic differentiation, Bangla continued to bear an interesting, fluctuating relationship with the canons of Sanskrit high literature, as Bangla writers sometimes tried to emulate the forms and delicacies of Sanskrit, and sometimes tried to

---

[2] The word 'ancestor' here does not connote unproblematic descent. Because the *caryapadas* are also claimed as the point of origin by other eastern Indian languages, several languages may have differentiated from this linguistic form. The Bengalis, accordingly, do not have an exclusive linguistic or historical claim to this ancestry.

[3] For the diversification of different styles of Sanskrit, of which Magadhi and Gaudi were the generally acknowledged east Indian form, see the chapter by Sheldon Pollock in Pollock 2003.

[4] One of the most influential views about the linguistic differentiation of Bangla from Sanskrit and Prakrit can be found in Dinesh Chandra Sen 1950: 10-20. He notes the particular features of the Gaudiya *riti* in Sanskrit as being full of *samasa* (compounds) and *sandhi* (euphonic combination), and marked by *sabdadambara* (erudite ornamentation, devoid of fluidity and grace).

consciously move away from the values of the Sanskrit universe and create independent literary criteria of their own. Historically, this literature gave rise to several corpora with peculiar cultural, religious, and literary sensibilities. It is impossible to analyse all of them in detail, but I shall flag the major phases and forms.

The literary historian Sukumar Sen considers the advent of the great religious personality Caitanya (1486–1534) a significant watershed in Bangla literary history, and he divides the tradition preceding Caitanya plausibly into three major sections, each with its own internally coherent literary concerns, forms, and styles.[5] The first segment consists primarily of renditions and transfers from the high Sanskrit canon. Its major texts are the *Ramayana* of Krttibas and the *Mahabharata* by Kasiramdas (both of uncertain date, perhaps fifteenth century), though these two texts are surrounded by a large literature seeking to translate Sanskrit texts into Bangla. The second segment consists of the large corpus of the *mangalkavyas* inspired by popular religious sects. Each strand of worship developed its own series of these texts, which had wholly original narrative lines celebrating the powers of popular deities in the context of a specific, local literary geography. Third, a considerable body of distinctive literature, often of great poetic sophistication, emerged in the pre-Caitanya era through the Vaisnava sensibility (of devotion to the god Visnu), associated with the works of Vidyapati and Candidas, the two great early composers of *padavali*: sequences of devotional lyrics. These poems worked primarily within the general narrative structure of the popular story of Krsna and Radha, the divine couple in Vaisnava culture.

After Caitanya, these primary currents of Bangla literary culture continued. But there was an enormous influx of strength and sophistication into the Vaisnava tradition, which produced a new literary genre that Sen felicitiously calls *caritasakha*, the 'biographic branch', specializing in presenting Caitanya's life as a divine narrative through a skilled combination of the mythical and the historical. The literary impulse associated with Caitanya's religion dominated Bangla literary production for nearly two centuries.

In the eighteenth century, as modern historians have pointed out, it is possible to detect the emergence of a new cultural sensibility

[5] Sen 1965.

that moved away from typical themes of mystical eroticism found in the literary culture of the Gaudiya Vaisnavas (Bengali devotees of Visnu) and gives rise to a new, more diverse and catholic, literary taste. This is reflected in the works of the major eighteenth-century poet Bharatcandra, whose large corpus of texts includes narrative *kavyas* like *Annadamangal* (a devotional poem on the goddess Annada, bestower of food) and the enormously popular *Vidyasundar* (Vidya and Sundar), but also many freestanding poetic works of a less traditional variety. The first history of Bangla literature must end in the eighteenth century with this literary culture.

The second history of Bangla literature begins in the nineteenth century with the coming of colonial modernity and the introduction of modern forms and themes, making Bangla the first distinctively modern literature in India. For the study of Bangla literary cultures, the early modern period is one of the most interesting, since there is a fundamental transformation of the literary world—from the definition of literary writing itself to the struggles to incorporate modern forms of narration and performance borrowed from the West, such as the novel or the sonnet, to the overarching problem of how to produce a literature that accepts the 'disenchanted' scientific view of the world. Yet this modern Bengali culture of the nineteenth century also made use of the basic repertoire of earlier literary traditions, and it eventually produced a literature that is distinctly modern yet has not lost its strong aesthetic connections with traditional techniques and forms. One of the challenges in the literary history of Bangla is to make sense of the relation between these two histories—the one that ends with the eighteenth century and the one that begins with the nineteenth—and the partial continuities and ruptures that comprise their complex relations.

With the rise of modern consciousness, of which the historical sense is an integral part, there was among nineteenth-century Bengalis an understandable historiographical concern with the origins of their language. The 'first beginning', marked by the *caryapadas*, like all such beginnings, was naive, not tortured by the specifically modern anxieties of reflexivity or accompanied by historical curiosity. After the 'second beginning' in the nineteenth century, the entire disparate, as well as temporally and spatially dispersed, corpus of texts and literary practices spanning the period from the tenth century to the eighteenth century was perceived as a *single* historical narrative, with a beginning and a characteristically provisional end in modernity. Naturally, this nineteenth-century exercise used implicit definitional criteria based on perceptions of identity. And curiously, in the early histories of Bangla literature, while Vidyapati (who wrote in Sanskrit, Maithili, and Avahattha) and Jayadeva (who wrote in Sanskrit) were seen to be firmly part of the basic definition of Bangla literary history, Islamic texts were often silently excluded.

The Conception of Literary Tradition

In any literary tradition there is always at least a minimal sense of the past. But the past is not a pre-theoretical thing that exists independently of literary conceptualization; the past is formed by concepts, and concepts of the past can differ from one culture to another, as also between different periods of the same literary culture. Evidently, modernity introduces a sharp break with previous concepts of the past; but it is important to understand exactly the nature of this break and not passively follow the trend that absolutizes this rupture. To absolutize is to argue that something that earlier did not exist at all came into existence—in this case, that 'something' is a new consciousness of history.[6] If we take this to refer to a historical consciousness in the narrow sense, this is true; but if we mean by this a certain *theoretical* attitude about how to use the past, this is false. It is true that before the nineteenth century a strict *historical* consciousness involving linear and calibrated notions of time—with calendrical indexing, which involved techniques of exact dating of events and texts that together constituted the essential ingredients of a modern historical sensibility—did not exist in literary-critical discussions in Bangla. But there was a strong sense of the presence of the past conceived as tradition. Since with modernity the concept of 'the past as history' gradually replaced the concept of 'the past as tradition', it is useful to analyse the differences between them.[7]

There is a radical difference in the significance of the temporal order of texts and literary sensibilities between these two senses of the past.

[6] For a strong argument about the newness of modern time consciousness, see Koselleck 1981, especially ch. 3.

[7] There are some powerful arguments suggesting that all societies, including the modern, require a tradition that is independent of 'scientific' history, and that history in this narrower sense cannot perform the functions of tradition. See, for instance, Gadamer 1981.

Tradition uses the facts of the past as evidence for the continuance of practices, suggesting that a particular way of doing things is still relevant precisely because it has existed for a long time. By contrast, the modern sensibility infuses its concept of the past with a strong sense of the discontinuity of practices, indicating that a certain way of doing things is no longer possible or appropriate. Significantly, the concept of the past as tradition was quite adequate for the purposes of the practical literary moves for which it was commonly invoked. A 'literature' (*sahitya*) was seen as a unitary field of texts that existed in a differentiated time, with those composed in the past living in a certain relation with those composed in the present.

For literary practice, living in a tradition meant two different things. At one level, there was a sense of a large and loose tradition that was given to 'everybody' in the literary world by virtue of their literacy: they had to be educated technically in the sciences of figures, metrics (*alankaraastra, chandahsastra*), and the like to be able to appreciate the major texts of Sanskrit literature. Literary cultivation of this *general* kind would consist in a set of technical competencies—knowing, for instance, the difference between simile and poetic fantasy (*upama* and *utpreksa*), the rules of alliteration (*anuprasa*), and the various kinds of *chandah*—that gave the cultivated a capacity to recognize, discern, and enjoy these elements in the texts. Usually, there was a simultaneous initiation into a narrower, more *specific* tradition, in most cases related to a sect—Shaktism, Vaishnavism, Shaivism—which constrained the tastes of writers and their audiences into a more limited horizon.

At the second level, authors had to know and relate their work to a recognized body of symbolic or iconic combinatory, narrative structures or conventionalized narrative lines. Medieval Bangla literature, for example, includes a celebrated tradition of Vaisnava *bhakti* poetry, generally known now by the name literary historians gave it in the nineteenth century: the Vaisnava *padavali*, or devotional verses relating to the god Visnu. These used a familiar narrative combinatory: compositions elaborated on the story structure around Krsna—not just any story, but ones drawn from the *Bhagavata* complex of texts, which emphasize the erotic interpretation of his life. Compositions, moreover, had to invoke certain continuities in literary themes (*visaya*), moods (*rasa*), and theologies in order to be recognized as parts of that tradition. Yet because of the gradual shift in Vaisnava theology towards the use of sexual union as a metaphor, and the slow legitimation of this metaphor as a vehicle for allegedly deep doctrinal meanings, these compositions could borrow from the luxuriant erotic tradition of classical Sanskrit, which was entirely secular and doctrinally indifferent—for instance, the wittily erotic ambience in Kalidasa, or the deeply sensuous play of language and sexuality in Bhartrhari or Amaru.[8]

This kind of deployment of past texts and literary resources evidently involved both knowledge of those texts and an implicit theory about how to relate to them for practical use. Obviously, this argument can be given a strongly structuralist form by suggesting that the structures of performed narratives or texts could be broken down into literary lexemes, which formed an underlying combinatory from which poets drew elements they required. The stretch of past time from Kalidasa to Bharatcandra, or from the ancient Sanskrit *Mahabharata* and *Ramayana* to the recent *Annadamangal* and *Vidyasundar*, is vast, and we can see at work the logic of what Pollock has called 'vedicization' in the case of literary texts as well.[9]

There are two interesting features in this traditional conception of a literary tradition. There is a certain element of gratuitous reverence for simple antiquity, and more recent compositions claim this value by a suppression of chronological indexing and a pretense of antiquity. Clearly, this constitutes a deft operation on temporality, primarily to stifle it or to erase its sense of linearity. This trick with time is in some ways exactly contrary to the modern orientation to time and its effects. To treat traditional literary doctrines as lacking a sense of the past, or a sense of what to do with the past, is thus false and unnecessarily patronizing. It is more worthwhile to bring out what they could and could not do with the past, given the way they conceptualized its existence.

The traditional literary sense of time was fuzzy and approximate, which made certain types of composing and reception practices

---

[8] Vaisnava commentaries on sacred texts would often explicitly acknowledge such influence, especially the inexhaustible conceit of the commentators at being able to bring out literally everything implicit in a text. Against the assumption of authorial spontaneity, commentaries set up a literature of meticulous erudition about internal references and allusions.

[9] Pollock 1989.

possible. Authors or critics would not have been able to tell exactly when the *Meghaduta* was composed, and would not have been excessively bothered if they failed. Even more intriguing, a text like the *Meghaduta* would have come down to them from a generalized past as part of an *agama*, a practice that tended to break down or efface the layers of time and in a sense placed literary texts in a common horizon of literary contemporaneity, or better, atemporality. It is important to distinguish between historicist contemporaneity (according to which a text is continuously refracted through a long succession of literary cultures, as, for instance, in the case of Greek tragedies in the contemporary West), and atemporality (which creates a kind of calendrically unstratified time in which all classical texts coexist in a temporally undifferentiated 'past').[10] Texts lack an ordinal sense of pastness. The meaning of something becoming a classic is precisely its rising above the indexing specificity of local culture and taste, thereby conquering the localizing and decaying effects of time—a meaning that still subsists in the English use of the term 'classic'. The concept of tradition, *parampara* (one after another)—a sense of things, texts, tastes being handed down in an unbroken chain of reception (not necessarily repetition)—therefore contains an implicit theoretical understanding of the pastness of literary texts. In this way of thinking linear succession is not progress, which makes it impossible to change order, but is turned into formal difference, which can be endlessly emulated and played upon as a repertoire. The most significant difference with the modern sense of time is that pastness does not lead to obsolescence; if anything, the hierarchy goes in the opposite direction, and a text tends to acquire greater value simply because of its alleged antiquity.[11] Kalidasa's excellence might be recognized as something impossible to repeat, but not because it is obsolete.

Literary Territoriality

In studying literary traditions in South Asia, the problem of historical anachronism assumes a form quite different from the problems

[10] See Gadamer's interesting discussion of textual temporality in Gadamer 1981: 356ff.

[11] This is reflected, for instance, in the traditional dichotomy of *pracina/arvacina* rather than the modern *pracina/navina*.

concerning historical anachronism analysed in recent discussions on social theory centred elsewhere.[12] This is illustrated by difficulties that arise regarding the notion of space—an obvious and unavoidable concern in this discussion—when we look for relations that tie bounded forms of territoriality to cultural and literary processes. Where does Bangla literary history take place? If we accept the anachronistic teleology normally implicit in the writing of modern Bangla literary history, that the main purpose of all previous history was to produce the present, then the answer becomes simple. Viewing the entire past of Bangla literature from the vantage point of the modern literature that arose in the nineteenth century, historians of Bangla literature often assume that the purpose of the whole of earlier cultural evolution was to 'produce' that literature. Given that teleological vision, the intriguing question of space or territoriality of literary culture—'How is the medieval structure or geographic spread of literature different from the modern?'—dissolves. It is replaced by a story of undeveloped, inadequate forms in a literary space that is left indeterminate, encouraging the casual assumption that it was the same as modern Bengal and that a long time is required for a literature to mature and take the modern form of a territorial linguistic identity. Teleological historical reasoning, especially popular with nationalist writers, thus obstructs the asking of some interesting structural questions.[13] Absolutizing a single territorial configuration—the one that the modern period demonstrates—turns all other previous evidence into a 'tendency toward' or a 'waiting for' that configuration. This often makes us forget that there was a different configuration of the territorial in earlier times that needs to be spelled out.[14]

Still, identifying the exact territorial boundaries of Bangla literary reception is a *question* for which it might be difficult to find a

[12] The most relevant in this context are the critical discussions about anachronistic reading in the works of Quentin Skinner, John Dunn, and J.G.A. Pocock, and the resulting controversy around the work of the Cambridge school. See in particular Skinner [1969] 1988.

[13] I have tried to analyse the most common forms of this kind of argument in Kaviraj 1991.

[14] Some of these issues have been discussed with great perceptiveness and scholarship in the special millennium issue (*sahasrayan sankhyā*) of *Des* (2000).

satisfying answer, given the state of knowledge about readerships or audiences of listeners in premodern Bengal. I have wondered about the lack of territoriality in premodern cultural structures, which appears so strange to modern observers because we consider such territorial grounding so utterly natural and necessary—almost an ontological condition for the existence of all cultural objects. Evidently, in precolonial times there were people who understood a clearly differentiated, identifiable Bangla language and had the necessary skills to recognize, read, write, and carry on literary practices in it. But the 'unity' of this language is itself an interesting concept. Unity of a language, Bhudev Mukhopadhyay observed perceptively, can mean two different things: a single language that a group of people *speak*, or one that they *understand*.[15] The structure of the linguistic world is often marked by the interplay between these two. In contemporary India, for example, there is a functional Bombaybased Hindi that is easily *understandable* to people in most parts of the country where these vernaculars are spoken (demonstrated with incontrovertible certainty by the vast popularity of Hindi films). However, more stylized and purified forms of Hindi or Hindustani used by native speakers of the language, which have greater overlap with Sanskrit or Persianized Urdu, are not as easily intelligible to others.[16]

In considering premodern Bengal, similarly, there are clearly discernible variations between the languages used by the *mangalkavyas* and by the Vaisnava *padavali*. Yet at another level the two show a

[15] Mukhopadhyay [1892] 1981. I have discussed his views in Kaviraj 1995a. Bhudev Mukhopadhyay is of course concerned with a different question: What can be a common language for India? His argument is that Hindustani is already a common language because it is the language the largest number of people in all parts of India would find intelligible, though this does not mean that they would be able to speak it. He distinguishes between a commonly spoken language and a commonly intelligible language.

[16] I have heard complaints that the Hindi used in All India Radio broadcasts is too artificially Sanskritized and therefore often inaccessible to Muslims and common people. Critics say that this Hindi is intended to create a speech community from which Muslims and subalterns are excluded. By contrast, the Hindi used in Bombay popular films has to find a level understandable to both Hindi- and non-Hindi-speakers. For an excellent analysis of the recent history of Hindi, see Rai 2000.

commonness not just in the words and their meanings but in the more complex registers of *alankarik* forms, iconic images, and the structure of *rasas* evoked. Another feature of the traditional culture helps literary intelligibility, based on these common attributes. In the premodern linguistic structure, Sanskrit was the universal high language, and understanding Sanskrit requires training in its grammatical rules. Sentences formed in proper Sanskrit are not immediately accessible to ordinary vernacular speakers. But Sanskrit has a more complex and subtler cultural function. The vocabulary of the literary vernaculars are based on Sanskrit, composed of words either identical to (*tatsama*) or derived from (*tadbhava*) words in Sanskrit. Sentences formed primarily with *tatsama* words, minimizing the use of verbs and drawing the poetic play as much as possible from the use of nouns and adjectives, bring the vernacular closer to Sanskrit and make it widely understandable. I suspect that one of the most interesting features of Vaisnava poetry was its use of that kind of 'dual' language, a kind of inexplicit Sanskrit standing behind the Bangla or Maithili, precisely because the region through which it circulated was much larger than present Bengal. It could be received as a Sanskrit–Bangla transverse composition, just as it could be received as Sanskrit–Oriya. It would ideally have had to be intelligible to the entire space of eastern Vaishnavism, which included Mithila and Orissa (and possibly also Manipur, through the extended influence of Gaudiya Vaishnavism). Take as an example Jayadeva's famous lines:

lalita-lavanga-lata-parisilana-komala-malaya-samire
madhukara-nikara-karambita-kokila-kujita-kunja-kutire.

This is evidently Sanskrit, but each word here can also be read as a Bangla *tatsama* of the same meaning. The undecidability of this ambilinguistic writing is enhanced for Bangla speakers by the final words of the lines, *samire* (where the wind) and *kutire* (in the hut), which can also be Bangla words with roughly identical meanings as locative singular. That is how a modern Bangla literary audience would hear these lines. This is an example of a Sanskrit composition that, paradoxically, can be *read* in Bangla. Compare, as an obverse example—that is, a Bangla verse that is almost entirely composed of Sanskrit words—a poem from the Vaisnava poet Jagadananda:

manju-vikaca-kusuma-punja madhupa-sabda ganji gunja
kunjara-gati ganji gamana manjula-kula-nari
ghana-ganjana cikura-punja malati-phula-mala-ranja
anjana-juta kanja-nayant khanjana-gati-hari.

In this stanza the Bangla language has already settled considerably, if we look closely at the rhetorical devices. For instance, in a later line (*lalitadhare milita hasa deha dipati timiranasa*) the two words *hasa* and *nasa* would not rhyme in Sanskrit, but would in Bangla (where *s* and *s* are pronounced more or less the same), and that is clearly intended. Similarly, there are alliterative passages that would work only with a Bangla pronunciation.

dasana kundakusumanindu badana jitala sarada indu.
bindu bindu sarame gharame premasindhu-pyari.

A recognizable literary culture exists here, but it stretches out on several planes. It is not merely a Bangla culture but is also inextricably associated with the universalizing presence of Sanskrit. First of all, there is a unity imparted by the appreciation of the high Sanskrit canon, ranging from religious texts like the *Bhagavadgita* to literary classics such as those by Kalidasa and Jayadeva. All those educated in Sanskrit would be able to relate to this canonical tradition. Below that overarching cosmopolitan culture, and with a more restricted spatial spread, is another literary culture based on eastern Vaishnavism. Within this culture, historically, the literary centre shifted geographically with the power of exemplary performances. Jayadeva had the apparent advantage of writing in Sanskrit; but Vidyapati wrote his *padavali* compositions in Maithili. Interestingly, however, this did not restrict Vidyapati's audience to the Mithila region. He had a vast and respectful audience in Bangla-speaking areas, where his verses were perfectly understandable, down to the modern period. In fact, his poetry was also actively imitated, which could not have happened without some element of overlap or indeterminacy. A whole group of accomplished Bangla poets composed *padavali* under the explicit influence of Vidyapati's compositions. This canon was so strong that the young Tagore in the late nineteenth century composed a whole book of poetic songs in Brajabuli (supposedly the mellifluous language of mythical Braja; actually, a passable imitation of Vidyapati), which are still sung with undiminished ardour in commercial musical performances in Kolkata. At school, historical collections of Bangla poetry for children, dearly intended to provide them with a poetic genealogy, standardly begin with famous verses by Vidyapati.[17]

This medieval Vaisnava literary culture was evidently held together by a combined configuration of religious devotion and literary forms. Court patronage must have been an additional source of sustenance. Royal patronage, however, was a fickle and unreliable support, undependable if the religious persuasion of the ruler or his successors changed. The tastes of ordinary householders were more reliable and more widespread. Stories told about lives of poets, even if exaggerated or wholly apocryphal, illustrate that the frontiers of principalities and religious cultures did not in fact coincide, and this helped literary figures or styles to escape excessively obtrusive supervision by political power. Poets often escaped the disfavour of their notoriously fickle patrons by moving to a competing court or another part of the same religious region. Competition between courts or dynasties also restrained capricious royal treatment of celebrated artists.

Schematically, there are two salient features of the structure of premodern literary space. One is that the 'sense of space' of each vernacular is quite distinct from those of others, yet it is also organized in a different way from bounded modern spatiality. A territorial configuration contains certain points, such as holy cities, birthplaces of saints, locations of important events, and sites of pilgrimage and festivals. From either single or multiple centres it radiates outward, and as one goes toward the outside, the sense of this particular space grows fainter and then changes into a strange space, no longer familiar. Distinctions come on slowly, not dramatically. The significant mark of this conception of spatiality is probably the use of broad distinctions between near and far, familiar and strange—different from the sense of

[17] For instance: *madhava bahuta minati kari toya/deyi tulasi tile deha samaalu daya janu chodabi moyd* (Madhava, I implore you, I have offered this body to you with basil leaf and sesame seed; please rescue me, in your mercy). This came in the school collection *Kavitanjali*, edited by a well-known modern poet, Kalidas Ray, and widely used as a 'rapid reader' in lower secondary schools (in class 7 or 8) in the early 1960s. Standard collections of Bangla poetry might formally begin with a perfunctory reference to *caryapada* verses, but the real business of appreciable literature starts with Vaisnava *padavali*.

a bounded, meticulously calibrated space to which we are accustomed. The latter, it must be noted, requires both a contiguity of space and a corresponding homogeneity of the cultural community—the 'we' who would call this space their own. The other feature of premodern literary space is that it is not a single plane on which all types of cultural practices take place. It has several layers, and the configuration of the space on one layer, say, Sanskrit, does not coincide perfectly with the others. The mappings are quite different on different planes, the ends and beginnings are divergent; yet it is a single lived world of literary cultivation. Modern thinking tends to split this into a Sanskrit literary map and a Bangla literary map, but people would have experienced it as a single literary culture.

Premodern Literary Cultures in Bengal

It appears that in many parts of India the rise of the vernacular literatures had a great deal to do with two primary factors: deep changes in religious sensibility and alterations in political authority, both of which sought a new language of cultural expression. The earliest form of the Bangla language separated off from the general North Indian linguistic form of late Middle Indo-Aryan known as Avahattha.[18] The first extant specimens of Bangla texts, discovered in the late nineteenth century by Haraprasad Sastri in Nepal and the lower Tarai areas, are primarily Buddhist poetical compositions, *caryapadas*. Buddhist religion had long showed an acute consciousness of the question of popular language, starting from the use of Pali and Prakrit, and it was entirely consistent with that tradition of religious sensibility for *caryapada* poets to compose their doctrinal songs in the emerging vernaculars. Written primarily by religious mystics, these expressed popular Buddhist ideas about conduct, occasionally in a symbolic and esoteric language.[19] The Buddhist *tantras* made

---

[18] The standard work on the linguistic origins of the Bangla language and the technicalities of its slow process of separation from the Avahattha is Chatterji 1970–2.

[19] *Caryapada* refers to *carya*, meaning conduct. There is considerable scholarly debate about the *caryapadas*: whether the language they are written in should be called primitive Bangla (see Chatterji 1970–2 and Sen 1965) or something else. For the state of this debate, see Kvaerne 1977.

abundant use of such special linguistic codes, referred to as *sandhya bhasa*—enigmatic or elusive speech. Like other forms of technical jargon, the mastery of this symbolic language served to distinguish insiders from the uninitiated. Among Buddhist tantric adepts, *sandhya bhasa* provided a means to articulate esoteric knowledge that was thought to be inexpressible in ordinary terms.

This religious context for the early use of Bangla points to a peculiar feature of the cultural development of Bengal. From the time of the *caryapadas*, the religious sensibility that has carried Bangla literature forward through successive stages has very often been associated with a nonBrahmanic strand, possibly because of the strong connection between Brahmanism and the ritual use of Sanskrit. It is not surprising, then, that all the major strands of early and medieval Bangla literature are associated with dissident traditions: Buddhism (*caryapadas*); cults of the lesser goddesses (the *mangalkavyas*, dedicated to goddesses like Manasa or Candi); and the reformist Vaisnava religious sects, which remained within the general limits of Hinduism, but occupied heterodox positions (*padavali*).[20] This trend was to continue throughout the history of the literature, with the emergence of practically every new literary sensibility being tied to some form of antiBrahmanical religious experiment. A transformation of religious sentiment through doctrines of *bhakti* produced a split in linguistic and literary expressions of devotion as well. The theology of Hindu sects changed, creating a different aesthetic conception of divinity, one that emphasized kindness, compassion, and accessibility that required expression in a different linguistic register. *Bhakti* images necessitated a shift from a language of distance, which could give appropriate expression to the *aisvarya*—the inconceivable and ineffable splendour—of the divine, to a language of *madhurya*, or emotional gentleness and sweetness, which could express intimacy with the deity.

The World of the *Mangalkavyas*

One of the primary strands of medieval Bangla literary culture is the genre known as *mangalkavya*: legends composed in celebration of

---

[20] For a detailed and scholarly discussion, see Dasgupta 1966 .

deities that were meant to bring religious merit to the lives of their devotees. The *mangalkavya* is clearly demarcated from other genres by its narrative form, literary stylistics, and peculiar brand of religiosity and representation of the social world. *Mangalkavyas* were intimately connected with large-scale religious changes, most probably a slow incorporation of lower-caste cults of non-Brahmanical deities into the orthodox tradition. The narratives normally suggest some kinship between the new deities (which were most often female) and well-known figures in the Hindu pantheon. The goddesses Manasa and Candi were the most popular subjects of *mangalkavya* composition, though there were instances of *kavyas* of the same genre to the glory of Dharma and other gods. The genre enjoyed a surprisingly long life, continuing down to the eighteenth century: Mukundaram Chakravarti's *Candimangal*, the masterpiece of the form, was composed in the mid-sixteenth century, and Bharatcandra composed the *Annadamangal* in the eighteenth century.

Though the narrative structure of the *mangalkavya* is known for its social role in championing relatively unknown subaltern deities, it is also significant for its internal literary features. In *Manasamangal*, for instance, the merchant Candsadagar, a devotee of Siva, is unwilling to offer worship to Manasa, the goddess of snakes. He goes through a string of misfortunes on account of Manasa's curse: fourteen of his trading ships laden with wealth capsize in storms; six of his sons die prematurely; and his last son, Lakhindar, dies of snakebite on his wedding night. His new daughter-in-law, Behula, a rural and subaltern Savitri, eventually brings the son back from the dead, forcing the reluctant merchant to accept Manasa's divinity. In Weberian terms, the religious spirit animating the *mangalkavya* stories leans toward the magical, in contrast to the more intellectual and rationalized preoccupations of orthodox or developed *bhakti* doctrines. The narrative crises are mostly resolved by explicitly supernatural means, and there is little effort at elaboration of philosophical doctrine: the stories' authors appear content to win a place for their divine protagonists in the Hindu divine order.

Mangalkavyas are primarily written in a rustic vernacular style, with a predominance of *desi* vocabulary over *tatsama* words, matched by relatively unambitious and uncomplicated metric composition. Dialogues often approximate the grammatical laxity of ordinary conversation. In the internal narrative economy of the genre, female characters acquire an entirely unaccustomed prominence, and often their behaviour is much less constrained than the social restrictiveness of the feminine roles of high Brahmanical tales: Behula and Sanaka in the *Manasamangal* stories, and Phullara in the *Candimangal*, offer a far more pronounced subaltern feminine than the classical images of Radha or Sita in the Bangla versions of the epics.

It is generally acknowledged that the *mangalkavya* tradition offers a detailed and reliable picture of a lower-class social world, reflected in the activities performed by the main characters, and so brings startlingly realistic depictions of everyday life into the highly stylized world of conventional literatures. It is entirely possible for *mangalkavya* characters to have uproarious domestic quarrels, and their colourful language makes use of forceful expletives—a linguistic order unimaginable in exchanges between characters of the *Ramayana* or the Krsna stories of the Vaisnavas. From the aesthetic point of view, too, the *mangalkavyas*, though often emotionally rich, present a world far apart from the more formal *rasa* conventions of classical literature. The *mangalkavyas*, therefore, represent a highly significant complex of literary sensibility-combining a distinctly subaltern religious spirit with the depiction of a peasant world of want and domestic troubles. Some sections of this tradition show a great awareness and representation of an Islamic social world, or at least a clear recognition of the mixed religious character of Bengali society.

The *mangalkavya* tradition might not be more impressive than others in purely aesthetic terms, but from the point of view of a social history of literature its significance is incalculable. They contain in an understated way a complete reconstruction of the conventional aesthetic world and its narrative economy. In nearly all significant respects, the classical order based on a Brahmanical view of the world—both social and narrative—is left behind, replaced by an order that rejects some of its most sacred conventions. The deities worshipped, the human characters portrayed, the story lines, the forms of fabulation, the nature and implements of literary and aesthetic enchantment, the implied audience—everything is different.

In conventional narratives, the central characters are individuals empowered by either ritual status or political authority: narrative exchanges are normally between Kshatriyas and Brahmans, and there are a number of side characters. In the *mangalkavyas*, by contrast, the central characters often belong to lower castes or inferior professions: Dhanapati and Candsadagar are wealthy, but they are *sadagars*, i.e. traders who are not conventional objects of poetic celebration. Kalketu is a *vyadha*, a hunter who kills animals for profit—a low, polluting profession. But by a combination of Candi's blessings and his own premiraculous qualities of strength and honesty, he earns the right to be ruler of a kingdom. In traditional narratives, adventure is the exclusive preserve of Kshatriya warriors: as they travel to unknown lands on military expeditions or personal journeys they meet and win beautiful women and fame. In the *mangalkavyas*, however, somewhat as in the Sinbad stories, some of these same elements are centred on the *vanik*, the seafaring merchant. As the merchant-heroes take over the Kshatriya qualities of bravery, however, they add to it a new element of seafaring adventure, a kind of subtle intelligence, the curiosity of the explorer. They, not the Kshatriyas, are the masters of space.

   In these narrative moves, the *mangalkavya* tradition seems to disregard the Brahmanical hierarchy of virtues. The stable, unworried system of established equations between castes and individual qualities and their professions is set aside, and boundaries are breached by a more radical imagination of possibilities. It takes the narratively significant qualities of bravery, steadfastness, resourcefulness, and subtlety and redistributes them among members of different castes and genders. The feminine characters of the *mangalkavyas* are often subtle, intelligent, and masterful in the management of their households and their world, being often gifted with a more penetrating awareness of the world's complexities than their husbands. Characters like Phullara and Khullana exude a much greater assertive femininity than do the inhabitants of the upper-caste *antahpur*, the women's quarters. They often assist their husbands outside the home (for example, the hunter's wife sells the hide in the market); they vociferously assert their disagreements on important domestic decisions; they fend off rivals in love—even Candi herself—by the simple force of their chastity mixed with some slyness; and at times of crisis they give excellent counsel to their headstrong or unsubtle husbands. The *mangalkavya* tradition therefore shifts the narrative world to a different social universe; the life of lower-caste society is brought into the sacred sphere of literature.

The *Caitanyacaritramrta*

A parallel process of growth of a new vernacular literary form can be found in the Gaudiya Vaisnava tradition, in a text poised between two moments of its historical development. All the three great religious biographies of Caitanya—those by Vrndavandas, Locandas, and Jayacandra—underscore Caitanya's divinity by telling with a sense of incredulous wonder how he made the miraculous happen. However, Krsnadas's *Caitanyacaritamrta*, the great philosophical text of the Gaudiya Vaisnavas, is filled with a different sense of Caitanya's divinity. At the time of this text, Caitanya was already in the process of being canonized. The Brahmanical tradition, which he defied so wonderfully, already recognized the need for reconciliation with his canonization; and reciprocally, his disciples acknowledged the advantages of accepting the high Sanskritic language and iconicity, and of transferring those techniques to a celebration of Caitanya's personality.[21] Thus, the evident humanity of the biographies—the narrative tension of which lies, for instance, in waiting to see what will happen in his contest with the *qazi* (civil judge), the symbol of political authority—is replaced by a text of a very different type. The narration of the same episode in the *Caitanyacaritamrta* is calm, not tense. Unlike Vrndavandas, its narrator is not conveying an unbearable

[21] By the time Krsnadas was composing the *Caitanyacaritamrta*, Caitanya's religion had already been reabsorbed into mainstream Brahmanical Hinduism. The story of the evolution of Caitanya's religion is complex. Several distinct types of associates and devotees were drawn to Caitanya. Nityananda was drawn from an *avadhuta* background, contemptuous of normal Hindu observances; on the other hand, there were sedate householders like Srinivasa Acarya who sought to bring Caitanya's doctrines back into the solid bases of respectability. Consequently, after Caitanya's death his religion gave rise to several sometimes mutually incompatible strands, all of which, however, treated the vernacular *Caitanyacaritamrta* as their main religious text rather than the more esoteric and Sanskrit texts of the *gosvamis* from Vrndavan. By reabsorption into Brahmanism I refer primarily to such cultural practices as the use of Sanskrit; the condensing of ideas into relatively esoteric *sutras*, which require learned commentaries; and the general use of an exclusivist literate apparatus. It is a cultural rather than a strictly religious Brahmanism that is at issue here.

anxiety through this unprecedented contest, but is entirely assured of the eventual victory of his lord. The episode becomes his play; literally, his *lila*.

The *Caitanyacaritamrta* is an astonishing document, situated between several literary models and written in a mixture of languages. It is still a biographical narrative of Caitanya's life, written with the evident claim of testimonial authenticity. Like Caitanya's other biographers, Krsnadas recounts what the master said after invoking the exact situational context. However, compared to the others, Krsnadas is far more interested in Caitanya's religious philosophy. Consequently, a great deal of attention is paid to Caitanya's sermons, to the intricate disputations with religious scholars who preferred other modes of *bhakti* worship or other strands of Vaishnavism, and occasionally to Caitanya's glosses of literary texts from the wider tradition of classical poetry. The historical-biographic narration throughout the text, including the master's dialogues, is in Bangla. Krsnadas rarely portrays him breaking into Sanskrit in ordinary situations, though it is generally acknowledged that Caitanya was one of the great scholars of the language in his time. So Krsnadas's decision to dilute his language into Bangla rather than retain a pristine Sanskrit medium is a denial of Brahmanical orthodoxy; it is a way of *doing* religion, a way of inviting people who are usually excluded from a high religious experience into its centre.

In Krsnadas's work we can see the workings of a philosophical reinterpretation of Caitanya's life. He recounts the tales of Caitanya's life in Bangla but is always careful to frame them in theological terms, providing first a preparation for the great event to be narrated and following up with a commentary that separates out the divine from the mundane, so that no unwary reader misses the cosmic significance in the apparently human drama. The commentary is in a heavy, because more technical, Bangla style, but the doctrinal framing is always in Sanskrit, using the entire apparatus of classical Sanskrit, from the learned exoticism of its vocabulary to the lofty skill of fashioning verses in complex meters like *mandakranta*.[22]

The mixed composition of the *Caitanyacaritamrta*—it is at once a biography and a doctrinal treatise, an account and a commentary,

[22] As for example *Caitanyacaritamrta*, Adikhanda 1, *sloka* 5.

incorporating Sanskrit and Bangla, high and low—helps us understand what medieval authors were attempting to achieve by writing in Bangla. Every time a religious movement had to widen its circle of followers, it had recourse to this linguistic technique. Thus, the historical process by which Bengalis became a people in a linguistic sense must be related to these periodic extensions, these successive 'democratizing' movements of religious ideas. At the same time, the linguistic texture of the *Caitanyacaritamrta* shows that the traditional structure of linguistic practice, in which individuals knew and used several languages, especially Sanskrit and Bangla, continued. Associated with these movements was the creation of a kind of bridge language, a form of Sanskrit that could be read from both sides. Accessibility from the Sanskrit side ensured that these compositions would have a wide circulation and make sense to those who understood Sanskrit or neighbouring vernacular languages; accessibility to Bangla meant that the works could also circulate among Bengalis who knew little or no Sanskrit.[23] This kind of mixed competence continued, certainly down to the work of poets like Bharatcandra in the eighteenth century.

The topic of mixed literary modes becomes more interesting and complex when the focus turns to literary practice: when we move from the question of what language the poets wrote in to what aesthetic structures were typically associated with each literary field. Was the act of writing in Bangla merely the translation of Sanskritic aesthetic processes, structures, feelings (*rasas*) into a lower, more accessible language? Or was the language shift the condition for writing an aesthetics that began to be different? Obviously, this question is closely related to a fascinating and awkward larger question: If the shift to writing in Bangla marks a rupture with the literary sensibility of early medieval times, should we treat it as the beginning of a certain kind of modernity?

There is a particularly intriguing aspect of Caitanya's religious teaching that might connect significantly with this question. Caitanya

---

[23] Many popular *stotras* (hymns) would seem to have this status: like the Rama *stotras* by Tulasidas, or the Vallabhacarya *stotra* to Krsna. Many versions of the *Caitanyacaritamrta* were found outside Bengal, in North India, and Tarapada Mukherjee argues that the text itself shows the use of Hindi terms. See his editorial introduction to the *Caitanyacaritamrta* in Krsnadas Kaviraj 1986.

constantly emphasized the metaphorical quality of the transgressive principle at the heart of his new doctrine: *parakiyatattva*, love for God with the intensity of a lover's desire for a loved one to whom he or she is denied social access—for instance, because the loved one is married to another, as in the case of Krsna and Radha. The emphasis on metaphoricity was taken up with great seriousness by Caitanya's later interpreters, such as the Vrndavan *gosvamis*. (The classical text that expounds the theory of *parakiya* love is Rupa Gosvami's *Ujjvalanilamani* [The Blazing Sapphire], *c.* 1550.) This interpretive strategy ensured that the doctrinal innovation could be immense without being socially disruptive. And turning supernatural or otherwise rationally inadmissible ideas into metaphorical keys is often the mark of a modern religious sensibility.

The World of the Vaisnava *Padavali*

Medieval Bangla literary cultures reveal two rather different, in some ways contradictory, aspects. Socially, the Hindu religious system was pervasively and punctiliously hierarchical. Yet culturally there was considerable scope for improvisation and innovation—a feature of much of Indian high culture, which allowed new religious figures and their followers to claim that they were trying to extend or explore ideas that were already part of the received tradition (*agama*). Loosely terming these as vertical and lateral relations, respectively, we can say that there was practically no tolerance for revisions of vertical relationships but considerable tolerance for lateral experimentation. For this reason many reformist trends started off with a disingenuous or at least misleading claim that they were engaging in a lateral extension of doctrine and religious experiment. A remarkable example from medieval North India is Tulsidas and his remaking of Rama in an image significantly different from Valmiki's.

There are partial parallels to this kind of reformism in the Bangla texts of the *Ramayana* and the *Mahabharata* by Krttibas and Kasiramdas, respectively. Though these texts are conventionally called translations (*anuvad*), what they do to the originals is actually more complex. They retell the story freely in Bangla verse—quite a different literary enterprise from what translation means in modern contexts. (In fact, a translation of this literal sort had to wait until Kaliprasanna Sinha produced his famous version of the *Mahabharata* in the mid-nineteenth century.) Because they are free translations, they provide their authors with ample opportunity for recreating, often quite dramatically, the narrative, literary, and *rasa* structures of the text. The tight structure of the narrative becomes loose and unfocused, and at times narrative complexity is sacrificed for a clearly linear popular story. The verse forms, though usually unadorned yet graceful in the Sanskrit original (as for instance the *anustubh* metre), are sometimes excessively simplified and onedimensional, as in the simplest Bangla metric form of *payar* (a fourteen-syllable rhymed couplet). Culturally, this accomplishes something quite significant: it brings the high epic text closer to people precisely by destroying its distancing grandeur. But it is doubtful that these adapted texts bring into being anything of great consequence aesthetically.

More interpretively intriguing from the point of view of aesthetic history, as well as more historically noteworthy, was the *padavali* poetry of the Vaisnava tradition. Medieval Vaisnavas in Bengal had a stock of resources to draw upon—a large, disparate earlier tradition of Hindu religious literature whose elements were dispersed across the texts and religious thought of the *Mahabharata*, the *Bhagavatapurana* (which it relied upon more than either of the great epics), and the more popular fabulist traditions around Radha and Krsna. They also had available to them the riches of the Maithili Vaisnava poetry of Vidyapati. But the specific configuration of images and narratives, along with the registers of aesthetic emotions, that the *padavali* gradually produced is quite unique. Elsewhere, I have explored the nature of this transformation of the *rasa* register of Vaisnava poetry, since it is so crucial to understanding modern Bangla.[24] It provided, in a sense, the template from which modern Bangla writers of the nineteenth century were to break away. Yet even while rupturing the *padavali*'s aesthetic template, the modern writers continued to value and deploy its elements so as not to let them disappear and become unobtainable. They used them constantly in their own literature as 'material'—as, for instance, in Tagore's famous interpretative poem 'Vaisnavkavita'.

The most striking transformation affected the literary character of Radha, the central erotic figure of the Gaudiya Vaisnava cult. In the works of earlier Vaisnava traditions, she seems to be very close to some of the images from earlier literary traditions, such as *prakrti*, or

[24] See Kaviraj 1995b: chapter 3.

primal nature—utterly indomitable, impossible to deflect from her decided 'natural' course of love. In earlier Vaisnava texts, Radha has the irrepressible quality of nature's great generative power, not merely in the crude sense of an endless willingness in love play, but also in the unconquerable lust for life that she represents in her resplendent sexuality. Ordinarily, conventional religious sensibility is coy and prudish, unwilling to speak openly about erotic enjoyment, but the early figure of Radha turns this upside down in the most remarkable fashion. Her existence is focused on sexuality; she seems to exist for nothing else. And her sexuality is so utterly open and uninhibited that it becomes, in an ironic but undeniable sublimation, strangely pure (the *Ujjvalanilamani* makes this point doctrinally). In her disloyalty to her husband and family, and to her social entanglements, there is a finality and power that can only be regarded as destiny. Ordinary mortals can only see her great spectacle and rejoice and hope that their own lives may be touched by a waft of this divine breeze.

The Radha of the Gaudiya Vaisnava tradition—not necessarily in religious doctrine but definitely in literature—still shows a struggle between two very powerful tendencies. One reflects and carries forward the *Bhagavata* icon of joyous abandon, and interestingly, whenever this aesthetic configuration is invoked there is a propensity toward rhetorical embellishment. When this Radha is going into the dark forest on a full-moon night, we must hear the jingle of her restrained anklets; the entire descriptive tradition of the *abhisarika* (the woman who braves the night to meet her lover), expressed in a grammar well understood from Kalidasa onward, is condensed in the depiction of her bodily movements and gestures.[25] The mandatory *anuprasa* (alliteration) and *utpreksa* (poetic fantasy)—the connection between literary ornamentation and this description of beauty, symmetry, fullness—is retained in the poetry of Vaisnava authors like Govindadas. But there is an unmistakable new contrasting tendency in the representation of femininity in the Radha of the *padavali*. This femininity is much less assertive; she is weak, constrained, caged, simply bewailing her fate and enlarging on her own vulnerability and misfortunes in love. At the same time, there is a distinctive new

[25] Detailed discussion can be found in Rupa Gosvami's *Ujjvalanilamani*, chapters 9, 10, 11, and 15.

development of character, an unconventional attention to the poetic exploration of inner mental states. Intricate, conventionalized mental states did form part of the traditional representational repertoire,[26] but the stirrings of individual subjective states in the Vaisnava *padavali* literature are of an entirely different kind: this avoids conventional typologies and begins to explore individual consciousness and its infinite, unpredictable variability. Accordingly, the tone of speech in the Vaisnava *padavali* texts changes significantly. The texts become primarily Radha's speech, but her speech has a strange character. It tries, in a sense, to take revenge on a new kind of incarceration through an interminability of speech. A second strand of Vaisnava *padavali* poetry, inaugurated by Candidas and continued by Jnanadas, which differentiaties itself from the Vidyapati strand, developed an entire metaphysic of loss and suffering that was represented primarily through feminine perception and metaphor. The representational, iconic figure of Radha signals a real transformation of the *rasa* aesthetics of this strand of *padavali* literature.

This new Vaisnava *padavali* poetry gave rise to a new canon of poetic performances, and some 'great poets' were selected among others less worthy of eminence. Its iconic material affiliates it to the story of Radha and Krsna derived from the *Bhagavata* and, in part, ultimately from the *Mahabharata;* its more directly literary ancestry is drawn from Jayadeva's *Gitagovinda* and Vidyapati's verses. But the aesthetics of this literature are completely distinctive. The structure of *rasa* it developed was unique—close to the range of emotions ordinary people experienced in their ordinary lives, and thus transforming the everyday with a touch of the divine.

From a literary-historical perspective, therefore, the Vaisnava corpus carried much greater significance than the adaptations of the epics. The Bangla versions of the epics, in my view, made an important sociological contribution by making the stories accessible, in a written vernacular form, to common people, but they gave up the heroic aesthetics of the original Sanskrit texts without discovering an aesthetic structure of their own. The *padavali* poetry, on the other

---

[26] The *Ujjvalanilamani,* for instance, follows up its ninth chapter on *harivallabha-prakcranam* with three immensely elaborate sections on the components of *rasa* analysis: *anubhava, vyabhicaribhava,* and *sthayibhava.*

hand, continued to work with elements of the Krsna narratives from past Vaisnava traditions, but it focused on the unheroic narratives of the episode in Mathura as a new axis around which all elements of the narrative economy could be rearranged, and a unique structure of *rasa* sensibility developed. Sociologically, this aesthetic structure enjoyed wide popularity and was continually performed in *palakirtans* in local temples in Bengal and major theatres of eastern Vaishnavism down to the 1950s.[27]

Through this particular instance, we might be able to grasp what the literary meant in this culture. Clearly, the literary was a sphere split into multiple layers, each requiring distinctive types of skills of composition and appreciation. The high Sanskrit level did not remain constant and unchanged. Precisely because it continued for such a long time, there was an incessant accretion of texts and textual materials. Because of its continuity and the constant need to cater to different tastes and skills, the Sanskrit layer was in some ways the most extensive and also the most internally differentiated. It vascilated through time between a tight, high Sanskrit corpus and a more accessible popular corpus meant for enunciative uses (e.g. chanting, which does not require pedantic grammatical mastery over the passages or stanzas). The lower levels of this Sanskrit stratum touched the boundaries of the Bangla stratum, which performed a different function. Bangla was used to produce a new form of literariness, closer and more accessible to popular sensibility, and exemplifying something of the doctrine of universality implicit in Caitanya's religious thinking. It at once brought the sense of the high religious within the reach of ordinary people and lifted everyday, ordinary life into contact with the divine—a distinctive feature of all *bhakti* movements.

This literary culture implies the existence of a circle of oral competencies, but we should guard against the usual, imitative superstition that the oral is always 'lower' than the written. At least

[27] The *palakirtan*, or recitation of the story of Krsna and Radha through a series of evenings to a group of devotees gathered in a specific temple, is an innovative form of religious practice that diverges from more traditional kinds of Hindu worship. Interestingly, the inventiveness of Caitanya's religion spread to all spheres. It developed not merely a new literary sensibility centred on a new story but also a far more communal form of the use of these literary forms in religious rituals than ordinary Hinduism.

one kind of literary orality is based on the idea that all texts necessarily have a representative function. Texts contain a possibility of meaning, but this meaning often waits on something that exists even before meaning begins—the sensuous, pre-semantic attractiveness of the aural or the musical. This stratum of the text must be brought into presentation (i.e. into aural presence) by means of oral mediation. In functions like the chanting of mantras in household worship or the enunciation of the *padavali* in a hymn (*kirtan*) performance, oral skills are crucial and aesthetically vital for bringing the right sound to a *sloka* or a song.

Vaisnava literature eventually broke down and reformed boundaries between literary languages in a radical fashion. Sanskrit was no longer the only prestige language, and the newly developed poetic Bangla tried imperceptibly to slide into a high status alongside it. In Vaisnava religious practices the use of Sanskrit for ceremonial purposes remained, but the new compositions in Bangla came to occupy a place of aesthetic prestige. A portion of Caitanya's enormous importance in history is that he taught the Bangla language to speak the divine.

The late-medieval Vaisnava rupture with traditional high culture was in one respect more radical than modernity's break with tradition in the nineteenth century. The nineteenth-century literary language enlisted Sanskrit on its side; it is very Sanskrit-near. The poetic language of the strand of medieval Vaisnava literature of Candidas and Jnanadas, however, is often consciously Sanskrit-distant. From the standpoint of a comparative sociology of literature, the Vaisnava break with tradition contained elements similar to the ruptures with traditional forms and literary practices that led to the earlymodern turn in Western literature: it was based on a crucial intervention in the religious sensibility of the society and was associated with fundamental religious and social reform. The congregation of the new religion provided its particular audience. A religion with a deep democratic impulse temporarily undermined the established authorities of orthodoxy and forced orthodoxy on the defensive. Acutely conscious of its newness, this religion sought a different aesthetic as well as a language appropriate for its anti-Brahmanical message. It used traditional aesthetic and literary constructs, like Sanskrit texts and anthologies (for example, Mammata's eleventh-century *Kavyaprakasa* was a favourite of Caitanya's and he returned to favourite verses for constant reinterpretation), but the cultural process at work was strikingly similar to what Pollock describes in his accounts of early Kannada. The use of Sanskrit cosmopolitanism is not surprising, because the new vernacular was created by a bicultural intelligentsia, and the Sanskrit world was a constant reference—either positive or negative—as a cultural structure to be emulated or abjured. Significantly, the vernacular culture that the new religion sought to establish, partly in competition with the Sanskrit, was meant to be cosmopolitan, not parochial.[28] It boldly innovated popular and collective aesthetic forms like the *sankirtan* (congregational singing, usually in a procession), where the musical performance did not happen in a specified, restricted space—in a temple, or a house—but moved through the streets of Navadvip in a new, open-ended 'public' spectacle. It also produced a literature that shifted the emphasis in the narrative discourse to the feminine subject in an astonishing inversion of conventions. Most significantly, it started to speak about the individual's state of mind in a new language of self-exploration. Yet there is no doubt that this stage in the history of literature passed without establishing durable institutions or leading to permanent modifications of the social world. The reforming energies of the social movement and the innovativeness of the literary forms were contained, eventually lost their way, and ultimately succumbed to orthodox restoration.

There is an apparent pattern in the history of relatively defined literary cultures like the Vaisnava structure. They periodically shake up the traditions of social and cultural orthodoxy without decisively

[28] See Pollock 1998. Although I do not find an exact parallel in Bengal to the role of patronage of political power in literary developments that Pollock demonstrates in the case of South India, there are strong parallels in other regards. Caitanya is clearly a cosmopolitan figure, having exemplary control of the Sanskrit corpus; and his travels in South and North India, particularly his disputations with other Vaisnava schools, is crucially facilitated by this. The religious sensibility he intends to set up is also cosmopolitan in character—intelligible to southern Vaishnavism as well as to northern devotees based at Vrndavan. Clearly, the redactions of the *Caitanyacaritamrta* that its editors, Sen and Mukherjee, analyse, show a vernacular cosmopolitanism—with versions collected from areas as distant as Rajasthan, the Braj region, and Orissa. See Mukherjee's introduction to *Caitanyacaritamrta* in Krsnadas Kaviraj 1986.

destroying them. As a literary culture gradually becomes cut off from the social process that generated it in the first place and gave it vitality, its active cultivation and continuation as a 'serious' literature suffer and degenerate, often falling into endless uncreative repetitiveness and a pointless exhibition of skills. Jagadananda's stanza quoted earlier is a good example of this kind of literary mannerism. As a composition, it demonstrates undoubted rhetorical skill, but its concern with formal features such as alliteration is obsessive, and its poetic imagination is feeble.[29] Its most significant feature historically is its slippage from the distinctive aesthetic structure of the Vaisnava *padavali* toward reabsorption into the sterile prosodic technicality of the standard Brahmanical erudition.

It would be entirely wrong, however, to conclude from the social decline of Vaishnavism that the *padavali* literary culture was erased without a trace. The peculiar intelligence of a tradition often prevents that eventuality, and its important creations are stored away in a kind of inactive inventory in literary-cultural memory. They survive not as living literature but within the living anthology of the tradition, available to be played upon by a new literary sensibility or a historically recreated consciousness. A tradition perhaps always exists as an archive for effective literary history, though the exact manner in which it produces these effects needs to be elucidated.[30]

There is evidence of a widespread anthological practice associated with the *padavali*, though materials were probably not collected in standardized, written anthologies. Thus a canon was formed that, though weak, still exhibited an internal coherence. Certainly, high points of performance were recognized, implying that some standards of judgement were applied by the collective spirit, which used these cultural items iconically. The compositions of Jayadeva and Vidyapati

---

[29] As in this *vyatireka* from the same Jagadananda poem, which is utterly standardized and unsurprising: *dasana kundakusumanindul vadana jitala sarada indu* (Her teeth put the *kunda* flower to shame, and her face is superior in beauty to the autumn moon).

[30] If we look at nineteenth- and twentieth-century Bangla appropriations of the Vaisnava *padavali* texts, it is clear that interpreters could invest them with a modern romantic sensibility and read them through a strikingly fruitful 'fusion of horizons'. This is quite self-conscious in Tagore's famous poem on the *padavali*, 'Vaisnavkavita'.

were treated as models by aspiring composers, though not by more Sanskrit-distant writers like Candidas and Jnanadas. The new poetry of emotion appeared to appeal increasingly to a more diffuse, undefined, and unorganized popular taste with a new criterion of accessibility. Beautiful poetry, it was realized, could be created by a string of mundane words, consciously abjuring the pedantic, rhetorical conceits of the erudite. Yet when the creative and social vitality of the Vaisnava culture waned, the strand that retained greater literary coherence was the one closer to the standard Brahmanical practices and pedagogies—which emphasized the sound (*sabda*) or the technical element rather than the distinctiveness of meaning (*artha*) that characterized the less academic style. The Sanskrit or Sanskrit-derived segment could securely defend its literary place precisely because it could go back to the strongly rehearsed pedagogy of the Sanskrit schools (*tol*) and their teaching of poetics.

To state a large and risky hypothesis: The movement of literary language in Bengal seems to have paralleled the movement of social, particularly religious, reform.[31] As long as the impulse for religious reform remained active, experimentation in literary technique and aesthetic structure continued. When that impulse died down, literary forms—like the religion itself—tended to be reabsorbed into orthodoxy. It appears unfair to characterize the forms of Vaisnava poetry like the *padavali* as medieval except in a purely chronological sense, since they display some elements of early modern literature; yet their eventual demise indicates that modernity is a matter not

---

[31] This is not meant to be a general statement about Indian vernaculars. I am sure Pollock is right that this line of argument has been used uncritically and often erroneously. In certain vernacular regions there is an obvious connection between the rise of new political power and the appreciation of the power of the vernacular, though in Bengal it is difficult to find such a direct connection. But two other lines of thought need to be explored more fully. First, the political ascendancy of Islamic rulers may have been associated with the writing of texts that used an Islamic cosmopolitanism. Second, religious reform is itself related to shifts in social power; so it might be prudent to avoid saying that religious reform involves religious but not political changes. Instead, we could perhaps argue that these changes are political through being religious. In that case, the boundary between a religious and a political explanation would have to be modified.

simply of sensibility but much more emphatically of institutions. If these sensibilities do not enable the crystallization of institutions that can provide them with practical, material form, they tend to decay, disperse, and eventually succumb to the silent but immensely powerful undertow of orthodoxy.

The Eighteenth Century: The Last of the Premodern

An analysis of the literary culture of the eighteenth century is important not because that culture produced a distinctive new literature but for understanding the nature of colonialism's impact. The works of Bharatcandra Raygunakar, one of that century's foremost writers, display the cultural forms that marked that period and show what it lacked in comparison with the forms of literary modernity introduced through Western contact. Bharatcandra's corpus is amazingly varied and full of technical virtuosity, starting from his early *Rasamanjari* to his three best-known works, *Annadamarigal, Mansinha,* and *Vidyasundar,* which form parts of a single poetic structure. These three texts together illustrate the strange geometry of literary culture in precolonial Bengal.

The *Annadamangal* continues the tradition of medieval *mangalkavya,* but its focus on Annada, or Annapurna, divine figure from the central Sakta canon, rather than on a relatively marginal goddess, reflects its adaptation to the high Brahmanical religion. The *Mansinha* recognizes the mixed social world of Muslims and Hindus, and, more crucially, the political supremacy of the Muslim elite. It portrays a world of Muslim political power in which Hindus like Majumdar, Annada's exemplary devotee, live by a combination of loyalty, cunning, and, when all else fails, miraculous assistance from Annapurna herself. In the *Vidyasundar* a romance takes place in the city of Barddhaman, which represents an urban context with a strong commercial element. The work's celebration of the power of money (*kadi*) confirms suggestions from recent historical research that the eighteenth century was a period of intense commercial expansion.[32] An old woman with privileged access to the princess in the forbidden space of the royal

---

[32] The extent of the exploration of new routes to social power in eighteenth-century India, after the collapse of the Mughal empire, is described in Bayly

antahpur (harem) consoles Sundar, the hero, by singing the praises of
money as the main implement in the pursuit of happiness: 'Money
buys what we eat; there is no friend except money. Money can buy
tiger's milk, and get an old man married. People die for the love of it;
it helps seduce respectable married women.'[33]

Bharatcandra was highly skilled in the use of metre and rhetoric,
and he experimented with producing in Bangla, with miraculous
virtuosity, the most difficult forms of classical Sanskrit prosody.[34]
Yet these experiments remain within the formal conventions and
rasa structure of a decidedly traditional literary sensibility; they are a
world apart from the struggles that were to convulse Bangla literary
culture in the next century.

Islamic Aspects of Bangla Literary Culture

A complex and contentious problem in the historical evolution of
Bangla literary culture is the place of Islam. Bengal as a region had
a long and continuous history of religious heterodoxy in which one
anti-Brahmanical movement followed another. After the decline
of Buddhism in Bengal, other strands of religious practice hostile
to orthodox Brahmanism found considerable support. Some
commentators suggest that Caitanya's followers were clearly divided
into several groups, and one of these, centred on the figure of
Nityananda, tried to carry on practices of heterodoxy abhorrent to
the ideologically timid mainstream, which wished to maintain the
respectability of the normal householder. Eventually, Brahmanical
Hinduism had major contenders in Islam on one side and in reform

---

1988, and in Subrahmanyam 1990 and 1994. For a general discussion, though
now somewhat dated, of this revisionist literature, see Washbrook 1988. A
readable translation of *Vidyasundar* is available in Dimock 1963.

[33] Bharatcandra 1950c: 202. The original reads: *kadi phatka chida dai
bandhu nai kadi bai/kadite bagher dugdha mile/kadite budar biya kadi lobhe
mare giya/kulabadhu bhule kadi dile.*

[34] Writing Bangla verse to the exacting specifications of some Sanskrit
chandas was considered technically difficult. Bharatcandra showed off his skills
by composing verses in metres like *bhujarigaprayata*. In modern Bangla, similar
skills were displayed by Satyendranath Datta, who composed in *mandakranta*,
albeit with some awkwardness.

or heterodox sects like the Vaisnavas on the other. The historical relation between Bangla literary culture and Islam is a question of immense complexity.[35]

Islamic courts often patronized composers of Vaisnava *padavali*, and there is considerable evidence of a slow extension of Islamic influence into various branches of Bangla literary culture. The Islamic strand of literary composition that developed, in turn, elaborated a cosmopolitanism parallel to the Sanskritic literary universe. Critical analyses of Islamic composition in Bangla point out that the language was full of loan words not only from Arabic and Persian but also from the North Indian vernaculars with which Islamic high culture bore a particularly close connection. Just as for Hindu literature Sanskrit was a vehicle for a high cosmopolitan culture from which vernaculars drew many of their literary principles, this Islamic literature shows a similarly transregional culture that gave its intellectuals access to an equally varied Islamic cosmopolis. They were the bearers of a second and parallel vernacular cosmopolitanism.

Other branches of late medieval literature carried obvious marks of a lively transaction between the Hindu and Islamic parts of late medieval Bengali civilization. Some observers consider it possible that Caitanya (who died in 1534) came into contact with Sufi ideas through some of his early associates, though the literary culture associated with him, at least in the form in which it was eventually canonized by the *gosvamis* of Vrndavan, shows little direct influence of Islamic language or forms. By contrast, both the language and the narrative content of Mukundaram Chakravarti's *Candimangal* (its first recitation, according to internal textual evidence, took place in 1555–6) shows an intimate knowledge of Islamic locutions and social practices.[36] Bharatcandra's *Mansinha* presented an Islamic side of the social and political universe with fluent familiarity. Mukundaram

[35] For reasons of space, it is impossible to analyse the scholarly literature on Bangla literary history in terms of their relative emphasis on Hindu and Muslim authors here. A comparison of standard history texts from West Bengal and from East Pakistan or Bangladesh would show the obvious difference in emphasis between the Hindu and Islamic sides of Bangla literary culture. It is interesting, however, to compare differences between the histories published in East Bengal before and after Bangladeshi independence in 1971.

[36] Sen 1965: 132.

and Bharatcandra are eloquent examples of Bhudev Mukhopadhyay's judgement at the end of the nineteenth century that orthodox Hindus should consider Muslims their *svajati* (own race or people) because the two, if divided by religion, were joined together by participation in a single material and social world.[37] In texts written by Hindu authors Muslim individuals and groups were seen, with increasing frequency and decisiveness, as part of a mixed social world—in Caitanya's biographies, the hostile *qazi* who was won over by his new religious dispensation; the mixed language of the *Candimangal*, which tells the story of the establishment of a Muslim area in the capital of Kalketu's kingdom; and the frequent appearance of Muslim characters in Bharatcandra's writings.[38]

It is by its contrast to this history of continuous and expanding transaction with Islam that the turn of events in the later part of the nineteenth century appears astonishing. The great Sanskrit and Bangla scholar of the second half of the nineteenth century Haraprasad Sastri, with his keen sociolinguistic sensitivity, put the situation of Bangla linguistic culture before the coming of colonialism quite accurately:

> In our country in those times three types of language were current in cultivated circles. Those *bhadralok* who had to deal with Muslim Nawabs and Omarahs used a Bangla with a great many Urdu words mixed in it. The language of those who studied the *sastras* contained a large number of Sanskrit words. There were many other people of substance apart from these two small groups. Both Urdu and Sanskrit words were mixed in their language. Poets and composers of *pancalis* composed their songs in this language. Broadly, there were three types of language for three groups: the Brahman pandits, people who dealt with courts, and ordinary men of property.[39]

More important than this linguistic taxonomy was the structure of linguistic and literary culture as a whole. It appears that through their

[37] Mukhopadhyay [1892] 1981: 13–16.

[38] Chakravarti 1977: 68.

[39] Sastri 1956, 1: 199. For a serious exploration of the class and cultural definitions of the Bengali *bhadralok*, 'gentle persons', see Bhattacharyya 2000. *Pancalis* were popular poetic compositions celebrating the glory of deities. They were used mnemonically by common people but were also read more formally in religious ceremonies, particularly in women's rituals.

respective forms of hyperglossia—Sanskrit and Arabic-Persian—the two sides of the Bangla vernacular had access to vast cosmopolitan literary spheres. These two cosmopolitanisms were not entirely exclusive; rather, people of high education acquired an asymmetric proficiency in both. Thus cosmopolitanism was not newly discovered by the modern intelligentsia; they were merely rearranging and redirecting a much older tradition of linguistic and cultural versatility.

In the age of Rammohan Roy (1774–1833), the cultivation of an upper-class Bengali included a mandatory initiation into Islamic culture and a fluent grasp of Persian. By the time of Rabindranath Tagore (1861–1941), roughly a century later, literary high culture had gone through a striking conversion to become a more solidly Hindu sphere. The cultural processes that brought on this transformation were driven by Western influences of all kinds, ranging from political liberalism, rationalist epistemology, and positivist sociology to modernist conceptions of culture.

Although a small Muslim political aristocracy had established itself in Bengali society through the distant and ever-weakening support of the Mughal empire, the Muslims constituted the bulk of the peasantry. Literacy skills were largely confined to the Hindu upper castes, who were the first to respond to opportunities offered by colonial rule. Certainly, this group of willing and enthusiastic collaborators did not represent the whole of Hindu society; their collaborative and reformist efforts faced stiff opposition from more traditional opinion. But it is significant that the conflict between the Brahmo Samaj (the 'society of Brahma', a religious reform group founded by Rammohan Roy in 1828) and Hindu conservatism was in some ways an internal affair of an elite that had learned to use the modern cultural apparatus—including schooling in the colonial education system, developing the skill of articulate debate in a literary public sphere, and highly intelligent use of the colonial legal system. Muslim participation in the early stages of this new modern culture was accordingly disproportionately small. It is to this new culture that we must now turn, for it constitutes one of the most fateful, complex, and contradictory transformations in the history of Bengal: the arrival of a colonial modernity in which formal principles were often universalistic but social practices involved enormous exclusions.

Literary Cultures of Modern Bengal: Colonialism and Linguistic Change

Undoubtedly, the greatest change in the history of Bengali literary culture happened after the firm establishment of colonial authority from the late eighteenth century. The entry of colonialism into Bengali society had a peculiar character that determined the manner in which Western intellectual influence spread in Bengali culture. It is wrong to portray the cultural impact of colonialism as exclusively coercive. The society into which competing European merchants and military adventurers entered was complex, and the defeat of the *nawab* of Bengal, Mir Kasim, in 1764 was not seen as a collective indignity. Some revisionist histories claim, not implausibly, that the eighteenth century saw the rise of powerful indigenous mercantile interests, who might not have been displeased at the defeat of greedy and capricious local rulers.[40] The British entered Bengali society slowly, as one set of players among many others in an arena of political turmoil. Their eventual victory over other contenders and the establishment of their authority led to the imposition of several new institutions. A significant feature of the Bengali response to colonialism was the remarkable enthusiasm shown by a section of the elite for the new institutions and knowledges coming from the West. Although the relations between a colonial authority and a subject people could never be free of tensions, the modernist elite, produced by early colonial processes in Bengal, developed surprisingly congenial relations with British authority.

In a development with important consequences for Bangla literary culture, Europeans early on started the process of framing grammatical rules for the Bangla language, copying and editing culturally significant texts and introducing a culture of print.[41] More detailed attention than is possible here should be given to the production of standard grammars by the British missionaries at Serampore (Carey

---

[40] See especially Bayly 1988.

[41] For searching analyses of these transformations by a near contemporary, see Haraprasad Sastri, 'Bangalar Sahitya', and his three presidential addresses, all of which deal in detail with institutional changes in Bangla literary culture: Sastri 1956, 1: 171–96, 211–83.

and Halhed), and the creation of the Bangla print script. Print culture immediately created pressures toward standardization in two fields,[42] tending as it does to privilege a particular dialect among the variety of regional forms that have traditionally flourished side by side. In this case, high Bangla was based partly on Calcutta speech but relied heavily on the style of the Nadiya-Santipur region, which was regarded as a 'pleasant' but not necessarily cultivated language. The transformation of this dialect into 'standard' Bangla met surprisingly little opposition—despite the fact that within a short time other speech forms were ascribed a subordinate status, and, in literary texts, dialogue in these dialects was soon marked as a 'low' form. A parallel pressure toward script standardization transformed the new print faces into models for writing, displacing the traditional diversity of calligraphic styles.

Out of this combination of intellectual influences, an entirely new kind of high Bangla was created, transforming the earlier, far less structured linguistic economy. And one of its most significant features was the deliberate adoption, out of the three forms delineated by Haraprasad Sastri and mentioned earlier, of the modified Sanskritic version of precolonial Bangla.[43] As Bangla tried to negotiate the intellectual demands of modern culture, the two modular languages with which it initially developed a strangely mixed relation of contention and emulation were Sanskrit and English. Sanskrit, after all, was the high language of the Hindu society's 'internal' practices, such as worship, marriage, and literary cultivation. English, by contrast,

---

[42] I am opposed to the casual, undiscriminating acceptance of Benedict Anderson's idea of print capitalism. While this idea applies to European historical examples, it is doubtful that the connection between print and capitalism is equally strong or invariable in Asia. In the Bengali case, it appears that, in principle, print increased the accessibility of both traditional and newly composed texts. In practice, however, it did not increase accessibility immediately. Initially, printed texts were not very cheap. The establishment of printing presses produced a flourishing business in chapbooks and cheap pamphlets on diverse subjects, and these were consumed primarily by the newly emerging urban lower-middle class.

[43] Ghulam Mursed has provided a detailed historical analysis of how this 'Sanskritization' of Bangla prose took place. See Mursed 1992.

was the language of a new kind of external practice, immediately associated with modern forms of power: law, administration, and new opportunities for external trade.

The Search for a Modern Aesthetic

Changes in literary practice, as distinct from language, were also fast and radical. The entire sphere of culture was powerfully affected by a new emulative imagination prompted by English education. This is clearly discernible in techniques of poetic composition. Traditional poetry had followed widely acknowledged and fairly stringent criteria concerning metre and style. These explicitly rhetorical elements gradually begin to fade from the serious attention of poets. Isvarcandra Gupta (1812–49), whose compositions exemplify the transition in poetic aesthetics, still worked with traditional norms of rhetorical virtuosity remarkably similar to those of Bharatcandra, but an astonishing change is revealed in his choice of literary subjects, which were mostly drawn from the urban life of colonial Calcutta. Gupta had found the secret of writing poetry about the ordinary, though doing so brought charges of frivolity, occasional obscenity, and lack of dignified themes (he wrote verses on entirely untraditional topics, like the gastronomic celebration of pineapples and *tapse* fish). But it is clear that his application of traditional forms to an urban, colonial, modern subject was already transient and unstable. The forms were inadequate for the subjects and were rapidly left behind in the search for more complex solutions.

Michael Madhusudan Dutt (1824–73), by contrast, emulated the aesthetic forms of the sonnet and the Miltonian epic in an attempt to create a high 'classical' atmosphere.[44] In Madhusudan, as in many of his contemporaries, we find the potent and unprecedented combination of elements from Sanskrit and English that marks the serious advent of modern literature: his narratives and characters are primarily drawn from the Sanskrit high classical tradition—Indrajit, Laksmana, Pramila, Ravana, and so on from the *Ramayana*; Tilottama and Sarmistha from the *Mahabharata*. But his great dramatic poem, *Meghnadbadh*, is a defiant declaration of independence from traditional Sanskrit poetry.

[44] On Dutt, see also Dharwadker, chapter 3, in Pollock 2003.

Madhusudan's language is highly Sanskritic, with several innovative elements, particularly in the use of verbs, which led to bitter debates in the Bangla critical world—his supporters considering them enhancements of the language, his opponents viewing them as travesties. Above all, *Meghnadbadh* is an excellent document of the paradoxical conjuncture in Bangla intellectual culture in early modernity. In one sense, *Meghnadbadh* was a radically new creation that turned all the values of the traditional epic upside down. It inverts the relation between Indrajit and Laksmana—and more indirectly, between Ravana and Rama—by treating the *raksasa* (demonic) figures as heroes and Rama and Laksmana as morally and practically devious. Yet seen from an alternative and equally plausible angle, it is a cultural artifact of the most dedicated imitation—an adaptation of Milton's *Paradise Lost* into Bangla culture, copying not only the narrative theme but also the metric form of blank verse (called in Bangla *amitraksar chanda*, verse of 'unfriendly' or non-harmonizing syllables).

Poetic excellence was now measured by the poet's skill in producing sonnets (*caturdaspadi*) rather than stately quatrains in quantitative-syllabic verse forms such as the *mandrakranta*. In a remarkably short time, elite pastimes such as *kavigan*—occasions, usually spectacular in nature, in which poets gathered to compose impromptu poems and passages, sometimes in competition with each other—were fatally undermined by a more introspective literary culture, marking a fundamental shift in the nature of the literary itself.

Kavigan was a poetic exercise that showed the conventional associations of poetry. It was performative, instant, part of a public spectacle, and required ready intelligence and quickwittedness from its composers. Its performance was exactly like that of music: the creator did not get a chance to revise, reflect, redraft, and present to the audience the product of an introspective and reflective private craft. Normally not written down, the compositions had no ambitions of permanence, though the most popular ones gained a form of oral immortality. Compositions by Madhusudan or Rabindranath, on the other hand, stood at the opposite end of the continuum of poetic forms. These were attentively crafted products, meant to be enjoyed primarily by a private reader. Above all, the culture of reading was fundamentally transformed. The presupposition of the silent reader introduced a series of interesting changes in poetry's technical structure, the most significant of which was the slow decline of the aural in favour of semantic delectation. This is reflected in the restrained, often almost embarrassed, alliterations in Tagore's poetry.[45] The overt representationality of performative poetry—its theatrical aspect—was entirely lost. Poetry now came to be enshrouded in a great silence of refinement.

Shifts of the kind evidenced in poetry formed part of a larger cultural change that instituted a new kind of boundary between everyday practices and crafts and the exalted sphere of the high arts. Recitation of the *Ramayana* or the singing of *padavali* as part of the seasonal and daily *kirtans* had intertwined that poetry with the unremarkable rounds of everyday activities, a relationship reflected quite often in the declamatory manner of reciting (often such recitation would be carried on alongside a mundane activity, such as doing everyday chores). The new poetry could not be used in this way—as part of religious ritual or community gatherings, or for inattentive mnemonic incantation in the household. Moreover, inasmuch as high literacy was a prerequisite, the new poetry was not equally available across gender.[46] Unlike some high poetry in North India that customarily functioned as part of sophisticated conversation, this poetry was unsuited for use in even the most elevated normal dialogue. It could not be approached without the inescapable sense that it was high art and thus separated from all other mundane pursuits.

Further transformations in literary culture came about as authorial practices changed in relation to reception practices. What had been a

[45] Tagore is again an interesting example here; he has undoubted mastery of metrics and figures of speech, and sometimes his use of this technical repertoire is strikingly original. But there is no demonstrativeness about it. Unlike traditional poetry, his works invite literary assessment not primarily on this terrain but on others. Nevertheless, it is not surprising that standard Bangla discussions of *chandas* use Tagore's poetic corpus almost as much as canonical Sanskrit examples. For a highly complex and deeply sympathetic appreciation of Tagore's metric originality, see Sen 1974.

[46] I do not mean there was something intrinsically gender-biased in these writings, but rather that modern education was initially almost entirely a male preserve. Subsequently, reading novels was often seen as a specially female literate activity, with many popular magazines directing their wares to a female audience.

local, participatory, communal collectivity, often gathered at a public spectacle, became for the first time an impersonal 'audience' of readers sitting and perusing texts in private, where the simultaneous enjoyment of others did not interfere with or determine their assessment of the text. As literature was turned into a primarily lonely pleasure, a series of institutional changes followed. Appreciation of literary objects (poetry in particular) changed form from the instant applause or coolness of the face-to-face audience to the scrutiny of modern criticism, which elaborately dissects the text at leisure and enhances both the prestige and the enjoyment of the text by a commentary that is itself literary, a literature supplementing literature.[47] A literary public sphere formed in the early nineteenth century around a group of journals, some of which were short-lived but immensely influential (like Bankimchandra Chattopadhyay's *Bangadarsan*, established in 1872), and the disputations in their pages determined the formation of canonical criteria for literary production. Literature now worked through a dialogue between the literary activity of poets and writers and the critical activity that offered aesthetic commentary and encouraged or inhibited various performative trends.

The creation of this literary modernity in Bengal, through the dissemination processes of printing and the creation of an impersonal literary public, was related to movements of political power in a fundamental way. In premodern India, political authority had a relatively marginal role to play in such important parts of life as economic activity, which was governed primarily by the rules of the caste order. It is not surprising that fundamental structures and institutions that helped cultural reproduction or commanded constitutive power over cultural form were also by and large outside the direct influence of rulers.[48] Those who ruled were routinely

[47] Significantly, this also affects the appreciation of traditional Sanskrit texts. Formerly, the only aids to the study of texts like those by Kalidasa were well-known commentaries; in the modern era, important literary figures wrote highly individual assessments of current works. This type of literary criticism produced a literary sense of taste that was far more individualistic, exploratory, and subject to periodic change than the heavy conventionality of the commentary tradition.

[48] However, in the light of the evidence Pollock (1998) puts forward, it appears that the relation between political power and cultural forms can be

praised, and they reciprocated primarily by providing patronage; this culture continued down to Bharatcandra's stay at the court of King Krsnacandra of Krsnanagar in the Nadiya region. By contrast, the colonial state, using the modern conception of politics brought from the rationalistic phase of European culture, laid claim to its territory and space in a radically new way, represented in its theory of state sovereignty.[49]

The British administration was naturally negligent about cultural life in its empire. The British did introduce cultural forms, which they saw as part of the civilizing processes of modernity, but they were hardly interested in producing in their imperial dominions something similar to the cultural homogeneity of nationalist Europe. From the late eighteenth century British power expanded with astonishing rapidity, and this prompted the question of clearly defined territorial structures to demarcate the jurisdictions of the British and the native princes' political authority. This habituated Indians to living in a stable, politically bounded space; but the connection between this space and its cultural content was still entirely accidental. As British rule extended westward, extensive Hindustani-speaking territories were added to the Bengal presidency. Bengalis duly developed sub-imperialistic delusions about themselves and considered other groups within the larger territory of the presidency their natural inferiors (these attitudes are reflected with particular clarity in the extensive travel literature produced by the Bengali elite). Except in a few extreme cases, they did not propose inclusion of these groups in the exalted realm of Bengali culture. Other linguistic groups could regard the lighted circle of Bangla literary culture with admiration or resentment, but they were not serious interlocutors. The delineation of the *cultural*

---

varied and complex: in contrast to the Bengali case, royal patronage obviously affected the direction of literary production in the case of South Indian empires. Wherever literature bore a strong connection with a polity through a common language, such pressures must have existed. Persian and Urdu writing had strong connections with North Indian courts. See the contributions by Alam and Faruqi, chapters 2 and 14, respectively, in Pollock 2003.

[49] Modern historians who have analysed the nature of premodern political authority have suggested the term 'segmentary state' to mark this difference, though not without controversy. See Kulke 1995.

boundaries of Bengal was the work, therefore, not of the colonial state but of the new Bengali intelligentsia.[50]

Separating Bangla from Other Languages

By the early nineteenth century, a separate modern linguistic identity was clearly discernible in Bengal. Naturally, what this language was and how its purely linguistic frontiers were drawn were major questions of internal contention in this early modern period. If we take early-nineteenth-century Bangla writing as an example of the state of thinking about the Bangla language, we find a remarkably complex ordering in the structure of linguistic practice. Speaking and doing things in Bangla had to make a place for itself in a world of many languages. An ordinary Bengali householder would speak to his family and friends and in the bazaar in one of the local Bangla dialects (these dialects are usually specific to relatively small regions, but they are framed in a more general division between western and eastern speech, referred to in Bangla colloquial usage as *ghati* and *banal*). But dealings with political authority, for instance regarding landholding or revenue, called for the consistent and skilful use of Persian.[51] Religious ceremonies—a constant part the household routine—involved the mandatory use of Sanskrit, though the average householder might have an insecure grasp over its grammatical intricacies. Any transaction with colonial power required knowledge of English. It was thus not uncommon for an educated Bengali to know all these languages

[50] But one should not put too benevolent a construction on this process of delineation of the boundaries of the Bangla cultural space. Some sections of the early Bengali intelligentsia claimed, for instance, that Oriya was not a separate language but a degenerate version of Bangla, and it would be better for the 'civilization' of Oriyas to learn and write standardized Bangla. There were serious suggestions that Oriya teaching should be abolished in schools in Orissa and replaced by Bangla. For details, see Mohanty 1986. Not merely cultural chauvinism but also hard calculation of material advantage were involved in making such aggressive subimperialist claims.

[51] For a fascinating collection of old Bangla letters, see Sen 1961. Not surprisingly, a large number of these letters discuss land transactions, and consequently, their Bangla language is heavily laden with Arabic–Persian terms.

with reasonable degrees of fluency. Each language performed clearly designated functions. If we classify these functions as high and low, then, interestingly, in the early nineteenth century Bangla was used for distinctly low functions. Serious business—concerning gods or kings or property—was dealt with in other languages.

The entrenchment of British power and the spread of Western education had the effect of simplifying this complicated triple hyperglossia with astonishing rapidity. English took over Persian's administrative function as records were converted into English, though record-keeping practices passed through a long period of administrative diglossia, and an otherwise English administrative discourse bristled with terms like *taluka, mouja*, and *patta*. The term *zamindari* remained in good semantic health until Independence, after which the institution was ceremonially abolished by legislation. Terms like *raja* and *maharaja* were severed from the original practice of rulership, which had been fatally undermined by the expansion of British rule, and became free-floating and available for adoption under British permanent settlement by middling *zamindars* without the faintest aspiration toward independent political authority. Earlier this would have been preposterously illegitimate as a social practice. A title like 'the Maharaja of Cossimbazar'—worn by a considerable player in factional politics in colonial Bengal—would have appeared completely ungrammatical in the context of the earlier map of social practice. (Appropriately, the ultimate resting place for the term *maharaja* is as a sign for a particular lifestyle, vaguely suggesting opulence, indolence, and geniality, in the famous advertisement for the national airline, Air India.)

It is a significant, if neglected, fact that the historical contact with colonialism was very uneven across the whole of South Asia. The Bengali contact with colonialism was peculiar for at least three reasons. First, Bengalis simply had the longest-running contact with modern British culture, and probably also had the longest time to devise a complex range of differential responses to British culture. Second, the nature of that contact differed in the case of Bengal. Since the British did not initially establish themselves with an unambiguous claim to state power, it was possible to see them as simply one force in a society in which several powers were jostling for position. The party of reform, led by people like Rammohan Roy, therefore could enlist

British support without moral scruples about surrendering to an alien civilization. Third, the entrenchment of British colonial power in India afforded upper-class Bengalis a great opportunity for sub-imperialist expansion and made them even more eager and inclined to ingest the Western cultural model. Consequently, the emulative enthusiasm of Bengali culture became particularly intense. From the start of the nineteenth century Bangla intellectuals were under enormous pressure to reinvent their intellectualism in a modern form, which altered the entire definition of what it meant to be an intellectual. Literariness played a specially significant role in this process. Not merely were creation and knowledge of literary texts in both English and Bangla essential skills for the cultivated; a certain clarity of syntax, chasteness of vocabulary, refinement of pronunciation—all operations influenced by literary texts—became mandatory constituents of the modern Bengali sense of cultivation.

One of the most striking features of literary modernity in Bengal was the rapidity with which the culture changed. There was an urgency to differentiate the modern period from the past, which was now seen as 'traditional' (that is, in the sense in which I used the term earlier: not as *agama*, or what is received from the past, but as part of *alita*, or the past itself). But although through its various stages of change—represented by Isvarcandra Vidyasagar (1820–91), Bankimchandra Chattopadhyay (1838–94), and Rabindranath Tagore, respectively—Bangla literature quickly became modern, it did not establish a stable, unworried pattern of either verse or prose writing, or of aesthetic structure.

Rammohan Roy is significant for two reasons. First, he exhibited in his own life a model of what Bangla education or cultivation meant during his time, particularly the almost mandatory inclusion of Persian skills and Islamic culture. The entire project of the putative upgrading of Bangla and the creation of a 'high' language was to erase this Islamic element in a surprisingly brief span of time. Within two generations, Bangla literary culture would become far more solidly Hindu—though in a rather complex way. Second, Roy is immensely important for the nature of his cultural project. He established the relatively liberal, strongly reformist Brahmo Samaj. Its principles, seen as a set of basic ideas or religious resources that would include metaphysical, philosophical, doctrinal beliefs, stocks of images, and iconography, stood in a very interesting relation to Hinduism. The Samaj played a foundational role in the creation of modern Bengali culture—from the devising of rules of ordinary *bhadralok* etiquette and the refashioning of the whole world of literary language through the works of Rabindranath to a revolution in women's dress.[52] If Hinduism is viewed in the structuralist fashion as a combinatory of elements, Brahmo improvisation responded to the challenges of the West, Christianity, and modernity by using with wonderful deftness some specific elements of this repertoire.

Hindu caste customs, rooted in texts like the *Manusmrti*, were utterly repugnant to progressive Brahmos, but they replaced those canonical texts with the equally canonical Upanisads. The Brahmos disliked the mutilation of classical Sanskrit by half-educated officiating priests and the utter aural disorder of worship in Hindu temples, but they replaced it all with the singing of appropriately solemn songs called *brahmasangit* (congregational singing of Brahma), and the adaptation of Vedic hymns. Doctrinally, it would be wholly unfair to accuse Brahmos of being more averse to Muslims than traditional Hindus. They were certainly seeking a more liberal religion, free from fanaticism. Yet their project for the creation of a high Bengali culture and literature looked entirely toward the repertoire of classical Hinduism for its resources.

The high culture of modern Bengal, created through the stunning originality of the nineteenth century, thus became a generally Hindu affair.[53] And this slow but decisive equation of the modern

[52] The introduction of the blouse to go with a new style of wearing the sari made it easier for women to come out of the *antahpur*. The traditional attire, though inviting romantic descriptions like Dusyanta's wonder at Sakuntala's appearance—*iyam adhikamanojna valkalenapi tanvi* (this slender girl looks even more beautiful dressed in bark cloth)—would not have promoted women's activity in the public sphere. On the historical transformation of dress, see Tarlo 1994.

[53] The Muslim responses to this new form of cultivation constitute a complex and large question. One kind of response was to acknowledge this culture as a historical given and acquire it: the language of many Muslim writers who adopted this solution is hardly different from that of their Hindu peers. But others felt the exclusion more sharply and suggested developing a 'Musalmani Bangla' whose predominant feature would be the frequent use of Arabic and Persian words to mark it off from Hindu high Bangla. After

Bengali self with a cultural gestalt associated with Hinduism was a fundamental reason for the gradual alienation of Muslims. One strand of nineteenth-century literary culture even showed explicit hostility to Muslims and, with the growing interest in history, began to represent Islamic rule as 'foreign' domination. References to Islamic rule as foreign are quite widespread and can be found in many Brahmo writings, apart from the unsurprising presence of this idea among more conservative Hindu texts. And hostility to Muslims in the works of highly influential writers like Bankimchandra played a significant role in this story. But to illustrate the crucial underlying problem I quote an extended passage from a famous essay, 'Indian History', by Tagore, who would not be suspected of communalism:

> Countries that are fortunate find the essence of their land in the history of their country; the reading of history introduces their people to their country from infancy. With us the opposite is the case. It is the history of our country that hides the essence of this land from us. Whatever historical records exist from Mahmud's invasion to the arrogant imperial pronouncements of Lord Curzon, these constitute a strange mirage for India; this does not help our sight into our country, but covers it with a screen. It casts a strong artificial light on one part in such a way that the other side, in which our country lies, becomes covered in darkness to our eyes. In that darkness the diamonds on the tiaras of the dancers flash in the light of the dancing halls of the nawabs; the red foam in the tumblers in the Badshahs' hands appears like red, sleepless, maddened eyes; ancient holy temples cover their heads in that darkness, and the high spires of the bejeweled marble mausoleums of the emperors' lovers try to kiss the stars. In that darkness the sound of horses' hooves, the trumpeting of elephants, the jangle of weapons, the paleness of tents stretching into the distance, the golden glow of silk curtains, the stone bubbles of mosques, the mysterious silence of the palaces guarded by eunuchs—all these produce a huge magical illusion with their amazing sounds and colors. But why should we call this India's history? It has covered the *punthi* of India's holy mantras by a fascinating Arabian Nights tale. No one opens that *punthi*. [But] children learn every line of that Arabian Nights tale by heart.[54]

Partition, the efforts of the Pakistani authority to impose Urdu brought on a strong reaction and a tendency to use a more Sanskrit-based high Bangla.

[54] Tagore 1968: 3–4. *Punthi* refers to a genre of Bangla literature centred on themes of ritual and myth. My intention in adducing this passage is not to revise the general opinion about Tagore but to illustrate a widely used

This striking passage presents a field of signs in which all the symbolic markers of the self are securely tied to Hindu culture and what is not of 'the essence of this land' is associated with Islamic and British history. The entire problem with modern Indian nationalism was that this way of representing history was not the preserve of Hindu communalists but was part of a far more common and casually commonsensical language.

The Making of Modern Prose

If Bangla was to be the basis for a restructured linguistic economy, it had to show itself capable of performing the high cultural functions, which at this historical juncture were divisible into two mutually opposed types. Some were connected to religious practice and were normally performed in Sanskrit. Others were associated with modern culture: the practices of science, law, and administration that had come to be associated with English by the late eighteenth century. The challenge facing Bangla was further complicated by the philosophical contradiction between these two spheres of high functions: acceptance of a 'scientific' view of the world was widely held as undermining orthodox Hindu religious life. To acquire a place of value, however, Bangla, incongruous as it seemed, had to be able to do both: it had to become a language capable of the high recitative solemnity of Sanskrit conventionally used at worship (*puja*) or ceremonials (replacing Sanskrit), and it had to acquire sufficient complexity and subtlety to become a language of law and science (replacing English). Finally, as a decisive mark of modernity, it had to acquire the capacity to produce a high literature (like both Sanskrit and English). Interestingly, the question of turning Bangla into a language of property-related jurisprudence was given less attention, illustrating that modern Bengalis, though poetically inclined, are characteristically negligent about pecuniary matters. Instead, a certain amount of Persianized language persisted in the practices of the revenue administration.

---

rhetoric. Tagore went on to write some of the most radically anti-communal and anti-Brahmanical poems in nationalist literature, generating a rare form of self-critical nationalism. In some of his late correspondence he recognized that his own earlier patriotic poems often shared a nationalist imagery that was revisionist by implication.

To perform all these functions successfully, Bangla had to enter into a peculiar relation of transaction with both Sanskrit and English. With the rise of early modern literature, two contradictory trends became immediately apparent. One sought the fluidity, lilt, suppleness, and liveliness of colloquial speech; the other resolutely faced the other way, toward borrowing maximally from Sanskrit vocabulary. Consider the opening sentences from Isvaracandra Vidyasagar's *Sitar Vanabas*, a major text in the founding of modern Bangla literature:

> ei sei *janasthanamadhyavarti prasravanagiri*. ihar *sikharades satatasancaraman jaladharapatalasamyoge nirantar nibid nilimay alankrta*.[55]

Grammatically, this is Bangla,[56] but the words are almost entirely Sanskrit—a string of *tatsamas*, or words borrowed directly out of Sanskrit. In the quotation, Sanskrit-equivalent words are italicized; if the *sandhis* and *samasas* were uncoupled, the number would be higher. The sentence structure is such that the main verb is hidden, which accentuates its similarity with Sanskrit.

Vidyasagar was engaged in a process of 'classicization' of Bangla. Indeed, in his writings the politics of the grammatical past is particularly intense and clear. He wished to create a Bangla that denied the language's somewhat mean and mixed medieval ancestry by making Sanskrit more *internal* to the Bangla linguistic structure. He supplemented this effort with his choice of the narratives that this newly formed 'high' Bangla was to present to its modern audience through institutionalized educational curricula. Vidyasagar's selection

[55] Sastri 1956: 1, 197–202.

[56] Haraprasad Sastri wrote a perspicuous essay on the strange hybridity of what passed for Bangla grammar, showing that what *vyakarana* meant in Sanskrit was different from the meaning of 'grammar' in English. Recent writers, he argued, made elementary mistakes by, for example, confusing 'parts of speech' with *vibhakti* (Sastri 1956: 1, 203–10). Although it is not central to my analysis here, I cannot resist noting that the casual celebration of 'hybridity' today sometimes tries to appropriate the creativity of the culture in nineteenth-century Bengal. I consider this totally illegitimate and thoughtless, perhaps prompted by a lack of familiarity with that culture in detail. People of Sastri's culture would have made a sharp and indignant distinction between cultural self-making and hybridity, and would have regarded the latter with some contempt.

follows an impeccable syllabus of early proto-nationalist culture—a combination of high Sanskrit tales like the *Ramayana* of Valmiki, *Raghuvamsa* and *Sakuntala* of Kalidasa, *Uttararamacarita* of the seventh-century playwright Bhavabhuti (all of which leave their traces on Vidyasagar's own storytelling), and Shakespeare (*Comedy of Errors* retold under the title *Bhrantivilas*). Given this reading list, the new Bangla civilizing process simply could not fail.

Vidyasagar's cultural strategy contained an important element of politics. Against the colonial argument that Indian traditional literature was vulgar and degenerate it asserted the exemplary character of the Sanskrit classical canon, which, however, was subtly reconstructed in a discernibly Western style through the surreptitious filter of 'modern' taste. There was clearly an enterprise to construct a past for Bangla that replicated the high classical past of the Italian Renaissance and ancient Greece that the British appropriated to their own literary culture. Vidyasagar's suggestion about what modern Bangla should be proceeded in the right modern direction: reinvented through the deliberate Sanskritization of its vocabulary, this new Bangla was capable of performing all the specialized functions expected of a modern high culture. It could easily perform the function of religious solemnity and worship precisely because these practices had traditionally been done in Sanskrit.[57] And by borrowing from the enormous wealth of Sanskrit's vocabulary and grammatical operations, it could also perform efficiently as a language of science, legality, and serious reflection.

In the period between Bankimchandra and Rabindranath there was intense and sophisticated discussion about what a 'genuine' high Bangla should be. The literary result of this discussion is seen in the grace, limpidity, and spontaneity of Tagore's mature language. But a purely literary reading of this process hides the highly interesting theoretical reflection on the nature of a modern language that continued for

[57] Brahmos were the only group that carried this logic through to its end. Others normally performed their *pujas* and marriage ceremonies in Sanskrit, but the Brahmos used Bangla translations of conventional *slokas* even for marriage ceremonies. They were also often the most particular about the purity of their language, taking enormous care not to slip English words into common speech—something that requires excruciating alertness.

nearly half a century. A key figure in this discussion was the linguist and scholar Haraprasad Sastri, who was given the affectionate title Mahamahopadhyay for his seminal contribution to a scientific study of the Bangla language. Sastri's linguistics were not merely technically excellent; they were also astonishingly alert to sociological contexts. In one of his influential essays, 'Bamla Bhasa' (The Bangla Language), Sastri sharply criticized the high Sanskritic style of two venerated figures of the earlier generation, Vidyasagar and Aksayakumar Datta (editor of the prestigious journal *Tattvabodhini Patrika*): 'The fact is, those who have taken up the pen in the Bangla language have never learned the Bangla language properly.'[58] Excessive Sanskritization affected what was perceived to be the natural, spontaneous rhythm of the language, and soon faced serious criticism. Sastri scorned the 'Vidyasagari' style as 'translation,' not 'creative writing': 'His Bangla is understood only by himself and his followers, no one else. How could they? After all, it was not a regional [*desiya*] language. It was a linguistic leftover [*ucchistamatra*] imagined by some translators.'[59]

Subsequently, the excessive Sanskritization of the Vidyasagar style was abandoned in favour of a more complex and versatile form developed by Bankimchandra, who wrote a spirited defense of the use of a mixed language for literature. Bankimchandra's Bangla was still full of Sanskrit words, but it was not defensive or ashamed of showing, through the verbs, that it was Bangla. This innovation freed written Bangla from the woodenness (*jadata*) of Vidyasagar's style; made it supple and sprightly; and allowed it to draw on the very different resources of colloquial, slang, and typically feminine speech. By the time of Tagore we find a fully developed and highly complex language, though in my view it was still weak as a vehicle of serious reflective prose compared to the strength of its ability to express sentiment.[60]

[58] Sastri 1956: 1, 197–202.

[59] Ibid.: 1: 198.

[60] There is considerable debate and reflection among writers of prose who, given the poetic obsession of the Bengalis, are often poets attempting a different mode of writing in their spare time. But the charge that the language Tagore used with incomparable grace was adept at sentiment yet weak in expressing serious, complex ideas is fairly common. In their various ways, writers like Pramatha Chaudhuri (primarily a prose writer), and Sudhin Dutta and Bishnu De (both poets and creators of deliberately 'complex' styles) experimented with

But precisely by going through this short period of experimentation Bangla had created for itself a history in capsule form, as it were: a high, sonorous, unpractical classicism that through modern influences was gradually unfrozen into the recognizable cadences of an ironic modern prose (to echo Bakhtin's idea that irony is a mark of all modern literature).

A second process in the creation of modern high Bangla had to do with English. Since Bangla is largely a Sanskrit-derived language, vocabulary could be taken unproblematically from that source. But a modern language expresses a world—material, social, intellectual, and aesthetic—that is structured by a different kind of complexity from that of premodernity. A significant element in this new sensibility is the determining, yet often subterranean, presence of science. This new rationalistic sensibility is often called in Bangla *pascatya bhav* (Western sensibility).[61] Bangla intellectuals understood quite early science's ability to produce a dramatic disenchantment with the world. In the Bangla context, the process of disenchantment was particularly brutal and dramatic; for, unlike in Europe, it did not occur over a long period through an internal dialogue within European culture, often within Christianity, through which religion slowly ceded intellectual problems and fields to scientific reasoning.

The total effect of intellectual changes in Europe over the seventeenth and eighteenth centuries was utterly revolutionary, but the actual experience was often incremental. In India, by contrast, this disjuncture occurred as a political clash between two civilizations, and any acceptance of modern science could immediately be denounced by conservatives as capitulation to alien ideas. Although Bangla modern culture was guided for about a century by religious and literary performances rather than scientific ones, science was clearly a subtle and ubiquitous presence.[62] Acceptance of the scientific, disenchanted

prose forms that were self-consciously distinct from Tagore's often mellifluous but weak later prose. Tagore's own prose went through what appears to me a regressive transformation.

[61] Bhudev Mukhopadhyay wrote a deeply perceptive and highly critical analysis of *pascatya bhav* in his *Samajik Prabandha* ([1892] 1981).

[62] For a discussion of the contradictions of colonial science, see Prakash 1999.

view of the world, even if implicit, made the practice of traditional literature impossible. Those who accepted this sensibility had to accept by implication a new map of the frontier between literature and scientific discourse.[63]

Science and Syntax

In modern cultures, science comes to have a paradoxical relation with literature. While it is differentiated from literature as a field of intellectual activity, it supplies in a sense the boundaries of literature, forcing literature to become more self-consciously aesthetic. The distinction between modern science, with its high and querulously sharp self-definition, and literature/aesthetics was thus another determining influence on the making of modern Bangla literary culture, especially prose.

Prose has become, in modern times, the privileged vehicle of science; and although literature can exclude itself from the strict regimes of expression required by science, by invoking that dichotomy it declares itself, after all, a literature in an irreversibly (if not entirely) disenchanted world. Prose, and generally all modern literature, carries this mark of disenchantment, which makes statements fallible and exudes a general

---

[63] Originally, the Brahmo critique of orthodox Brahmanical Hinduism was developed on the basis of rationalist arguments: modern Hindus should only entertain ideas compatible with modern rationalism, it was argued, and therefore it was essential to reject traditional superstitious beliefs. A striking example of this belief in scientific reason was Tagore's famous rebuke of Gandhi for his claim that a devastating earthquake in Bihar was God's punishment for the practice of untouchability. See Tagore 1996. While most writers and opinion-makers agreed about the crucial importance of science, views differed about the best means of acquiring it. In addition to reading the latest scientific material, extensive translation and writing of general science texts were greatly encouraged. Bhudev Mukhopadhyay, who as an inspector of schools had special title to speak on these matters, pointed out with characteristic perceptiveness that the spread of science required a true laicization of knowledge, as in modern Europe. It was unlikely, in his view, that this could happen without imparting science education in the vernacular. To him it appeared that Bengalis were learning not science itself but 'stories of science'—a much inferior substitute. See Mukhopadhyay [1892] 1981.

sense of cognitive skepticism.[64] To effect this, in the case of Bangla, required new kinds of sentences expressing a provisionality entirely untypical in traditional syntax. For example, sentences beginning with *yehetu* (since/because), indicating a strong relation of causality, were required for expressing inductive generalizations or subsuming particulars under general laws; *yadio*, or in earlier versions the more Sanskritic *yady api* (while/although), indicated an open-endedness of judgement, registered a contradiction, or indicated a measured sense of qualification.[65] Though initially authors felt a certain awkwardness with these syntactic forms and sometimes used them as flags of stylistic rebellion, within a short time, as the nature of discursive practices changed, they became commonplace. By Tagore's time, at the turn of the century, they were being used with great ease and style, as in Tagore's famous poem 'Duhsamay'.[66]

Probably the most striking use of the kind of syntactic structure at issue, applied with a deliberateness impossible to ignore, was in the conscious urbanity of Sudhindranath Dutta (1901–61), who was famous precisely for the excess (to some) or the fluency (to others) of his mixture of obscure Sanskritic terms with obtrusively English syntactic form (a style that is also seen in striking forms in the poetry of Bishnu De). This combination, and especially the internalization of these syntactic structures, became the mark of both the maturity and the modernity in all types of writers, irrespective of political

[64] It would be wrong to say that earlier secular literature did not, at times, show a highly refined sense similar to rationalist skepticism. One of the best examples would be Ghalib's famous couplet: *ham ko malum hai jinnat ke haqiqat lekin dil ke bahlane-ke liye yah khyal accha hai* (I know the real truth about paradise, but for beguiling the human mind it is an excellent idea).

[65] The obvious exception to this was the esoteric language of technical philosophy.

[66] *yadio sandhya asiche manda manthare*
sab sarigit irigite thamyid
yadio sarigi nahi ananta ambare
yadio klanti asiche arige namiya.

Though the dusk is approaching in slow steps,
All singing has stopped at some strange signal,
Though there is no companion in the unending sky,
Though weariness is slowly numbing your limbs.

or artistic positions. Other, subtler uses of the element of surprise in language occurred in poetry. To take a random example, in two apparently simple lines of Jibanananda Das's (1899–1954) famous poem 'Cil' (The Kite), there is a startling use of a possessive case, creating a delectable effect of inversion:

hay cil, sonali danar cil, ei bhije megher dupure
tumi ar kendo nako ude ude dhansidi naditir pase.

The second phrase in the first line, *sonali danar cil*, inverts the normal relation of possession: instead of *ciler dana*—the kite's unproblematic possession of its wings—the poem chooses to speak of *danar cil*, the golden wing's relation (possession/metonymy) with the kite. The phrase *bhije megher dupure* (the afternoon of wet clouds) in the next phrase has a similar, though weaker, effect.[67]

Disenchantment and the Prose of the World

Self-consciously artistic prose writing led to the slow discovery of the poetics of prose. Traditionally, most compositions aspiring to attention and claiming intellectual seriousness were composed in verse, no doubt partly because the mnemonic element supported the pedagogy. As the conception of knowledge became more secular, such mnemonic devices were less required, though the importance of memory in Indian learning continues even today. With the breakdown of the caste-based order with regard to occupation, arrangements for storing and imparting knowledge needed to be more impersonal. There was a shift from the tightly controlled system of Brahmanic pedagogy to a written, impersonal, accessible knowledge.

For analysing the world in a disenchanted manner, whether in everyday or scientific discourse, prose was increasingly seen to be the 'natural' form. Prose assisted a calm, unexcited, and exact recording of things. Prose was also the language of sober and recursive reflection. As the general picture of the world became more scientific and was rendered increasingly prosaic, the character of the literary was affected

[67] Because English admits phrases of this kind, their effect when rendered in English is considerably diluted. Fortunately, there is an excellent study of Das's poetic art available in English: Seely 1990.

in a process similar to transformations occurring in the world of useful objects. It is often suggested that in the traditional world art and craft were not separated by a definitional distinction but existed at two points of a continuum. A certain kind of artistic craft could be encountered everywhere: from the applique work on *kanthas* made from old rags to carvings on ordinary household utensils. Modernity, however, tends to divest useful things of this additional gratuitous artistic dimension and subject them to a minimalist, utilitarian design. Crafts become increasingly functional, while high art is given a more formalized presence. The general map of cultural practices is fundamentally altered.

So also, as the literary world was given over to prose, and an underlying, commonsense scientific criterion came to govern prose writing, literature gained at once a more restricted and a more exalted place. Literature could no longer happen unexpectedly and anywhere: it became highly formalized, prized, precious precisely because it was made the subject of an increasingly specialized profession. Though authors in the nineteenth century could not survive by taking literature as an exclusive profession, as Michael Madhusudan Dutt's tragic fate demonstrated (he lived out his days in abject poverty, depending entirely on support from his friends), literary writing was clearly seen as an extraordinary activity. Its task was to recreate enchantment in a world that had finally been desacralized and disenchanted. In social terms, this development paralleled the rise of a new concept of entertainment—in a lifestyle increasingly dominated by temporal regimes driven by work.[68]

Disenchantment and the Transformation of the Fantastic

Nothing reveals the enormous and ineradicable impact of science on literature—how science imperceptibly determines the conditions of possibility for literary forms—better than the fate of the fantastic. A

[68] There is unfortunately not much systematic study of the distinction between work time and leisure time under conditions of modernity, but some provocative thoughts on the significance of *cakri* (salaried employment) are found in the work of historians like Sumit Sarkar and Dipesh Chakrabarty. See, in particular, Chakrabarty 2000.

major constituent of literary enchantment is the work of the fantastic, in the form of the wondrous affairs of the supernatural. In classical literature, interventions by the supernatural are common and often occur in ways that appear gratuitous to modern literary taste. At times, the intervention of the supernatural plays an astonishingly complex role, as, I think, in the climactic point of the *Mahabharata*, the disrobing of Draupadi.[69] In common traditional stories, especially in the *mangalkavya* tradition, supernatural intervention is often the most necessary point of the plot, as the relevant deity magically dispels an inevitable disaster. With the goddesses Manasa and Candi, accomplishing supernatural miracles was almost routine. And Annada unleashed her goblin army to terrorize Delhi's inhabitants and force Jahangir to recognize the merits of her devotee, Majumdar.

A modern sensibility immediately brings embarrassment, if not straightforward disrepute, to such literary conventions. Within the short span of a century, Hindu deities completely lost their abundant capacity of interfering with natural causality—particularly their proneness to appear theatrically in order to invert the narrative scene. Now they could only come to Calcutta within the clearly protected formal space of humour, as in the famous popular story *Devganer Martye Agaman* by Durga Charan Ray (1886), in which the gods plead their inability to help the goddess Ganga against British technology, which has humiliatingly spanned her with the steel arches of the Howrah Bridge.[70]

The civilizing process of modern culture included the formation of a specialized literature for children, and the fantastic, driven from adult stories, found refuge in that literary space. However, even the children required scientific, rationalistic education, and the traditional stories of goblins were increasingly replaced by a different kind of fantasy, one associated with the mythical and historical past. Tagore arranged for publication of a collection of 'grandmothers' tales' (Daksinaranjan Mitra Majumdar's *Thakurmar Jhuli*) to prevent the disappearance

[69] This is one of the most difficult and complex episodes of the epic to interpret. Is Krsna's intervention—rescuing Draupadi and scorning the efforts of Duhsasana—to be taken literally, or does it show that, because of the magnitude of its immorality, the episode is impossible to bring to words and literary representation?

[70] Ray [1886] 1984.

of that tradition. And children's literature came to be dominated by the writing of Sukumar Ray—most notably his nonsense verse in *Abaltabal*—and the wonderfully colourful recreations of the past by Abanindranath Thakur, the celebrated painter, in Thakur's *Rajkahini*. The only place where the fantastic could find a secure sanctuary, entirely protected from the charge of being antiscientific, was in a hugely popular and expanding literature of science fiction, because here fantasy could in fact ride on science itself.[71]

Technologies and Transactions

Not surprisingly, the coming of the new high literature altered the nature of the audience for literary productions. Some traditional texts, like any written narrative, were meant for huge, partially anonymous audiences—like the two adaptations of the *Ramayana* and the *Mahabharata* mentioned earlier, or the *mangalkavyas*—but their sense of audience was quite different from that of modern literature. Indeed, extending and modifying Gadamer's theory of textual representation in *Truth and Method*, it could be argued that a text like the *Ramayana*, even when translated and written down, could not find its appropriate audience without going through various procedures of representative mediation.[72] The *Ramayana* would not be read at one sitting or in a series of sequential occasions, the way a modern story is read. Parts of it would be either collectively read by communal audiences or enacted by mediating poets or performers, who would draw on their own narrative imagination in the theatrical depiction, the selection of words, and the composition of dialogues. The story could not 'come to life' without their representation on each narrative occasion.

At a level lower than the 'universal' literature of the epics were entirely episodic creative forms. One example would be the *kavigans*

[71] Arguably, the act of putting Daksinaranjan Mitra Majumdar's tales into the textually inflexible format of a modern book was itself a fundamental change. It dispensed with the esoteric knowledge of the grandmother—and in most cases, with the grandmother herself—since literate children could now read the stories straight from the book. Children's science fiction made a triumphant start with *Ghanddar Galpa*, by the well-known writer Premendra Mitra, and was pursued by a distinguished string of front-ranking writers, down to the stories by Satyajit Ray.

[72] See Gadamer 1981: 91–127.

mentioned earlier—contests of extempore verse composition, which people enjoyed immensely, but which were also entirely ephemeral. The compositions were not meant to survive the day and therefore did not face the kind of scrutiny of form, substance, and style that a written text-object would face in a primarily written culture. There was no way of retrieving them except in unreliable reports from memory, and the performance was appreciated for the astonishingly spontaneous creativity of the versifiers. Obviously, the *kavigan* was a total experience for the audience, who could appreciate it only firsthand; and they had to be familiar with the utter contingency of occasions to which much of the humour would refer.

Some premodern texts were of course canonized, but with such strong associations between the authors and the gods they praised that the authors were turned into mythical figures. Somewhat like Vyasa or Valmiki, they were not individualized precisely because their achievements were so immense. Although we can certainly detect personal styles among the Vaisnava poets—for instance, the very different styles of Candidas (who emphasized the semantic and the emotional) and Govindadas (who stressed the aural and technical craft)—the authors were not individuated in the modern sense. This was partly because the finished literary product did not reach directly from the author to the reader (another reason, of course, is the paucity of information we have about these authors). These songs, poems, and stories formed parts of *padavali kirtan* recitals, where the narrative could be inflected by the improvisations of the narrator (*kathak*), who would exploit the immediate surroundings to enhance his presentation. The text in the strict, written sense was thus a core structure on which the narrator would build his personal rendition of the tale.

This improvisational performativity was entirely removed from the modern text, which was fixed, nonperformative, and supposed to reflect, in the European style, the author's individual sense of life.[73] In other words, the earlier texts allowed—and in some cases required—the representation of the textual content by a mediating performer, exactly like the mediation of a dramatic text by actors. Modern texts, on the other hand (like lyric poems or novels, the two

---

[73] For an illuminating discussion of the Western context, see Taylor 1989.

literary forms considered paradigmatic of a modern cultural sensibility, centred around a cult of 'authenticity', such as the one that quickly dominated Bangla), created a unified, singular authorship in place of such secondary authorly functions; by their very form, these did not allow any other subjectivity to interpose itself in the private exchange between the author and his reader. The best and most perverse example is perhaps the imposition of an utterly fixed performative structure on Tagore's songs, on the grounds of a largely spurious sovereignty of supposed authorial intention. It would create utter consternation among the Bangla *bhadralok* audience if the rendering of Tagore songs deviated from the musical notation (*svaralipi*), while in the case of many other songs of comparably recent origin singers were allowed a great deal of performative liberty.

Thus the meaning of the literary, as also of the community of readers, was significantly transformed: it shifted from an event performed face-to-face before a relatively intimate community, to an abstract, objective textual object, emphasizing the individuality of both author and reader and the impersonal nature of that relation.

In modern Bangla culture, for reasons that ought to be explored sociologically, literary work—often generically referred to as 'writing' (*lekha*)—soon came to be especially valued among modern intellectual practices. Haraprasad Sastri, observant as ever, noted that to place Bangla literature on a firm foundation writers had to become professionals (in other words, work as full-time writers), though paradoxically, in the nineteenth and early twentieth centuries this was possible only for aristocrats. Successful early writers of those days belonged to the colonial elite. Bankimchandra was a deputy magistrate, and Tagore, who came from a *zamindar* family, was happily exempted from the need to earn a common living. But even Tagore, one of the most celebrated writers worldwide in the early twentieth century, found difficulty financing his university at Shantiniketan through royalties.

Only in the 1940s did serious literary writing descend socially to become primarily the work of petty bourgeois individuals living on small office jobs. Saratchandra Chattopadhyay's unprecedented popular success as a novelist allowed him to become a professional author, but in his time this was still an exception. Jibanananda Das, perhaps the most remarkable and distinctive poetic voice after Tagore, was shadowed by lack of professional success his whole life, and he worked as a college lecturer in obscure institutions in Calcutta and rural Bengal.[74] He died in a tram accident that was as heartbreakingly urban as some of his poetry. After his time, the modern associations of Bangla high literature, in which the subject and object are both petty bourgeois and its predominant theme is an oppressive, unfulfilling urban modernity, were firmly established.

Cultural traditions are hard to obliterate, however. Although they were dislodged from the high grounds of literature, some of the older, oral processes of literary delectation were preserved in the great Bangla institution of the *adda*, an informal gathering typically devoted to conversation on matters of literature and culture that became the source and seat of judgement of much literary production. The *adda* was not an impersonal public sphere; rather, it was an unstructured and private literary association, access to which was controlled by common taste, technical style, or political ideology. The *adda* itself was predictably degraded after the 1940s, turning into a mandatory activity for aspiring young writers, often focused on radical departures in little magazines.

Reminiscences of literary personalities show a clear change of location, style, and context of the literary *adda*. Initially, important writers attracted groups of admirers and collaborators around them. Haraprasad Sastri reminisced about conversations with Bankimchandra in his house at Kanthalpara during which drafts of Bankim's novels in progress were read out and discussed. Similarly, a large and varied circle of literary and artistic personalities gathered around Tagore, the institutional setting of Shantiniketan giving the group a particular stability. Subsequently, important trends in poetic writing, like the post-Tagore iconoclasm of the group associated with the journal *Kallol* or the attempt to fashion a radical left-wing literature around the journal *Paricay*, came out of literary *addas*. These groups were complex and heterogeneous, consisting of creative writers,

[74] See Seely 1990, which contains—besides critical appreciation and biography—admirably translated passages from Das's most important poems. Amazingly, Das was dismissed from his position as college lecturer in Calcutta because of uncomprehending and unfair reviews of his poetic work: see Sen 1965: 330).

literary critics, and ordinary men of literary taste—a kind of inner and privileged audience. The writers themselves were often quite a mixed group, including poets, novelists, and short story writers. Later, when some groups became affiliated with political ideologies, they expanded to include writers of political commentary. The first *addas* were held in the opulent and quiet interiors of upper-class homes.[75] Access to and membership in these gatherings were therefore rigorously restricted. Literary friends gathered in the houses of eminent poets or writers and discussed literary works by way of unstructured conversation. By the 1940s, non-elite versions of such things were already in place—for instance, in the offices of the Communist Party or the Progressive Writers' Association, or in editorial offices of journals like *Paricay*, where access was not socially restricted yet was largely ideologically determined.[76]

By the 1960s, literary *addas* also spilled over into more public places, like roadside cafes or the famous Calcutta Coffee House in the College Street area, which single-handedly housed the editorial boards of hundreds of highly interesting though ephemeral journals. By that time, literary careers went hand in hand with the unemployment of the educated lower-middleclass youth, or, in cases of the more talented or fortunate, with a turn to professionalism usually supported by publishing groups that marketed popular magazines of huge circulation.

As Bangla literature established itself, it became part of a wide world of cultural transactions. Surrounding the 'death of Sanskrit', of which Pollock has written, there were other subtle deaths, one of them being the death of medieval Bangla.[77] Most significantly, the medieval tradition of literary cosmopolitanism, in which Bangla had ingeniously selected elements out of Sanskrit culture and recombined them into something of its own, was replaced by a modern version, in which Bangla began to imitate Western bourgeois forms. It also imitated Western forms of canonicity. As modern Bangla literature established

[75] Datta 1985.

[76] *Paricay* was started around 1931 by a group of literary aesthetes, but was taken over later by Communist and left-wing writers.

[77] Pollock 2001.

itself, it became part of a wide world of cultural transactions within the cultural space of South Asia. Bangla began to have immense influence over literatures of adjacent regional languages, though not surprisingly this was a rather fraught and ambiguous relationship of emulation and resentment. The works of Bankimchandra, Rabindranath, and Saratchandra were translated in huge waves all across India. In this brief early phase, Bangla contentedly accepted its position as a 'hegemonic' literature in India, casually presuming its pre-eminence among other vernacular literatures. But even in this context Bangla placed itself in a clearly recognizable cosmopolitan hierarchy ranging from the local to the global.

Bangla was seen as positioned in the middle of a literary 'world' in which European literatures—English and French especially—stood at the top, *above* Bangla in some sense, and the other Indian literatures stretched away below. This helps us understand the flow of traffic in translations. Very little from other Indian literatures was translated into Bangla, and little of what was translated became popular. In this condition of relative isolation Bangla resembles English, with its sense of being privileged and having little to learn from others. For instance, a Bengali child given a fairly careful literary education could grow up in the 1950s without hearing a reference to *Godan*, the great Hindi novel by Premchand; however, Bangla versions of even minor European novels of adventure or romance were quite plentiful. A children's writer, Nripendra Krishna Chattopadhyay, almost single-handedly presented the entire canon of European classics to the young Bengali reader. An average middle-class child in a small town could easily grow up with his imaginative world populated on the one side by characters from the Sanskrit story collections *Kathasaritsagara* (Ocean of Stories) and *Vetalapancavimsati* (Twentyfive Tales of the Undead), and on the other *Ivanhoe* and *The Three Musketeers*. Children's editions of both kinds of texts were equally popular as gifts in school prize-distribution ceremonies.

Until the 1950s, cultivation did not sever connection with the high classical past. Kalidasa at least, and some common classical literary texts, were mandatory parts of a fastidious literary education. From the 1940s, due to radical influences, there were attempts to accord *literary* recognition to folk traditions which had been treated with indifference if not contempt by the early creators of a high Bangla. This is reflected in an interest in the recovery and inventorization of Baul songs and tales told by grandmothers.

It is interesting to consider what the divergent values embedded in this literary cosmopolitanism produced in terms of the Bengali 'habits of the heart'. In the 1950s, there was a wave of translations from Western literatures other than English. But these translations had a metaliterary purpose. They were meant not only for simple delectation but also to assist in reflection on the nature of literary modernity in the context of a debate about what was modern poetry and whether Tagore's poetry qualified. One of the most striking documents of this discussion was Buddhadev Basu's essay justifying his translation of Baudelaire as an example of what *modern* poetry, with its vision of a city of 'steeples and chimneys', should be. Radical leftwing political influence regarded this strand as degenerate and balanced it with equally energetic translations of poetry from an astonishingly cosmopolitan spread of sources from Pablo Neruda to Nazim Hikmet (the latter was translated by Subhas Mukhopadhyay, at the time a young and promising poet with the Communist Party). In the 1960s came a second wave of translations, which focused on European drama—Chekhov's *Cherry Orchard*, Pirandello's *Six Characters in Search of an Author*, Brecht's *Three Penny Opera*—intended not for a reading public but for a very appreciative theatre-going audience with highly eclectic taste. All these translations have since played to consistently full houses in Calcutta's theatre district. What the Bengali inhabitant of a declining modern Calcutta has found so absorbing in these plays is an interesting question for the understanding of cultural translation.

Tagore and the Problem of the Modernity of Literature

Early-modern Bangla literary practice—the second 'origin' of Bangla literary culture—raised a set of questions: What was the meaning of modernity in the literary field? Was it simply a temporal marker, indicating merely that this literature existed effortlessly in the 'present'? Or did modernity have some substantive content: acceptance of a general cultural sensibility, a background understanding of the world taken from modern science, or some literary principle like individuality and rejection of convention? Since the work of the early-modern writers developed in the context of an implicit contest with colonialism and the prestige of English, they had to claim that Bangla possessed the dual distinctions of having a classical past and being able to produce a high literature in the present. In Vidyasagar's time it was easy to claim the first by reinventing a Bangla artificially proximate to Sanskrit; but the second task was obviously more difficult. There was a growing sense of a strange historical chasm between the pasts of Bangla literature and its present, an uncomfortable but inescapable feeling that those pasts were enabling factors for the growth of modern literature yet were aesthetically discontinuous from the modern literary enterprise. Quite often the solution was daring and ingenious: instead of finding modern subjects for aesthetic presentation, authors chose ancient narratives but handled them in distinctly modern ways.[78] By the time Bankimchandra wrote his prose works to complement the considerable riches of Madhusudan's poetry (mid-nineteenth century), modern Bangla could claim a distinctive and distinguished body of new literature.[79] It was the works of these two writers in particular that became the 'classical' texts of modern literature, occupying the strangely dual status of 'modern classics'. The more modern literature evolved, reaching a mature stage in the later works of Rabindranath Tagore (in the first part of the twentieth century), the more its difference from traditional literature became transparent.

The entire line of Bangla literature from Bankim to Tagore was modern in some ways, but its central aesthetic ideals and principles

[78] This important question calls for careful and separate analysis. But the main point can be illustrated by Madhusudan's choice of themes: the stories about Meghnad, Tilottami, and Sarmistha; and Tagore's reworkings of classical moral dilemmas in his long narrative poems in *Katha O Kahini* (1900), discussed later.

[79] Interestingly, Haraprasad Sastri made the astonishingly chauvinistic claim that the historical situation of modern Bangla was unparalleled in the world. He believed that modern Bangla writers' access to the traditions of both Western and Indian antiquity as well as the great variety of modern European literature would spawn a literature of unequalled glory. In other words, literary writers for the first time had before them the dual ideals of Kalidasa and Shakespeare.

remained 'classical'. The ideas and techniques that animated that literature were similar to the principles underlying Shakespearean drama, nineteenth-century English romantic poetry, and the Victorian novel. From the 1940s onward, however, a new intellectual anxiety forced more reflection on what constituted modernity in literature. Exposure to contemporary European art led to the birth of a new, more complex form of modernism. It became evident by this time that the principle of 'modernity' was curious; it represented not a single set of literary criteria but rather the principles of motion, displacement, and openness toward transformation and experimentation in literary values. However modern a form of literature was, it was not immune from challenge by forms that spoke in the name of modernity against any existing body of texts. Many 'modern' writers and critics found this aspect of literary modernity deeply unsettling. Modernity turned into a problem because of the rapidity with which both poetic and prose conventions were threatened with what some considered undeserved obsolescence.

By this time, one peculiarity of the literary modern must have been clear to its more perceptive practitioners. In traditional literature, temporality had a clearly different form. In ancient and medieval literature in Sanskrit the making of new classics at a later period did not cancel out, transcend, or, more significantly, 'make impossible' writing in an earlier style. Jayadeva in the twelfth century and Vidyapati in the fifteenth did not make their predecessor Kalidasa obsolete; in fact, Kalidasa's style was a canonical option for later poets. Classic texts, once they were admitted to this exalted status, shared a common immortality. Clearly, this kind of temporalization was not happening to modern Bangla. The classicism of Bankim and Madhusudan was highly individual, in that other authors could not follow them without appearing unoriginal, and their works became stylistically or aesthetically obsolete relatively quickly. Although Madhusudan's poetry and Bankim's fiction and satires had already achieved the status of classics, they lacked some of the attributes possessed by acknowledged classics in traditional literature.

True, modern Bangla literature slowly developed a canon of 'great texts', but these texts and their concerns and styles soon became unrepeatable. Classics failed to become conventionalized as literary practice—as parts of a repertoire of acknowledged styles in which literary writing could be carried on for the indefinite future. Even Bankimchandra's admiring contemporaries apparently found it impossible to write like him; so it is not surprising that his concerns with Indian, Hindu, and Bengali history, his powerful Sanskritic language with its great internal differentiation, the manner in which his characters conducted themselves, the dramatic structure of his novels, and the sketchiness of the world depicted inside his stories were all inimitable to Tagore's generation. This was so not merely because of the power of his imagination and its peculiar individuality, but also because of the subtle sliding away of his aesthetic world—a double obsolescence of both that world and its aesthetic forms.

Tagore's pervasive influence on modern Bangla literature was subtly present even in work that strove to break away from him. His younger contemporaries, including rebellious poets associated with the iconoclastic urges of the *Kallol* group (formed in 1924), could not deny that the language they used had been fashioned by him. Yet even Tagore was not immune to the accelerated obsolescence that haunted modern 'classicism'. Critical discussions about Bangla poetry gave compelling reasons why it was impossible to 'write like Tagore' any longer, and by the 1940s even Tagore was firmly, irrevocably in the past. In fact, the novel *Seser Kavita*—his brilliant attempt to find an answer to the insidious challenge of literary modernity, his refusal to belong to a literary past during his own lifetime—in a paradoxical fashion, tragically illustrated his failure. The craft of the novel shows his unparalleled skill with words, proving that he could write colloquial prose if he chose with a poetic fluidity far surpassing the young writers. He could portray youthful, 'modern' characters whose romantic sensibility was quite different from the usual figures in his own mature writing. Yet *Seser Kavita* was the best refutation of his own claim that he was, by the standards of the gritty and melancholy 1940s, a literary contemporary. It represented a magnificent failure to be modern by the current criteria. By contrast, a single line of Jibananada Das's gloomy poem—in which he quickly sketches the habituation of despair in the posture of an Anglo-Indian prostitute puffing smoke under a dim street light while waiting for some indefinite American soldier in Calcutta's twilight—contains a deeper expression of the moods of post-war urban despair and its awkward demand for an aesthetic that could make poetry out of degradation. This was beyond the moral possibilities of Tagore's aesthetic, despite his extraordinary technical virtuosity. What had been demanded was a change not in style but in the fundamental aesthetic itself.

After Tagore, this kind of historical obsolescence, as if by definition now part of the modern literary condition, was routinely acknowledged. Accomplishment in poetic or novelistic writing was noted for the individuality of style but was never expected to be conventionalized in the manner of traditional literature. There was an underlying critical sense that the movement of literature consisted in bringing each new literary aesthetic to its limits, and then crossing them by making literature take account of subjects that had been impossible to talk about in a literary way before. The claim of novelty among the post-Tagore poetic generation was focused entirely on this problem.

Modernity presented writers with two different literary worlds, one drawn from Indian traditions, the other from the West. Authors improvised by using elements from both aesthetic alphabets and produced new forms that were irreducible to either. Numerous examples can be drawn from Tagore's poetic work to illustrate this and to show that what he eventually produced was not an imitation of Western forms, but a distinctively Indian/Bangla species of the literary modern. However, it would be wrongheaded to celebrate this as a case of aesthetic 'hybridity', in line with current postmodern appropriations. In fact, poets like Tagore had a well-articulated conception of what hybridity was and believed that aesthetically hybrid forms were produced by a fundamental failure to reconcile contradictory traditions. This can be shown by reference to several aspects of Tagore's work. Under the pressure of modern intellectual influences, he fashioned a language that could express the complex urges of modern subjectivity. In several poems, he reflects on the nature of the unity of his self—a question forced on him clearly by the pressure of a modern conception of the subject coming from Western literature—but he answers through a complex combination of themes and elements drawn from Indian literary-philosophical sources.[80]

---

[80] Several of Tagore's poems are titled 'Ami' (I). One of these, in his *Parises*, asks with exemplary precision:

I wonder today if I know this person
whose speaking makes me speak,

The same virtuosity is shown in Tagore's handling of the past. In a group of poems written in his middle period and gathered into a book called *Katha* o *Kahini*, he takes up poignant occasions or scenes from ancient Indian literature, like the conversation between Karna and Kunti, the mother Karna never knew, on the night before the battle of Kuruksetra; the appeal by Gandhari to her husband Dhrtarastra against her son Duryodhana; and an astonishingly intense inquiry into the nature of moral responsibility for one's acts through an encounter in hell between King Somaka and the priest who had advised him to sacrifice his small child in a *putrestiyajna* (sacrifice for obtaining a son).[81] A third example is Tagore's artistic reflection on suffering and evil in the world, which required both Western ideas of the tragic and Hindu/Buddhist conceptions of *duhkha* as theoretical preconditions, though they were not direct sources of his thinking.

A mark of modernity is the increasing reflexivity of its literature. Artists and writers think more self-consciously about what they are doing; interpretation of form enters into writing itself. It became clear as time passed that Tagore represented a form of the modern in sharp contrast to everything that had gone before. Yet there was simultaneously a gathering sense of dissatisfaction precisely with Tagore's literary immensity, and an attempt, faltering at first but increasingly more assertive, to find ways of going beyond him.

Two tendencies, discernible from the 1940s, attempted to escape Tagore's limits—which were also the limits of Bangla literature—and

---

whose movement makes me move,
whose art is in my painting,
whose tunes ring out in my songs,
in this my heart of strange happiness and sorrows.
I thought he was tied to me.
I thought all my laughter and tears
had drawn a circle around him and bound him to all my work and play.
I though that he was my own:
it would flow down my life to end at the point of my death (1964: 172–3).

There can hardly be a more precise elaboration of the nature of individual subjectivity than this.

[81] The relevant poems are 'Karnakuntisamvad', 'Gandharir Abedan', and 'Narakbas'; all figure in *Sancayita* (Tagore 1972).

to start questioning the nature of modern aesthetics.[82] The first was reflected in the style of poetry associated with the journal *Kallol*, which began to carry the works of some of the best post-Tagore writers; the second was linked to the political radicalism of the Communist cultural movement. At the time, these two strands treated each other with the ruthlessness reserved for the ideological enemy, in a grotesque local reenactment of the Cold War. Yet, in historical retrospect, there was a strange complementarity in their distinct efforts to take literature beyond Tagore's overwhelming but limiting presence. Aesthetic critics of Tagore experimented with formal properties of poetry that went beyond his art, absorbing the most diverse cosmopolitan influences—Buddhadev Basu looking at Baudelaire, for instance, or Jibanananda Das using surrealist imagery. An example of the latter is Das's famous line, *harinera khela kare tara ar hirar aloke*—'Deer play in the light of stars and diamonds'; even a prosaic translation shows how utterly different this is from any contemporary poetic idiom in Bangla writing. Radical writers sought a literature that transcended Tagore by crossing social boundaries, by making the poor, the marginal, and the disheartened legitimate objects of literary enunciation.[83] But both

[82] Some of the most intellectually searching discussions on why Tagore was indispensable and at the same time had to be gone beyond can be found in Buddhadev Basu's essays: Basu 1966.

[83] In 'Aikatan' (Orchestra), one of his most historically perceptive late poems, Tagore sought to give a preemptive answer to these arguments. He listed what his poetry had failed to cover and, with great regretful honesty, said that he had at times stood outside the courtyard of the next neighbourhood but had entirely (*ekebare*) lacked the strength to step inside (*majhe majhe gechi ami o-padar pranganer dhare/ bhitare prabes kari se sakti chila na ekebare*). But he warned against what he saw as 'a fashionable working-classness': 'to steal literary fame without paying the price of real experience' (*satya mulya na diyei sahityer khyati kara curi/ bhalo nay, bhalo nay, nakal se saukhin majduri*). He also presciently invoked the poet of a lower order of human experience, which had escaped him:

iso kabi akhyata janer nirbak maner
marmer bedana yata kariyo udhar
ganhin e-desete pranhin yetha caridhar
abajmar tape suska nirananda ei marubhumi
rase purna kari dao tumi.

trends critiqued Tagore on the same significant point: his art looked away from the everyday slovenliness, degradation, and the problem of evil in modern life, an evil that was mundane, banal, inescapable. A major task emerging from this aesthetic and sociological criticism of the limitations of Tagore's immensity was the search for an aesthetic in the increasingly grimy city life of Calcutta. Tagore wrote two famous poems on Calcutta as a sign of modernity: 'Nagarsangit' (Song of the City) in his relatively early phase, and 'Bansi' (The Flute), his late attempt at capturing poetically the everyday bleakness in the life of the average clerk. But in both his face is averted; he despairs of Calcutta being in any possible sense an aesthetic object. Therefore, among post-Tagore writers, finding an aesthetic of the indigent, restricted life of the urban lower-middle class became the centre of artistic contention.

Some of the most interesting arguments about modernity and its aesthetic expression turned on the reading of Baudelaire's poetry, which had been translated into Bangla, with a defiant and insightful introduction, by Buddhadev Basu.[84] This brought into Bangla literary debates one of the central questions of literary modernity: Can evil be at the centre of an entire aesthetic? A seriously reflective rejoinder to this argument—which preferred Baudelaire's engagement with evil over Tagore's detachment—was offered in Abu Sayid Ayub's essay *Adhunikata o Rabindranath* (Modernity and Rabindranath). Ayub deplored the tendency of modern literature to centre its artistic reflection on the problem of evil. Ayub translated the concept 'evil', with an instructive awkwardness, as *amangalbodh*,[85] but this was

---

Come, o poet who would recover the deep pain in the speechless minds of unfamed men, this songless land where it is lifeless all around, this joyless desert dried by the heat of neglect/ignominy, fill it with enjoyment. 'Aikatan, Janmadine,' Tagore 1972, 823–4.

[84] Basu 1961.

[85] If rendered with pedantic accuracy, *amangalbodh* could mean a sense (*bodh*) of the inauspicious, which raises an interesting problem of *Begriffsgeschichte* in literature. The duality of good and evil could be rendered in more colloquial Bangla as *bhalo* and *manda*; but when authors sought a more philosophical term, they tended to opt for the more religiously laden distinction of *mangal* and *amangal*.

entirely appropriate: Tagore in his 'Song of the City' called the earth
outside of the city *sundar* (beautiful) and *subha* (auspicious), indicating
the fundamental internal relation between these two concepts in his
aesthetic. The poem almost implies that the city is external to what the
earth normally is. Ayub restated this philosophy of art, claiming that
two features of modern literature are especially significant: first, 'the
intense attention to the literary form' (*kavyadeha*; lit. the external or
formal 'body' of literary art); and second, 'the excessive consciousness
about the presence of evil in the world.'[86] Ayub conceded that
Baudelaire was a poet not in a mere formalistic sense but in a 'vedic'
(i.e. philosophic) sense: he was *satyadrasta*, a seer of truth.

> Particularly, when those gifted with subtle and sympathetic understanding
> observe the helplessness of the human condition, their imaginative minds
> come under the shadow of limitless despair and sadness. Baudelaire has
> given form to this shadow in his poetry. . . . All this is acceptable. Still I
> would like to state that Baudelaire is an incomparable poet of a certain
> mood, a certain *rasa*, not more.
>
> My greatest complaint against Baudelaire is that he is a talented poet,
> but he has used his amazing genius to bring himself and all of us to
> perdition.[87]

Ayub then went on to prove that Tagore's poetic world does not
show a naïve denial of evil, but places its unquestionable presence in
the more complex pattern of an ultimately metaphysical optimism.

Despite the intricacy and subtlety of this debate between critics
and defenders of Tagore, and Ayub's attempt to argue the continued
relevance of Tagore's aesthetic, the subsequent evolution of Bangla
poetry shows that historically the verdict went against Ayub. Bangla
literature eventually found an answer to the problem of evil in another
way. In certain respects this solution is reminiscent of Baudelaire
himself, because it too is a poetry of a soiled, degraded world, a poetry
in which chimneys and drains outnumber steeples and temple spires.
But it is also quite different. The Calcutta of post-Tagore poetry is
not just a faint copy of Baudelaire's Paris; its evils and provocations
are not derived but authentic—like the poets' voices that eventually

---

[86] Ayub 1968: 9–10.
[87] Ibid.: 8, 12.

speak about it. In Baudelaire there is still a vestigial classicism in the heroism of the poet's loneliness. He faces an evil that is grand and metaphysical without assistance from anyone, least of all from the women who poison him and help him forget.

Baudelaire's poetry offers a subtle monumentalization of evil, which Jibananda's poetry utterly lacks. Even this consolation—the grandeur of the evil that is the poet's eternal enemy—is denied to the tired, lower-middle-class worker of Calcutta, who, unlike the upper-middle-class professional, does not come home at 'the violet hour'. His life has no violet hour. His life faces an evil that comes in small, unavoidable pieces—indefinable insults and disappointments that become routine, the attrition of everyday life. To paraphrase a famous line, life ebbs like water dripping from a dirty, leaking tap. It is the repetitiveness and unremarkableness of this destiny that makes it so difficult to turn into poetry: but this precisely constituted the aesthetic challenge that Bangla literature after Tagore tried to address. A wonderful poetic statement of this melancholy is the title of Sunil Gangopadhyay's recent title poem: 'The Beautiful is Depressed, and the Sweet is Feeling Feverish' (*sundarer mankharap madhuryer jvar*).

Practical Contexts of Literary Practice

My discussion of literary traditions would not be complete without some analysis of the social contexts of literary practice: journals, societies, coffeehouses and tea shops, and the ubiquitous *addas*—places characterized by an inextricable mix of unemployment, literary ambition, subtle taste, and loafing.[88] Though this topic warrants a whole discussion by itself, some points can be made briefly.

At its earliest stage, the new literature relied on two types of support. First, many writers came from the upper crust of the colonial elite and had the means to publish their own work. Their efforts were assisted by a kind of social collegiality of class, and since the elite collectively longed for a high Bangla literature, they felt it was their social responsibility to support this literature by becoming its audience. Financial support for commercially unviable literary enterprises

---

[88] On the significance of *adda* for Bangla literature, with some persuasive and a few startlingly excessive claims, see Datta 1985. A more general and perceptive analysis is offered in Chakrabarty 1999.

came through donations, subscriptions, and at later periods through influential supporters securing highly profitable advertisements. Eventually, as Bangla literature developed in variety and confidence, a market for it grew. But it is significant that as late as Tagore's mature period literature was not profitable. Even Tagore's literary earnings—phenomenal compared to other contemporaries—were too meagre to support a substantial institution.

It appeared for some time that the imitativeness of modern Bangla literature would lead to the emergence of literary institutions along British or European lines, in the form of *sahitya sabhas* (literary societies) and the formalization of university and school syllabi. But the law of early and rapid decay in Bengal's travestic modernity ensured that such institutions rapidly declined. Even august bodies meant to represent the interests of Bangla literature or native learning, like the Bangiya Sahitya Parisad (Bengal Literary Society) and the Asiatic Society, appear to have gone into terminal decline from the 1960s. Only the *addas* and the inclination of young intellectuals to publish small magazines have survived; individual projects have tended to sink quickly, but the authors have consistently regrouped into new journals and genres.

Two other developments that have affected the literary scene since the 1950s are the coming of the modern newspaper market and, subsequently, of the film narrative. With the rise of popular journals with large circulation, like the legendary weekly literary magazine *Des*, popular novelists started writing serialized novels and stories especially for the annual *puja samkhya* (the autumn festival number). This affected the structure of the stories: formless length was more readily tolerated, and the stories could be cut up into small episodes like television serials. The criteria for judging these stories, which were often bestsellers, were also utterly different from those applied to the self-consciously artistic prose compositions of earlier times. The effect of film aesthetics on literature is an important potential area for analysis, since the transaction of influences is reciprocal. Just as films depend heavily on the narrative resources of literature, so literature is affected by the presence of film. As literary culture turns into an interactive element in a very different cultural economy it enters into yet a new phase. It appears that since the 1960s Bangla literary culture has been in a serious process of restructuring, of which only the broad terms can be specified. First, the linguistic economy that emerged through the nationalist movement with its political diglossia has been seriously modified by the structural developments after Independence. People at high levels under both national capitalism and state socialism prefer to speak in English, and through the increasing power of the state and the market English has found a much wider domain of use compared to the linguistic economy of the 1960s. A new middle-class elite has developed that uses English as its only serious language, and the literary production of this social group has tended to be in English. The relation between vernacular literatures and this new domain of literary English is being gradually negotiated, displacing in some significant ways the earlier relation between nationalism and vernacular writing. It affects the claims of vernacular cosmopolitanism particularly seriously. Cultural changes have also restructured the audiences for the various vernacular literatures.

References

Anisuzzaman. 1971. *Muslim Manas o Bamla Sahitya*. Calcutta: Muktadhara.
Ayub, Abu Sayid. 1968. *Adhunikata o Rabindranath*. Calcutta: Dey's Publishing.
Bandyopadhyay, Shibaji. 1986. *Bamla Sahitye Ora*. Calcutta: Papyrus.
Basu, Buddhadev. 1961. *Baudelaire o Tanr Kabita*. Calcutta: Navana.
———. 1966. *Kabi Rabindranath*. Calcutta: Bharavi.
Bayly, C.A. 1988. *Indian Society and the Making of the British Empire*. Cambridge: Cambridge University Press.
Bharatcandra. 1950a. Annadamangal. In *Bharatcandra Granthavali*, ed. Brajendranath Bandyopadhyay and Sajanikanta Das. Calcutta: Bangiya Sahitya Parishad.
———. 1950b. Mansimha-Bhabananda Upakhyan. In *Bharatcandra Granthavali*, ed. Brajendranath Bandyopadhyay and Sajanikanta Das. Calcutta: Bangiya Sahitya Parishad.
———. 1950c. Vidyasundar. In *Bharatcandra Granthavali*, ed. Brajendranath Bandyopadhyay and Sajanikanta Das. Calcutta: Bangiya Sahitya Parishad.
Bhattacharyya, Tithi. 2000. Rethinking the Political Economy of the Intelligentsia, Bengal 1848–1885. Ph.D. dissertation, School of Oriental and African Studies, University of London.
Chakrabarty, Dipesh. 1999. *Adda*, Calcutta: Dwelling in Modernity. In *Alternative Modernities*, ed. Dilip Parameshwar Gaonkar. Special issue of *Public Culture* 11 (1): 109–45.

————. 2000. *Provincializing Europe*. Princeton: Princeton University Press.

Chakravarti, Mukundaram [Kavikankan]. 1977. *Candimangal*, ed. Ksudiram Das. Calcutta: B. Chanda.

Chatterji, Suniti Kumar. 1970–2. *The Origin and Development of the Bengali Language*. 3 vols. London: Allen & Unwin.

Das, Sisir Kumar. 1984. *Gadya* o *Padyer Dvandva*. Calcutta: Dey's Publishing House, Calcutta.

Dasgupta, Sasibhusan. 1966. *Bharater Sakti-Sadhand o Sakta-Sahitya*. Calcutta: Sahitya Samsad.

Datta, Hirendranath. [1985]. *Sahityer Adda*. Calcutta: Sahityam.

Des. 2000. *Sahasrayan samkhya* (special millennium issue).

Dimock, Edward C., ed. and trans. 1963. *The Thief of Love: Bengali Tales from Court and Village*. Chicago: University of Chicago Press.

Gadamer, Hans Georg. 1981. *Truth and Method*. London: Sheed and Ward.

Kaviraj, Sudipta. 1991. The Imaginary Institution of India. In *Subaltern Studies 7: Writings on South Asian History and Society*, ed. Partha Chatterjee and Gyanendra Pandey. Delhi: Oxford University Press.

————. 1995a. A Reversal of Orientalism. In *Representing Hinduism*, ed. H. von Stietencron and V. Dalmia. New Delhi: Sage.

————. 1995b. *The Unhappy Consciousness*. Delhi: Oxford University Press.

Koselleck, Reinhart. 1981. *Futures Past*. Cambridge, Mass.: MIT Press.

Krsnadas Kaviraj. 1986. *Caitanyacaritamrta*, ed. Sukumar Sen and Tarapada Mukherjee. Calcutta: Ananda Publishers. Kulke, Hermann, ed. 1995. *The State in India 1000–1700*. Delhi: Oxford University Press.

Kvaerne, Per. 1977. *An Anthology of Buddhist Tantric Songs: A Study of the Caryagiti*. Oslo: Universitetsforlaget.

Majumdar, Daksinaranjan Mitra. [1908] 1981. *Thakurmiir Jhuli*. Calcutta: Mitra o Ghosh.

Mammata. 1980. *Kavyaprakasa*, ed. Sivaraja Kaundinnyayanah. Delhi: Motilal Banarsidass.

Miller, Barbara Stoler, ed. and trans. 1977. *Love Songs of the Dark Lord: Jayadeva's 'Gitagovinda'*. New York: Columbia University Press.

Mitra, Premendra. 2000. *Ghanadar Galpa*. In *Ghanadasamagra*. Calcutta: Ananda Publishers.

Mohanty, Nivedita. 1986. *Oriya Nationalism: Quest for a United Orissa 1866–1936*. Delhi: Manohar.

Mukhopadhyay, Bhudev. 1957. *Bhudev Racanasambhar*, ed. Pramathanath Bisi. Calcutta: Amar Sahitya Prakasan.

————. [1892] 1981. *Samajik Prabandha*. Calcutta: Paschim Banga Pustak Parishad.

Mursed, Ghulam. 1992. *Kalantare Bamla Gadya*. Calcutta: Ananda Publishers.

Pollock, Sheldon. 1989. Mimamsa and the Problem of History in Traditional India. *Journal of the American Oriental Society* 109 (4): 603–10.

———. 1998. The Cosmopolitan Vernacular. *Journal of Asian Studies* 57 (I): 6–37.

———. 2001. The Death of Sanskrit. *Comparative Studies in Society and History* 43 (2): 392–426.

———. 2003. *Literary Cultures in History: Reconstructions from South Asia.* Berkeley: University of California Press.

Prakash, Gyan. 1999. *Another Reason: Science and the Imagination of Modern India*. Princeton: Princeton University Press.

Rai, Alok. 2000. *Hindi Nationalism.* Delhi: Orient Longman.

Ray, Durga Charan. [1886] 1984. *Devganer Martye Agaman*. Calcutta: Desh.

Rupa Gosvami. 1965. *Ujjvalanilamani*, ed. and trans. Haridas Das. Navadvip: Haribol Kutir.

Sastri, Haraprasad. 1956. *Haraprasad Racanavali*. 2 vols. Ed. Suniti Kumar Chattopadhyay. Calcutta: Eastern Trading Company.

Seely, Clinton. 1990. *A Poet Apart: A Literary Biography of the Bengali Poet Jibanananda Das (1899–1954)*. Newark: University of Delaware Press.

Sen, Dines Candra. 1950. *Bangabhsa o Sahitya*. Calcutta: Dasgupta and Co.

Sen, Prabodh Candra. 1974. *Chanda-Jijnasa*. Calcutta: Jijnasa.

Sen, Sukumar. 1965. *Bamlar Sahitya Itihas*. Delhi: Sahitya Akademi.

———. Ed. 1971. *Vaisnava Padavali*. New Delhi: Sahitya Akademy.

Sen, Surendra Nath. 1961. *Pracin Bamla Patra*. Calcutta: Calcutta University.

Skinner, Quentin. [1969] 1988. Meaning and Understanding in the History of Ideas. In *Meaning and Context: Quentin Skinner and his Critics*, ed. James Tully. Cambridge: Polity Press.

Subrahmanyam, Sanjay, ed. 1990. *Merchants, Markets and the State in Early Modern India*. Delhi: Oxford University Press.

———. Ed. 1994. *Money and the Market* in *India, 1100–1700*. Delhi: Oxford University Press.

Tagore, Rabindranath. [1900] 1938/39. *Katha o Kahini*. Calcutta: Visvabharati-Granthalaya.

———. 1964. Parises. In *Rabindra Racanavali*, vol. 15. Calcutta: Visvabharati.

———. 1968. *Bharatvarser Itihas*. Calcutta: Visvabharati.

———. 1972. *Saricayita*. Calcutta: Visvabharati.

————. 1996. *Selected Letters of Rabindranath Tagore*, ed. and trans. Andrew Robinson and Krishna Dutta. Cambridge: Cambridge University Press.

Tarlo, Emma. 1994. *Clothing Matters: Dress and Identity in India*. London: C. Hurst.

Taylor, Charles. 1989. *The Sources of the Self.* Cambridge: Harvard University Press.

Vrndavandas. 1932. *Caitanyabhagavata*. Calcutta: Sri Gaudiya Math.

Washbrook, David. 1988. Progress and Problems: South Asian Economic and Social History *c.* 1720–1860. *Modern Asian Studies* 22: 57–96.

4

A Strange Love of Abstractions
The Making of a Language
of Patriotism in Modern Bengali

To think of possible indignity to a land composed of mountains, forests, and rivers, this essay argues, is not a natural thing. Conceiving of nature as having a life similar to human beings and as being the object of emotions is a historical fact—something that happens when the modern emotion named nationalism appears in societies. It is under very specific cultural circumstances that such emotions can be projected on to the natural world, or indeed the natural world can be seen as a singular entity to which the entire apparatus of human emotions can be applied. The ideology called nationalism engendered unknown forms of affection—for unprecedented and abstract things.[1]

Although it goes strongly against our intuition to admit this, emotions are historical. This is especially true of public emotions

---

[1] I am using the term 'abstract' in the sense in which Benedict Anderson uses the idea in his *Imagined Communities* (Anderson 1983). The people who constitute a nation must remain, for each individual nationalist, a group of abstract members whom he will never meet. Yet the emotion he cultivates for them is one that is similar to his feeling for individuals he meets and deals with face to face in his immediate life-world. It is this allegorical transposition of intimate emotions of affection, loyalty, and devotion which makes the feeling of nationalism so strange. But it is also one of the most remarkable features of our world that this strange and unnatural process has become the most unsurprising feature of modern history. The study of the symbols and language of nationalist discourse is an examination of the intellectual techniques by which this strange and unprecedented thing becomes possible.

like patriotism. People use a language of emotions meant for natural communities like the family, and kinship for an abstract modern association with the nation. Here I want to argue that an emotion like patriotism (which is a deeply ironical misnomer for any Bengali and shows the inescapable slippages of writing in English, because a Bengali can, strictly speaking, only be 'matriotic') does not come naturally. People living in a space, in a territory, and in nature may universally admire the bounty of the world around them, but that does not amount to feeling the specific emotion called modern patriotism. Yet, the fact that it is *historical* does not make it, in Gellner's sense, fraudulent. Rather, this raises a question central to the work of modern historians of nationalism on the precise meaning of the *historicity* of nationalism. Historicity, strictly speaking, is a two-sided, somewhat paradoxical notion: to suggest that something is historical is to suggest that it draws upon the past; yet, it also suggests that it is something that emerged at a particular and specifiable time, and did not exist before.

The literature on nationalism has struggled with this conceptual problem. Is there a previously established ethic, which acquires, under the pressures of modern history, a new kind of self-valuing consciousness? Or does the response to a sense of political indignity associated with foreign occupation bring forth a new sense of identity where none existed before? Is the identity old but the sentiment new? Or is the identity itself forged by a new configuration of history, leaving us with no possibility except to treat the sentiment towards this new object as unprecedented? There is no necessary reason why there must be an invariant, general answer to this question. Here I offer an answer that is parochially valid, correct for the Bengali, and presumably by extension for the Indian case. Recognition of objects in the social world requires the prior existence of a language crafted to capture precisely those objects. A nation can begin to exist when both a descriptive and an evaluative language for it has been fashioned. It would be an inaccurate historical representation to say that authors created a language of veneration for a nation that already existed pre-linguistically. In fact, it is the forming of a language of emotion regarding the nation—in this case, the symbolic figure of the land-mother—that makes the descriptive figure of the nation imaginatively visible. I argue that the creation of a language appropriate for the expression of this new emotion, both linguistically and iconically, required a great deal experimentation; and that, even when it was consolidated in the period of high nationalism, there was always potential for instability in this image. There were significant variations in what people saw as their country, the ways in which they imagined its form, and the exact kind of emotion they felt for it; and these variations were not merely formal—each form determined its political implications. Nationalism is a particularly interesting field for the study of the politics of seeing.

At one level, the analysis here is straightforwardly Durkheimian. All societies, Durkheim argued, must have a language in which they value themselves, since one of the central devices for the maintenance of societies is this mechanism for collective self-reverence. But social worlds change historically. Transformations of modernity must therefore create a crisis in this language of selfreverence, for a modern social world is populated by social and political objects of a different kind of construction from earlier ones. One of the central questions here is the paradox of sacredness: modern institutions always seek to deploy and use for their own purposes the established languages of sacredness: from the way in which ceremonies for battle martyrs imitate religious rituals, to the way palaces of modern power try to copy styles of ancient architecture. Modern institutions, however, are often secular, and their use of the language of the sacral is always plagued by some awkwardness. The language of sacredness which these societies used successfully in their traditional past would not easily relate to those objects that modern people like to value. And Durkheim was quite right to acknowledge that modernity has had persistent difficulty with fashioning a language of value entirely its own. This may have to do with the difficulty of retaining sacredness in isolated areas in a world which is gradually becoming desacralized.

Here I will try to follow the alterations in this reverential language and analyse the techniques by which this was brought about in the case of modern Bengali nationalism. What was the nature of this language before the coming of modernity? What exactly were its resources? Exactly what sort of operation was done on those resources to make them adequate to the demands of a modern, mundane sacredness in a world in which other sacrednesses were slowly fading? I shall try to show how writers and imaginative creativity moved the traditional language of piety and its associated iconography to the modern sacredness of the nation. I hope this will also reveal a central irony of modern nationalism: its state of indecision between on the one hand the demands of a rational calculation of selfinterest, and on the other an equally insistent need to constantly appeal to something not based on self-interest at all—an indefeasible community. Modern nations are perpetually uneasily poised between these two, partly contradictory, conceptions of the collective selves.

In purely formal and rational terms it is impossible to induce people to make large sacrifices for the diffuse and uncertain glories of national pride. Conventional arguments of rational choice can be adduced to make the nation still more mysterious. As the objectives of national uplift or eventual freedom from colonial rule are indivisible goods, it is rational for individuals to act as free riders on the sacrifice of others. When India won freedom from British rule, it was impossible to reward with freedom only those who had acted for its achievement, and exclude, for example, those who had worked as British civil servants. When freedom came, all Indians became free, irrespective of whether or not they had supported the freedom struggle. This would appear to have rewarded the free riders particularly well. They enjoyed the benefits of collaboration with the colonial authorities while foreign rule lasted, and shared the freedom of the nation when independence arrived. According to a particularly strong version of such reasoning, this must make the emergence of nationalism particularly problematic.[2]

Nationalism requires, as a supplement, a language of identity of a particularly excessive kind, by which the motherland is not merely valued but valued above all else. This perception of the unique value of the motherland is matched by the excessive demands for exemplary action in her cause. This transition to action is usually prompted by the emotion of nationalist devotion, which is created, in a quite literal sense, by literary operations on existing symbolic repertoires available to a specific culture. From this point of view, the 'creation' of a language of nationalist affection can be seen, to use Ian Hacking's

---

[2] That is, if we extend to the nation the kind of arguments Mancur Olson, for example, uses to explain the absence of class action among Western proletarians.

luminous phrase, as an enquiry into 'historical ontology'—of a new way of seeing things, and a new way of being among individuals.

Some Peculiarities of Bengali and Indian Nationalism

The argument I am suggesting here refers primarily to the emergence of a nationalist language in Bengali culture; but this idea could possibly be generalized for other Indian languages as well, because their historical conditions were similar. Bengalis, and Indians generally, lived a life of contradiction in their education in the nineteenth century. The ideas they absorbed through their college education exhorted individuals to see themselves as choosing and maximizing individuals, but their poetry asked them to lay down their lives if their country called. The process of the creation of this second language, of a poetry of affection for an abstract entity called a political nation, is of great interest to students of political culture. I shall try to unravel the great diversity of intellectual influences that goes into its making, and the evolution of its unstable repertoire of images, and follow historically its major iconic and literary equilibrium as it emerges in the works of Bankimchandra Chattopadhyay. I try to show that in Bankim it expands and suggests its own language of excess, which brings a reaction in the form of a strangely deprecatory nationalism in Tagore a generation later, and, as independence reduces the poignancy of its images, its excessive character turns it into an object of disillusionment and parody.

The Making of a Language: Bankimchandra and *Vande Mataram*

A new emotion requires a new language to express it. And it is not an exaggeration to suggest that Bankimchandra Chattopadhyay devised the elementary aspects of this new language in an awkward song placed inside one of his last novels, which enjoyed an extraordinary career in the history of modern Indian culture.[3] It is often said that Bankim's

[3] Chattopadhyay 1964b. For an admirable English translation with a critical edition of the text, see Lipner 2005. This contains an excellent, detailed Introduction about the history of both the composition and reception of the song. For a scholarly account of the career of the song, see Bhattacharya 2002.

iconography in *Vande Mataram* is traditionalist and conservative. I find this seriously misleading; the idea can be entertained only if we take a casual and inattentive view of the word and image texts. Any serious attention to the texts of *Vande Mataram* will show on the contrary that it is a highly innovative composition both in linguistic and iconic terms.

There are two different ways of reading the text of that song, both plausible in their own ways. Its first textuality is within a novelistic, narrative frame: its meaning circumscribed and fixed by what it does for the narrative and its internal fictive characters. It is a song sung by specific figures in the contingent narrative circumstances of that specific story. But the longer and larger history of that song must take account of the process by which it floats free of that narrative frame, and becomes a free-standing song of first Bengali and then Indian patriotism, invoked, like others of that genre, in their characteristic abstractness. That historical fate does something strange to the original story. That story is both erased and multiplied: erased because it does not have to be invoked as a specific manner of acting and being in the world, precisely because it has become generalized for the putative inhabitants of the new nation. It has not been forgotten because its spirit has gone into oblivion, but forgotten because it is taken for granted. The unprecedented sentiment it creates through the contingent events of that story later become the generic atmosphere of a patriotic consciousness. After some time, the song does not need the story any longer, because that story had been written into the silent breathing of that culture; that narrative is forgotten because its spirit has become unforgettable. To work, to convey its meaning, the song does not need the narrative frame.

I wish to tell three stories regarding that song. First, the story of its writing, which is instructive because it shows how innovative the literary composition was. Second, the story of the novel within which the song appears and is sung, the narrative preparation of that *bhava*. And finally, the story of the song itself as the origin of a free-standing iconic world full of internal figural iconicities of its own, and its deeply ambiguous inheritance.

The first point to note is the feeling of surprise that this song comes from Bankimchandra, one of the most resolutely unpoetic of Bengali writers. After some early misadventures in rhymed poetry, Bankim realized his mistake and never left the more secure poetics of literary prose, which could incorporate some stylistic attractions of poetry in a more controlled form within the capacious powers of prose writing.[4] In stylistic form, he never strayed into poetry again, except on this utterly memorable occasion. But this breaking into poetry, in a literal sense, is highly significant. It shows a crisis in the narrative, a point where the new emotion of patriotism has reached an unbearable intensity, when its unrecognized and unsuspected cadences become too powerful even for Bankim's prose, like emotion breaking into tears; this powerful, new, half-recognized, unknown emotion breaks for this first time, in its own celebration, into poetry.[5]

But this first-ever occasion of breaking into poetry was not free of trouble. In formal terms, only the emotion is undeniable, and its irresistible expressive power is tangible; in terms of the crafting of a literary form for it, it was awkward and, in some ways, flawed. Educated Bengalis, cultivated in the literary arts of three languages— Sanskrit, English, and Bengali—were not slow to recognize its formal problems. A younger contemporary and admirer, Haraprasad Sastri, records a revealing incident in his autobiography.[6] A small group of gifted young writers and admirers used to gather for weekly hearings of the text when Bankim was composing *Anandamath*. When he read the narrative segment in which the song first appeared, there was stunned silence, not because the highly cultured audience thought the song wonderful, but because they could not bring themselves to

---

[4] As one of the first writers in modern Bengali, Bankim had to be a most self-aware user of language. His relation to modern Bengali is a paradoxically dual one: it is true that he writes in modern Bengali, but it is equally true that what we call modern Bengali is made to appear precisely through his writing. He does not have a pre-existing language called modern Bengali in which he writes his works. Rather, it is through his actual writing, he shows that something like this language is possible. He wrote an intriguing essay called 'Bangala Bhasa' (Bengali Language) which explores the various forms of Bengali idiom and techniques of their complex combined use in literary prose (Chattopadhyay 1964a).

[5] For a more detailed analysis of the narrative framing of the song, see Kaviraj 1995: ch. 4. See also the detailed discussion of the relation between the song and the narrative in Lipner 2005.

[6] Sastri 1980.

believe that Bankim, the greatest writer in the language, could, at the height of his imaginative powers, produce something so replete with infelicities. Their alarm was not unjustified. The song begins with solemn Sanskrit:

Vande mataram
sujalam, suphalam, malayajashitalam, sashyashyamalam mataram.

Yet after a few stanzas it reaches a point of poetic climax and breaks ungrammatically into Bengali. To his startled audience this appeared not an invention but a slip. The more courageous among them, like Sastri, drew Bankim's attention to the formal and grammatical awkwardness, because they thought it might expose Bankim, despite his unassailable stature, to ridicule. Bankim, usually more forthcoming in discussion, Sastri tells us, simply said they could not convince him; of course what they said was true, but 'the song was right'. This is an extraordinary incident, if true, because Bankim was the most rationalistic of writers, never at a loss for providing entirely impeccable and reasoned justification for his beliefs. But here he seemed to have no rational grounding of his conviction, only an inexplicable faith in the song's rightness in some inexplicable sense.

Obviously, there was a distinction here between what was grammatically and poetically correct. But beyond its poetic propriety, Bankim wished to say that it was *politically* right. Yet, to say that he needed a language of that politics—and Bankim's defence of himself remained inarticulate because he could not find that language—to say he was himself only halfway towards making it take form. I think the relation between the Sanskrit and vernacular in the *Vande Mataram* is similar to the discrepant tone of the last chapter in Machiavelli's *Prince,* a fault of form from the point of view of consistency of composition, but a triumph in finding a new linguistic register of an unprecedented emotion. As Federico Chabod asserts, without that last stylistically inconsistent chapter *The Prince* would not have been *The Prince*;[7] without that stanza in Bengali, *Vande Mataram*, equally, would not have been the song that made history.

We have now become so used to the image of the land-goddess that it is somehow inconceivable to think of a time when this was

[7] Chabod 1958.

unknown. The tradition of devotion in Hindu religion has a great variety of goddesses, some of whom bear a maternal-feminine form, but are *not* the land. It is necessary therefore to see how this particular image is put together from an earlier iconic field. There are two parallel processes of image-making going on in the novel: in the song the image of the mother is being slowly built up in words; but in another scene of the novel a directly iconic image is also built up directly through a play on imagic forms of various Hindu religious sects.

The Mata to whom that song is sung is not entirely an abstract image of words; it is correspondingly portrayed in a visual image of icons. Mahendra, one of the main characters in the narrative, goes down into the underground temple of the *santans* and is presented with an image of baffling complexity.[8] Consider the primary form of the icon. It is, first of all, a composite image: the main image was a statue of Vishnu (Bankim's preferred deity among the large Hindu pantheon), but there is an image of Shakti in his lap. This composition is of course wholly ungrammatical; both Shaktas and Vaishnavas in Bengal would have found worshipping such a composite image doctrinally unacceptable. In the Bengali tradition of iconic composition, there were occasional instances of the combination of Kali and Krishna into an androgynous image, called Krishnakali, using the darkness of complexion and playing on the stark opposition of the two forms—one masculine, the other feminine. But such images were not very common, although there is evidence of imaginative variations being played on the depiction of individual forms like Durga or Kali or Krishna. Thus, although both Vishnu and Kali came from the formal repertoire of image-making, Bankim's peculiar way of putting them together was highly untraditional. Besides, his construction of this image is not meant as an object for traditional prayer; it is meant specifically for a modern worship of a new object, the motherland, uneasily poised between a metonymy and a metaphor. This is a classic example of 'writing upon writing'.[9] Its *elements* are taken from earlier iconic forms and their language, but its actual figural form is not sanctioned by that pre-existing language: it defies

[8] Lipner 2005: pt I, section 11.
[9] I have made a more detailed argument about the ingestion of external influences in intellectual history in Kaviraj 2006.

the rules of conventional pre-modern iconic syntax. Yet there cannot be an entirely new language; the new expressions must mould the old language into a new one precisely by the repetitive and insistent use of such ungrammatic vision. To be intelligible, it must carry on with its pretences and semblances of continuity; hence the Sanskrit, hence the literary form of the *stotra*. But there is, surrounding all this, an unmistakable sense of displacement, a search for something that is really unprecedented, unthinkable, and really ungrammatical—a distinctly secular sacredness.[10]

Even in Bankim's work this expression of a nationalist emotion does not appear suddenly, without some confused prefiguration. Indications of some interesting preparation for these displacements can be found in his earlier work. What Bankim uses for this invocation is the form of the *stotra* or *stava*, a classical format of worship that works through exaggeration of a deity's powers and beneficent disposition. Conventional religious *stotras* were meant for a specific kind of religious act, for the quiet or noisy worship of the Hindu devotee to his deity, a process marked by an indelible selfishness. A devotee offered the prayer either in the privacy of his worship room, or else the different form of privacy of the silence of a river at dawn, to his personal God. Occasionally, Hindus would worship together in a temple, where many devotees would chant a common prayer, but each was offering his own deeply individual application for mercy and compassion. So the collective, to use Marx's contemptuous phrase, was a sack of devout potatoes, not a political community. Nor did it possess a conception of itself with any form of collective agency. Bankim wished to create a song that would be entirely different from this traditional *stava*, in its literary, formal, point; a song in which the enunciation would not be by discrete individuals, but instead where the invisible lines of separation amongst the tiny circles of their single destinies were erased, enabling them to see themselves as collective makers of a single enunciation. To accomplish this, the song must have a character such that its words would become futile were they not spoken with this new, unknown, unfamiliar, exhilarating togetherness. In this sense, the traditional *stotra* was essentially personal, the political anthem equally essentially collective.

[10] To capture the precise shock of this kind of newness we can use a phrase Hacking culls from Foucault: see Hacking 2003.

I have argued elsewhere that, paradoxically, literary humour had a role in creating the artistic space for this intense solemnity.[11] Humour creates an undermining effect; and any literary form that is subjected to humorous treatment is partly subverted. In Bankim's case, oddly, a humorous device accustoms the audience to the possibility of play, of using a form for purposes other than conventional ones. There is a formal, poetic preparation for such a displacement of the *stotra* form in one of Bankim's humorous essays in *Kamalakanter Daptar*. Its protagonist, a destitute Brahmin opium-eater, Kamalakanta, reports a dream. In one of his inspired sequences of dreaming, when essences appear unbidden to his sight, freed by the power of opium from the distractions of everyday life and when he can directly read truth and history, he initially saw a golden idol floating away in the swirling waters of a dark river. On paying attention, he realized that the image and the river were not common images but powerful metaphors. The icon was the image of the goddess Durga on the *saptami* day, the joyous middle point of the autumn celebration of Durga Puja, golden both as a metaphor of the harvest and of glorious plenty, and of an unspecified national opulence. She was being carried down the streams and waves of an equally metaphorical river—of time, dark because its waters are cognitively impenetrable, and irresistible because there is no point in straining against those currents of time and mortality.[12] Kamalakanta writes one of the most powerful passages of his nationalist construction immediately after evoking this image; and it is also characteristic that, in that piece of writing as well, Bankim's emotions overpower his writer's discipline. What is remarkable is that this emotion makes him not only use infelicitous words, most uncharacteristic in someone who habitually shows sedulous attention to rules and grammaticality, but to leave those uneasy words in the printed text. This could only be because he thought that they expressed, despite their 'faulty' character, something immensely significant which it would be wrong to erase merely because it was grammatically suspect. Bankim thus sensed that something of immense historical import was happening through his writing, in his text, which he had no power to edit out. This idol was

[11] Kaviraj 1995: ch. 2.

[12] In Hindu mythology and philosophical doctrine, *kala* (time) is often analogically linked to a *srota* (torrent/current) in a recurrent metaphor of *kalasrota*. Bankim's dream simply evokes a direct picture of that metaphor.

so precious because she was, in his words, *navaswapnadarsini*, one who made it possible to see new dreams. After this inspired passage, as is the formal style in *Kamalakanta*, the writing again lapses into the frivolous and the travestic, but in a significant manner. Kamalakanta begins to invoke the *aryastotra*, a traditional incantation to goddess Shakti. Curiously, after some proper lines from the canonical composition, he inserts an inimitable mark of his travestic humour: the all-powerful mother is thanked—among others of her proper world-sustaining tasks—with the successful sustenance of Kamalakanta in the midst of the many predicaments of colonial discipline. Kamalakanta is a man without a profession, an income, even a proper and stable address, the essential ingredients of middle-class humanity in a colonial world; and his sheer survival in a world of these omnipotent structures, a fugitive from all its intended disciplines, can only be attributed to the mercy of the omnipotent mother. But the humour, or the irony, is two-sided: while making fun of the regimes of colonial discipline, it also makes fun of the *stotra* as a form, takes liberties with it by inserting an utterly frivolous line into a high classical text.[13] I suspect that there is another, more complex operation at work here. By means of this humour, it prises the *stotra* free of its classical function in traditional sacrality; and as a free-standing form then, a form which retains its sacral character and aura but which is dissociated from its locus in traditional codes of worship, it becomes available for surprising untraditional applications. Only someone who was prepared to take such liberties with traditional forms could put it to more pressing and innovative use.[14]

The *stotra* to the Mother 'returns' in an altered form as *Vande Mataram*, a patriotic song, in *Anandamath*. Indeed, even the narrative framing of the song is indicative of its newness. It is sung by one of the rebel leaders, Bhavananda, to an astonished Mahendra, who gets more mystified as the lines unfold. After a couple of stanzas, Mahendra expresses his surprise: 'but this is not my mother, this is my land'; and implicit in this question is the astonishment of the traditional

[13] *Jaya ma kamalakantapalike.* (Victory to the Mother, protector of Kamala-kanta.)

[14] This analysis is simply taken from my discussion of the *stotra* in Kaviraj 1995.

hearer of *stotras* at the projected transfer of the sentiment of devotion to an unprecedented new object, a land-mother. Mahendra's aesthetic and sentimental perception initially objects to this unaccustomed connection—between the intense worshipping and protective love that a mother deserves from her child, and the uninteresting givenness of the land, which was always taken for granted, and unremarkable, but is now suddenly turned into a complex object of such reverential vision and sentimental devotion. It is not surprising that Mahendra is the great survivor in the final battles in the novel. Others make their impact and fade into the mistiness of time, but Mahendra, the ordinary good man, survives, although transformed. At the end of the novel, in one sense, nothing has changed in external historical reality; in another everything has changed inside the mind. Satyananda, the elusive guru appears at the end of the climactic battle, and advises reconciliation to the establishment of British power. Yet, the consciousness of people has changed, because they have learnt to see a new dream—navasvapnadarsana—which makes this acceptance historically impossible. The whole point of the novel, of its narrative jangle, of its cut and thrust, is the education of the common man in Mahendra; his political transformation by learning a new aesthetic of *deshbhakti*,[15] a stark neologism that would quickly become a commonplace of nationalist discourse. He learns a new optics, a new *vision* of his land, and is given the gift of imagining it formed as a mother, and a language to worship her. The untraditional nature of this aesthetic is therefore marked in the novel itself; Bankim provides an *internal* interpretation to what he was doing narratively, inside the narrative: within the novel the relation between Bhavananda and Mahendra represents the relation between the writer and the reader.

What is left behind and what is aesthetically new can be found by comparing the *aryastotra*, the source, and *Vande Mataram*, the product. In my reading the *Vande Mataram* is the *aryastotra* transformed by the stress of living through the violent, desecrating chemistry of colonialism. The traditional song is to the Mother conceived as the mother, sustainer of the world. It is an imaginative and aesthetic conception of a premodern world which does not know of abstract space, a world populated by other peoples, alien and different. It

---

[15] *Deshbhakti:* a worshipful devotion to one's country.

is an invocation of a Mother to all that exists in this world, and a hymn to her glory. She is the Mother of a world that is close, near, homogeneous, close to hand, comfortable, full of familiar things and people. It is wrong to call this attitude a spirit of generosity. It simply does not have a conception of a world that is large enough, diverse enough, differentiated enough to hold other people and other gods, fundamentally, abstractly different from 'ourselves'—the worshippers of this mother of familiar things. It is perhaps false to say that premodern people had no sense of a mapped world, but even if it was a form of mapping, that was done on very different principles. Those were not maps that showed the indubitable existence of Tahitians, without a person knowing empirically or immediately very much about them. The intense presence of the immediate world, with which persons can interact directly, occluded much of the abstract world beyond it. In modern mapping, the immediate world is only a small part of the abstract mapping of the earth., and can claim no geographic privilege

Vande Mataram is a hymn to a Mother who is created in the image of her worshippers, whose characteristics are all related to their collective self. She is emphatically a Durkheimian goddess, not different from the human beings she sustains and protects; she is simply a resplendent re-description of themselves. She is the glorious form of the nature they inhabit, of the people they are. It is a glorification that bends back towards the self, the ultimate object of this devotion. Implicitly, the ontology of the social world has become wholly different. The song sees the world as abstract space, all parts of which are not equally hallowed. It is a world of maps and peoples, of frontiers and divisions, of selves and others. It is animated by an emotion which presupposes the world created by modern geography and history books; in that conception India is not the world, but a part of the world, and presently an unjustly oppressed part. The emotion of devotion that this elicits is a fundamentally transformed emotion; from one of wonderment, satisfaction, supplication, and gratitude at being allowed residence in this wondrous scheme of things, it is now a tense emotion of grandeur, enthusiasm, and only barely concealed animosity. In the case of the first Mother there were no references to power because she symbolized all the powers of the world; in the case of the second Mother, unjustly diminished and insulted, there is a need to remind her children of the great, irresistible power that she can command:

> *abala kena ma eta bale?*
> *bahubaladharinim, namami tarinim, ripudalabarinim, mataram.*[16]

All the characteristics of the Mother are combative; her stance has been changed from a universal and sustaining repose to an avenging energy evoking conflict and victory.

Sculpting a Goddess of Secular Strife

Clearly, what happens inside the song is similar to the sculpting of a figure using words as material. Linguistic newness is a strange thing: nothing that uses language for intelligibility can be, on the one hand, entirely new; on the other, although the intelligibility of the discrete linguistic elements is a condition of the possibility of new creations through language, by forcing words into carrying unaccustomed meanings authors are able to bring new linguistic possibilities into existence. The idea of sacredness is intelligible only through its separation and distinction from the profane. Yet nationalism manages to create a new language which performs the impossible; it habituates people in using a language of sacrality while referring to entirely profane objects.

Closely observed, the song has two parts, describing two separate types of imagery. Usually, in Hindu religious iconography, the deity is worshipped in a state of peaceful repose, even though he or she is often the invincible last resort of vulnerable and terrified human beings.[17] The god Rama, for instance, despite his heroic exploits in the *Ramayana*, is always traditionally in a calm and reposeful state, devoid of exertion and anger. The underlying idea is that although evil might be temporarily, contingently powerful, in a cosmically

---

[16] 'Why are you so powerless, Mother, despite such power?' Translation taken from Lipner 2005. This is also significantly the uncharacteristic Bengali line in the poem. But the song immediately after this slip composes itself and resumes its more stately imposing cadence in the next line.

[17] Rama is often invoked as *nirbala ke bala Ram*—Rama is the strength of the helpless.

well-ordered world the power of goodness incarnate in various godly forms deals with such challenges. To describe the almighty in a state of agitation would be a kind of sacrilege, a lack of confidence in his/her invincibility. Only in some particular traditions, like the text *Candi*—much loved by Bengali devotees of the goddess Shakti—is the divine shown in an actively fighting state, her wrath depicted iconically in slaying figures of evil. Bankim's song draws upon both these iconic systems equally. The first part of the song is placid, reposeful, continuing the usual conventions of depicting the calm, unagitated majesty of a deity, though her attributes are surprising: the waters, the fruits, the soft cool breezes, the abundant harvest. This too is an iconic invocation of power, but in a state of calm. In the second part, however, this power changes form into something that can be a force of a very different kind, a force fighting against oppression. This force is marked by the numbers of her willing soldiers, their raised weapons, the menacing roar of millions of voices raised in her defence. It is true that this awesome power is to be used only in their just defence against subjection and dishonour; but this is a startling and surprising transformation of one aspect of a deity. The goddess has undergone, in these few sentences, a fateful transformation: she is now literally made up of human beings, and the purpose of her incarnation is also an entirely mundane business—a fight against injustice. She is a new goddess of strife in a disenchanted, political world, participating awkwardly in fierce exchanges of mundane power in the modern world. She does not give sustenance and benefaction to all human beings; her divine invincibility is partial to her own people.

In Bengali religious thought there is a rich tradition of conceiving of the supreme being as a mother, a sustaining, protective, unconquerable force. But sustenance and protection are somewhat different ideas; or at least they give the same general idea somewhat different inflections. In the religious tradition of Shakti worship, there are two different iconic representations of these differently inflected ideals. In purely iconic terms, the Vaisnava tradition developed the image of the goddess Shri, who sustains the world, including her suppliant children, in an attitude of infinite affection: and her iconic representation describes her as *karunagravanatamukhi*, leaning forward a little in a gesture of pity very similar to the Christian images of Pieta. In the Shakta tradition of divine imagery, the emphasis is more on protection from evil, which takes the unconquerable feminine ideal into a more contestatory field of representation. Evil is given an embodied form; and the invincible mother takes on an appropriately warlike image as the triumphant Durga, who is depicted at the moment of her triumph against demonic images of evil, the *Mahisasura*. As is well known, she can also take a darker form, as Kali, who is violent, cognitively impenetrable, terrifying in her unpredictability, and pitiless like time (*kala*), which merges invincible power with the ability to deliver indiscriminate death and destruction.

Two Times of the Song: The Question of Interpellation and the Analogical Logic of Narration

Since it first appeared the *Vande Mataram* has never ceased to evoke controversy. Some literary and political critics point out, in their overall political reading of Bankim's work, that there is a strong element of animosity towards Muslims in his thinking.[18] I do not wish to contest this claim entirely, though I feel Bankim is aware of the problem and it occasionally troubles his otherwise liberal conscience.[19] But a communal reading of this song faces several interpretative problems: it makes the meaning of the song rather confused. If the invocation of the goddess is entirely in order to free her world of Muslim misrule, it becomes an insoluble mystery how the song can be the pre-eminent anthem of anti-British nationalist sentiment. Did Bankim's readers misjudge his authorial intention entirely, and turn a song meant as

[18] Lipner's Introduction gives a detailed and reasoned account of these controversies, and also suggests that my study of Bankim avoids this problem (Lipner 2005).

[19] See, for instance, the appendix to the revised version of *Rajsinha*, the last fictional work of his life Bankim Rachanabali, Volume II, 555–662. This passage is significant, in my view, because it uses a device that is also at work in the enunciation of *Vande Mataram*. The novel's last edition ends by saying: 'let no reader think that the purpose of this work is to make a distinction between Hindus and Muslims. Hinduas are not always good and Muslims bad, or Muslims good and Hindus bad. Good and bad elements exist in equal measure among both groups. Rather one has to admit when the Muslims were rulers of India for somany centuries, Muslim rulers are superior to their Hindu contemporaries.' (Chattopadhyay 1984: vol. II, 661.)

anti-Muslim tirade by a loyal British subject into an unintended anthem of opposition to British rule?

Even dedicated critics of Bankim, who regard him as the originator of Hindu communal discourse in modern India, would not commonly deny that the song had a triumphant career as an anti-British nationalist anthem. How was that possible? I wish to suggest it was made possible by a literary device—of playing with two temporalities of enunciation of the song. Diegetic time is often a complex form of dual temporality—of a time *inside* the narrative interacting through the story-telling device with the time *outside* the narrative, the always contemporary time in which the text is read.[20] Narrative temporality is often this double time—produced by the artistic device connecting character time with reader time. To yield to the narrative pretence, in this case, the song is being uttered/sung by a fictional character inside a fictional historical narrative placed in the eighteenth century, just before the secure establishment of British power. This is the *time of the character*. But the song is also being read in the *time of the reader*, in the late nineteenth century, in the privacy of the interiors of Bengali households. In this second time, the time of the reader, the oppressive regime is not Muslim but British, and the abstract, general question— 'why are you helpless in spite of such potential power?'—resonates in this context with a very different meaning. The historical novel in that sense is not historical at all; it is simply an elaborate pretence of writing about the present using a historic code. It is problematic to suggest that the whole of the novel is written in a consistent code of camouflage of intentions—that we can simply substitute the Muslim figures by British ones to complete our grasp of the sense of the novel. Literary critics also often point out the obvious difference between the utterance of characters and the utterance of the author. Anti-Semitic beliefs in characters are not necessarily the opinion of the author, so anti-Muslim sentiments of characters inside a novel are not necessarily those of Bankim. These arguments are technically justified, but besides

[20] To take an example from Dickens, in *A Tale of Two Cities*, the time of the characters is the time just before the outbreak of the Revolution in Paris, and time of the reader is a time afterwards. So the characters in the story have no means of knowing that they are moving into Paris before a historic storm; equally, the readers have no means of not knowing this.

them is a wealth of sayings by the author within his novels, and in his more unambiguously assertoric essays, which show he had absorbed a modernist-Orientalist understanding of the medieval period of Indian history. By this I mean that he saw political conflicts anachronistically, as hostilities between large collective actors—states or entire peoples who were subjugated or liberated. There is a sullen underlying hostility towards Muslim rule that is undeniable, though he has a sufficiently vivid realization of the demands of modern liberal universalism to feel troubled about it.[21]

Yet this element of hostility to Muslim rule makes the question of the historic 'meaning' of the novel more complex. The meaning of a literary text exists between its authorial intention and the intentionality of reading, and every individual reading is in a sense a contingent fusion of the authorial and readerly horizons. There is no doubt that, in the last novels, Bankim was preaching what his admiring contemporaries coyly called *anusilantattva*, the theory of defiant discipline, which consisted of two parts. On one side, there is in all these novels a repetitive creation of a theatre of action marked by injustice and the oppressive power of *vidharmi* rulers. *Vidharmi* signifies something more complex and more intense than 'alien' or merely descriptively foreign. It indicates something morally alien, a moral vision that subjugates, defiles, and destroys the settled moral habits of a people. Despite his liberal expressions of unease, Bankim's novels are strewn with too many fictive scenes of Muslim oppression. The total effect of reading his novels is certainly an appreciation of Muslim rule as morally oppressive and repugnant; but there is also a subtle and not entirely surreptitious incitement to analogical reasoning which would regard British rule, on identical grounds, as both oppressive and repugnant. Bankim certainly had a change of mind about the cultural implications of British rule. His early works, while alive to the indignity of foreign rule, tend to regard the intellectual offerings of modern Western culture as positive. Towards the end of his life he comes to a much darker perception of cultural influences from the West, and seems to regard the emancipatory ideas themselves as causing a deeper and more troubling form of heteronomy. Precisely

[21] For instance, in the postscript to *Rajsimha*. Chattopdhyay 1984: vol. II, 661.

because of their universalist form, it was possible for natives to accept and own them, and offer rationalist, emancipatory grounds for their acceptance of these ideas. But that made it impossible to discern the essential difference between an unforced acceptance of rationalist ideals and a submissive, colonial adoption of the mores of foreign rulers. In humorous sketches like the *Ingrajstotra*, Bankim plays with this difficult theme that was central to controversies about religious conversion as well. Both in Christian theological discussion and Islamic doctrine, there is a persistent worry about the connection between power and morals within the conversion process. Real conversion from one religion to another, thinkers point out, must be an uncoerced choice, an adoption on purely moral grounds of a religious ethic seen by the converted as superior. Power within the equation contaminates this decision, with either fear or the expectation of mundane advancement which power can guarantee to the converted. Conversion affected by either fear of punishment or calculations of preference cannot be seen as real religious transformation.[22] Despite its comic tone, Bankim's *Ingrajstotra* raises an identical problem in a nonreligious, colonial context: how can one be sure that the acceptance of rationalist ideas is because of their purely rational powers of persuasion, and not a self-interested adoption of the intellectual fashions of colonial rulers? His intensifying suspicion of a secret heteronomy at the heart of emancipatory crusades of liberal rationalism inclines him increasingly towards a form of rationalized Hinduism, which stands at the heart of his new doctrine of patriotism. In the fictional world of the novels, this is converted into a logic of analogic thinking about historical situations: the dominance of the Islamic rulers is unjust and is opposed in the novels by characters displaying exemplary patriotism. In the world outside the novel, the world of its reading, not the internal world of its actions, it is easy to infer that there is a similar existence of dominant alien rulers; but now, in his later years, alien in this more complex and moral sense. The act of reading is therefore a double

---

[22] Arguments of this kind can be found among liberal thinkers within many different religious traditions. In early-modern political theory, Locke advances arguments of this type in his *Essay Concerning Toleration*. In Indic Islam, very similar considerations can be found in Abul Fazl's collection of the emperor Akbar's thoughts in the final sections of the *Ain-i-Akbari*.

one, of two readings: a reading of the internal fictional fact, and an analogical, real fact of current subjection.

The reading thus has little trouble in analogically extending its meaning to the present. The song *Vande Mataram* operates on a similarly analogical register: the nation, an unspecified 'we', occupies the place of the oppressed in both equations; in the eighteenth century the place of the oppressor is occupied by the Muslim ruler, in the nineteenth by the British, and the song clearly points to the appropriateness of a similar sentiment against both types of subjection. But as the reading, and a virtual singing, occurs in the present, those words enunciate a patriotism directed at the present and real enemy. The beautifully crafted hatred of this song achieves a fascinating transposition, changing the image of the British from a race of political protectors, intellectual instructors, and cultural allies in rationalism to a race of political enemies. But the logic of analogical hatred is curious and complex; the transposition of hostility to the British does not erase its uses against Muslim rulers of the past. Thus, it is plausible to suggest that two acts of hatred happen in the singing of the song. Although it is increasingly turned into a song of nationalist defiance of British colonial rule and is the first literary creation to set this new dark emotion to music, there is an analogical reference to Islamic oppression in the very act of singing it. By making colonial oppression unforgettable, it also makes Muslim rule ineradicably alien.

The Meanings of the Song

There has been a huge controversy about the meaning of this song in the interminable debates about Indian nationalism and its present significance. Seen from the point of view of intellectual history and cultural theory, the contending readings have commonly presupposed a restricted view of the many possible meanings of an artistic object. Some philosophical views maintain that textuality is integrally historical, that is, to be a text is to be open in principle to historical reinterpretation. It can be argued, following Gadamer's work on inter-pretation of art, that a meaning does not inhere in the object of art. What inheres in a text is meaningfulness, the potentiality of bearing meaning, as distinct from a single or a specifiable set of meanings. A text always waits for representation—in both senses of the term.

To be meaningful, it has to be represented by some act of meaning-creation, like the actor's actual declamation of the lines of Macbeth. Before that act of representation, of bringing something abstractly wordy into something that is uttered and meaningful, the text is not, strictly speaking meaning-bearing. Secondly, since each instance of bringing it to meaning is contingent on its performative context, every text is capable of re-presentation—of being presented anew—in a different context, bearing a differently inflected meaning. For a theory of interpretation drawn from Gadamer's version of historicism, a text is merely a structure of possibilities, not a structure of performed meaning: it always exists poised between the meaning-creating act of the author in his horizon, and the meaningcreating act of the reader similarly embedded in his. This opens up the possibility of a distinction between an authorial meaning, and a performative meaning, which encompasses the acts of singing, discussing or reading which are all, in Gadamer's view, equally representational acts. Extending Gadamer's analysis, we can then distinguish between a compositional meaning focused on what the author intended to say, and a performative meaning centred on the separate, but equally meaningcreating activity of the readers, singers, users of the text—which are linked but can, and in fact often are, quite discernibly different. Reading, on this account, is not a passive reception, or re-cuperation of the authorial meaning; it is an independent activity in which the reader brings to the reception of the meaning of the text his own intellectual and cultural formation, his own context of reading and authorial intention. When the textual object is a song, and its reception is itself an occasion of public singing, often in political context, the *taking* of the song has, irreducibly, a large component of *making* by the singer; its interpretative mediation is crucial. It therefore becomes possible, precisely because of the abstractness of the song's locution, to transpose a different context from the narrative one. A large section of Bankim's admirers, who sang the song regularly, would have been able to receive it as an anti-British patriotic text. At least, it is odd to suggest that Rabindranath Tagore, who is usually above suspicion in matters of communalism, set the song to its common tune because it was a fluent vehicle of anti-Muslim communal rage. The complexity of *Vande Mataram's* audience, its circle of reception, testifies to its complex historical meaning. Gadamer faces the problem that arises from this argument of literally following each reception-event of the text as a meaning-creating act: it raises the question: Is the meaning of a text always plural, so diffracted among its many performances? Or can we say there is in some historically plausible sense a meaning of a song that is singular? Gadamer suggests that, in each historical stage, the context of performances, contemporary aesthetic taste and current social preoccupations would impart some similarity to separate individual performances, which he calls in his distinctive sense a 'structure'.[23] It is possible to suggest that for a large audience during the national movement, *Vande Mataram* acquired a primarily nationalistic 'structure' of meaning. Within the song, as a free-standing text, there is no reference to Muslim rule, only a general and abstract reference to the Mother's capacity to stop her enemies (*ripudalavarinim*). It is also remarkable that the objection to the song from the Muslim and secularist intelligentsia is about its use of a Hindu iconic language: its composition in Sanskrit, its assimilation of the *stotra* form of adulation, its constant references to the Mother-goddess. Ironically, if the general deployment of a Sanskritic-Hindu semiotic is the basis of the objection, few nationalist compositions could, strictly, pass the test. Tagore's famous patriotic songs, '*he more citta punyatirthe jaga re dhire/ ei bharater mahamanaber sagaratire* or *janaganamanaadinayakajaya he*', would fall by the same criterion. The only song capable of passing such a secularist test would be the famous preamble to, or a selection of articles from, the Indian constitution, set to a fetching tune.

Yet precisely because of its narrative context of hostility to Muslim rule, precisely because the authorial meaning is at least the first meaning of a text, *Vande Mataram* always attracts a different audience, a communal Hindu reception. This audience responds powerfully to the song precisely because of the duality of the adversaries within its abstract meaning, precisely because the image of the Mother who is *ripudalavarini* signifies a triumph over both the British and the Muslim. In a historical paradox, precisely because the purpose of fighting the British is now obsolete, its valence would retain, to this audience, primarily an anti-Muslim inflection.

They like the song because within this broader form of modern patriotism it always folds a longer and more insidious enmity, and because in this finely-crafted text hatred does not merely point to the

---

[23] Gadamer 1960/1989: 105ff.

British but also makes the other hatred unforgettable; and the re-enactment of this, present, proximate contest always reminds people of, and connects to, the other conflict in Indian history. This is the second 'structure' of meaning of *Vande Mataram*; and the destiny of the song has been a conflict over these two powerful structures of interpretation. When Nehru decided to call this India's national song rather than its anthem, he subscribed to the first structure; but the Bharatiya Janata Party's (BJP) insistence that it be chanted in all Indian schools seeks to incline its meaning towards the second. *Vande Mataram* wanted to create a battlefield with foreign rulers at a time when such a battle could happen only in a political dream; but it inadvertently started a cultural battle over its own meaning which is far from settled.

There is another remarkable confirmation of the real complexity of meaning of this text. The authorial meaning evidently inheres in the complete text of the song, and the narrative frame which animates the words with their meaning. The first distanciation from this complete authorial intention occurs when the song is set free of its narrative architecture, and taken as a separate and independent composition by its admiring singers. But the interruption of authorial meaning does not stop there. As controversies start swirling around the full text of the song, various political groups suggest that only the first stanza of the song, which simply offers worship to the sustaining form of the motherland, should be sung as an anthem, not the offending second stanza. Again, this is a remarkable example of a group of receivers seeking to impose *their* meaning on the song irrespective of the authorial intent. Many poetic compositions which have come to acquire a political destiny have had such reception meanings imposed over the authorial meaning. Tagore's composition, which was eventually adopted as the Indian national anthem—precisely because of the absence of such suggestions of offence—went through this tussle between the composition and reception meaning. The song as a whole was regarded as too long to be an anthem, and only the first stanza, which helpfully enumerated the major states of India's federal constitution, was made the anthem. Still, what was poetically was not necessarily politically correct. Its mention of Sindhu—a reference to the region of Sindh—remained an inconvenient oddity: if it was a reference to a region, this might be read as an irredentist desire for the province of Sindh, lost at Partition to Pakistan; if it meant Sindhi-speaking people, they were certainly part of India's immense melange of languages. Political interventions into the verbal body of the songs always demonstrated the play of two meanings—the authorial and the receptional. While the author's meaning was foundational to the text, it was not, in case of these compositions which became political with time, its only or determinative meaning.

Nature, Space, and Residence

Bankim's immense innovation lay in bringing together in a miraculously effective combination three unconnected ideas that existed in earlier Indian thought. Traditional Indic culture had highly elaborate images of the goddess Shakti— in the shape of philosophical conceptions of nature, a very different tradition of aesthetic delectation of natural beauty, and an entirely prosaic understanding of space. The crucial point is that these were disparate, discrete, and entirely unconnected. The goddess' images did not include nature. Aesthetic appreciation of natural scenes had nothing to do with the sacred; rather, in poets like Kalidasa, depiction of nature runs very close to a witty erotic vision of the world. Space is mundane, entirely bereft of emotional significance. Bankim creates a new language of nationalist worship by joining these unconnected strands into a convex symbolism. A neutral space, the country now comes to be marked by natural features of striking beauty. Nature now merges with the figure of the divine mother, so that it becomes possible for her inhabitants to be transformed into her children, grateful recipients of her natural and divine sustenance. Within traditional thought, these overlaps would have appeared ungrammatical, gratuitous conflations of discrete languages appropriate to disparate fields of reflection. Whereas for the moderns, after the shock of the new is absorbed this becomes the only language that can express a nationalist sentiment.

The new emotion is inextricably linked, in all nationalisms, to a theory of charged, significant, sacral residence. Space has to be given a new kind of sacredness. Traditional thinking in Hindu culture had a great richness of ideas about nature, or rather the nature of nature. Nature was thought of as *prakrti*, also the name of woman—agitated, generative, fecund, creative, restless, irrepressible. She is therefore the image of a primal, unconquerable force. But again this was an enveloping conception of nature seen as a precondition of human existence, and viewed as a source of general preservation and sustenance. It was not an image of a nature over which people could throw a *possessive* relation, a nature that was inextricably part of our self, or a selfness extended to nature and its neutrally existent features—such as rivers, mountains, paddy fields, and ponds. Undoubtedly, the romantic poetic and artistic imagination had something to do with this new intensified idea of domicile; our living inside this world making it special, just as living inside it made us sacred. Rain and sunshine, the cycle of seasons, the mundane business of sowing of seeds and harvesting grain, instead of being unsurprising, quotidian, grey processes, became aesthetic events. They became happenings, on the way to becoming sacred, their very occurrence a mark of peculiar speciality, precisely because these rains and sunshine, these hills and rivers, these grains and fields were those of the self. It is interesting to note how the new geography of abstract space—the space which is beyond the individual's immediate apprehension, but which he knows exists—plays an important part in this transformation. It does not require much argument to show that things like rivers and mountains are not natural objects of love; and it requires a refiguring of the imagination to achieve affection for this intense and immediate nature, these inanimate objects. In earlier cultures, these may have been aesthetically admired, but not loved with such intensity. Poetry accomplishes the astonishing function of what can be called the selfing of nature. In this mapped and diversified world of neutral and natural space, one part with clear boundaries now becomes precious, sacred, emotive, and valuable: it becomes a moral home, the Motherland. Residence in the physical world is made sacred, and poetry becomes the privileged expression of this feeling.

After Bankim, the image of the Mother is invested with an immense fulness, and the figural form of the country as Mother, the image of the Mother-Land, so insecurely and polemically established in Bankim's late fiction, once established, is never dislodged again. Constant addition to her descriptive richness slowly makes for a change, at least a potential change in the axis of this image. This will be evident if we compare the constituents of the images of the Motherland in Bankim and some others who followed him in the tradition of Bengali poetry. Even in the process of creation of value in nature, turning it into a home, the homeland, there are clearly discernible stages. While Bankim is still engaged in the basic process of iconic transfer, shifting the associations of the sacred image of the mother on to the unaccustomed features of the homeland, still trying to convince the puzzled audience of Mahendras, he is simply conferring characteristics of *shubha* (auspicious) or *su* (good) on apparently unexciting objects, convincing the Mahendras that this natural world, always present and available to us, is nevertheless something that deserves thanksgiving; and that it has to be regarded again through a complex aesthetic optics, taken partly from the sensuousness of classical Sanskrit poetry but transformed by lacing into it a new sense of the self's residence.

Classical Sanskrit poetry saw nature only as a thing to savour, enjoy, take pleasure from—as something that enhanced the human idea of sensuousness, a nature that adorned and complemented women's beauty. Using similar descriptive tropes, the new aesthetics converts nature into something valuable and anthropocentric in a new sense, connecting with a more urgent emotion of gratitude for its bounty, and invoking, at the edge of that palette of feelings, more darkly *rudra* emotions like resentment at her humiliation, the spirit of sacrifice, an avenging anger. Compared to the earlier aesthetic of nature, the new aesthetic is sadly limiting. It represents an appreciation of nature which is more intense but more parochial. Earlier, nature existed in two forms—a universal form in which it offered its beneficence to everyone, and a particular form when some of its features—like specific scenes—excited a very definable sense of pleasure. The new emotion that envelops nature is different from both these traditional perceptions. Formerly, the beauty of nature, its sustenance, its mysteries, were supposed to be universal. They beautified the lives of all human beings, or, in Kalidasa's aesthetics, of those who had the sensitivity to appreciate the beauty it made so abundantly available. Now, nature's beauty and bounty is felt more intensely, but not as a gift to all men; rather the special sacredness is of a special part, and to a special group of recipients. It is a mapped world, aesthetically and emotionally, intensely conscious of its boundaries, a world not joined by nature's universality but broken by a humanly parochial sacredness. It is already disenchanted, to use Weber's modernist phrase: from a world governed by God, it already appears like a world governed by the United Nations. This nature is also not particular in the sense in which romantic painting presented it—as a highly specific response of an artistic self to a particular landscape: a scene, a time of day, a strange play of light which was intense but individual. The new visual and iconic celebration of nature is collectivistic, its beauties are visible to its particularly favoured children.

I have argued elsewhere that this Mother is decisively created by the census, and commented on Bankim's great and surprising artistry in putting statistics at the heart of a poem.[24] The Mother is not merely gifted with natural qualities, but also with the modern power of numbers: her children, who also make up her body, can roar with seven crore voices in her glory, just as much as they, somewhat unpractically, raise fourteen crores of hands bearing swords in her defence. The corporeal image of her in Bankim's poem is very similar to the image of the Leviathan on the frontispiece of Hobbes' *Leviathan*, except that she was a woman, and there was a combination of the characteristics of the bountiful with the terrible. The carrying of two swords by each counted Bengali may be militarily inconvenient, but its point lies elsewhere, in the sense of invincibility and power that this counting produced. Bankim was wonderfully ingenious in turning the implement of colonial counting into a weapon of the nationalist imaginary.

Subsequent Adventures of the Nationalist Icon

It is interesting to see how, after Bankim's founding move, this image grows and changes at the same time. The only thing that stabilizes after Bankim's inspired intervention is the impossibility of patriotism for Bengalis and later for Indians. Figurally, their patriotism is always referred to a Mother, made out of these very diverse elements of tradition, from the theological and aesthetic imagination of the *rupa* (a term that denotes simultaneously *appearance* and *beauty*) of *shakti*, to the unrelated strands of aestheticizing nature in erotic poems of the classical Sanskrit tradition. Bankim invents not a new optics of nature, but a new *function:* he invents a *political* nature. He was, after all, the inventor of modern politics in Bengal, not in the form of debating

---

[24] Kaviraj 1995: ch. 4.

societies, parliaments and legislatures, or movements—those variously visible theatres of politics. His greatest gift was to suspect and then show the subliminal presence of politics everywhere in colonial society. His response to the colonial suppression of politics led to the invention of a politics that was ubiquitous. Even nature was political.

After this founding moment, nearly all self-respecting poets compose songs to the glory of the Motherland, who then slowly acquires, through an intense exchange of iconic signification between literary and artistic representations, a highly typified figure of Bharatmata whose image dominates not merely fields of literary-poetic writing but also painting, and eventually the popular Hindi film. As later poets add to the reasons and characteristics of the Motherland's incomparable splendour, these features become too full and diverse, and the image is in a sense ripped apart by this fulness of determinations. As a consequence, the single mother image gets distributed into several, even competing ones.

I shall briefly mention only a few to tell the story of the afterlife of these patriotic icons. Two lines of development emerge from this founding imagination. As the past glories of Hindu civilization are discovered and enlisted in support of political nationalism, in one strand of nationalist poetry the features of the Mother's glory become historical. This country is glorious and great not only because of its rivers and mountains, for its bounty in the harvest, its full fields, but also because of its shining historical past. But this historical memory could go in many different, potentially conflicting, directions. In some cases, it went in the direction of a narration that was resolutely Hindu, and in odd cases, not perhaps wholly unnaturally, prided itself on its own past history of colonizations to put beside the more recent successes of the British.

But history is always an unreliable basis for glorification. In the case of more critical writers, the journey into history could also take a surprisingly self-critical form. Brahmo writers often undermined Hindu narratives of glory by counterpointing to them a narrative of indignity and injustices internal to Hindu society, and asserting that, more than British power, Indian society was fatally weakened by dishonor inflicted on its own people. In the generation after Tagore, two poets produced two extraordinary texts poised at different ends of the continuum of this increasingly contradictory poetic discourse on historical memory. Satyendranath Dutta, a young poet greatly loved for his rhythmic artistry, wrote a hymn to the land of Bengal with both strands of hyperbole, natural and historical, without a trace of any criticism. In one of Dutta's patriotic poems a long line of Indian conquerors is indiscriminately enlisted, placing Asoka's non-violent conversions beside military conquests of Sinhala and South East Asia.[25] At the other end there was an early and immature poem by Sukumar Ray (the incomparable writer of nonsense and children's verse) with the misleadingly patriotic title *Atiter Chhabi* (images of the past). The title, in the long tradition of patriotic poems from *Vande Mataram*, invites an expectation of natural and historical glory; but it delivered a savage critique of the Hindu caste system and its diminishment of humanity by setting up an ever more intricate system of denials. On this view, British colonialism simply used the divisiveness of Indian society and punished it for its own sins.

Not surprisingly, the poetic discourse of Bengali nationalism slowly developed the language of excess common to nationalist literatures. Mother India is not merely glorious but globally incomparable. Nearly all poets and literary figures participate in this celebratory language of excess.[26] It should be remembered, however, that poetic propositions have a distinctive status in such language. Poetic language is often conventionalized; tropes of excess carry a conventionalized

[25] Satyendranath Dutta composed a famous patriotic poem which had lines like the following: '*amader chele bijaysingha helay lanka kariya jay*' (Our son, Vijaysingha, who conquered Lanka without effort). Datta 1973: vol. II, 359.

[26] Even Tagore, who would subsequently turn deeply critical of modern European nationalism for its militarist enthusiasm, and begin to suspect more excessive forms of Indian nationalism as well, was not immune from this conventional use of the trope of incomparability. One of his poems on Bengal, *Sarthaka janam amar janmechi ei dese*, goes on to say: *kon desete janine phul gandhe eman kare akul, kon gagane othe re cand eman hasi hese* (in which other land do fragrant flowers fill the heart with such longing, or the moon rise in the sky with such a smile). Tagore 1970: 24, 257. Atulprasad Sen writes of India as *adijagatajanapujya* (the original object of worship of the whole world— song 72) and, in another favourite of the patriotic canon, *bharat abar jagatsabhay srestha asana labe* (when India will again take the place of the finest in the assembly of the world—song 73). Sen 1996: 89, 91.

meaning rather than a meaning following its precise literal locution. Thus it is easy for even usually restrained thinkers to venture into the conventional language of excessive admiration when writing nationalist poetry. One of the best examples of such deeply felt and conventional admiration of the motherland in a language of excess is a composition by Dwijendralal Roy, a contemporary of Tagore's. His is a particularly popular song of patriotism in which the lyricism of patriotic exaggeration, in a way, consummates a tendency of excess long implicit in poems of nationalist enthusiasm. Ray's song goes into not unfamiliar raptures of exaggeration:

> *dhanadhanye pushpe bhara amader ei basundhara*
> *tahar majhe ache desh ek sakal desher sera*
> *se je svapna diye tairi se desh smrti diye ghera*
> *eman deshti kothao khunje pabe nako tumi*
> *sakal desher rani se je amar janmabhumi*

There is a land that is evidently the best among all countries in this bounteous world; it is made of dreams and bounded by memories. The song carries all the classic marks of nationalist imagination that modern theories emphasize: the connectedness of collective dreams of the future, and of common memories of the past. In the most unrestrained phases of its rapture, the song asks where else one can find such affection from brothers and mothers (*bhayer mayer eta sneha kathay gele pabe keha*), where else are lands with flowers so fragrant, where else is moonlight so cool. It is understandably unenthusiastic about a historical tour of the past, since the Brahmo attacks on that memory had proved so devastating, making it deeply inconvenient territory. Aggressive nationalist imagination therefore came back to an essentially unreasoned glorification of the self, which became mystical as it became excited and enthusiastic.

Tagore and a Double Language of Nationalism

Interestingly, in the next phase of the complex history of Indian nationalism, two sceptical reactions emerged to this tendency towards intensifying cultural chauvinism. In the expanding nationalist literature, this iconic image of the motherland acquired both fulness and troubling features of internal complexity. First of all, in many cases of Bengali nation-worship,[27] there remained a complex, partly ambiguous relation between Bengal and India as two possible conceptions of this glorious place of residence, and the iconic image of the Motherland was ambiguously placed, not very inconveniently, between India and Bengal. Politically, this was enabling rather than inconvenient because it found, incongruously, a music expressing the complex stratified form of mature Indian nationalism which saw no incoherence in evincing patriotic emotion for both Bengal and India. Individuals could be proud of being both Bengalis and Indians, and the iconic images of the two figures were at times indiscernibly similar. But the growing image of Mother India had become bafflingly complex: it was an image that contained too many attributes, and eventually this turned from a single identifiable image into a repertoire out of which people could construct images of their Motherland after their peculiar ideological and iconic preference. To keep using the language of images and visions, the Mother that these songs and poems invoked and glorified, really differentiated into several images, invoking distinct predominant *rasas*, quite different constructive possibilities. Interestingly, these figures could also cancel out each other or quarrel among themselves, since the ideological visions of the Motherland that they expressed became different, often even contradictory.

At the height of successful political nationalism, from the 1920s, we can observe at least three forms of a feminine, iconic nation with somewhat different inflections in their symbolic imagery. The first is essentially the original figure of a human collective form given to nature—bounteous, sustaining, resplendent, but not aggressive; expressing a sentiment that simply wished to worship its own collective self through poetic self-glorification. The second was an iconic embodiment of intense, aggressive, exclusionary nationalism

---

[27] This refers to patriotic compositions—poems or songs—written in Bengali, but in the worship of Mother India (Bharatmata). There was a parallel strand of similar emotive writing about Mother Bengal: as in the song by Rajanikanta Sen, another prolific and talented composer of the time: '*Banga amar, janani amar, dhatri amar, amar des/ kena go ma tor chinna vasan, kena go ma tor malin ves.*' Tagore also composed poems in praise specifically of Bengal, one of which, *Amar sonar Bangla, ami tomay bhalobasi*, became the national anthem of Bangladesh.

that stressed history more than nature.[28] It only recognized a Hindu self and a correspondingly Hindu past. More alarmingly for critical intellectuals like Tagore, it was incapable of criticizing anything in its own past, constantly urging a recovery of past glory that was already threatening to turn into the kind of political ugliness that Tagore had seen emerging in Europe. For some Indian intellectuals, this transformation of nationalism constituted a particularly heartbreaking betrayal. This showed that the ugly excesses nationalism in Europe— the imperial nations' defence of the enslavement of others, and the Fascist states' military aggressiveness—could find a parallel in colonial countries in the form of a divisive, exclusionary nationalism which regarded a part of the native society itself as its enemy. Tagore wrote in passionate condemnation of aggressive, parochial nationalism, and saw in this 'a crisis of civilization'.[29] This second form of Indian nationalism did not show a way out of the crisis, either in the world or at home: that was merely India's contribution to an incomprehensible epidemic of a degenerate form of belonging.

As an ugly form of nationalist enthusiasm became more apparent, Tagore experimented with an unprecedented interpretation of nationalism which turned from enthusiasm towards deeply felt self-critical guilt. Even in his poetry, with its predominant tone of reflexive self-absorption, Tagore had a capacity to blend in a profound sense of sadness over social issues. Untouchability and internal indignities troubled his spirit and were even expressed in rapt and entirely private relations with his God. He had a peculiar ability to subvert standard

---

[28] In the 1860s some perceptive thinkers had expressed alarm at the emergence of this trend. The conservative Hindu thinker Bhudev Mukhopadhay stressed in his reflections on collective selfhood that emphasis on nature and material culture went towards a perception of commonness between peoples of all religion, because, despite doctrinal differences, they resided in the same nature and developed the same material ways of dealing with its conditions. English education, he observed, influenced some new intellectuals to develop a divisive perception of the historical past and regard Muslims as their historical enemies. Bhudev's reflections demonstrate that all Hindu thinkers were not necessarily hostile to Muslims. See Mukhopadhyay 1981.

[29] See Tagore 1941/1950. Some of these themes are also developed in his lectures on nationalism.

tales of heroic splendour by noting deep malaises in Indian society. His reinterpretation of the spirit of patriotism found a direction directly opposed to the standard enthusiasm for the past, and counteracted such exaltation by focusing on a collective feeling of guilt. A poignant presentation of such critical patriotism can be shown in his famous invocation of 'his unfortunate land', which did not deserve to be freed until she became equal to those whom she had treated with indignity. The ideas and ideals of this new form of self-critical nationalism have the directness and unattainable simplicity of his best poems, and can be rendered into unpretentious prose:

> O my unfortunate land,
> you have to be equal in indignity to those
> you have treated with contempt;
> you have denied them the right to be human
> you have made them stand in front of you
> but have never allowed them to come to your embrace
> those you have pushed down would drag you down with them
> those you have left behind would keep pulling you backwards.

An equally eloquent articulation of this inclusive nationalism was in another poem evocatively titled *Bharat-tirtha*: India—the land of pilgrimage, which turns the image of pilgrimage into a metaphor for a cosmopolitan nationalism.[30] The earth of India is holy not because—as he himself had averred earlier—it gave to the world its great religions, but because it invited streams of humanity to mix and unite. This is in a sense, within its covering of poetic obscurity, an extraordinary inversion of what is of value in the nation—not its claim to purity, of its origins, of its uniquely valuable culture, but the opposite and more complex attraction of mixture and an ability not to be dogmatic. In the same poem he similarly switched and inverted the principles of ritual purity and touch, the twin principles of caste Hinduism, in an astonishing poetic move. The peculiar generosity of 'Indianness' invites the Aryan and non-Aryan, Hindus and Muslims, the Christians, and even, surprisingly, the English.[31] Peculiarly for a

---

[30] See Tagore 1972: 506.

[31] For a discussion of the question 'who is an Indian?' see the sensitive exposition of this point of view in Khilnani 1997, and the defence of this kind of complex perception of identity in Sen 2005. A collection of Tagore's songs

patriotic poem, it repetitively and unremittingly connects the political and the social, the indignity of colonial slavery with the indignity of caste degradation, and asserts that a nation which treats its own people so appallingly has no moral right to political independence. In one of its most remarkable moves, the poem invites the Brahmin to hold the hands of all others—but *after* he has purified his heart (*eso brahman shuchi kari man dharo hat sabakar*).[32] It calls the fallen (*patita*) and asks him, effectively, and remarkably, to forgive.[33] They must all hasten to a coronation of 'the mother', a ritual occasion conceived in the Hindu fashion as culminating in a final ablution, the pouring of holy water on the crowned head. In Tagore's inversion, the water poured on the mother enthroned is to be rendered holy in a strange ritual. The water, which would purify the mother herself, waits; for it will not be wholly pure until it is hallowed by the purifying touch of all (*sabar parase pavitra kara tirthallire*).[34] This is the final ritual of inclusion and seeking forgiveness.

I hesitate to call this inverted Hinduism 'liberal'. Despite the undeniable influence of a liberal moral imagination, it seeks a form of critical thinking that works on principles internal to the domain of Hindu thought. It forges its critical arguments not by drawing on Western liberal principles—with which its ideals largely coincide—but on deliberate inversions of traditional Hindu arguments. Instead of declaring that henceforth all lower caste people shall be treated as legal equals, it suggests using a language of asking for forgiveness from the untouchables for their historical repression. Like Rammohan Roy's

---

in excellent translation, which stresses the nationalist cycle of songs, *Svades*, is Bardhan 2008. Though it is a trifle odd to extend this kind of generosity of feeling towards the British at the height of the nationalist conflict with colonial power, this is not uncharacteristic in Tagore's intellectual evolution. Much of his prose writing had been concerned with the question of how best to be an Indian, and his famous novel *Gora* is entirely concerned with this conundrum of identity. Gora, the protagonist, who initially believes he is the purest breed of Brahmin, is eventually revealed to be the son of an Irish couple. His insistence on being an Indian eventually leaves only such a wide, cosmopolitan definition as the possible way.

[32] Ibid.

[33] '*Eso he patita kara apanita sab apaman bhar*'. Ibid.

[34] Ibid.

decision in the previous century to respond to Christian and rationalist criticism by rationalizing Hindu doctrine and staying within its imaginative world, this is a similar decision not to abandon religious discourse but to expand its horizons and to invert its hierarchies. Tagore may have argued that to abandon Hinduism and take one's stand on the different fundamentals of liberalism was too easy: it would purify the deciding self without wading into the filth of social ills.[35] To become a liberal is to step aside and avoid this necessary internal struggle. This is a penance inextricably connected with Hinduism's history. It could come only out of Hinduism's struggle with its own history, not through imitation of some alien generosity. But one must recognize—despite our admiration for this icon of a Mother not sullied but instead purified by the touch of the lowest castes, and thus created by this moving gesture expiation of Hindu society's historical guilt—that it is one figure among many.

Strictly speaking, the nationalism of any society is not a single coherent structure of ideas, but a repertoire; its emotion is not organized around a single image but an unstable array of possible images mined by different groups for their own peculiar iconic purposes. And the untidy memory that nationalism creates for its people through its successes, failures, compromises, and prevarications leaves its field of iconic representation always provisional and open towards new figurative possibilities. History and memory are deeply ambiguous fields, precisely because they are diverse and inexhaustible in their own ways. It is precisely the constant renewal of appeals to history which shows it is never final, never settled forever. Although this appears counterintuitive, the past as memory always remains unstable. In the case of Indian nationalism, the more history is used in this imagination the more it is fragmented and shown to be capable of alternative constructions.[36] Two lines of this past, two clashing types of memory—the glorious and the guilty—remain unreconciled to the end, bitterly contesting and cancelling each other in these poems and icons, which, as nationalism gains ground, come to acquire canonical status. One evokes the memory of a past about which

[35] In the long and passionate intellectual exchanges in Tagore's novel *Gora*, these questions are taken up repeatedly and worked out in detail.

[36] No matter.

Indians could be proud without any sense of guilt—remembrance of the Vedas, the classical literature, the empires, the power and the glory that was India. But there is another memory that follows this as its dark shadow, constantly reminding nationalists of the failures of this civilization—a past of untouchability, caste coercion, oppression of women, superstition, sati. This version of nationalism argued that it is impossible to be rationally proud of the necessarily mixed record of past times, but only of a reconstructed nation, without these deforming flaws, which can only appear in future. Patriotism thus remained a deeply ambiguous, if generally uplifting, sentiment, one strand drawing its poetry from the past, the other from an unrealized future.

The Patriotism of Disenchantment

At the time of Independence, Gandhi made the famously risky remark that his aim was 'to wipe every tear from every eye'. In an analysis of Gandhi, Ashis Nandy shrewdly observes his use and exaltation of the ideals of femininity, his celebration, against the grain of a more masculine form of patriotism, of the woman-mother's peculiar pity and caritas. Nothing reveals his feminine conception of emancipation more clearly than this phrase, a typical mother's remark. The subject of this utterance could only be the Motherland created by a long process of iconic crystallization. But as Independence arrived and became soiled by its disappointments, as the tears remained unremoved, this image of a Motherland taking care of her children began to falter and attract travesty. The decline of this exaltation of sentiment began to show in two ways: in an increasing indifference towards such images and musical exhortation to collective sentiment. Independence Day celebrations at schools and town squares, which elicited a vivid and spontaneous emotion, in the early years began to look routine, tired, and deserted. In cinema halls, once, the national anthem at the end of a movie brought all viewers instantly to their feet; by the 1960s, people started shuffling out while the anthem played forlornly to emptying theatres. By making the iconic forms of nationalism ubiquitous, the state also made them banal.

But something more remarkable also began to happen. Bakhtin's famous discussion of the laughter of the lower orders in the European renaissance showed how iconic representations that were slowly sculpted by the upper classes, and which represented the fundamental values of the society, were undermined by what he called the irreverent 'popular laughter of a thousand years'. In India, the laughter of the lower orders began to puncture and undermine the solemn rituals of state nationalism. As the lower classes are less literate and lack control over the theatres of cultural production, this kind of sceptical unbelief could only express itself episodically, in surprising scenes of writing, in anonymous forms of production. I shall mention only one of them from my own experience. An extension of cosmopolitan nationalism occurred in the literary and cultural productions of the first two decades after Independence. Under the influence of Nehru's recension of nationalist sentiments, Hindi films produced immensely popular songs which emphasized that strong nationalism was not necessarily opposed to internationalism. One of its most popular examples was a song sung by a character who claimed:

> *Mera juta hai japani, yeh patloon inglistani*
> *Sar pe lal topi rusi, phirbhi dil hai Hindustani*

> My shoes are Japanese, the trousers are English,
> the red cap on my head is Russian, but my heart is Indian.

This elaboration of the theme of a paradoxically cosmopolitan internationalism interlaced with a saddening sense of material deprivation was extended in another famous Hindi film song:

> *Chino arab hamara, hindustan hamara*
> *Rahne ka ghar nahin hai*
> *Sara jahan hamara.*

In this complex text a number of iconic allusions intersect, making it particularly thick with emotive references. It says, in a gesture of internationalism that can be adopted only by the dispossessed:

> China and the Arab lands are ours,
> India belongs to us
> We have no place to stay [because] the whole world is ours.

The song plays particularly on sentences taken from another celebrated patriotic poem by the Urdu poet Mohammad Iqbal, set to tune by the musician Ravi Shankar, which runs: *sare jahan se accha hindustan hamara, hum bulbulen hain iske, yeh gulistan hamara* (this India of ours is the best in the world; this is our garden of paradise, and we are its nightingales/singing birds). The song plays on, and against, this famous predecessor in several ways. Against its affiliation to India, the latter song emphasizes an ardent internationalism, though it does not forget to stress that its more universal sense of belonging (*chino arab hamara*) is not at the expense of a deeply felt Indianess (*hindustan hamara*). But it declares its affiliation to a radical universalism, against an elite nationalism, by claiming that though we have no place to stay the world as a whole belongs to us.

This parodic operation was still within the orbit of educated culture: it is a case of radical writers contesting the interpretations of patriotism of an earlier generation more intensely focused on the national, less aware of the world, and assuming a comfortable disregard of troubling questions of the poverty of those who make this nation, and thus of the poignant paradoxes of nationalist belonging. I saw an unforgettable parody of the earlier language of Indian nationalism inside a bus in Delhi, almost like graffiti, which expressed with wonderful economy and wit its rebellious sarcasm against this entire tradition:

rahne ka ghar nahin hai,
kahte hain hindustan hamara.

We have no place to stay:
but they say India belongs to us.

It was written by a subaltern poet, a bus painter with a tenuous command over Hindi spelling. But he showed the confidence of one who possessed a poetic truth, incorrectly spelt but politically poignant, trying to capture the life experience of a disinherited generation. It showed a miraculous mastery of allusions, its affect understood only if seen, like lines of graffiti, as a writing against previous writing, as lines written both in continuation and defiance of the entire previous tradition of nationalist sentiment, a piece of writing that stood both inside and outside the language of nationalism. Against the earlier, long, solemn, loving poetry that turned rain into beneficence, land into a home, this was a fatal exclamation of disenchantment. Precisely because of that great condensation of metaphors into the Motherland's iconograph, this homelessness was transformed into a desolation much greater than not finding shelter in a large city. By turning the language of *sare jahan se achha hindustan hamara* against itself, it managed to express a much greater collective, historic, dispossession. Against the secure sentiment of nationalist glory that the educated classes take for granted and set to uplifting music, this expressed the bafflement of the poor asking what's so great about belonging to a great nation.

References

Abu al-Fazl ibn Mubarak. 1873. *Ain i-Akbari.* Trans. H. Blochmann. Calcutta: Rouse.

Anderson, Benedict. 1983. *Imagined Communities: Reflections on the Origin and Spread of Nationalism.* Revised Edition. London and New York: Verso, 1991.

Bardhan, Kalpana, ed. 2008. *Songs of Love, Nature and Devotion: Selected Songs of Rabindranath Tagore.* Delhi: Oxford University Press.

Bhattacharya, Sabyasachi. 2002. *Vande Mataram.* Delhi: Penguin.

Chabod, Federico. 1958. *Machiavelli and the Renaissance.* London: Bowes and Bowes.

Chattopadhyay, Bankimchandra. 1964a. 'Bangala Bhasa'. In *Bankim Rachanabali, Volume I: Sahitya.* Kolkata: Sahitya Samsad.

———. 1964b. *Bankim Racanabali (BR), Volume 2: Upanayas.*

Dutta, Satyendranath. 1973. *Kavi Satyendranather Granthavali*, ed. Bishu Mukhopadhyay. 2 vols. Calcutta: Bak-sahitya.

Gadamer, Hans-Georg. 1960/1989. *Truth and Method*, 2nd edn. London: Sheed and Ward.

Hacking, Ian. 2003. Making Up People. *Historical Ontology.* Cambridge, Mass.: Harvard University Press.

Kaviraj, Sudipta. 1995. *The Unhappy Consciousness: Bankim Chandra Chattopadhyay and the Formation of Nationalist Discourse in India.* Delhi: Oxford University Press.

———. 2005. Outline of a Revisionist Theory of Modernity. *European Journal of Sociology*, XLVI, 3.

Khilnani, Sunil. 1997. *The Idea of India.* London: Penguin.

Lipner, Julius (ed. and trans.). 2005. *Anandamath, or The Sacred Brotherhood by Bankimchandra Chatterji.* Delhi: Oxford University Press.

Locke, John. 1993. *An Essay Concerning Toleration* (1667). In John Locke, *Political Writings*, ed. David Wootton. London: Penguin Books.

Mukhopadhyay, Bhudev. 1981. *Samajik Prabandha* (Essays on Society), ed. Jahnavi Kumar Chakrabarty. Kolkata: Paschim Banga Pustak Parshad.

Sastri, Haraprasad. 1980. *Atmacharit*, in *Rachanasamgraha*. Kolkata: Paschim Banga Pustak Parishad.

Sen, Amartya K. 2005. *The Argumentative Indian*. Delhi: Penguin.

Sen, Atul Prasad. 1996. *Gitigunja*. Kolkata: Sadharan Brahmo Samaj.

Tagore, Rabindranath. 1941/1950. *Crisis of Civilization*. Calcutta: Visva-bharati.

———. 1970. *Gitabitan Akhanda*. Kolkata: Visvabharati.

———. 1984. *Sancayita*. Kolkata: Visvabharati.

5

Tagore and Transformations in the Ideals of Love

On the Languages of Love

Is it possible to write a history of love?[1] A sceptical response would be relatively easy to understand. First of all, emotions are notoriously intractable to analytical discussion. It is eminently possible, it can be argued, to write about love in a literary way, but difficult if not impossible to write about it analytically, with historical reliability and precision. Underlying the apparent universality of the emotion lies the bewildering variety of the social forms in which it exists and is experienced by human beings. Despite these arguments, I wish to suggest, it is possible and fruitful to think about love historically. In doing so, however, we should keep in mind the concerns of the sceptical view, and try to exercise methodological controls which answer the main points of its scepticism.

To write a history of love is possible in three different ways. We can write a history of love as a concept or language, as a social institution, and as an artistic ideal. These three techniques would yield three distinctive products—a conceptual history of love, a social history, and an artistic history. In this essay, I shall concentrate on some points regarding the conceptual and the social history of love through the prism of Rabindranath Tagore (1861–1941). Tagore's artistic reflection on love evolved through clearly identifiable stages and constitutes a vast and complex field. I shall focus on the historical shifts in the

This essay was first published in Francesca Orsini, ed., *Love in South Asia*, Cambridge: Cambridge University Press, 2006.

[1] Our seminar proposal began with this question taken from Philippe Aries's masterful account of private life: Aries and Duby 1987–8.

framing concept of love and in the rules of expressive conduct, and I will ask what broader shifts in social and aesthetic mentality these changes suggest.[2]

If we turn the original question around we can get an interesting starting point: why should it be difficult to write a history of love? It can be difficult, presumably, for two rather different reasons. One, because love is a matter of emotions and irretrievably private acts of intimacy, and such things are difficult to grasp conceptually and put accurately into analytical forms. Love is, after all, famously ineffable. There is a second, more interesting, reason: it can be argued that we cannot write a history of love because it is a universal emotion; therefore, love does not have, and does not require, a history. Love is universal, but the idea of universality can have different forms. The kind of universality we ascribe to love is like the universality of human languages: all human beings have language, but not the same specific language. Language is present everywhere in the human world, but not in the same form. Similarly, in all societies and historical stages, love exists; but the forms of social conduct and the conceptual system through which people think about it and represent its variations are different. There is a famous anthology in Bengali, conventionally used as a mandatory present to newly-married couples, entitled *Hajar Bachharer Premer Kabita* (Love Poems of a Thousand Years). Its contents reveal that love poems were indeed being written for over a thousand years, but not that what constituted love remained unchanged.

Within this generally conceived continuity, we can find several distinct languages for representing and reflecting on love in pre-modern India, and it is probable that in each of these traditions, on closer examination, we shall be able to locate several restructurings.[3] Ancient and medieval Sanskrit literary culture contained a powerful tradition of aesthetic theorizing and poetic compositions on *srngara*, the axial concept which framed these artistic practices and connected

---

[2] For some excellent recent studies on the social relations aspect of these questions, see Raychaudhuri 1999, especially his long essay 'Love in a Colonial Climate'.

[3] Literary scholars have tried to do something on these lines in Pollock 2003.

the literary to the plastic arts in a larger cultural structure. The Islamic tradition of '*ishq*, especially of Sufi-inspired poetry, became highly influential in North India, extending into magnificent compositional forms about mundane love (*muhabbat*). Besides these 'high' literary traditions, there were diverse, locally powerful traditions of folk aesthetics which presented elaborate reflections on the social and personal experience of love. These were expressed through traditions of folk poetry and artistic forms often extending into semi-classical music, like the *thumri* and the *barahmasa*.[4] Obviously, a highly significant refiguration occurred in these languages with the coming of the artistic sensibility of modernity in the nineteenth and twentieth centuries. Schematically, this represented a shift from an erotic conception of love to a primarily emotional one, and Tagore's poetic and narrative art played a determining role in the constitution of the language of modern love in Bengal.

The Concept of Love

In the historical transformation of the discourses of love, Rabindranath Tagore was a major performer and his work constituted a principal site of the transition from one aesthetic structure to another. In convenient shorthand, this change can be simply designated as a change from *shringara*, conventionally translated as erotic love, to *prem*. This immense aesthetic transformation had a pronounced interstructural quality, an interconnectedness of the various things that were participating in this process. Everything associated with the conceptualization, reflection, and representation of this universal and primal emotion underwent a transfiguration, starting from the central aesthetic concepts and their precise meanings to narrative, poetic, and musical forms.

The easiest and most obvious place to start from in trying to understand this change is to look at the shifts in the meanings of conceptual terms, the surface vocabulary. At this level, it reflects the slow decline, in two senses, of the term *shringara* and its associated

[4] For *thumri*, see du Perron 2002. Muzaffar Alam suggests that the *barahmasa* was introduced as an innovation in Persianate Islamic poetry: see Alam 2003.

terms, like *adirasa*, the 'first *rasa*' (see below). First, through the emergence of a new kind of aesthetic theory, this conception of love is devalued and consigned to a lower, coarser level; consequently, the occurrence of the term *adirasa* becomes rarer until, at the end of this historical process, it is reserved only for pejorative use. This constitutes the surface, linguistic sign of a shift from one entire aesthetic structure about love to another, a shift not merely in the natural language terms, the words *shringara* to *prem*, but, to follow formal structuralist semantics, a transfer from one linguistic structure to another, a shift in the whole conceptual language. For the words derive their full meaning not in themselves, as freestanding individual terms, but through their associations, the system of differentiations of which they form a crucial part. The word *shringara* is mentioned less frequently, less positively, until, in the end, it comes to designate something that the refined, modern Bengali aestheticism cannot mention without a shudder of revulsion.

A good example of this socio-aesthetic shift can be found in the work of Bankimchandra Chattopadhyay (1838–94). Bankim understands and appreciates the pre-modern *shringara* structure, and often deploys its resources with great skill,[5] but he strongly disapproves of the dominance of *adirasa* in pre-modern literature as aesthetically monotonous and, in addition, morally degrading. It is clear that his objection is more intense about the second feature of that literary tradition. Although Bankim denounces the 'deluge of *adirasa*' in the works of the twelfth-century poet Jayadeva, in the most astonishing places within his own novelistic oeuvre he refers with evident appreciation to famous erotic descriptions by Kalidasa. When a Mughal princess hears the news of the death of her illicit lover in a battle she is described with a celebrated Sanskrit line from the famous lament of Rati after the death of the god of love in Kalidasa's *Kumarasambhava*.[6] Bankim's work is transitional. It combines a residual appreciation of the forms of traditional aesthetics of love

[5] I have tried to show how Bankim's depiction of feminine figures draws upon pre-modern literary norms: Kaviraj 2005.

[6] Chattopadhyay 1985a: 660. The verse is '*vasudhalinganadhusarastani vilalapa vikinrnamurddhaja*' ('sprawled on the earth, so that her bosom was grey with dust, [she] bemoaned [her fate], making the woods share her grief'), from *Kumarasambhava* IV.4.

with a new social disapproval of its implied morals of sexual laxity.[7]
In Bengali literature, the principal place of aesthetic approval is slowly
occupied by the word *prem* (Sanskrit *prema*). For this to happen some
strict semantic shifts were required.

Prem is a Bengali *tatsama* word, i.e. 'identical with' the Sanskrit
prema, but in modern usage we can detect a definite narrowing of
the exact meaning of the term. In conventional literary vocabulary,
in both Sanskrit and traditional Bengali, the term *prema* had a much
wider and indeterminate connotation. *Prema* meant an indeterminate
form of love and could be linked to all kinds of relations and *rasas*.
Of course, there was always a form of *prema* which was linked to the
adirasa, for instance, the *prema* that Radha feels for Krishna; but there
was no paradox in using *prema* for other objects of affection, affiliated
naturally to other types of emotions: the *bhratrprema* or 'fraternal love'
Bharata shows towards Rama, the *prema* that Hanumana has for Rama,
or the *prema* of *sakhya* (friendship) between Krishna and Arjuna in the
Mahabharata. In the narrative cycle of Krishna, Yashoda's *prema* for
the little Krishna is linked to the *rasa* of *vatsalya* or parental love. It
can even be linked to *karuna* (compassion) in the form of the *prema*
that the Maker—in the form of Annapurna or Shri or in his formless
self—feels for his often misguided, always vulnerable creatures.[8]

Erotic relations are only one particular class among many to which
the term *prema* can be applied: it can even be attached to inanimate
things. By the late nineteenth century, these other connotations have
practically fallen off. There is a careful differentiation of the linguistic
register to suit and describe a more modern palette of emotions.
Terms like *prem*, *pranay*, and *sneha* start getting differentiated into
more specific use, and there is a clear tendency to reserve the term
prem primarily to designate a new romantic attachment between
individuated selves, a relation that slowly gains a high ethical priority.

---

[7] Though it must be stated that, in pre-modern Sanskrit poetry, there are
two opposed strands on eroticism and its relation with social norms. While
one strand implies that sexual liaisons are enjoyable in general, irrespective of
whether they are within socially sanctioned marriage, another clearly celebrates
both eroticism and matrimony. The *Kumarasambhava* is a good example of
the second.

[8] In some of Tagore's verses, this earlier meaning of prem still occurs.

One particular cycle of Tagore's songs can thus announce without any hesitation or fear of misunderstanding that they are about *prem*—about love.[9] Only one kind of love is left to enjoy this pre-eminence.

Love in Traditional Aesthetics

In conventional Sanskrit and classical Bengali aesthetics, the very designation of *shringara* as the *adirasa*, the 'original' or 'first' *rasa*, accords to it a pride of aesthetic place. But by the time we reach Bankim, the word *adirasa* has become almost a term of abuse. It indicates lewdness, vulgarity, prurience.[10] Strewn throughout Bankim's comments on traditional literature are remarks about the supposed vulgarity of traditional shringaric tropes, and he evidently absorbed the Orientalist argument that the historic decline of the Hindu civilization, its enervation, is signalled by a descent into pointless erotic playfulness. In *Krsnacaritra* (1886) this argument appears with particular sharpness, as Bankim's reconstitution of Krishna's figure is simply impossible without a direct assault on this sensibility. Though in his literary criticism Bankim treats Kalidasa with enormous respect, comparing him, for instance, with Shakespeare, his preference for the more muted and less shringaric artistry of the *Uttararamacarita* shows this subtle movement of aesthetic taste.[11]

In technical terms of literary aesthetics, this transformation is composed of several complex interconnected shifts: I shall take up only one of these for illustration. This is the question of *rupa*, of the shringaric conception of beauty. *Shringara* in traditional aesthetics cannot derive its full meaning without a connection with *rupa*—beauty of the physical form, primarily, though not exclusively, associated with feminine figures. The shringaric aesthetic does not regard looking for physically and materially beautiful things and people as problematic, or even remotely shame-inducing. Pre-modern literature often dwells on the various proper emotions or dispositions

---

[9] The *Gitabitan* is divided into three volumes. The first deals only with the theme of *puja* (worship), the second with the related themes of *prem* and *prakrti* (nature), the third is an assorted collection with patriotic and ceremonial songs mixed in with those taken from the dance dramas.

[10] See Chattopadhyay 1985b: 464.

[11] Chattopadhyay 1985b: *Uttararamacarita,* 159–85.

of heroines or *nayikas*; a sense of shame (*lajja*) is regarded as a greatly desirable feminine trait, but it is associated with propriety and modesty in social contexts and it can be entirely compatible with a sense of value in one's beauty, perceiving beauty as a great gift. If we look at the continual, mild eroticism that accompanies Kalidasa's descriptions of nature in the *Meghaduta* (The Cloud Messenger), we can understand the unashamed openness of this eroticism, almost its indispensability for any aesthetic perception of the world. Notice of beauty is everywhere, and comes up in the most surprising places. Apart from the famous erotic descriptions in Kalidasa, or the more narrowly erotic poems of Amaru which refer to mundane figures, or slightly extra-mundane ones like *Meghaduta's yaksini*, this form of description is unproblematically extended to figures who are objects of religious devotion.[12]

However, though Kalidasa is undoubtedly part of this shringaric aesthetic, like all great writers he transcends its narrow confines. His reflection on sexuality—of *rupa*, *shringara*, love, and fulfilment in life—does not merely display the poet's technical versatility in versifying and technical knowledge of sexuality. As Tagore repeatedly shows in his essays, Kalidasa's heroines are often beautiful, but they work towards a self-realization and realization of love which surpasses the value of simple physical beauty. This happens in the case of Shakuntala and, more dramatically or graphically, in the case of Parvati in the *Kumarasambhava*. Despite this, I think it will be correct to say that there is an aesthetic way of seeing the world which is shringaric. It sees the beauty of the feminine form and the beauty of the world as interchangeable, and thus allows the constant double movement of metaphors in which Kalidasa excelled. Consider the following examples. In the *Meghaduta* the beauty of natural things is always reminiscent of feminine beauty. The darkening evening light on a hill looks like a breast—'*preksaniyam avastham madhyesyamah stana iva bhuvah sesavistarapand uh*'.[13] The waves of the Betravati river

---

[12] In pre-modern literature, male figures like Rama and Krishna are often described as persons of great beauty, particularly Krishna. Many of the crucial narrative elements of the Krishna cycle of stories depend on this particular feature of Krishna.

[13] '[The mountain] with its sides covered by wild mango trees shining with ripe fruits will certainly attain the state of being looked at by pairs of gods, for

are like the rippling eyebrows of a woman turning up her face to be kissed. The full line of the white sand beach of the river against the blue line of water is like the glimpse of a leg when a blue sari is waved away by the wind. In all these cases the direction of the metaphor is from the natural things towards a suggestion of the female body. In the *Kumarasambhava*, for instance, Parvati is described as: '*avarjita kincidiva stanabhyam vaso vasana tarunarkaragm*' (With the red cloth, of the colour of the rising sun, disturbed and showing a bit of her cleavage, she is like a flowering tree that walks, slightly bent forward, it is so heavy with blooms).

In Vaishnava literature, the obvious example of *rupa* is the figure of Radha. The classical texts in this tradition arc some sections of the *Srimadbhagavata* and Jayadeva's *Gitagovinda*, both in Sanskrit.[14] But it can be argued that in these cases the figures of Radha and the *gopis* hover ambiguously between mundane literariness and explicit divinity. In other cases the figures are more unambiguously divine and there is much less occasion for the devotee to observe the deity's beauty, as in the invocations to Sarasvati, but still the shringaric aesthetic mentions exterior physical features. Even in the Chandi *slokas*, where we arc supposedly celebrating the immense and invulnerable power of our mother who is going to defend us when we cower in terror before evil, we are not meant to forget the beauty of her figure. Besides, as the Durga images in Bengal remind us, the *raudra rasa*, the physical expression of the emotion of anger, imparts a strange and fascinating heightening of feminine beauty. Beauty, in short, is a happy miraculous gift, to be enjoyed by its possessor and by those in its presence. This is a broad and general argument. It does not mean to suggest that the Sanskrit literary tradition has no complex reflection on the social effects of beauty. On the contrary, in the high Sanskrit tradition there are exceptional cases in which beauty is not seen as an unmixed blessing. The *Mahabharata* is a great and unclassifiable example: Draupadi's life shows beauty as a kind of curse. In general, however, the shringaric aesthetic sees *rupa* as a pivotal motif, and it is

---

it resembles the breast of the Earth, black in the centre and pale white in the surface.' Kalidasa 1927: 78–9, v. 18.

[14] For the *Gitagovinda*, see Miller 1977. For the *Bhagavata Purana*, also called *Srimadbhagavata*, see Tagare 1976–86.

rupa which qualifies individuals, especially women, to be celebrated in literary texts.

The Decline of the *Shringara* Ideal

To illustrate my point about the history of conceptual change I shall use three examples from three different stages of Bengali literature— the narrative poem *Vidyasundar*, written by Bharatchandra in the eighteenth century; Bankim's novels, written in the middle of the nineteenth century as an intermediate stage; and Tagore's works, written mainly in the early twentieth century. Tagore already lives in a literary world that enjoys the consequences of the Bankim moment, and is entirely divested of the earlier shringaric associations of love; indeed, in Tagore there are some aesthetic experiments which seek to take this logic to its extreme point and dissociate *rupa* from *prem* altogether.

The first example is fairly simple. In Bharatchandra's *Vidyasundar*, the aesthetic reflection on love is clearly traditional. Vidya and Sundar are attracted to each other by their physical beauty. Their raptures are described in great and graphic detail, and the insertion of the *Caurapancasat* into the text simply confirms the argument that the aesthetic of love is primarily one of eroticism.[15]

In my book on Bankim I simply commented on the tragic vision in Bankim's novelistic art and its great aesthetic power.[16] However, it now seems to me that Bankim's tragic aesthetics has a certain connection with this long-term historical change. It appears that Bankim performed a significant reorienting operation on this traditional aesthetic structure and crucially turned it in a modern direction. Bankim's art is brilliant, but from the point of view of an aesthetic conceptual history, a *Begriffsgeschichte*, unstable. In terms of aesthetic theory, he has abandoned the *shringara* language and, as mentioned, denounced the excessive sensuality of its high texts, especially the *Bhagavata Purana* and *Gitagovinda*. Although it is clear that Bankim knows and perhaps secretly loves Jayadeva's poetry—it would have been unnatural if he did not, since his work is so utterly replete with

---

[15] For the text, see Bandyopadhyay and Das 1950. For the English translation, Dimock 1963.

[16] Kaviraj 1995: esp. ch. I.

the classical tropes of poetic rhetoric—his formal judgements about Jayadeva are severe. The best example comes from his discussions of Krishna's character, where Bankim cannot simply evade the questions of divine sensuality. He decides to tackle the problem head on and produces a powerful reinterpretation of the episode of the stealing of clothes, the *vastraharna*, in the *Bhagavata* narrative. Out of the different interpretations of the *Bhagavata* he decides to follow the commentary by Sridharasvami, which systematically translates eroticism into a code of metaphors of inextricable devotional union. What is remarkable is Bankim's textual treatment of the lines describing the appearance of the *gopis* in front of Krishna. He finds the lines so offensive to his literary taste that he refuses to provide a translation, as they are *aslila* (obscene), and unfit for a wide reading public.[17] Yet if we enter Bankim's created universe of novels and the central theme of love in them, we find a clear paradox. Although there is a strong sense that the bodily in its overt form is *ashlila* and is therefore unmentionable in literary compositions, the central dynamic remains a reflection on exceptional *rupa* and its effects on ordinary lives. Exceptional beauty is still accorded a kind of literary homage when feminine characters are described in the novels: there is a discernible heightening of the descriptive language, the subtle and complex use of poetic tropes. But the narrative consequences of such extraordinary beauty are usually tragic. Bankim's reflection on love and beauty can be thus seen as a strange, and fraught, historical operation of a new emotional sensibility playing upon a traditional and still active field of subjects, particularly *rupa*. This sensibility finds the effects of *rupa* on the world to be largely destructive, giving rise to melancholy and a sense of tragedy. *Rupa*, physical beauty, and the fatal attraction it exerts on people who encounter it is everywhere—starting with Ayesha's beauty compared to Tilottama's in *Durgesnandini*, Bankim's first Bengali novel (1865). In fact, Ayesha is more of a classic Sanskrit *shringara* heroine than Tilottama, and it is

---

[17] 'Krishna would not easily return the clothes to the gopis—he intends to return them the just desserts for their action (*karmaphal divar icha ache*). What transpired after that we cannot divulge in a Bengali intelligible to women and children. Therefore I quote the original Sanskrit without translation.' Chattopadhyay 1985b: 462. For an extended treatment of 'obscenity', see also Gupta 2001.

not surprising that Tilottama, in spite of representing the auspicious ('*mangalamaya*') form of the beautiful, eventually fades, and the emotional conflict is centred on Ayesha's beauty and the curse it carries with it. I am tempted to argue that the repetitiveness of this connection between beauty and tragedy in Bankim, the eventually fatal ruinousness of physical beauty, is linked to this historical shift. In his emotional and ethical sensibility Bankim has moved into a far more modern kind of thinking on love, yet his narrative and artistic imagination remains chained to *shringara* aesthetics: Ayesha, Manorama, Mrinmayi, Shaibalini, Dalani, Rohini, Kundanandini, Indira, Lavangalata, Zebunnisa, Kalyani, and Shri are all exceptionally beautiful women, and they are invariably destructive in their effects on social relations around them. However, to understand why the general narrative and fictive mood is so melancholy we must notice what kind of social relations are being destroyed. This will also help us understand the underlying connection between literary aesthetics and ethics. The extraordinary beauty of these women is destructive to the new relationship of intimate, emotional conjugality—which is the hidden, or rather the counter-punctual, norm. Within all these 'historical' settings there is always a straight, uneventful, wholesome, positive (*mangalamay*) unit—a kind of emotional love, not based on physical enchantment and obsession, which produces benign results. In Bankim's aesthetic world this love is always counterpointed against the aesthetic of *shringara*, and his narratives therefore validate the new emotion by negative example.

Thus, despite remarkable similarities in purely formal terms, this is not Kalidasa's aesthetic at all: it is full of beautiful women, of explicit erotic attraction, of tropes and descriptive conventions straight out of the Sanskrit high canon. But the Sanskrit high tradition is a classical structure with its internal equipoise between constitutive aesthetic principles: beauty is linked to expectations of calm enjoyment, of a general fulfilment and enhancement of life. When Kalidasa begins the poem by saying—

Prac]andasuryah sprhaniya candramah sadavagaha ksatavarisancayah
dinantaramyobhyupasantamanmatho nidagha kaloyam upagatah priye

Here has approached, dear, this hot season, when the sun is fierce,
the moon becomes desirable,

one can continually bathe in the ample waters, evenings are delightful and the feeling of love is allayed.[18]

—we do not expect, as in Bankim's world, a sudden tragic turn, like the appearance of the dangerous and mysterious Kapalika in *Kapalakundala* (1866). Instead we expect a continuation of erotic enjoyment: eroticism at peace with itself. In Kalidasa and the high Sanskrit canon we find not just an erotic way of looking, but more a way of being in the world. In Bankim some purely literary features of this cultural structure are still present, still centred around *rupa*, but his overall literary thinking places it in a world which makes it conflictual, tense, constantly upset, constantly fearful of this curse of beauty. In Kalidasa beauty is an inexplicable gift, a mundane miracle, not a curse leading to dark events. This nocturnal aspect of *shringara* in Bankim stems, I suspect, from the modern transformation in the nature of emotions. In Kalidasa's world, beauty—of ordinary women, of the *yaksa*'s distant lover, of Parvati—is not merely a piece of great good fortune in itself. Its effect on the world is generally benign; it is always a means to good fortune, it is part of an unruptured structure of good things in the world. In Bankim's art, this kind of beauty works increasingly as a curse, almost always a prefiguration of emotional disaster. The direction of change in social sensibility is clear. The artist's own ethical preferences coincide with the new course, although his formal artistic structures are still entangled in traditional aesthetics.

If we take Bengali literary production as a whole, we observe that, after Bankim's intervention, *rupa* has already receded; it has already become the less important part of an emotional conception of *saundarya* (beauty), so that even if great attention is still paid to the depiction of physical beauty, in the presentation of the body it is the face that gets much greater attention rather than the conventional description of the sexual allure of the body. For the face is regarded as the theatre in which 'inner' emotions play and find expression. Tagore's depiction of beauty is often facial and emotional in this way, and the eyes play a particularly large part. These eyes are entirely different from the shringaric eyes of the traditional view. Compare the playful erotic eyes of a *shloka* about the women of Ujjaini in Kalidasa's

---

[18] Kale 1916: v. 1.

Meghaduta with a song by Tagore, in which the eyes typically figure as the metonym of beauty:

vidyuddamasphuritacakitaistatra pauranganam
lolapangair yadi na ramase locanairvancitohsi

Life will be wasted if you do not linger with the ladies in the city, whose glances quiver at the play of lightning.[19]

bidhi dagara ankhi yadi diyechhila
se ki amari pane bhule paribe na.

If the maker gave you such large eyes,
Couldn't they fall on me, by chance (or by mistake)?[20]

It is entirely appropriate that the verb for the cloud's appreciation of the women's eyes in Kalidasa is *ram-*, with unmistakably pronounced erotic suggestiveness. To play on a word from the *Meghaduta* itself, and one that Tagore notices pointedly in his poem on *Meghaduta*,[21] the new eyes of emotional beauty are 'inexperienced in the play of the eyebrows'—*bhruvilasanavignah*.

Such changes as outlined so far were not confined to literary creations alone. Literature after all describes physical beauty in language; and it is not surprising that these ideas come to influence the direct representational portrayal of beauty in painting. In this, Tagore's thinking runs closely parallel to the search for an emotional version of beauty in the work of painters of the Bengal school.[22]

Love as Individuation

By Tagore's time, this transformation of *rupa* into emotional beauty and of erotic love into a more emotional and romantic love—in other words, a transformation of the emotional world of art—had been accomplished precisely by the lessons and deeply stringent morals of Bankim's literature. Bankim's novels, through their tragic endings and through a technique of negative implication, had already celebrated

[19] Kalidasa 1984: II, 10, v. 27.
[20] Tagore 1970: 894.
[21] Tagore 1964: 196.
[22] The work of the painters of the Bengal school has been analysed with much attention to their connection with social and political ideas in the writings of Mitter 1994 and Guha-Thakurta 1992.

and idealized the new kind of romantic love. In Tagore, the evolution of the new aesthetic structure of love moves one step further: this new universe of emotions, and the social world the emotions can create and in which they can feel at ease, can be subjected to further literary elaboration. Tagore's heroines are strikingly different from Bankim's: they are individuated as persons, seeking through something of a *Bildungsroman* their own individual destiny. As readers we do not feel, as with Bankim, that, at least in physical terms, we are encountering a type—the literary type of the beautiful woman. Women are much more individuated precisely because of the author's awareness that an excessive attention to *rupa* contains the danger of slipping into that literary type. Their depiction is now primarily in terms of their internal, emotional attractiveness, rather than any exterior, physical beauty. Individuation in the novel is thus a double process, both physical and psychological—they are unlike any other both in their looks and their characters. In Bankim's *Durgesnandini*, Ayesha's entrance into the prisoner's chamber starts with a long dissertation on *rupa*—what it means, its various forms, a fine distinction of the beauty of the three lovely women who are central to the story. At the end of this analysis Bankim offers an indirect description of Ayesha's beauty:

> Just as the lotus is at the centre of the garden, Ayesha is at the centre of this story. So, I want the reader to have an imaginative conception of her appearance [*avayab*]. Had I been a painter, had I been able to hold a brush, I would paint that complexion: not the champa, not red, not the white lotus, but one in which all of them are mixed, that is the colour I would paint her; if I could draw that forehead, curved but wide, a theatre of love; on top of that I could draw the clearly defined line of her hair; if you draw that hairline, following that clear forehead equally well drawn up to her ears, if I could make it bend round her ears, if I could paint the hair resembling black silk, if I could paint the thin clear parting, if I could describe her coiffure, if I could draw those dense eyebrows, first the point where they come close to meeting, but not quite, from there they widen towards the middle and taper towards the end into needle thin lines, if I could paint those darting, soft, eyelids, like clouds full of lightning; if I could show their wide lines, the beautiful curves of the upper and lower lids, the blue light of those eyes, and their still large irises . . .[23]

[23] *Durgesnandini* in Chattopadhyay 1985a: 40–1.

The description continues for almost a whole page, sculpting Ayesha's image in words, and it is clearly filled with conventional descriptions of beauty from classical Sanskrit literature. Now take the female protagonists, the two sisters Sucharita and Lalita, in Tagore's *Gora* (1910): in physical terms they are sketched quickly and briefly, and the description of their physical appearance is done by deft touches, without serious elaboration or the kind of pleasure of description Bankim lavishes on his heroines. The introduction to Sucharita in *Gora* is short and mundane, deliberately inattentive to eroticism:

> There was a mirror in the room, and standing behind the girl Binoy gazed at her reflection . . . He had never known any womenfolk outside his own family circle, and the picture he now saw in the mirror fascinated him. He was not skilled in scrutinising feminine features, but in that youthful face, bowed in an affectionate anxiety, it seemed to Binoy as if a world of tender brightness had unfolded before him . . . She then turned to Binoy.
> What wonderful eyes! It never occurred to him to ask whether they were large or small, black or brown: At the very first glance they gave an impression of sincerity. They had no trace of either shyness of hesitation, but were full of a serene strength.[24]

Sucharita and Lalita are remarkable, yet ordinary, women: they do not have the gift of exceptional beauty. And any physical characteristics that are mentioned, in fact, go in the opposite direction, they point to their ordinariness rather than an inflation of their beauty. Sucharita is briefly described as comely, pleasant-looking; Lalita, in the only reference to her appearance, is described as darker than her sister, and the entire point of the writing underlines the fact that they are women of unprepossessing looks. Against this underdetermination of their physical appearance stands the constant emphasis and elaboration of their emotional character: their perceptions, ways of feeling, ways of thinking, and their personal development through the staple of the *Bildungsroman*—misunderstandings, moral examination, and eventual resolution. Through these elements pertaining to the techniques of literary aesthetics they are individuated as characters, moulded by the length of time and space allowed to novelistic narratives into highly specific distinct individuals who cannot be mistaken for anyone else,

[24] Tagore 1924: 2.

unlike the highly repetitive resplendence of women of natural beauty. Verse describing the pre-modern feminine type can often be used almost interchangeably and applied to figures like Sita, Draupadi, Parvati, Radha or other more human *nayikas*. But, even within the confines of a single novel, descriptions of Sucharita cannot be transferred to Lalita, though they are sisters, and much in sympathy about the ethical matters central to their lives. Individuation has something of an internal connection with the inner world of emotions and the refinement of sensibility. The outcome of this process is a new conception of beauty, which figures like Sucharita or Lalita eventually attain at the end of the narrative, but it is a form of interior beauty. In Bengali, the word *antar* (Sanskrit *antara*, 'inner') figures more and more prominently in this discourse. At the end of the story, their experiences in the short couple of years that the novel describes deserve to be regarded as 'extraordinary', just as they themselves, as individuals, stand out as remarkable. As in the general theory of the *Bildungsroman*, this is because of a dual process of cultivation.[25] They were not extra-ordinary characters to being with, but the narration describes a process through which they emerge as morally remarkable—not in the sense that others would find it hard to emulate their achievement, but rather because others in similar situations ought to, and probably will. Thus the novel plays on a contradictory but entirely intelligible combination of the attributes of ordinariness and extraordinariness. Starting out as ordinary individuals, the two young women evolve through their sentimental education, bring refinement to their own characters, and ultimately become distinct and remarkable. Although eventually Sucharita's ideals come to coincide entirely with her father, Pareshbabu's, she retains her distinctness. We get the feeling that though people like Sucharita, Pareshbabu, Gora, and Binoy might form a close-knit circle of friends, the moral basis of their community is founded on respect for the individuality of each person rather than because they share in common the traditional features of the same religious community. It is of vital narrative significance that Binoy decides against conversion to the Brahmo faith of his fiancée, and Lalita finds in herself the ability to respect him despite this. Parallel to this runs the sentimental education of the reader, whose sensibility

[25] Bakhtin 1994.

is similarly heightened and refined, so that at the end he or she is also able to recognize this 'happening' inside the story and inside the figures in the narrative. Reading a novel of this kind, a typically powerful *Bildungsroman*, is expected to cause a similar effect on the reader's personality as well. The refinement of the characters is a disguised refinement of the reader of the novel. There is in this simultaneous ethical and aesthetic reflection an increasingly strong connection between themes of ordinariness, individuality, and interiority. This point could be elaborated indefinitely by drawing on examples from all sides of Tagore's creative work—poetry, songs, and novels.

Narrative Exposition of the Emotive Ideal: Three Stories

This transformation in the aesthetic structure of beauty was a question central to Tagore's artistic consciousness. The general aesthetic-emotional attitude I am referring to can also be found constantly in his songs. To Bengalis it is immortalized in the lines:

Ami rupe tomay bholabo na, bhalobasay bholabo
Ami hat diye dvar khulbo na go, gan diye dvar kholabo

I won't bewitch you by beauty, but by love,
I won't push the door open by my hand; but by my songs, make you
    open it to me.[26]

In these lines, the first occurrence of *bholabo* has a strong conventional suggestiveness because *rupa* is meant for seduction. Bankim wrote famously: 'Beauty was created to cause enchantment' (*rupato moher janyai haiachhila*). But the meaning of the second occurrence of *bholabo* is already displaced into something more emotional, ethereal, and, in this mode of thinking, refined. Besides constantly commenting on it in his poetry, Tagore made this question a central problem in some of his narrative poems and drama. We shall look at three of his narratives. The first comes in two versions: as a narrative poem *Parisodh* (Cleansing), later turned into an unceasingly popular dance

[26] The verb *bholabo* combines meanings suggesting seduction, enchantment, and winning someone's heart by deception: from Tagore 1970: 307.

drama called *Shyama* (1939), with the added expedient of musical interpretation of the narrative moments and movement. Second, we shall look at the interpretation of love in the plays *Raktakarabi* (Red Oleander, 1926) and, finally, the dance drama *Sapmocan* (1939), where this line of thinking on love is taken to an experimental limit-form.

Parisodh/Shyama

In *Shyama*, an unsuspecting handsome young traveller, Vajrasen, enters a city in uproar about a theft of jewellery from the royal household. The unscrupulous *kotwal*—the chief police officer who is under pressure to find the thief—falsely implicates the traveller and sentences him to death. When he is being taken from the jail for execution, Shyama, the head dancer of the royal court, sees him from a distance and is instantly enchanted by his appearance. She seeks to persuade the *kotwal* to free him, but the *kotwal* needs a victim. Shyama, blinded by passion (*kama*, though Tagore does not use that term: it is too gross even for mention in his high aesthetic), turns to Uttiya, who has long nursed unrequited love (*prem*) for her. Uttiya decides to link his life inseparably to Shyama by dying in Vajrasen's place, confessing to the theft and going to his death. While making the decision, Uttiya sings a famously moving song of love, a mixture of emotional devotion and besottedness:

> *Nyay anyaya janine janine janine,*
> *Sudhu tomare jani, tomare jani, ogo sundari*
> *Cao ki premer parama mulya*
> *Debo ani, debo ani.*

> I don't know right from wrong, lovely girl,
> If you want the ultimate price of love
> I shall present it to you.[27]

Innocent Vajrasen knows nothing of this, and is somewhat bemused by his inexplicable release, and content with his great fortune in love. Shyama is briefly united with the traveller, and they start on a journey of love on a boat. Vajrasen periodically wonders about his release and asks how she managed to set him free. Eventually, Shyama

[27] *Shyama, Gitabitan*, in Tagore 1970: III, 740.

tells him, confident that he is enough in love with her not to leave. In revulsion, Vajrasen leaves her and goes away on his travels. But at night, the shadow of a very beautiful woman hovers near the boat in the darkness. Initially Vajrasen is overcome with desire and calls her to himself, but then he recovers and finally rejects her, and she fades away from the story. Vajrasen is stricken—by desire, but more by a deep moral guilt at his failure to forgive, expressed in one of the most poignant dramatic songs in Tagore's entire work: he laments the weakness of love, and asks for forgiveness from God for his failure to find forgiveness in his heart.[28] He acknowledges that the god who takes the sinful in his care would forgive Shyama, overwhelmed by her guilt. But perhaps he would not forgive Vajrasen who was not able to extend kindness. This wonderfully rich song dominates the meaning of the narrative, and obviously raises deep and interesting questions about the limits of the duty to forgive: was the traveller right in not forgiving Shyama for her crime? He was, after all, the main beneficiary of her wrongdoing and could not absolve himself in any other way. But was Shyama not deserving of forgiveness? Is God's forgiveness ampler, but also different, from man's? This reflection on love represents a simple but powerful operation on the distinction between *shringara*

---

[28] *Ksamite parilam naje ksama he mama dinata, papijana sarana prabhu*
mariche tape, mariche laje premera balahinata, papijana sarana prabhu
priyake nite paraini buke premere ami henechi
papire dite sasti sudhu papere deke enechi
jani go tumi ksamibe tare je abhagini papera bhare
carane taba binta
ksamibe na ksamibe na amar ksamahinata, papijana sarana prabhu.

I failed to forgive, O lord who gives refuge to the sinful,
Forgive my baseness, O lord. Love's helplessness is dying of remorse, dying of shame, O lord.
I failed to my love into my heart. I violated love itself.
I tried to punish sin, and brought sin upon myself.
I know you would find forgiveness for her who is at your feet bowed by her guilt
I know my want of forgiveness/compassion would not find your forgiveness.
O lord, refuge of the sinful/guilty.

—Tagore 1970: 750.

and *prem*. Bankim's conventional themes of *rupa* and *moha* permeate the entire story, as the unfulfilling nature of a love based merely on desire. And, curiously, at the end of the play we could say to all three of its characters what Bankim, in a strange eruption of an external authorial voice at the end of his novel *Candrasekhar* (1875), says to its main character, on the point of his imminent death: he is on his way 'to that eternal place where beauty does not cause enchantment, love does not cause sinfulness'.[29]

Exterior and Interior Vision: *Raktakarabi*

In two other dramatic narratives Tagore returns to the same theme, with some alterations in the structural features. Once again the recursiveness of the themes, and their recurrence in free-standing texts like songs, appear highly significant. There are some striking similarities in the two plays and in their treatment of the enigmatic development of love for an indistinctly seen character. The two plays also develop a new theme about emotions absent from the sketchy treatment of love in *Shyama*. In *Raktakarabi* Tagore again creates an enigmatic, symbolically complex, feminine figure: Nandini. The play is placed in a strange setting of cavernous mines from which indistinct

[29] Tagore 1957: 86—'Then be on your way, Pratap, on your way to that eternal place where beauty does not cause enchantment, love does not lead to sinfulness. Even if you get a hundred thousand Shaibalinis at your feet, you would not want to love them.' ('*Tabe jao Pratap, sei anatadhame jao . . . jekhane rupe moha nai, pranaye pap nai . . . Laksa Saibalini padaprante payileo bhalobasite cahibe na . . .*'), Chattopadhyay 1985a: I, 424. This is a strange and puzzling sentence. The first part is a wonderfully concise reflection on the moral essence of his story; but the last clause is odd. In my reading, it shows the peculiar unease in Bankim's mind between the traditional shringaric fascination with rupa, mere beauty, and the new ideal of individuation. An empirical case of love—like the instance of Pratap and Shaibalini in the novel—is uneasily poised between these two ideals. It is eventually unclear if Pratap falls in love with Shaibalini because she is beautiful, in which case, he could have fallen for other equally beautiful women; or because she was herself, an unsubstitutible individual, in which case, he could not have loved anyone else. In this context, to speak of 'a hundred thousand Shaibalinis' suggests that she is replaceable with a thousand other beautiful women, gestures towards the traditional aesthetic.

masses of human beings excavate sources of wealth, supervised by a powerful but remote king who knows everything, whose voice is heard, but who cannot be seen. Clearly, the king represents power and wealth: he exerts enormous control over people and things, but he does not control happiness; indeed, he is consumed by an incessant yearning for it. Nandini is an obviously symbolic naming: it means someone who delights and brings happiness, though it is unclear both in the name itself and her narrative movements whether she delights by her beauty or her character. Yet it is clear that Nandini is the centre of a complex geometry of desires. The king evidently desires her and hopes forlornly to win her by a combination of power and occasional spells of self-reflection, when he wonders if exercising power is meaningful or an intolerable strain and he should simply leave everything. Nandini is also desired by a symbolic poetic figure, Bishu, who is mad, entirely unattached to pursuits of mundane power and wealth, even of everyday domesticity, and who wishes to win her simply by the ethereal powers of music and longing. It is evident that, wherever she goes, she excites desire, though in this highly symbolic play that does not mean erotic desire in the material sense. In some of his later plays Tagore, under the influence of some abstract strands of modern Western drama, evolved a highly symbolic register in which protagonists were not realistic or representational characters but signs or figures embodying ideals and principles. *Raktakarabi* is written entirely in this kind of shadow language, in which characters are both signs and embodiments of ideas. They are signs, but they also excite and feel emotions themselves. As if in a shadow play, but within language, the protagonists are indistinct, and their gestural language is one of stylization and exaggeration. Despite this highly charged sign-language, the meaning of Nandini's being is unmistakable: Nandini is simply happiness. Not surprisingly, she is desired by everybody, her nature is construed by each in his own way, and each has his own sense of how to attain her. The king wants to attain her through power and, to a lesser extent, through wealth; but his intelligence is sufficiently rich to tell him that these are not the means by which he can bring her within his grasp. Bishu, the poet, wishes to shackle her with music and aesthetic creativity, but he lacks weight and commitment and he, too, realizes deep inside him the inadequacy of this path to happiness.

Nandini constantly entices and eludes everyone, yet she, or rather the search for her, is central to everybody's life. What brings meaning to human life is the search for love, not its attainment—a theme that resonates in much of Tagore's literary and religious reflection. Bishu devotes a song to her which runs: 'I want to sing you a song, you who awaken sorrow in my heart; I want to sing you a song, you who wake me up from my sleep. In the middle of my work, you don't let the stream of tears stop. You come and touch me, you fill my heart with bliss, only to move away. You stand screened behind my pain.' Happiness in the abstract, or in the wonderful figural form of Nandini, comes and touches our heart only at certain moments, but the pain or sadness that fills the rest of our time is transfigured by those miraculous instances of fulfilment. Happiness therefore always stands beyond a screen of sorrow, sadness, pain, through which we can catch a hazy glimpse of it. But it is that hazy certainty of its presence which makes life a constant search for Nandini. This is, of course, in dramatic form, a philosophical reflection on human happiness rather than on love in the narrower sense. But the figural contest between various characters who desire love contributes to the continuing thought about love, desire, and eroticism. Love in *Raktakarabi* is enveloped by a deep and serene aestheticism of great lyrical refinement, with carefully chosen words, a slow and beautiful cadence, restrained and wistful music—a thoroughly new and different world compared to the aesthetic that celebrated shringaric love.

Vision and Emotion: *Sapmocan*

One of the most startling narrative techniques in *Sapmocan* is that the king, the central character in the play, is never seen on stage. The story begins with a highly conventionalized justification for fantastic occurrences. Customarily in Sanskrit drama, human stories would start with a prologue telling how a superhuman figure—*apsaras* or God (*devata*)—had attracted a curse from some powerful deity and been condemned to the sorrows of a human birth. Tagore's story uses this convention as a subterfuge. Two dancers, one male and one female, in the main dancing hall of paradise commit a mistake and are punished by the king of the gods to suffer the contrariety of a human life. As the prophecy states: 'go down to earth, where you will cause and endure suffering'.[30] The female dancer is born as a princess of great beauty,

---

[30] *Gitabitan* in Tagore 1970: III.

the male as a disfigured king. Kamalika is wed to the great king when she grows up, but her husband never meets her except at night, when there are no lights. Kamalika yearns to see him, but he persistently refuses. On the day of the spring festival Kamalika watches a dance from her window. In the circle of handsome dancers she watches a repulsively deformed man; and in their nocturnal conversations, she mentions her disgust to the king. When he reveals himself to her, she initially recoils. But through the movement of the narrative she eventually overcomes the delusions of human vision and is granted the vision to see love. In the play, absence is the great central formal device. The king is central to the drama but he has to be visually absent. His voice is heard, usually played, following Tagore's authorial intentions, by an actor with a deep, pleasant voice. But in the world of this play his presence disposes with the most obvious means of presence, i.e. vision. Thus the play effects a rupture between presence and vision. In both *Raktakarabi* and *Sapmocan*, there is an essential play on the distinction between two conceptions of love, one based on vision and the other on emotion—respectively, *rupa* and *prem*. In both cases the hero is never seen, except accidentally, by the heroine, and the entire drama is one of the development of vision, of a deeper form of seeing: when love has been nurtured by emotional intensity the subjects are enabled to see their lovers as 'beautiful', something they could not do only with an exterior vision. One could speak of exterior and interior vision, or of a seeing by the eye and a seeing by the mind, a subtler visuality of emotion. Again, Tagore must have thought about this distinction deeply as it reappears in his songs, with an independent, free-standing contemplation of vision and enchantment:

> *Cokher alloy dekhechilem cokher bahire*
> *Antare aj dekhbo jakhan alok nahire.*

> I had seen you by the light of my eyes in front of me
> Today when there is no light I shall see you inside my heart.[31]

In both cases the heroines are eventually won by deeply enigmatic heroes who never come into view, who never become an object of external seeing or *darshan*. Tagore is playing here with the semantic

---

[31] Ibid.: 110.

complexity of the very concept of darshan—only when an internal, intellectual as well as emotional, seeing supplements the seeing with the eye, when a non-visual vision of consciousness brings truth to the vision of human sight, can it be said that a person has had the darshan of an object. The repeated visits to a temple to see a deity are not darshan itself, but a preparation, an aspiration to achieve it some day. It can be said that Kamalika had merely *watched* the king dance on the day of the formal festival of spring: later, only when she is able to *see* him through her love, not her eyes, does the real spring festival arrive.

Although the three Tagore narratives are all ostensibly traditional, what is happening through them is an irreducibly modern aesthetic manoeuvre. The movements within these narratives, where very little actually happens in terms of events, bring about a reconstitution of an emotion, a vast displacement of the aesthetic meaning of the emotion called love. The narratives do not show us how, in fantastic or ancient contexts, a beautiful woman came to love a deformed man, but how modern individuals should interpret and practise emotional intimacy. The stories are preparations for emotional modernity, establishing with enormous grace a new aesthetic ideal.

Romantic Love and Surrounding Relations

At the beginning of this essay I suggested that the ideal of love has a dual character. It is simultaneously an aesthetic and a social ideal. The emotion of love thus constituted can be experienced and enacted in real lives only if the social world is transformed in deeply significant ways. As social relations exist in a structure, a revolutionary change in the nature of love and marriage such as that outlined so far could not happen without all the other relations surrounding the couple also undergoing changes consistent with the central shift. The task of the good parent now is not to find a match for the daughters, but to help them understand themselves, to help them 'listen to their heart'. Pareshbabu, the softspoken, self-effacing, but highly principled father in *Gora* is the exemplary figure in this revaluation of parental responsibility. He has already developed an altered relationship with his daughter, whereas his wife, despite being a doctrinal Brahmo, has not changed her social role accordingly. Her understanding of a good marriage for her daughter is still that of finding a suitable match in purely pecuniary terms, irrespective of the tendencies of the heart. And, evidently, even after marriage (a period that literary narratives seldom explore with the same curiosity) conjugal relations between such romantic lovers cannot conform to the old conventional Hindu custom of feminine supplication.[32]

Individuation, Ordinariness, Interiority

Several principles are established through this collective literary reflection on the nature of love. In its most fundamental redefinition, love does not mean a universal desire that men and women feel for each other, particularly the attraction of physical beauty. It is now an emotional bond which one individuated 'soul' feels for another, and both feel it is precious and peculiar. Sexual attraction is a subordinate part of this feeling of emotional companionship. This literary principle is then elaborated indefinitely, with writers exploring its various forms, variations, and consequences. In a society still full of repressive restrictions, especially on the elective behaviour of women, such emotional love often takes an excessively platonic soulfulness, where the initial emotional attraction between young people is routinely frustrated by unavoidable social norms of unelective, arranged marriage. But in literature stories of such emotional attraction—eventually successful or failed—come to be accepted as the norm. Further, in modern literature, particularly in modern fiction, the ordinary is constantly celebrated: ordinary emotions of entirely ordinary persons. Literature thus comes to impart a subtle impulse towards democracy. Finally, the theatre of love is now the infinite extension of the interiority of the mind, not the play of sexual desire. The shringaric ideal, still unwittingly discernible in Bankim's art, is finally laid to rest. It cannot be revived except as a parody, as deliberate anachronism, or as simple curiosity about the antique. Kalidasa's writing is still read and enjoyed at the time of Tagore but, to use vernacular concepts, as *atita*, not as *agama*—that is, as enjoyment of a

---

[32] But see some later short stories by a Bengali writer which, presenting a casuistry of marital relations, problematize the aspiration to conjugal love: Bandyopadhyay 1994.

form of literature of a distant, antiquated past, not as conventions that are creatively meaningful. The shringaric conventions have become the literary equivalents to a museum piece.

In Bengali culture, as elsewhere, there is a strong historical connection between this emerging literary aesthetic and a new social ethics of individuality and domesticity. A serious, and often acrimonious, discussion on the nature of social ethics takes place in Bengali intellectual culture in the nineteenth century: some of its central questions are similar to the issues raised in German social philosophy between Kant and Hegel. The impact of European rationalism on religious thought produces arguments strikingly similar to Kant's ideas about 'religion within the limits of reason', placing great reliance on the idea of a common practical reason. The reading of European philosophy and contemporary intellectual debates, which were part of a modern education, plays an important part in this process of moral conversion. The new individualistic ethics is, of course, initially read, then imagined, and finally practised in actual personal conduct only by an adventurous, privileged, and often aggressive minority within the modern elite. Despite their statistical insignificance, however, their imaginative influence on the society was immense. Initially, these examples of individualistic personal conduct remained heroic examples of leading a self-conscious individual life in a society that looked with sullen disapproval at the 'outlandish' ways of a privileged modernist minority. In the colonial context, with its early signs of nationalist resentment, such behaviour was often condemned as apish flattery of the Englishman. Bankim's brief but vicious comic sketch, *Ingrajstotra* (A Hymn to the English), is a very powerful expression of such mockery.[33] But, significantly, engaging in romantic love does not figure among the modes of conduct Bankim satirizes in the piece. By contrast, Bhudev Mukhopadhyay's essays on the family (in *Parivarik Prabandha*, 1882), are an entirely serious philosophical contestation of this new mode of emotions and social conduct.[34]

As long as such conduct remained confined to a tiny minority among the elite and the vast majority in Bengali society calmly

[33] *Ingrajstotra* in Chattopadhyay 1985b: 9–10.
[34] Mukhopadhyay n.d.

carried on practising arranged marriages, these modes of behaviour remained merely individual, and extraordinary. It could deserve the honour of moral heroism but it could not be called 'an ethical life', simply because it lacked the effortless, taken-for-granted quality of real, embedded (*sittlich*) ethical norms. The literary idealization of this model of conduct contributed to their becoming *sittlich* in the historical long term.

At first, literary texts like novels produced a powerful intellectual argument through the narratives themselves. Bengali novels are strikingly discursive in their texture. Inside the narratives, characters do not merely fall in love. In Tagore and Saratchandra Chattopadhyay's novels, they spend what appears to be an utterly disproportionate amount of time intellectually debating what falling in love means ethically, and whether it can be justified. Novels do not merely present fictional events of love, but in doing so show how fulfilling such ways of behaving and experiencing emotions can be. Secondly, novels tended to create an impression of the commonplaceness of such actions and behaviour, giving them a misleading aura of ordinariness, i.e. such things as engaging in love relationships happened all the time in novels in a society in which these things happened only rarely. Fictional characters become in a sense shadow people in this social universe, performing, despite their unreality, the immensely powerful function of setting examples, giving arguments, and providing advice for real individuals on the point of falling in love. They contributed to a fictional normalization of such conduct. Thirdly, literature produced a new sensibility in which this love becomes a literary, aesthetic, idealized norm. Couples married by solid familial negotiations would go devotedly to watch Bengali romantic films with Uttamkumar and Suchitra Sen, the two most popular actors of this genre. They would either exult in the fulfilment such love gave to marriages, or condole the tragic failure of such love and the consequently unfulfilled lives of the cinematic characters. Through such fictional experience their own conjugal relationships would be transformed in small, imperfect and partial ways.

Literature, in other words, both recorded and contributed to this fundamental social change. Tagore's narratives record the historical equilibrium where such individualism has become common, almost normal.

References

Alam, Muzaffar. 2003. The Culture and Politics of Persian in Precolonial Hindustan. In Pollock 2003: 131–98.

Aries, Philippe and George Duby. 1987–8. *A History of Private Life*. 4 volumes. Cambridge, Mass.: Harvard University Press.

Bakhtin, Mikhail. 1994. The Bildungsroman and its Significance in the History of Realism. In *Speech Genres and Other Late Essays*, trans. Verne W. McGee. Austin: University of Texas Press.

Bandyopadhyay, B. and S. Das. Eds. 1950. *Bharatcandrer Granthabali*. Calcutta: Bangiya Sahitya Parishat.

Bandyopadhyay, Manik. 1994. *Wives & Others*. Trans. Kalpana Bardhan. Delhi: Penguin India.

Chattopadhyay, Bankimchandra. 1985a. *Rajsimha* (1882). In *Bankim Rachnabali (BR)*. Vol. I: *Upanyas*. Calcutta: Sahitya Samsad.

———. 1985b. *Krsnacaritra* (1882). In *BR*. Vol. II. Calcutta: Sahitya Samsad.

Dimock, Edward C., Jr. 1963. *The Thief of Love: Bengali Tales from Court and Village*. Chicago: The University of Chicago Press.

du Perron, Lalita. 2002. 'Thumri': A Discussion of the Female Voice in Hindustani Music. *Modern Asian Studies* 36.1: 173–92.

Guha-Thakurta, Tapati. 1992. *Making of a New 'Indian' Art*. Cambridge: Cambridge University Press.

Gupta, Charu. 2001. *Sexuality, Obscenity, Community: Women, Muslims, and the Hindu Public in Colonial India*. Delhi: Permanent Black.

Kale, M.R. Ed. and trans. 1916. *The Ritusamhara of Kalidasa*. Vol. I. Bombay.

Kalidasa. 1927. *Meghaduta*. Trans. K. Ray. Calcutta.

———. 1984. *Meghaduta*. In *Works of Kalidasa*. Ed. and trans. C.R. Devadhar. 2 vols. Delhi: Motilal Banarsidass.

Kaviraj, Sudipta. 1995. *The Unhappy Consciousness*. Delhi: Oxford University Press.

Miller, Barbara Stoler. Ed. and trans. 1977. *Love Song of the Dark Lord: Jayadeva's Gitagovinda*. New York: Columbia University Press.

Mitter, Partha. 1994. *Art and Nationalism in Colonial India*. Cambridge: Cambridge University Press.

Mukhopadhyay, Bhudev. n.d. *Parivarik Prabandha* (Essays on the Family). Chuchurah: Bhudev Publishing House.

Pollock, Sheldon. 2003. *Literary Cultures in History: Reconstructions from South Asia*. Berkeley: University of California Press.

Raychaudhuri, Tapan. 1999. *Perceptions, Emotions, Sensibilities*. Delhi: Oxford University Press.

Tagare, G.V. (ed.). 1976–86. *The Bhagavata Purana*. Delhi.

Tagore, Rabindranath. 1924. *Gora*. English trans. London: Macmillan.

———. 1957. *Sapmocan*. In *Rabindra Racanabali*. Vol. 22. Calcutta: Visvabharati.

———. 1964. 'Meghdut', *Sancayita*. Calcutta: Visvabharati.

———. 1970. 'Akhanda', *Gitabitan*. Calcutta: Visvabharati.

6

The Poetry of Interiority

The Creation of a Language of Modern Subjectivity in Tagore's Poetry

Before Rabindranath, I would like to suggest, Bengalis were, poetically at least, 'self-less'. His literary art is the first to delineate a problem of modern subjectivity for poetry to explore.[1] The achievement of this new problem shows the necessary complexity of these processes, both the ambiguity of such beginnings and their incontrovertibility. New literary or philosophic concepts, new problems, new ideas do not find an easy, unproblematic entry into a culture in the way a simplistic, material conception of 'inside' and 'outside' would suggest. Ideas from the 'outside' do not come into an empty linguistic field. They enter a pre-existing conceptual language of literature and have to express themselves by altering the earlier language 'from within'. To be even articulated, so that it can be thought, a new idea needs to twist, manipulate, cajole an older language to express itself. There is

---

This essay was first published in Bharati Ray and David Taylor, eds, *Politics and Identity in South Asia*, Kolkata: K.P. Bagchi, 2001.

[1] I do not wish to deny that elements moving in this direction can be found in earlier writers, but these are mere elements. I would assert that the fully developed problem of subjectivity does not appear in Bengali writing before Tagore. Before him, Bankimchandra's characters sometimes reflect upon their own situations, and, in a manner generally admired at the time, show conversations between two sides of their mind. Michael Madhusudan Dutta, over the latter part of his career, repeatedly reflected on his destiny and wrote formally autobiographic poems. Biharilal Dutta discovered that explorations of the mental or psychological states of the mind constituted an important poetic subject.

no prelinguistic, undistorted, primal beginning of ideas from which they are expressed through concepts, words, languages, styles. These languages, which are the ideas' means of expression, also constitute the ideas. It is generally acknowledged that one of the fundamental themes of modern literature is the exploration of the self, or of subjectivity. If subjectivity means simple self-reference, or a certain clear conception of authorship, these things existed in premodern literature as well; but modern subjectivity is marked by several distinctive features—its individuality, its mentalism, its interiority. Earlier traditions of philosophical or literary self-exploration in India did not have a language which could accomplish this modern task. Rabindranath, I should like to argue, draws on some earlier languages of the self to make this possible, by employing their terms, but displacing their meanings by carefully modulated untraditional use.[2] Finally, I should like, further, to assert that although the idea of the self that he invokes could not have arisen without an encounter with modern Western notions of subjectivity, what he eventually places inside this self is significantly different from the solutions favoured by aesthetic individualism of the Western variety. In an age in which the aggressive triumphant individualism of modern Western thought is growing weaker, and losing its hegemony as a model for cultural self-realization, it is interesting to explore what this distinctive imagination of the self was like, and what it offered. (That is, not simply showing how it is different from the standard Western models and criticizing it for this failure, for this inability to be something other than what it was.)

I

In all social worlds people effortlessly are. But as social beings people are various things. They inhabit certain regular, commonly intelligible descriptions which fit them in specific ways. They are Brahmins or Shudras, Tamils or Bengalis, Hindus or Muslims, in a recourseless sort of way. These descriptions have a dual character: first, these constitute the ways in which these individuals conceptualize their

---

[2] The question of linguistic change has been given much greater attention in discussions of social practice. But literary practices also require, at least in cultures like the modern Indian, a sensitive exercise in historical semantics *(begriffsgeschichte)*.

own social beings; and second, these represent the complementary and confirmatory ways in which others act towards them.[3] There is a common argument in modern social theory that modernity introduces into this matter of social identity of people a concept of subjectivity, or, on a milder version of the same thesis, although ideas of a subject and some notions of reflexivity might be present in earlier cultures, modernity introduces a new meaning of the subject and his reflexive capacities. This argument has the greatest significance for moral philosophy and literary history, for this new 'self' opens up two new fields of exploration, enjoyment, adventure, and reflection on subjectivity—first, a new domain of subjectivist, i.e. individual-centred, morality; and second, the exploration and description of the psychological states of this subject in the literary forms of the modern novel and lyrical poetry. I will here follow the philosophical significance of the semantic transformations of the pronoun 'I' (*ami*). Even the first person singular is a fascinating subject for *begriffsgeschichte* (historical semantics); and I suspect that careful analysis would show that we are ourselves in a distinctly different way from our traditional forebears. But this transformation of the 'I' bears an intimate connection with related, if not similar, transformations of the sense of we, or of collective identities. These two processes of subjectivation, being individual and collective subjects, can be connected with a reasonable historical theory. Elsewhere I have argued that modernity has an irresistible logic of change which leaves no identity untransformed, collective or personal;[4] and the essential point of connection is that modern collective identities can be composed only on the basis of a substratum of modern individuality.

One of the main principles of this modern 'bourgeois' individuality is famously the one of choosing: the idea that individual lives are lived and constituted through choice. This idea could take, and often did, two rather different forms. In its utopian-ideal, or some might say ideological, version, it suggested that individuals lived the lives

[3] This does not mean that others' handling of my identity is entirely confirmatory of my proposals about it. If their handling differs sharply from mine, I am forced to take note of that and respond. In actual social practice, what we call the identity of an individual is always transactive.

[4] See Kaviraj 1992.

they chose to—an unpractical and historically naïve conception of modern society as a realm of unimpeded choice. This served to show how this conception of an individual life based on choice was not a free-standing singular idea; it evidently depended on several other typically modern notions. For instance, thinking of an individual life in that radically elective way presupposed a conception of the world and its social relations as fundamentally alterable, not fixed and entirely immovable. All presentations of the principle of individuality were not so naïve; it was capable of more complex and, aesthetically, much more compelling forms. The principle of individuation could be played off artistically against an acknowledgement of rigidities of social structure. It could be said that the principle of choice marked human lives, but societies often obstructed its realization, and tragedies occurred in modern times primarily through this form. In any case, the primary narrative tension in most modern Bengali novels arises from the conflict between a recognized value of the principle of individuation, at least in matters of the heart, and placing such strongly individual personalities within the framework of a society which is extremely rigid. Even in lyrical poetry and songs, which ordinarily do not have a narrative form, and are thus less suited to the expression of this conflict, there is often a pervasive sense of melancholy arising out of this sense of interdiction against spontaneous affection.[5] Charles Taylor has argued that there were two interconnected domains in which this new ethic of choice was worked out in its fulness—in new theories of personal morality and in literature, and it is theoretically interesting to explore this connection itself.[6] In both its forms, at any rate, this was deeply connected to a new ideal of responsibility, indeed a feeling of responsibility towards a person who was not, according to earlier moral conventions, a normal object of responsibility—a responsibility towards oneself. But this change in attitude was not

[5] To take a random example from Tagore's own songs, one can think of this early one:

sakhi bhavana kahare bale
sakhi jatana kahare bale
tomra je bala dibasarajani bhalobasa bhalobasa!
sakhi bhalobasa kare kay
se ki kebali jatanamay.

[6] See Taylor 1985.

practically painless or conceptually simple: for this to occur, some associated conceptual changes were also required. An individual could be said to be responsible for himself, or towards himself, only if his life was seen or constructed in a new, morally rather peculiar fashion. A person could be said to waste his life if his actions did not conform to certain ideal trajectories constructed through morally and imaginatively compelling models only if it was assumed that that kind of life was in principle open for every single individual to live under the historical conditions modern societies provided. But the principle of choice also implied that there were many different options about ways in which the right kind of life could be pursued. Individuals in the real world faced serious obstacles in living the lives of their choice.

These obstacles were of two types. Some came from the acts of others, usually socially powerful agents, who lived according to traditional norms which in principle denied the rule of choice and sought, with the collusion of a traditional society, to impose these rules on rebellious romantic lovers. Impediments of aristocracy, or caste, or parental disfavour usually based on one of these grounds, constituted the primary examples. But obstacles could also rise, in a wholly liberal, non-traditional world, from the clash of wills or individualities where individuals were not impeded in what they wanted for their happiness by the presence of traditional structures or norms, but by the equally free and unconstrained will of others who happened to want the arrangement of the world to be different—a clash this time not between subjectivity and tradition, but between subjectivities. This terrain was described in great aesthetic fulness by modern novels.

It was essentially because of a half-perceived understanding of this historical conflict that the reading of novels as such, and not of any specifically offending ones, was considered undermining in traditional Bengali households. This was I suppose why the novel was by definition political, however formalistic or aesthetically superior its literary craft. To anxious traditional parents, the consequences of an untimely reading of even classics by Bankimchandra and Tagore could be as dangerous to the moral training of young girls and boys (in that order) as any salacious or improper narrative by morally unrestrained novelists. I realised much later why my grandfather considered listening to the most inane *adhunik* songs morally polluting for young adolescents under his charge, though the only worrying feature I found in them was the puerile nature of their lyrics.[7] I conceded later that he was a much better sociologist than me, and he saw in these nondescript jingles an intolerable and dangerous celebration of the principle of subjectivity, of the terrifying idea that his daughters, especially, could live their lives as they chose rather than the way others had lived before them. Both these types of conflicts abound in Rabindranath's novels, and their complexities are explored aesthetically—between subjectivity and tradition and between incompatible subjectivities. Occasionally, as in *Gora*, he introduces enormously delectable complexities—like Gora's attempt to express in a language of choice a life pattern which ruled it out, a traditional sense of life disguising and expressing itself at the same time through the language of subjectivity.[8]

The first narratively significant feature of this modem aesthetic is the association of the principle of choice with the living of lives. Especially in a society ruled by the system of castes, this is an emphatically novel and unsettling idea. The system of castes was of course subject to the historical pulls and feints of human ingenuity, and people who lived in what must appear to us, with our non-caste view of the world, as positions of unbearable moral disability managed to formulate strategies which used to their full the flexibility that the system afforded in practice. Still, the idea of living one's life according to one's choice went against the grain of the central principles of Indian society. This meant not merely that people could not deviate from largely set social trajectories in the actual lives they lived.

One consequence of that social arrangement was that lives were not individuated in the modern sense. Individual lives were often considered narratable; but that was primarily because they illustrated

[7] *Adhunik* means, literally, modern. *Adhunik* songs were a genre of popular love songs which often celebrated the feeling and deplored the impossibility of its consummation in repressive Bengali society. It was precisely the universality and unindexed character of their utterance which made them appear so dangerous. Their expression of desire could be transferred all too easily from the protagonists in film stories to ordinary adolescents in real life.

[8] In the first part of the novel, before he comes under the influence of a liberal Brahmo family, Gora, the central character, espouses an aggressively traditional form of Hindu religion, but defends it, in an interesting complexity, in a language of choice. He had, in effect, elected to reject the principle of election. See Tagore 1910.

some social principle, associated with a certain walk of life, or trade, or occupation, carried to its extreme and noblest limits. Stories were told of individuals who exhibited exceptional fidelity as wives, or loyalty as servants, or constancy as friends, or trustworthiness as soldiers. However, these could not be treated as stories of individuation in the modern sense. Nothing happened to their lot which did not to somebody similarly socially placed. What was surprising and therefore narratable was the extraordinary intensity of their devotion to their roles and their internal values, but not the trajectories themselves.

With the coming of modernity, society does not of course change obligingly all of a sudden; but the principle of plasticity of individual fates and destinies is recognized. This also involved a fundamentally new way of looking at an individual's life. Life was an opportunity, a time which lay undetermined in front, to be filled up with acts and events of one's own making.[9] Such elected lives, to the extent they are possible (and it would be much later, with the infusion of socialist critiques of capitalist modernity, that the sense of the limits imposed on choice would appear clearly to the Bengali intelligentsia and find articulation in its literary world), exemplify a process of singularization, making each life interestingly different from others. Singularization in this sense was, in these days of early bourgeois ideology, both a descriptive fact and a moral ideal. Individuals who lived their lives inside the social contexts of modern cities were seen to be singularized in this sense; their lives moving through a series of unpredetermined events in previously unthinkable and self-created trajectories. But this fact of descriptive sociology was shadowed, or hallowed subtly by the presence of a normative ideal. Colonial modernity created, because of the perverse impartiality of the British rulers, a field of careers open to talent in modern India/modern Calcutta (indeed this confusion between India and Calcutta was very

[9] The idea of self-making is slightly different and potentially distinct from the idea of an elective life. This could, at least, avoid some of the worst forms of the elective ideology. Self-making could mean an individual's attempt to live his life steadfastly accordingly to some guiding principles, often in face of the irrationalities and oppositions of real society. The self that is eventually made is an accomplishment precisely because of the dangers and difficulties attendant on it.

persistent; but it was also pardonable because 'modern' India was really
for a time modern Calcutta), within which individuals could seek their
individual social and moral destinies. There was a close connection
between this change in the way people looked at lives and told stories
about the more interesting cases.

The singularization of individual lives, or individuation, raised
some problems of practical narrative aesthetics. Traditional literary
forms in India worked on a standard and easily recognizable theory
of narrative eligibility of characters. The artistic repertoires of poets or
other literary practitioners could be used to celebrate only exemplary
lives or their combinations. This exemplariness was defined quite
clearly. The life of Rama satisfied this criterion of narrative eligibility
precisely because it was an exemplar: in subtle ways it managed to
show how a life should be lived both for kings and celebrities, and also
for ordinary householders. The *Ramayana* was so significant for the
delineation of the Hindu moral world precisely because it presented
such a number of exemplars in combination—of Rama, of Sita, of
Laxman and Bharat, and Hanuman, each in their own way carrying
a certain individual principle of human relationship to their point of
ultimate excellence.

Narrative eligibility according to the modern idea became completely different. Aesthetic principles of the new literature retained the
theoretical connection between exemplariness and narrative eligibility;
it was still something exemplary which made a life or a part of it a
fit object for literary representation. But in modern aesthetics what
made a life or a slice of it exemplary was displaced in a most radical
fashion. It also, at the same time, altered the meaning of ordinariness
and its connection to literary representation. To the new aesthetic
consciousness lives were exemplary not because all individuals of a
relevant class were alike and the protagonists' story showed the essence
of the story of all lives. Rather, behind their mask of ordinariness all
individual lives were unique. It was this certainty of their being unique
and narratable in a non-heroic sort of way which made them fit for
such literary attention. Modern novels especially presented the results
of this new aesthetic principle by making narratively interesting the
lives of individuals who were unremarkable by traditional norms.

Choice, the element of election, brought in a rationalist logic
into the living of individual lives; and one implication of this was
an accompanying rule of corrigibility. Bourgeois individuals had

eminently corrigible selves. Just as the bourgeois, literally, learnt from mistakes in mercantile transactions and altered their commercial ways, early modern narratives of subjectivity constantly portrayed the corrigibility of selves who ceaselessly renegotiated relationships. Stories in early modern novels are full of misunderstandings, misjudgements, clarifications, reconciliation—between parents and children, between friends, and of course paradigmatically between people in love. In all such acts and incidents they were actually searching for ways of finding their selves, what they truly were.

This kind of recursive and corrective reflexivity required an enormously significant conceptual object, which is a precondition for this kind of living of individual lives, a requirement for all its adventures, misunderstandings, soul-searching, and sorrows. This is called the self—the conceptual representation of the individual's life which the individual could return to in thought and constantly revise. Living this kind of life practically required a conceptual representation of individual life-histories as peculiar stories to which the individual bore a dual relation as actor and narrator. This relation is of course apotheosized in the literary form of the autobiography; and not surprisingly this civilization, practised in reticence about one's own exploits, suddenly burst in the nineteenth century into a veritable cackle of autobiographic voices—of how singular individuals found, lost, regained, regretted, confirmed the lives they had led. The autobiography was ubiquitous. They were written, remarkably, by writers, politicians, civil servants, actors, actresses (a considerably daring feat in the early years), teachers, housewives, even *darogas* (petty police officers).

Under the bewildering variety of individual life-stories was the invariable sense of the pleasure and surprises of individuation—of individuals escaping the rigid destinies of caste society for the astonishing uncertainties of a world being remoulded by colonial power. Even in the oddest circumstances, the autobiography was a celebration of autonomy. Partha Chatterjee has shown how child widows, denied the most important accompaniments of a full life, would, with amazing ingenuity, turn their lives by reflection into triumphs of subjectivity.[10]

---

[10] See Chatterjee 1993. The subject of women's autobiographies has been an astonishingly fertile subject in recent years, with important contributions by Malavika Karlekar, Jasodhara Bagchi, and Tanika Sarkar.

They would very often illustrate another feature of this new conception of the self for recounting their narratives of subjective autonomy. In the literature on autobiography, there is considerable discussion about the creation of this sense of an interior self. First, the privileged place of the self, the site where the self was created, or marked, as it were, was, as Locke famously proposed, the site of individual consciousness; mental states. Second, these mental states, and particularly the consideration of moral dilemmas, was regarded as a process which went on inside the mind. This interiority did not merely mean that what went on in someone's mind could not be seen from the outside. This mental inside was also gradually seen as an expanse universe in itself, distinct and separable from the worldly universe outside, a recourse and a retreat from its tribulations.[11]

This principle, particularly essential in repressive and illiberal early modern Bengal, was the translation of autonomy into interiority. Women were its greatest aesthetic and practical proponents because they were so often the most repressed and disprivileged elements in society; and with astonishing ingenuity, some remarkable individuals among them turned this interiority of the self into the realm of their unconquered autonomy. And the literary form of the autobiography was the realm of their spiritual triumph over a society which still kept them under strict repressive surveillance. This is why the autobiography, the organization of memory around an abstract individual self, was so central to the development of the cultural styles of modern subjectivity. A life contained innumerable and potentially recoverable incidents of varying degrees of significance. The autobiographical form turned this infinite stretch and chaos of a life into a history, in much the same way as histories brought a form and intelligible structure to the infinite stretch of the past of a people. Like history, the autobiography was also subtly, subliminally, and ineradicably political. It sought to privilege one particular narrative of this life over other possible ones, and thus implicitly it made a distinction between simple memory, the recall of incidents of the past by a subject, and its organized form, which edited and structured it explicitly for presentation as a *bildungsroman*.

Another feature of this new subjectivity was that it introduced gradually, through unconscious and subtle ways, sometimes

[11] Taylor 1985 gives a particularly felicitous account of the development of these ideas in the Western tradition.

through the sheer exigencies of translation of English thoughts into unaccustomed Bengali phrases, a new language of possession in the depiction of this subject. Undoubtedly, the basic determinants of this process in Bengal were fundamentally different from those in Europe. It is generally accepted that in European thought and linguistic practice, the attributes of a person, which would have been traditionally considered integral, that is indivisible from him, came to be seen gradually as his properties, i.e. belonging to him. And this term, initially more ambiguous and general, eventually slid towards a firm coincidence of meaning with the idea of possession. As a consequence, the attributes of an individual were seen as his properties, in the sense of being his possessions, making possible the unprecedented alienation of attributes which would have been inconceivable under earlier social and linguistic organization. The strangeness and peculiarity of capitalism lay in the fact that it made possible the alienation not only of properties that were present in an individual, but even his future properties, like his ability to do labour in the future. This in turn made possible a whole range of new productive arrangements of capitalist modernity.

It would be unhistorical to suggest that it was similar large-scale transformation of the Bengali economy under colonial capitalism that altered this language of description of individual attributes. The economic changes brought in by colonial administration were far removed from this kind of thoroughgoing capitalism, which would have required a corresponding transformation of language for the enforcement of labour laws and contracts. Yet, although unforced by such economic changes, there is an unmistakable introduction of the language of subjectivity through primarily cultural and literary means. Asok Sen grasped a fundamentally significant truth about the intelligentsia in colonial Bengal when he argued in the 1970s that it desired the cultural arrangements of capitalism without its basic economic transformative processes.[12] It was a highly cerebral, and naturally highly idealized version of bourgeois subjectivity introduced through literary forms of self-constitution.

Literary subjectivity stressed the peculiarity of each individual life, and of its attributes; but it also required a language in which these

---

[12] See his contribution to the debate about the nature of the 'Bengal renaissance' in Joshi 1979; and Sen 1977.

attributes, and these incidents could be conceptually detachable from the person. This was required if individuals had to reflect on their own lives as narrators, judges, and evaluators; if they had to arrange a relation with events and experiences of their own lives which was both interior, because no else could have the same privileged relation to it, and at the same time external, because they required to have towards their own lives the impartial attitude of the narrator and the judge. The language of possession made all this possible. It was crucial not merely for the success of contracts, but also for autobiographies. Thus this language, which speaks commonsensically, of one's experiences, events of one's life, and one's attributes as one's possessions—not in a way that these could be alienated, but that they could be narrated—was a fundamental precondition for the origin of some types of modern literary forms. We do not sense the utter peculiarity and newness of these linguistic conventions, because we have been so used, in the last hundred years, if not to the experience of living in a capitalist society, at least to the conventions of describing ourselves as neutral attributeless selves to whom attributes are added later on.[13]

There was another aspect of this conception of subjectivity which was significant for literature. This self is considered a kind of interior space, but not a narrow space in which only the physical or other attributes of the individual were kept tightly together. Its attributes were also psychological. One of its fundamental capacities was to have mental states, reflect on them, evaluate them, vary them, return to them in memory and moral judgement. The mentalist features of the modern self invested this interiority with a new quality. This self contains many marks of creative ambiguity. From the outside it might look like a point, existing with other such points of subjectivity in the wide social world; but it contains precisely because of those qualities of the individual consciousness an internal immensity unheard of in earlier cultures. This self is conceived as a whole new universe added to the external universe outside, but infinite in its psychological slates and thus equally intractable to adequate description. Just as it was natural science which could give us adequate intimations of what the

---

[13] The most well-known discussion of this process of minimalization of the self into an abstract attributeless point is Sandel 1974.

outer world was like, the interior world required a new language of literature to be described with any adequacy. Selves thus stretch in the form of life histories—stretching from either birth as a point of origin or some other elected time as a point of origin of consciousness, with the time given to it stretching undetermined in front, with a space-like quality to this virgin time which was to be filled with appropriate events. Explorations of this inner universe of the self occurred in two different literary modes. Novels described and interpreted events and gave their fulness an aesthetically intelligible form. Poetry was the form which specialized in exploring its complexities not through the tangibility of incidents but by depicting states of emotion.

These changes happened in a period of about fifty years in modern Bengali literature, and in these changes Rabindranath's art played a decisive role. He created the language of this new poetry, expressing with greater success and complexity this self-directed poetic emotion. He also fashioned a language adequate for the mundaneness, complexity, and psychological subtleties of the modern novel.[14] It goes without saying that he also created a new language of poetry, so palpably modern in its diction, tone, tropes, and images that it encountered intense resistance and ridicule from traditionalists when it first emerged and was looking for its own distinctive poetic accent. Inevitably, Tagore's poetry involved an obligatory exploration of this self. But the novelty of his exploration does not end there. It is not merely the subject of the self which is entirely new, but also what he eventually puts inside that subject, the way he eventually defines it in his poetic art. In reading Tagore I am surprised by the turn that this exploration of the self takes after a time, making his resolution of the problem of self quite distinctive, and very different from the standard norms of bourgeois subjectivism.

Tagore did not merely present this new object of poetic aesthetics

[14] Although Bankim undoubtedly created an aesthetic of modernity, his attention was drawn almost exclusively to large, political, in a sense public questions, like history and colonialism. Bankim had little time for this kind of exploration of subjectivity. His novels consequently have more of the aesthetic and narrative structure of drama, rather than the descriptive fulness of the distinctively modern bourgeois novel form. In that sense Tagore is really the maker of the modern novel in Bengal.

in Bengali literature; in the course of presenting it, he had to fashion
a new language which could be an adequate vehicle for its expression.
He did so not by inventing new words, but by displacing through
imaginatively unconventional deployment the meanings of older ones.
Not surprisingly, the world at the centre of this invention of a new
vocabulary was the word *ami*, the Bengali term for 'I'.

But the fact that Bengali had this term did not indicate that it
had any previous conceptual tradition of self-making in the modern
sense. All languages have grammatical forms of self-reference,
arrangements that allow speaking about the speaker. But the idea of
this 'I' is not philosophically equivalent to the modern conception
of the self. I think it is indicative of something significant that any
translation of the term 'self', as a free-standing noun (i.e. not as an
adjectival prefix, like *atma-jivani, atma-katha, atma-jignasa*, etc.), is
still plagued by an acute linguistic awkwardness.[15] My hypothesis is
that the word *ami* earlier referred to the grammatical 'I' which did not
have an association of a vast an explorable interiority which poetry
and novelistic prose could illuminate. Gradually, in Tagore's hands,
it shifts and complicates its meaning, and comes to mean the self, or
the philosophic-psychological 'I'.

But I wish to make a further point as well. Although, undeniably,
the question of the self in this form arises through a contact with
modern subjectivist literature from the West, his poetic sensibility
moves away from Western individualistic solutions. What he takes
from the West is essentially the technique of drawing an outline
of the concept, what he places inside that to give it content comes
from an intelligent and constantly searching reading of indigenous
traditions which spoke of the self in different religious and theological
contexts. These indigenous sources were primarily, for Tagore's poetic
biography, the Upanishads; the aesthetic of restrained tragedy (or
tragic moderation) he found in Buddhism—which sees in death
and suffering an aspect of the meaningfulness of life (and death as

[15] For instance, I have considerable trouble thinking of a Bengali version of
the title of this essay: 'Tagore and the Self'. I have to get round it by making
it self-questioning or self-making, *atma-rachana* or *atma-praniti*, but that
precisely is to be avoided. Pradyumna Bhattacharyya suggests *atma*, literally
self, but it looks unfinished, bare, and unnatural, waiting uneasily for a suffix.
Pradyumna Bhattacharya, personal communication.

suffering in its ineffable, inexpressible form); and Bengali traditions of syncretistic religiosity, especially the songs of *bauls*. I shall try to show the outline of this question and the sources of the answer by reading one particular poem. Its title is *ami*, in *Parishesh*, written on 11 February 1931, roughly ten years before Rabindranath's death.

II

This poem is actually one of several called *ami*, which Tagore composed at different points of his prolific poetic life: it is indeterminate between the grammatical and the psychological 'I', between the thin 'I' and the deep self. But although I shall focus on one single poem, it may be useful to present a short genealogy of these poems within Tagore's poetic oeuvre. His poetic evolution shows something interesting about the connection between the search for the language and the search for this object, indeed their inextricability. In a very early poem in 'Sandhyasangit', which by his own later evaluation was before he had found his distinctive poetic voice, already shows the problematic of the self in an inchoate form. It is still not a self which is distinguished from its own living experiences, seen as a being to whom experiences happen, and who therefore possesses it; but it already shows the possibility of this distinction within one's undifferentiated 'I' through the play of memory. The poem is intriguingly titled '*amihara*',[16] which indicates a lost 'I', but also implies underlyingly the presence of a part of this 'I' which is the subject of this loss, a part at least of this 'I' which has done the losing, and can therefore express its sadness at this alienation from its self.

But the loss of the self is arranged by a temporal division. It is an interesting idea, because it suggests that the 'I' is a moment, not the entire stretch of the person's life or experience. When we say 'I' it refers only to the transparent self-consciousness of that particular moment, a kind of existential self-consciousness of immediate being. From the vantage point of this point-like self, it then becomes possible to reflect

---

[16] The title is untranslatable in a straightforward way. It means a subject who has lost himself. But the intriguing and interesting thing is that the modern self is incapable of losing itself in quite this way (*harayechhi amar amire*) except in spells of irrationality or failures of memory.

and deplore the loss of earlier selves. Selfmaking is thus a synthetic activity, it is done by a point-like consciousness of the present, but it can at will distance earlier states of its own life and mind, or assimilate them; it asserts a curious sovereignty of this immediate point-like self in time over the entire material of its own past, which it can use for remembrance. But this is not otherwise mysterious: 'It is the bud of my childhood', it is my innocent self; 'the two of us have travelled after losing our way.' I have thus 'lost my I' (*harayechhi amar amire*); and it is not surprising that 'at times, on evenings my lost companion comes back for a moment into my heart.' This theme of self-interrogation remains with Rabindranath to the end of his life, a constant sense of surprise at the experiences of sorrow that waited for him and the strategies by which he was able to overcome and sublimate them. He expressed this beautifully in one of his songs:

> *apnake ei jana amar phurabe na*
> *sei janar-i sange sange tomay chena.*

I am not concerned here with his process of self-recognition, only with the manner in which he fashioned a natural and conceptual language for this, the resources from indigenous philosophical traditions which he used in this interrogation. He wrote two poems with the title *ami*, both in the later stage of his poetic career, one in *Parishesh* and the other in *Shyamali*. It was the latter he decided to include in his selection of poems called *Sanchayita*. Both of these poems enter into an explicitly philosophic exploration of the self, but I have a preference for the one in *Parishesh* because while it seems to show most of the basic traits of the modern bourgeois individuality in its question, it tries to provide an answer that is distinctly non-individualistic. This was by no means his last or testamental utterance on the problem of the self. Rabindranath famously returned to the question of 'who am I' in his last poems, in a *Shyamali* poem, and most poignantly in two or three poems immediately before his death, 'Pratham Diner Surya' or 'Rupnaraner Kule'. But I think in his reflection on the poetic self the poem from *Parishesh* is particularly important, because it gives us some clues to the sources of which he constructed his sense of the self.

III

The poem

I wonder today if I know
Him who speaks in my words,
Who moves in my movement,
Whose art is in my paintings
Whose music rings out in my songs
In pleasure and sorrow and happiness
Day after day in the varied space of my heart.
I thought he was bound to me.
All the laughter and tears of this heart
Have bound him to all my work and my play.
I thought this I was my own.
It will flow down my life to end at my death.
Who do I remember then in inexpressible delight
At the touch and sight of my love,
On the further shore of an unfathomable sea of happiness
Again and again
I had met that I beyond my self?
I know thus
That-I is not imprisoned within the limits of my being.
In the greatness of the heroes of epics,
Losing my self,
I find that-I within me, crossing in a moment (great gulfs of)
Time and space.
I find in the illumined annals of the saints
The acquaintance of that-I which lies hidden behind
Shadows in my mind.
That-I has learnt about itself in the
Words of poets down the ages.
The rain comes down in the horizon
With blue clouds and the dank gusty wind.
I think
This I from one age to another,
In countless forms,
In countless names,
Crosses countless births and deaths
Countless times.

I shall watch this I today within
The endless indivisibility of man
Which takes inside the past and the future (what has
Happened and what has not)
In silence,
This I who exists everywhere.

Aj bhabi mane mane tahare ki jani
jahar balay mor bani
jahar chalay mor chala
amar chhobite jar kala
jar sur beje othe mor gane gane
sukhe dukkhe dine dine bichitra je amar parane
bhebechhinu amate se bandha
e praner jata hasa kanda
gandi diye mor majlle
ghirechhe thare mor sakal khelay sab kaje
bhebechhinu se amari ami
amor janama beye amar marane jabe thami
tabe kena mane pade nibid harashe
preyashir darashe parashe
bare bare peyechhinu tare
atal madhuri-sindhu-tire amar atita se amire.
je ami chhayar abarane
lupta haye thake mor mane
sadhaker itihase tari jyotirmay
pai parichay
Jani tai se ami to bandi nahe amar simay
juge juge kabir banite
sei ami apanare perechhe janite
digante badal-bayu-bege
nil meghe
barsha ase nabi
base base bhabi
ei ami kata murti dhare
kata janma kata mrityu kare parapar
kata barambar
bhut bhabishyat laye je birat akhanda biraje
se manab-majhe
ebar dekhiba ami se-amire
sarvatragamire.

There is, I believe, a clear architecture in the poem. It is structured in the form of a question, and an answer, or at least an attempt at one, both of which are quite explicitly philosophical, their philosophic sources or roots, i.e. where the question and the answer come from, are also quite evident. The poem sets up the question of the self, in the first stanza, to a first suggested individualist answer to it (second stanza); shows why that is not satisfying, and offers the outlines of a non-indivdualistic solution (the last stanza). Consider the first stanza: *aj bhabi mane mane tahare ki jani* . . . The question itself is obviously unprecedented in literary terms. Traditional people could have wondered about the difficulties of knowing others, but not knowing one's self. And this has firm foundations in the social world in which they lived. If one person's life experience is mirrored by those of others, particularly in the absence of a psychologizing notion of the self, the certainty, familiarity, repetitiveness of experience does not require a questioning.

By contrast, two features of modern existence constantly give rise to questions about the coherence of a self. First, the twists and turns of careers which can throw individuals into new and unfamiliar situations and contexts, disrupt the continuity of their lives, and raise the question of what they are making of the life given to them. (It seems Ramakrishna was adept at turning the minds of his followers constantly towards this threat of inconstancy.) Second, with the acceptance of an idea of a psychological self, a mind which is sufficiently detached from its own experiences to be able to reflect on and criticize them. It is in fact increasingly seen as an intellectual responsibility of this self to reflect critically about the life story that is unfolding before it. It also turns its own psychological states, additionally, as an object of its reflection. This is what turns the self, the 'I', the person who is closest to oneself, into a problem. The unproblematic quality of the pronoun as it was seen traditionally is thus fractured, and replaced by something that is less homogeneous, and containing a multiplicity of relations inside itself, between itself as the subject of experience and the narrator, between the narrator and critic, between present and past selves. The direction of the solidly integral 'I' which is required for even asking this question is wholly new, and to do this the literary language of Bengali is hardly equipped or practised. Tagore has to make words do unaccustomed things; but the added difficulty is that within this poetic diction he does not have time or circumstance to offer a philosophical introduction to this novel use of bits of language. It has to be done while using the language itself. Poetry does not have the luxury of an interruption, a reconstruction of the necessary language before it is put to use. In poetry, language has to be used and its use altered at the same time.

We find both a connection and a disjunction between this and the earlier poem, 'Amihara'. The early poem plays the later self against the earlier in a temporal sense, using the infinite divisibility of the life of the subject, and asserting in a sense the representational immediacy of the point-like temporal present, the transparency and the presence of consciousness to itself. In that sense 'Amihara' is not a poem which is experimenting with a radically new language of the self. It is simply using a narrower definition of the self, the immediate, present sense of the 'I', and differentiating from similar immediate self-perceptions of earlier times; the access of the self to itself is not in doubt or unclear, or complicated. It is simply that it is the focus of an accumulation of experiences, and the self, because of its finitude, is condemned to live in a kind of permanent present. It loses its earlier presents. Its only way of setting up a relation with those moments is through memory, which is not a presence but a loss.

In the poem in *Parishesh* the self that is disengaged and conceptually posited against the flow of experience is clearly more philosophical, not one temporal segment of a life reflecting on its relation with another, and deploring its subtle, inner decline. Here, by contrast, it is a properly reflexive self; that is, the self that must be distinguished and posited as distinct if the self of 'amihara' has to bring its own temporal presence under reflection. The problematic thing is not about the past, but the present, not what the self has lost but what it is. This clearly shows the reflexive self of the distinctly modern subjectivity, distinguishable from the experiences of the individual's life, which, as it were, looks on them, and reflects on their meaning. It is the presence of this self which makes experiences capable of recall and representational organization. It is indeed the self which is the essential writer of autobiographies, distinct from the person whose life is reported on.

The proper topic of reflection for this 'I' is the swathe of experiences of its own life; but that requires this awkward and linguistically unprecedented disjunction. It is interesting how resolutely Tagore stays within the terms of the Bengali vocabulary and syntax, how he avoids recourse to the Sanskritic terms *atma* (self). Michael Madhusudan had before him immortalized a particular autobiographical use of this term by writing his poem 'Atmabilap'. The Tagore poem stays obstinately within the vocabulary of Bengali, avoiding the temptation offered by the Sanskrit *atma*, so that the term *ami* is obviously directed. To indicate both the person who speaks, and what he speaks about, the poem has to use the pronoun *ami*; but the necessity and pressure of this distinction forces it to prefix it as this-I and that-I (*ei-ami/sei-ami*). The use of the third person pronoun creates not merely a sense of discreteness between the two, but also a strange effect of distanciation, in the strict sense an objectification of the subject; and the deliberate awkwardness of language reflects the philosophical awkwardness of putting the same person on two sides of the cognitive equation. And the very first sentence shows the difficulty of this peculiar effort at knowing, which ought to be the easiest of all to know (*aj bhabi mane mane tahare ki jani*).

There are two further moves in the poem. The first is to suggest an individualist answer to the question of the site and limits of the self. But the locutions of the stanza itself makes it clear that this is inadequate. However, the manner in which the phrase 'I thought' is used suggests to me that there is perhaps a more complex hint in it towards both its unsatisfactoriness and plausibility. It is clear from the decisiveness of the phrase '*bhebechhinu*' that it is a way of thinking that the poet has put behind him; at the same time, there is a subtle hint that there was nothing surprising about thinking like that. It suggests a rise in stages of self-cognition, as if the individualist conception of the self is a natural stage in this understanding, but one that would be eventually transcended. The second stanza of the poem displays all the characteristic features of an individualist self-perception. This self has a finite, bounded site of existence; it is anchored and bounded inside his life, a combination of the themes of fulness of experience and boundedness within its determinate events. A life is determinate, with a clear boundary; it is made of precisely those experiences and no other; and that is the entirely privileged private material on which an individual's memory plays. The singularity of individual lives is marked by what it contains inside itself, and how its boundaries are marked by the two uninfringeable, ineffable points of origin and end, birth and death. It is this that turns the necessary raggedness and unnarratable infinity of actual lives into the bounded intelligibility of a life-history.

Most interestingly, in its unobtrusive and understated way, which makes it almost likeably lyrical, it also employs the language of possession—*bhebechhinu se amari ami*, this I, I thought was my own, which in Bengali has an ineradicable sense of the phrase 'I thought I owned it.' It is important to recognize the plausibility of this thesis. The entire educational training of the middle-class Bengali disposed him towards this individualist solution to the problem of his individual identity. Also, the background assumptions of literary practice, of the writing of novels, of lyric poetry, reinforced this definition. Most significantly of all, the entire thrust of modernist discourse went against traditional philosophic thought which seemed to posit metaphysical concepts like brahman, god, or all-pervading consciousness, all fatally undermined by the triumphant march of scientific rationalization. People were obliged, in this disenchanted world, to accept their finite, delimited, individual selves. It is this solution that Tagore finds troubling and seeks to transcend; the rest of the poem is devoted to this task.

As the poem moves on, this individualist subjectivity is slowly questioned and shown to be inadequate; but characteristically, Tagore avoids direct polemics and the superseding of this individual sense of the self is done through the characteristic gentleness of interrogative sentences.[17] And the reflection on the self moves through three levels of mediation. The features of the concept of the self slowly abandoned/ undermined are its boundedness,[18] its definitive enclosure into the inside of the individual,[19] and its relation of possession to the subject.[20] In a strange manner, I think it reflects the movement of literary themes in Tagore's own poetic life. It discovers that the creation of one's own

[17] *Tabe kena mane pade nibid harashe preyasir darashe parashe bare bare peyechhinu tare, etc.*

[18] *Bhebechhinu amate se bandha ... gandi diye mor majhe bendhechhe tahare mor sakal khelay sab kaje*—these are all verbs of binding and boundedness.

[19] *Gandi diye mor majhe.*

[20] *Bhebechhinu se amari ami.*

self is something like a discovery, even the startling discovery of one's own emotions, in their astonishing and startling range and depth, which depends on another through romantic love.

Later, his poetry advances from *Gitanjali* onwards to an appreciation of much subtler, much longer, deeper relations with 'others' in history and memory and culture. Tagore's poetry from *Kadi-o-Komal* onwards, as he himself recognized, emphasized that some of our deepest inner experiences involve the existence and mediation of the other, the duality of romantic love. In this again there is an interesting play of indigenous and Western themes. While the emphasis is on the choosing self, the individual who is in a sense a victim of his own caprice of love, he/she has no control over whom she falls in love with because there is a strange magic net of love stretched across the world (*amra jalasthale kata chhale mayajala pati*). A result of modern notions of individuality, this can quickly intermingle with familiar themes of theological doctrine of self-knowledge through one's other. In the Gaudiya Vaishnava tradition, to take only a proximate example, Krishna famously created Radha because, according to the *Chaitanyacharitamrita*, he wished to understand his own self, and 'taste' it.[21] True, the self is an interior reality, and it is full of precious, significant, inexpressible moments of poignancy of experience. It can reflect on these aesthetically and philosophically; but those experiences, although they in a sense reside deep within us, could be possible only in a relationship with someone else. Krishna can reflect and refine his understanding of what his self is; but this knowledge is not self-standing; it is utterly dependent on the consciousness of Radha, and the essential mediation of their relation.

In personal relationships, similarly, for Tagore, the individual comes to realize and understand his self even in terms of his emotions, because these emotions cannot arise in him unaided. They arise only through an emotional intentionality, through their directedness towards someone else we love. It is true that through these emotions and the relationships we come to understand our own selves better, but at the same time we are utterly dependent on that mediation. This is also why we are never complete; our lives are constantly open towards more experiences. Interiority therefore does not negate relations

---

[21] *Svado kidrsho va madiya*, etc. Kaviraja 1995: sloka 6, 1.

with others; its boundedness, its apodectic certainty about itself, if construed in a hermetic way, is entirely misleading. These experiences happen to the individual and are preserved in his consciousness; yet these are not intrinsic, but relational. In other poems, which I do not wish to bring in too fully into this discussion, Tagore also suggests the inevitable textuality of our own relation to our experiences. These experiences of love, even the experience of sight, are given to us not by the physical eye, but with the assistance of images which are sedimented in our consciousness through texts. The way I see a woman is therefore textual. Those texts, invisible but real, lie in the charged distance between her and me.

These experiences, as all readers of Indian poetry know, are sources of pleasure that are limitless, because the mind can return to them always in memory. Much of romantic or erotic poetry in classical Sanskrit is devoted to the ambiguity of a remembrance, the returns in memory, their strange mixture of reality and illusion.[22] What gives firmness of form to individual lives is the organization of memory—because this inner self constitutes the present out of elements which are drawn from both its temporal supplements, by the mind reviving the events of the past and reflecting on the possibilities of the future, both aspects of this inner self. But memory again is an entirely private individual affair, although it is deeply personal and irreducibly interior. We do not have a wholly private language of our memory, or a repertory of images. The private memory and fantasies of individual selves requires a language-like template of collective memory out of which our self-interpretative moves are created. Like individual memory, it does not present all the events of history at the

---

[22] One of the permanent favourites from classical Sanskrit poetry would be

Kalidasa's lines in *Abhijnanasakuntalam*:
ramyani biksya madhuransca nisamya sabdan
paryutsuke bhabati tatsukhitohpi jantuh
taccetasa smarati munamabodhapurvam
bhavasthirani jananatarasauhridani.

But a more poignant one, again a favourite from Chaitanya onwards, is from Mammata's *Kavyamimamsa* attributed to Silabhattarika:
yah kaumaraharah sa eva hi barah sa eva caitraksapa . . .

same time, but only those elements which illumine the particular moments that need recall and interpretation. This interior self is thus a text, an object of reading;[23] and it is appropriate that Tagore will seek implements by which his self can be 'read' in this sense.

The final move of reading the self is the oddest of all. One central principle of the individualist construction of modern subjectivity is its 'this-worldliness'. This-worldliness does not merely rule out confusingly mystical ideas about extensions of the self through rebirths, etc., it also centres on a strong connection between this-worldliness and hedonism. One of the primary capacities of this individual subject is his ability to take pleasure from the world, the self's ability to extract enjoyment from life.[24] Inevitably, the autobiographic account becomes

[23] Although it cannot be stated at all fully in a footnote, I wish to suggest that we should take the verb 'reading' here in a rather imaginatively expanded sense—to mean all the things we do with the texts, not just a passive relationship with its marks. I suggest elsewhere that in the Indian tradition of living with texts, a great number of paratextual activities are allowed which are not merely receptive.

[24] This idea of this-worldliness was a constant terrain of conflict between Indian writers of the nineteenth century and their image of Western thought. In their view, Western thought was homogenized around a core of materialist, eudaimonist ideas. Individual thinkers saw different implications of this persistent hedonism of Western civilization and sought to reject its claims in various ways. A very common move was to concede the material superiority of the West but claim a compensating spiritualist eminence for Indian civilization. Bhudev Mukhopadhyay, Tagore's senior by two decades and one the most theoretically perceptive Bengali intellectuals, connected the militarist character of Western modernity with its insatiable appetite for material goods and pleasures. He also thought that this increased internal conflicts between classes, as much as external conflict between states. Gandhi's critique of Western modernity, several decades after him, closely resembled Bhudev's arguments. Tagore followed a somewhat different route. He accepts the idea of this-worldliness, the idea that there is no otherworldly supplement to the life lived on earth, nothing that can dilute or complement its finality. Yet he constantly played on some of the metaphysical ideas of Hinduism to give them an aesthetic meaningfulness. He also emphasizes the significance of an ability to take pleasure from life, but turns it in a direction of a Buddhist ethic rather than the materialistic, hedonist interpretation of this idea in modern Western thinking.

a recounting of these joyous moments around which the contours of a life are built. The temporal boundedness of this self and its this-worldliness therefore make this notion of the self strongly opposed to ideas of afterlife or *janmantar*—a succession of births through which human beings find fulfilment of their existence, which is a notion that suffused Indian traditional thought, common to both the Hindu and the Buddhist traditions. Tagore evinced a deep suspicion of some of the central metaphysical ideas of Brahminical Hinduism, and *janmantar*, with its association with the justification of caste-practices through deserts of an earlier, invisible life, is particularly repugnant to the Brahmo consciousness. But as his thought on these questions evolves, it develops a strange capacity to transcend the parochial conflicts between Brahmos and Hindus. Tagore seeks to construct his own individual model of an Indian tradition, which is typically modern, and extremely eclectic between its various constitutents. The move in this direction is clearly indicated in the long but subtle and fascinating polemics in the pages of *Gora*. Both Gora and Panubabu are seen as dogmatic and narrow-minded, in which Gora's depiction is not surprising, but from a Brahmo intellectual the depiction of Haran as a bigot, little better than orthodox, caste-ridden, Brahminical Hindus is a startling departure. Some narrative episodes in *Gora* also suggest that Tagore was bothered by the Brahmos' eagerness to stress the similarities between their religion and Christianity. The more Tagore constructs an eclectic Indian tradition, the more he renders the local disputes between Hindus and reformers redundant. He therefore turns away from the Brahmo reading of Hindu metaphysics in purely theological terms. Accordingly, in his mature work there is an immensely expansive, inexhaustible playfulness about that idea of *janmantar*—of the after-life. In reading the concept in its theological literality, as Brahmo polemicists tended to do, he saw the waste of an aesthetically suggestive idea. Thus he engages in this poem in something which can be seen as a strong and repetitive tendency in his works, a re-translation of Hindu theological ideas into an aesthetic register, giving it a complex and quasi-historical significance.

His poetry is full of the themes of an elusive return, which is sometimes just an intense longing and confirmation of his experiences in life, sometimes a play on memory. At times this is simply a wish that confirms the idea of this-worldliness:

Email Boarding Pass (Web Check-in)

E

As a courtesy to fellow passengers please place your carry-on items in the overhead bin above your own seat.

SPECIAL SERVICES

NIL

Name :

MR DR PURNENDU CHATTERJEE

Name	**MR DR PURNENDU CHATTERJEE**	
From	Mumbai → To	Kolkata
Flight No.	6E 395	
Boarding Time	16:15 PM	**Date** 17 Dec 15
Sequence No.	48	**Departure Time** 17:00 PM
Gate No.		**Class** K **Seat No.** 3D

PNR : **CBVNPA**

Flt No. : **6E 395**

Seat No. : **3D**

Seq No. : **48**

C.S.I. Airport Mumbai
7 DEC 2023
SECURITY CHE

Boarding gate closes 25 minutes prior to the departure time. Boarding gate numbers are subject to change, please check flight information screen for latest updates. Checking of hand baggage is a mandatory procedure. Passengers are requested to co-operate with IndiGo and the relevant authorities. Have a pleasant flight.

abar jadi iccha kara abar asi phire.[25]

But it is clearly marked in this wish itself that this is not materially or theologically possible. It is a theological idea displaced into a wonderful aesthetic meaningfulness. Or take another poem of this strange return: *Chira-Ami*, which says despite his not being there after he takes his leave,

> *takhan ke bale go sei prabhate nei ami*
> *sakal khelay karbe khela ei-ami*
> *natun name dakbe more bandhbe natun bahur dore*
> *asba jaba chiradiner sei-ami*
> *takhan amay nai ba mane rakhle.*[26]

Translation

Who can say I shall not be there in that dawn?
I shall be a part of all its play
I will be called by a new name, bound in the embraced of new arms
The same me—the me of all times—will come and go
Would not matter if I am no longer in your memory.

But the fact that he is not remembered does not matter any more, because he will be present in his absence, in the continuing life of others. Yet the most interesting feature of all this is a resolute refusal to slip into metaphysical or mystical vagueness. The continuity of life is interpreted in an almost material fashion, through the presence of a person in others' memories, his ability to affect others' experiences even beyond his death.

> *Aji naba basanter prabhater anander leshamatra bhag*
> *ajikar kono sur bihanger kono gan ajikar ei raktarag*
> *anurage shikta kari pari jadi pathaite tomader kare*
> *aji hate shatabarsha pare.*[27]

Translation

If I could send to you even the tiniest part of the joy of this dawn,
Any tune of today, any of its birdsongs, this [sky's] red glow

[25] *Gitabitan* in Tagore 1972.
[26] Ibid.: 728.
[27] Ibid.: 268.

If I could drench them in my affection and send them to your hands
A hundred years from now.

This is an emphatic assertion of the continuity of life after death.
Yet it is done through a completely credible play of memory. The
aesthetic translation or the idea of *janmantar* also figures in this poem
and results in undermining or transcending all central markers of the
individualist construction of the self—the bounded time in which the
life is lived, the name which gives it an indelible mark of singularity,
the limits of death as a final horizon. Even in entirely material terms,
a life cannot be said to have ceased if its consequences are still active
in the world. If he is able to present the resonances and the colours of
an evening sunset to readers after a hundred years,[28] his poetry, such a
central part of himself, certainly has not ceased to exist. Dying is not
thus ceasing to exist; and birth signifies only in a shallow, superficial,
uncomplicated sense, an origin of one's consciousness. What is
gratifying to historians is the fact that what he invokes most effectively
against atomic individualism is no metaphysical mystical idea of the
interconnectedness of individual to universal life through brahman,
etc., but an essential principle of historicity of selves.

III

The poem seems to me to have a fundamental central idea. The
first stanza enunciated a question; the second offered it the standard
individualist answer. The third puts it into question and goes on to
provide three examples, which have one thing in common. They all
show that the deepest experiences of the self, which mark the self as
what it is, which provides the reflexive capacities of the self with the
experiential material on which it reflects and to which it returns in
memory, are not created by its own self-enclosed activity. These, which
are the most intimate personal markers and constituents of the self, are
all produced by its mediation with others. The mediation first invoked
is that of love, in which the most inner and precious feelings of this
self are generated by the presence of the lover. In a way, this also calls
in question the idea of the other being distant rather than near. This

[28] 'Aji Hate Shatabarsha Pare', ibid.: 268.

shows that in some cases there is an 'other' who is also the nearest to the self, so agonizingly close as almost to be its part. Tagore's language also shows something more interesting: the most intense contact with our being, our selves, is not casually achieved; these do not have a self-evident presence like our body. We come to touch and capture it at rare moments—*bare bare peyecchinu tare*, I received that touch of my self at times. It is not securely and physically given, this intense sense of the self has to be achieved. And what is rarely achieved thus has the most astonishingly awkward and astonishingly beautiful locution *amar atita se-amire*, the 'I which is beyond this I.' There is a symmetrical paradox in the manner of getting to this larger self. To get one aspect of that self, in the glories of the great heroes of the myths, the small, enclosed, bounded self has to lose itself to get its larger form: *apana haraye, tare pai apanate deshkal nimeshe paraye*, which makes a clear play on the two verbs of losing and finding (*paoa and harano*). To find that larger, fuller, more fulfilling self, the narrower self, which imprisons an individual within his life, has to be lost.

There is a most interesting aspect to the third moment in the poem which affirms a non-atomistic conception of the self in the last stanza. It recovers a whole range of locutions from the language of transmigration of souls, but these are now divested of their metaphysical grounding in a karmic theory of responsibility and moral causality of fates. The new sense of the self can transcend the enclosing of time, it can move across ages (*juge jugantare*), it can reincarnate itself (*kata murti dhare*), it can go beyond deaths and lives (*kata janma kata mrityu kare parapar*). It can do all that not because there is an immortal unliberated soul which is caught endlessly in the ineradicable imperfectness of our living a human life. It does so because it recognizes two fundamental things about its self: its most intimate experiences are created in transaction with others; and the language through which he can relate to the world outside and the universe within himself is a gift of his language. But this language is what it is because it is also the language of others, including others in time, and contains a memory that is not individual but cultural. It can thus find its place in a great seamless continuity of historical being (*bhut bahbishyat laye je birat akhanda biraje*). It can go anywhere. Thus the two attributes of the almighty—being *antaryami* and being *sarvatragami*—are now transposed to this human self.

A most interesting feature of this self-exploration is that it accepts and acknowledges a final disenchantment of the world. It recognizes that for a modern consciousness the path of return to the metaphysical beliefs of traditional Hinduism is closed But that does not mean that there is a fully articulated alternative system of beliefs with its ready rationalistic language into which he can transport himself. Tagore's thought reduces the metaphysical ideas but translates them into a historicist and aesthetic register, and finds reasons for believing in them without shame or defensiveness. *Janmantar*, the great central concept of Hindu metaphysics, turns into a metaphor of memory, and asserts a position very similar in some respect to German historicism. He does not abandon his language—either in the sense of the natural language, or the conceptual one. He does not reject Bengali, with its inextricable Sanskritic memory, as inadequate for a modern sensibility, and begin to live in English. Nor does he abandon ideas like *janmantar* as being disreputable relics of superstition. He improvises a displacement of their meanings and turns them meaningful again by a translation that is historicist and aesthetic.

This also serves another important purpose, quite central to the Indian nationalist discourse about modernity. It does not accept a world in which the search for meaning has become meaningless and undermined. It argues that the world must be re-enchanted by poetry. It acknowledges that there is no way back into the language of tradition. That does not force it to simply plagiarize the West and reproduce a lisping imitation of Western languages, but to improvise an idiom of its own peculiar sense of the modern. Tagore, like most of what is modern in India, cannot be understood without the language that comes from the West as much as the language that comes from his past.[29]

If we turn the reflection of this poem into the less delectable language of social theory, it asserts that the inescapable historicity of

---

[29] This is by no means an exhaustive discussion of Tagore's attempts at poetic self-exploration. In his later writings, especially a series of poignant last poems, he returns to this theme of knowing the self, but occasionally with a more radicalized doubt about the question itself. The two last poems, written actually during his last months, 'Rupnaraner Kule' (May 1941) and 'Pratham Diner Surya' (July 1941), take up the same theme, but with a final

existence makes atomistic individualism a false theory of the self. True, we do not have other lives and their memories, as in karmic theory; but our lives, the lives that we live in intense privacy and selfishness, rely on other lives and memories, which are internal and inextricable from them. Our deepest experiences, which both mark and define our selves, happen, or are brought to language, only through the mediation of others, breaking in many interesting ways the bounds of the narrow, bounded 'I'. We live our own lives through others' words and memories; and others' lives and memories, because they are indispensable to our negotiation of the world outside and the universe inside us, continue to exist through our own. To live a fully human life we constantly interpret ourselves, but our conceptual and interpretative means come from a larger memory than our own. Individual lives are therefore in a certain sense unbounded and unconcluded. At least the standard atomist conceptualization and accounting of its happiness and suffering is shown to be unsatisfactory. We discover eventually that the sense of the poem, if its meaning is displaced into the language of social theory, is that the individual subject, despite the uniqueness of his inner life, is not a monadic, windowless unit, but an ensemble of historical relations.

References

Chatterjee, Partha. 1993. *The Nation and Its Fragments*. Princeton: Princeton University Press.

Joshi, V.K., ed. 1979. *Rammohun Roy and Modernisation of Bengal*. New Delhi: Vikas.

Kaviraj, Sudipta. 1992. The Imaginary Institution of India. In Partha Chatterjee and Gyanendra Pandey (eds), *Subaltern Studies VII*. Delhi: Oxford University Press.

Kaviraja, Krishnadas. 1985. *Chaitanyacharitanrta*. Ed. Sukumar Sen. Kolkata: Ananda Publishers.

---

detachment: the rising sun on the first day of life had asked, 'who are you?', without an answer; and the setting sun on the last day of life asked again, 'who are you?', but found none. Does this mean it is impossible to answer the question altogether, or that it is always incomplete and therefore always inadequate and false? Tagore 1972: 832, 833.

Sandel, Michael. 1974. The Procedural Republic and the Unencumbered Self. In *Political Theory*, 12 (1984), 81–96.

Sen, Asok. 1977. *Iswarchandra Vidyasagar and His Elusive Milestones*. Calcutta: Riddhi.

Tagore, Rabindranath. 1910. *Gora*. Kolkata: Visvabharati.

———. 1972. *Sanchayita*. Calcutta: Visvabharati.

Taylor, Charles. 1985. *Sources of the Self*. Cambridge: Cambridge University Press.

7

Laughter and Subjectivity
The Self-Ironical Tradition in Bengali Literature

By the grace of the Almighty an extraordinary species of sentient life has been found on earth in the nineteenth century: they are known as modern Bengalis. After careful analysis zoological experts have found that this species displays the external bodily features of *Homo sapiens*. They have five fingers on their hands and feet; they have no tails; and their bones and cranial structures are indeed similar to the human species. However, as yet there is no comparable unanimity about their inner nature. Some believe that in their inner nature too they are similar to humans; others think that they are only externally human; in their inner nature they are in fact beasts.

Which side do we support in this controversy? We believe in the theory which asserts the bestiality of Bengalis. We learnt this theory from English newspapers. According to some redbearded savants, just as the creator had taken atoms of beauty from all beautiful things to make Tilottama, in exactly the same way, by taking atoms of bestiality from all animals he has created the extraordinary character of the modern Bengali. Slyness from the fox, sycophancy and supplication from the dog, cowardliness from sheep, imitativeness from the ape, and volubility from the ass—by a combination of these qualities He has made the modern Bengali rise in the firmament of history: a presence which illuminates the horizon, the centre of all of India's hopes and future prospects, and the great favourite of the savant Max Mueller.[1]

---

[1] 'Anukaran', Vividha Prabandha, in Chattopadhyay 1968: vol. II, 200-1.

T o be tormented without a clear definition of the self is a distinctly modern affliction. Apparently, human beings lived moderately contented lives for long periods in history with what must appear to us moderns rather perfunctory images of what they were. Presumably, they did not feel such urgent need to form themselves into something they had imagined through reflection, and did not feel anchorless in their existence because they lacked such pretensions. What happens in modern history that makes a picture of the 'self' such an essential part of social and individual being? Do all men living in modernity feel this need? Or only those who are not only accidental inhabitants of modernity but also ideologically modern? Do all those who enter a late modernity, already soiled by its historical pioneers, become selves in the same way and to the same extent as their enlightened European predecessors? Or do subtle deflections occur in this assumption of selfhood?

It is a common claim that modernity imposes on individuals and communities an historical requirement of self-reflection.[2] A lyrical form of this idea would look upon the whole of history as the rise of man to self-consciousness and making his historical existence transparent to himself. The claim appears exaggerated if transparency is meant to imply that in modern times human beings, both as individuals and collectivities, understand what they do, have a clear sense of the intentions which go into the making of events, retain control over the acts which constitute them, know that the consequences obey the purposes, and that if they do not actors can analyse the difference and bring the course of events under control at a subsequent stage. Though it is quite evident that human beings living in modern times achieve nothing resembling such transparency, the idea of selfconsciousness is obviously central to the project of modernity.[3] Thus in a more modest and historical form, the idea of self-consciousness in both its senses—(i) as a gradual reflexive clarification of the nature of the self that already exists, or (ii) the crystallization of an idea of a self which

---

[2] For an illuminating analysis of the connection between modernity and identity, see Taylor 1992; and in a different, more sociological direction, Giddens 1992.

[3] I have dealt with some aspects of this problem, as it affects marxist thinking, in Kaviraj 1992.

did not exist earlier—must be seen as being central to the history of modernity.

Modernity imposes the necessity of historical self-reflection on people undergoing its unfamiliar transformations; and this imperative of self-reflection is unavoidable because what undergoes transformation is the self, the way people *are* what they are. The historical processes of modernity involve the introduction of a sense of choice, in two ways. People can choose to be what they are—Hindus, Muslims, Bengalis—in a new way, and make what they are have new consequences; or they choose to be what they were never before—for example, Indians. I have argued in my work on Bankimchandra Chattopadhyay that different societies arrange this process of self-reflection in varying forms.[4]

In the West the primary form of this kind of historical reflection was social theory, in which various schools took significant phases of history through a kind of slow replay and explained what they thought had happened through these happenings. In India, reflection on modernity came primarily through literature.[5] It was through literary texts that Bengalis came to form historical ideas about what had happened to them through colonial processes, and imagined their collective selves—through various suggestions by literary writers about what was central to their self and what was lacking in it (if of course such an instance of cultural perfection as the modern Bengali could be said to lack anything at all). Literary humour, in particular, discussed how they could acquire what they lacked, and become even more perfect than they were. The Bengali self is thus a deeply historical construct, always unfinished, always under negotiation, formed and unformed at the same time.

The literary search for the self turns out to be a dual process, seeking the self at two levels: the individual self, and a more collective identity shared by all—at least all educated—Bengalis. Curiously, contrary to plausibly individualist theories of society, the individual selves are not first discovered and then put together in a collective, social self.[6] Probably the pressures of living under colonialism, endowed

---

[4] In Kaviraj 1995.

[5] For an excellent discussion on the historical course of such self-reflection, see Chatterjee 1986.

[6] There is clear evidence of a search for a collective self, which would qualify

with a new sensibility which taught them to value autonomy, made it inevitable that the search for the collective self would occur first. It is somewhat later, with the coming of Tagore's introspective literary sensibility, that they discover that the inner life of the individual, despite his apparent inconsequentiality, is also a universe, and that its enormous and unending mysteries can be explored through the psychological novel and lyrical poetry.[7]

I wish to suggest that in this historical construction of the Bengali self a tradition of literary self-irony played an irreplaceable part.[8] For this irony provided a centre to two types of significant historical processes—the large, visible, spectacular actions through which people sought to reconstruct their political world; and equally, the almost invisible readjustments of behaviour in the everyday—the inescapable world of etiquette, civility, conversation, those unspectacular events which nevertheless fill up most of individual and social lives.

Laughter before Bankim's *Kamalakanta*

Irony was by no means new in Bengali literature. Literary humour came from several sources: classical, folk, and the peculiarly derisive wit that the fragile prosperity of colonial Calcutta gave rise to—the humour of a people who were themselves somewhat bemused at their own historical good fortune, a subtle anxiety about the rapidity with which they were elevated, by their association with British rule, to

---

to be called by the English word 'nation', in the works of Bankimchandra Chattopadhyay; but the fashioning of a language for the interiority of the individual self had to wait till the maturer works of Rabindranath Tagore. I have tried to analyse the shaping of this language in Tagore in Kaviraj 1994 (reproduced in the present volume).

[7] It is thus not surprising that Tagore returned repeatedly to write poems on '*ami*' (I/Me), and his late poetry is full of reflection on the ambiguity, inconclusiveness, and unboundability of his personal self. Many of his celebrated novels and stories do of course explore the nature of the individual self and the mysteries of self-consciousness: e.g. *Gora, Ghare Baire, Jogajog, Strir Patra.*

[8] I have stated this argument more fully in Kaviraj 1990, and Kaviraj 1995: ch 2.

positions of evidently undeserved eminence.[9] This produced a genre of local town humour which consisted not only in lower classes satirizing the more fortunate, but also the babu bantering his own breed,[10] a trend luxuriating in witty, often somewhat smutty songs. Colonial opportunity for self-advancement created inexplicable cases of rise to fortune which attracted acerbic comment.

Modern Bengali literature did not start laughingly. The language awkwardly drawn out of the integuments of Sanskrit by Ram Mohan Roy (1772/4–1833) and Iswarchandra Vidyasagar (1820–91) was sombrely serious. In Ram Mohan, it had the function of disputing theological and philosophic abstractions with missionaries and Hindu conservatives, and had little occasion to laugh, least of all at itself. In Vidyasagar, the new, highly formal Bengali language was slowly extended towards literary texts. Its extension was deeply paradoxical: it was difficult to make out if it was trying to differentiate itself from Sanskrit or merge back into its enormous grandeur. Vidyasagar had little literary imagination, only an urge to devise a language of great art for Bengali culture. This resulted in an ironic originality. He never invented a story worth the name; indeed, the textbook he devised for Bengali children,[11] which assumed essentially that to be good at Bengali one must be good at Sanskrit, was a massive example of a dramatically limited imagination. His attempt was to show that Bengali could be a high literary language, not because wonderful stories could be dreamed in its medium, but because well-known and well-loved classical tales could be retold in it without diluting the high serious tone of the originals. His Shakuntala and his Sita therefore were somewhat more sombre and mournful than the original heroines of the

---

[9] Apart from literary writing, and probably before that, this corrosive banter against the pretensions of the babu, a political and cultural creature of colonial rule, appeared in popular songs.

[10] A term denoting the middle-class educated elite of colonial Bengali.

[11] *Varnaparichay* (Vidyasagar's primer for children) contrasts particularly with the artistically imaginative treatment in Tagore's *Sahaj Path* (Tagore's primer, which was based on an entirely different pedagogic theory, and emphasized the fact that children must learn to read the world both literally and artistically), though of late this has offended the anachronistic sensibility of leftist cultural commissars.

Sanskrit texts. It would be uncharitable to suggest that Vidyasagar did not appreciate the *rasa* of humour: he did an adaptation of the *Comedy of Errors*.[12] But as Bankim observed in a discussion about Pyarichand Mitra, his narratives were irremediably derivative.[13]

Stories always came from the two high traditions early Bengali literary intellectuals regarded with admiration: either from high Sanskrit or from high English, preferably from Kalidas and Shakespeare.[14] Literary imagination came to be unchained in Madhusudan Dutta (1824–73). For although his narratives were still taken from the high classical tradition of the Hindus, his poetic imagination had the daring to invert their messages, partly no doubt through inspiration from English high-tradition texts.[15] Madhusudan also wrote two short farces, both concerned with Bengali babus, *Buro Shaliker Ghare Ron* (1860) and *Ekei ki Bale Sabhyata* (1860), making fun of the fun-loving parasites of colonial Calcutta and asking, despite the flimsiness of the storyline in the second play, a large and inescapable historical question. For the title of the play raised the central problem of colonial culture: Is this what should be called civilization?

Bankim created a different kind of laughter. It had undoubted connections with earlier strands of humorous literature, but with each of them it instituted a subtle rupture, such that it is misleading to see him as a humorist who continued any one of these traditions. Before his *Kamalakanta* (1875; enlarged 1885), Kaliprasanna Sinha had produced a forceful ironical portrait of Calcutta society in his *Hutom Penchar Naksha* (1862) which declared, in a typical mixture of acknowledgement of responsibility and renunciation, 'I have not used a single idea that is fanciful or untrue in my sketches. It is true

[12] Vidyasagar 1869.

[13] 'Bangala Sahitye Pyarichand Mitra', in Chattopadhyay 1968, ii: 862–3.

[14] A good example of this idea of exalted canons is the topic of Bankimchandra's famous essay in literary criticism, 'Shakuntala, Miranada evam Desdemona'. See Chattopadhyay 1968: vol. II, 204–9.

[15] Madhusudan Dutta's *Meghnadbadh Kavya* (1861) is an excellent example of how creatively writers could exploit the possibilities opened up by the conjunction these two high canons. The narrative is taken from the *Ramayana*, but is read through an inverting interpretation which owes much to *Paradise Lost*.

that some people might discover themselves in its pages, but I need hardly add that these are not themselves. *All that I can say is that I have not aimed at anyone, but observed all.* Indeed, I did not forget to include myself in these sketches.'[16] Apparently, *Kamalakanta* is similar to these writings: the major difference is that although the problematizing of the self is lightheartedly mentioned in Sinha's agenda, it remains unrealized. And the tone of the entire piece is too frivolous to raise serious discussion, beyond acerbic social banter. In Kaliprasanna Sinha's case the phrase 'I have not forgotten to include myself in these sketches' goes beyond the reality. He did not realize the gravity and the tragic taste of turning banter towards the self. Sinha is speaking of an insignificant individual, personal self, which, while included in the collective portrait of the Calcutta babu, must retain a certain distinctiveness from them for his utterance to become philosophically and formally possible.

Yet there is an insubstantiality, an insignificance in this banter when compared with the irony of Bankim's *Kamalakanta*. I suggest that this arises for two different reasons. Bankim's irony is informed by a much deeper and intricate understanding of the public fate of his people, a darkly ironic sense of history achieved through reflection upon the benefits and impositions of Western modernity. Historical reflection on modernity was not an easy intellectual pastime for writers of his time. Bankim's generation was brought up on a narrative of European modernity which, partly mythically, partly justifiably, described it as a process of attaining autonomy and selfdetermination.[17] The economic, social, and political achievements of the modern period were primarily the effects of that miraculous philosophic principle.

This made the offer of modernity implicit in their history deeply paradoxical. Reflection on colonial modernity revealed a tragic dichotomy: either autonomy without modernity or modernity with the acceptance of subjection. It was the section of the Bengali intelligentsia which could not answer this question simply, without contradiction and regret, that had recourse to a self-ironical laughter.

[16] Sinha 1862: Introduction (my emphasis).
[17] For an interesting discussion on Bankimchandra's view of the West, see Raychaudhuri 1990. Partha Chatterjee analyses Bankim from a different angle: Chatterjee 1986.

Those who could make simpler and less tragic choices did not need this form of self-understanding.[18] The sound of this laughter could be heard from Bankim through Tagore's early works down to the most enigmatic product of the Bengali literary enlightenment, Sukumar Ray (1887–1923), the creator of its most admired nonsense verse, a poetry which did not make sense in single sentences or verses but captured some of the most fundamental historical meanings of middle class Bengali mentality when seen as a whole. After his time, this form of self-ironical writing gradually declines, spluttering ineffectually in the works of occasional imitators in later generations.[19] But after the arrival of a leftist sensibility, which was to dominate Bengali intellectualism for nearly half a century and encourage it towards enormous moral simplifications, it disappeared into the untroubled certainties of leftist politics. By becoming entirely serious, one-dimensional, radically self-righteous, Bengali literary reflection slowly lost its taste for the ineradicable contradictoriness of being. Its great tragedies were no longer related to subtle ironies of self-construction or experience, but the winning and losing of municipal and state elections. I shall discuss simply three moments of this tradition, starting briefly with Bankim, followed by two verses from Tagore and Sukumar Ray. In all of them the central figure is of course the babu, the educated middle class Bengali, the image of intellectual perfection.

Bankimchandra's *Kamalakanta*

Bankimchandra showed, in the formal aspects of his writing, a consummate mastery of traditional *alankaric* aesthetics,[20] and a decided preference for the *alankara* of *vyajastuti* or counterfeit praise.[21] This does not, however, make his art traditional in the ordinary sense. Bengali humorous writing had long used *vyajastuti* with great skill.

[18] For example Gandhi.

[19] A good example of poetry which is closely imitative of Sukumar Ray, and marked by both technical similarity and utter philosophic difference, is the enjoyable but altogether less beguiling poetry of Sunirmal Basu.

[20] Most generally, an *alankara* can be termed a literary or stylistic embellishment. But the term also generally means a combination of rhetoric and poetics.

[21] *Vyajastuti* is the technical form of an *alankara* which consists in wordplay producing counterfeit praise, or praise-abuse.

Bharatchandra (*c.* 1712–60), the eighteenth-century poet, chose to use *vyajastuti* to display technical virtuosity in versifying, and more significantly to show that the metric and semantic complexity of Sanskrit rhymes could be emulated in Bengali verse. But Bharatchandra's objects of humour were solidly traditional. One of his most famous poems was to Shiva, a traditional object of such ironical devotion.[22]

In Bankimchandra's time this form was revived with great success by the poet Ishwarchandra Gupta, whose work, in formal terms, sometimes strongly resembled Bharatchandra's.[23] But by the nineteenth century the literary culture had changed fundamentally, and this was reflected in the controversial reception of Gupta's poetry in babu literary society. Ishwar Gupta attempted a daring combination of form and content: he used traditional alankaric techniques to describe with derision the manners of the Calcutta babu, and mixed with these undoubtedly classical resources a taste for bodily humour commonly found in vulgar literature. The literary reception of Gupta's poetry showed an enormous change in taste. His poetry was increasingly condemned as trivial and obscene, unfit for public consumption, and particularly ineligible for inclusion into the canons of literary sensibility of the new Bengali intelligentsia. Literature was meant to induce cultivation and enlightenment, not merely to entertain, and although Gupta's undoubted mastery of technique might be diverting, its vulgarity made it unfit for the new reading public, which incidentally included the newly-educated women. To be sure, the babu still retained a great interest in the prurient and the vulgar, but was increasingly unwilling to admit this taste; as in Victorian England, this taste was supplied by a flourishing underworld of *battala* literature, furtively circulated, widely condemned but surprisingly widely consumed.[24]

[22] In his *Annadamangal*, there are some famous stanzas in which Daksha, Sati's father, denounces Shiva in the presence of his guests. This part is prefaced explicitly by the poet with the lines: *Bharat Shiver ninda kemane barnibe/ nindachchale stuti kari Shankar bujhibe* (How can Bharat write abuse of Shiva? I shall praise in the disguise of abuse: Shankara will understand).

[23] For an excellently well judged criticism of Ishwarchandra Gupta's poetic works, see Bankim's 'Ishwar Gupter Jivancharit o Kavitva', in Chattopadhyay 1968: vol II, 835–60.

[24] Literally, under the Banyan tree; but standing for a genre of disreputable, salacious publications.

The reception of Ishwar Gupta was not a matter of literary success in the case of an individual; it indicated a historic transformation of literary canons and taste. The legitimate objects of laughter in traditional aesthetics were the follies of individuals, or idiosyncrasies, any object or act that could be called, in terms of the *Natyashastra, viparita*—other than what is commonly done.[25] A certain form of *hasa*, of a much subtler kind, was often associated with the erotic, the transience of the pleasures of the flesh and the forgivable follies surrounding it.[26] The Indian literary tradition had always given a central place to the materiality of the erotic.

But the public appearance and enjoyment of eroticism imposed requirements of obliqueness in the presentation of sexuality. The arrival of a Victorian aesthetic put an end to this complex aesthetic of presentation of the erotic. It bifurcated this realm into two wholly different conventions of literary composition. On the one hand it produced a prudishly saintly high-literary style—which made its readers wonder if Bengali heroines were gifted with the powers of immaculate conception—and turned matters of courtship and love into exchanges of philosophical or aesthetic ideas. On the other side, quite an unrestrained traffic of petty vulgarity went on profitably in a sub-literature of obscene tales. Bankim commented directly on the pretentious dishonesty of this divide between public and private enjoyment in one of his humorous sketches in which a babu, returned from the exertions of his office, has a conversation with his wife on the pleasures offered in the Bengali language. Characteristicially, he expresses contempt for serious Bengali fiction but finds vulgar stories enormously diverting. In any case, irony had fallen on bad days. It was a mark of frivolity, unworthy of a serious aesthetic, let alone a vehicle of serious social reflection.

With Bankim's *Kamalakanta* (1885),[27] irony makes a triumphant return; but it returns transformed, as irony about the self, or double irony.[28] It has achieved a new subject, a new reflexivity, and has

[25] Shastri 1956: ch. VI, 312–17.

[26] The best example of this is of course the poetry of Kalidasa.

[27] *Kamalakanter Daptar* (1875) was enlarged in 1885 as *Kamalakanta*.

[28] I have discussed the function of this double irony in Kaviraj 1995: ch. 2.

learnt the more complex and mature pleasures of self-criticism. It asks what the self is, what its historical and aesthetic possibilities, suggesting a distinctly modern anguish because it is only the modern sensibility which knows how to be troubled about the self, at least in this form.

Purely formally, irony makes a transition from the highly mannered and restrictive metric forms of verse to the free seriousness of prose. Earlier, verbal playfulness was associated mainly with verse. Bankim demonstrated that many of the delectations of verse writing could be captured in imaginative prose. But prose could offer other pleasures which verse, at least of the traditional sort, could not. Most significant among these new enjoyments was the attitude of reflection that prose expressed. From being a vehicle of frivolous enjoyment of insignificant objects in the world, and of the exploitation of the infinite resources of punning and *shlesha* on things like the *tapse* fish or babus (who for altogether contingent reasons incurred the hostility of Iswar Gupta),[29] irony came in Bankim to have a serious object, indeed an object beyond which nothing could be more serious for modern consciousness. Instead of discussing trivial things in a world not fixed with a historically serious gaze, it now reflects on three objects not entirely distinct from each other, all implicated with the historical world. These are the self, the collective of which the self is a part, and the civilization of colonial India which formed the theatre in which this darkly comic spectacle of the search for the self unfolds. Irony has achieved a new dignity; from the vehicle of unserious mirth (*upahasa*, *atihasa*) it has now turned into a vehicle of something so serious as to be nearly unsayable. It is hardly surprising that the elaborate taxonomies of traditional *hasa*, of even the great *Natyashastra*, do not have a name for this new laughter.

The obsessive object of the *Kamalakanta* text is the babu: he is what is being written about, and he is also the self who does the writing, as well as the more elusive experiment in escaping from the babu self by and through the act of writing itself. Bankim is trying to teach the Bengali educated person how to write himself out of babuness. He is thus the constant object of Bankim's sparkling humour in all

---

[29] *Shlesha* is an *alankara* that comes closest to irony in the classical Sanskrit repertoire.

its varying moods, from the vicious to the gentle to the forgiving. And the babu is not a new theme brought in for a display of this new humorous form in the *Kamalakanta* texts; indeed, he is Bankim's first love. Two of his earliest pieces discover this abiding object of his sarcasm, the collective self with which Bankim has such a fertile relationship of contradiction. He is undeniably a part of this group, yet he cannot accept he is, leading to his founding the tradition of Bengali self-irony.

The early *Ingrajstotra* (Hymn to the Englishman), with a helpful subtitle, 'translated from the *Mahabharata*', at once establishes both the form and the content of this humour.[30] The *stotra* (a rhymed incantation) form would undergo, via experiments at Bankim's hands, the whole gamut of sentiments from the ridiculous to the sentimentally uplifting. Bankim was to reshape this fundamental form of invocation in the Hindu tradition to startlingly novel purposes. To be a *stotra*, however, a composition must conform to some purely formal properties of style. Incomparability of the deity to whom the *stotra* is offered is conveyed by the mannerisms of descriptive excess. *Stotras* also exhibit an usually circular, repetitive movement, coming back, after each cycle of excessive praise, to the signature phrase describing the essential attributes of the object of worship. In Bankim's early travesties of the *stotra* style there is a certain deliberate debasing of this form which can come only from a shrewd familiarity of its formal precepts, just as a successful cartoonist would generate laughter by exaggerating the credible features of a face. Early parodies like the *Ingrajstotra* are therefore pieces of convex satire which pour sarcasm in several ways: directly on the babu, the reciter whose discourse it encapsulates, indirectly on the Englishman the object of worship, and subtly on the doctrine of excess of the *stotra* form. Stylistically, this immediately applies Bankim's favourite ironic means, the *alankara* of *vyajastuti*; and its content is a double description: of the Englishman, the object, but in terms which throw more light on the character of the subject, a self-description of an ascending or intensifying servility.

> O one who can divine what is going on inside our minds! Whatever I do is meant to win your heart. [Though the Bengali verb *bhulaibar janya* is more double-edged and can mean, equally, to deceive you; so the correct rendering of the meaning of the sentence would be 'to win your heart by

---

[30] Chattopadhyay 1968: vol. II, 9–10.

deception']. I donate to charities because you may call me an altruist. I study so that you may call me learned . . .

If you so wish (or because you wish it) I shall establish dispensaries; for your applause I shall set up schools: according to your demands I shall give subscriptions. I shall do whatever you consider proper. I shall wear boots and trousers; put spectacles on my nose, eat with knife and fork, dine at a table. Please keep me in your favour.

I shall renounce my mother tongue to speak your language; abjure my ancestral religion and adopt the Brahmo faith; instead of writing babu use Mr as a prefix to my name, be pleased with me.

I have given up meals of rice, and taken up eating bread: I do not feel properly fed until I have partaken of some forbidden meat [beef]; I make it a point to take chicken for snacks; therefore, O Englishman, please keep me at your feet.

Please grant me wealth, honour, fame, fulfil all my desires. Appoint me to high office, a raja, maharaja, raybahadur, or a member of the Council. If you cannot grant these, invite me at least to your at homes and dinners; nominate me to a high committee or the senate; make me a justice or an honorary magistrate. Please take notice of my speeches, read my essays, encourage me; then, I would not take heed of the denunciation of the entire Hindu society.

Clearly, there are two levels of meaning in this false hymn. At the first level, there is a caricature of both the collaborating babu and the British who confer honours on him. Characteristically, Bankim goes straight to the heart of the matter, cutting through the pretence. Only in appearance is colonial society a realm where career is open to talent; in fact, the colonial administration does nothing to encourage merit. The Englishman can give anything he likes literally to anyone: the arbitrariness of his conferments is emphasized, which makes the babu's supplicatory self-abasement its entirely proper complement. High honour in colonial Bengal is hardly recognition for desert, public service, or ability, but of competitive servility. Colonialism endows the ordinary British official with mystical powers of nomination: he can name anything into existence; and the essential point is to be so named by the right authority. The English can rename all social and moral descriptions.[31] In all this, the babu's adoption of reform

---

[31] Bankim wrote an immortal satire on this process of the rise of a Bengali to eminence in the colonial world in his *Muchiram Guder Jibancharit* (1880), Chattopadhyay 1968: vol. II, 113–28.

and rationalism is shown for what it is. He is a rationalist out of opportunism, and entirely unclear about how a rationalist argument is to be grounded. He would do all the right things—accept modernity, break tradition, adopt altruism—always for the wrong reason, not because he can show or believe that these are the right course of action but because the British consider them praiseworthy. The babu's adoption of Western rationalism is fundamentally marked and tainted by this heteronomy.

Two types of acts can be behaviourally indistinguishable: but whether it is an act of altruism or servility can be decided only by looking into its rational grounding. The upside down, travestied character of colonial modernity is etched in briefly and powerfully through this supplicatory refrain: 'I shall do everything you ask for', turning the right actions into wrong ones. Acts of apparent subjectivity are really ones of the deepest heteronomy. That is why colonial society is such an appropriate field for sarcastic demystification. Even seemingly highminded action must be probed by this sarcastic mistrust, until the true motives are revealed. It is the unapparent, indistinct intention which can tell an act of kindness from one of imitative servility, verbal posing from genuine intellectual conviction.

This was an early piece from Bankim's satire, and compared to his more mature irony it is somewhat unrefined. Its significance lies more in the fact that it sets a pattern, a structure, and it is curious how little this structure of babuness was to change in Bankim's mind. This is followed by a piece of such sustained satirical excellence that it is doubtful if even Bankim ever surpassed it.[32] Like the hymn, this too is purportedly taken from the *Mahabharata*, turning its claim to all-seeingness, using and travestying it at the same time. Vaishampayana, the sage who recites the *Mahabharata* at Janmejaya's court, is caught in the early part of his performance, and the king, with great curiosity about the historical future, requests him to recite the *guna* (qualities) of those who would be known as babus and adorn the earth in the nineteenth century.

Not in vain were the author and reciter of the epic called *sarvadarshi*, all-seeing. He compresses the historical features of the babu into an

---

[32] *Babu*, in Chattopadhyay 1968: vol. II, 10–12.

unsurpassable portrait. An approximate idea of Vaishampayana's characterization can be found from some of the passages, though translation misses the insistence of the series of adjectives in Bankim's writing:

Babus are invincible in speech, they are proficient in foreign languages and hate their own; indeed, there would appear some babus of such amazing intellect that they would be altogether incapable of conversing in their mother tongue . . . The babus are those who would save without purpose, earn in order to save, study in order to earn, and steal question papers to do well at examinations. Indeed, the word babu would be many-splendoured in its meaning: those who would rule India in the *kali* age and be known as Englishmen would understand by that term a common clerk or superintendent of provisions; to the poor it would mean those wealthier than themselves, to servants their master. I am however celebrating the qualities of some people whose only aim in life would be to spend a fittingly babu existence. If anyone takes it in any other sense his hearing of the *Mahabharata* would be fruitless; in a subsequent birth . . . he would be born as a cow and constitute a part of the babu's dinner Anyone devoid of understanding about poetry, with an execrable musical taste, whose only knowledge is confined to textbooks crammed in childhood, and who regards himself as omniscient is a babu . . . Like Vishnu, the babus would incarnate in ten forms: clerk, teacher, Brahmo, broker, doctor, lawyer, judge, landlord, newspaper editor, and idler. Like Vishnu, in every incarnation, they would destroy fearsome demons. In his incarnation as a teacher he would destroy the student, as station master the ticketless traveller, as Brahmo the small priest, as broker the English merchant, as doctor his patient, as lawyer his client, as judge the litigant, as editor the ordinary gentleman, as idler the fish in the pond . . . Any person who has one word inside his mind which becomes ten when he speaks, hundred when he writes, and thousands when he quarrels is a babu. One whose strength is one time in his hands, ten times in his mouth, hundred times in his back, and absent at the time of action is a babu . . . He whose household deity is the Englishman, preceptor the Brahmo preacher, scriptures newspapers, and place of pilgrimage the National Theatre is a babu. One who gives himself out as a Christian to the missionaries, as a Brahmo to Keshabchandra, a Hindu to his father and an atheist to the Brahmin beggar is a babu. One who drinks water at home, alcohol at his friends', receives abuse at the prostitute's, and kicks at his employer's is a babu . . . O king, the people whose virtues I have recited to you would persuade themselves that by chewing *pan*, being prone on the pillow, having bilingual conversation, and smoking tobacco they will regenerate their country.

Apparently an astute observer of men and their manners, Janmejaya had formed a clear idea of what sort of beings the babus would be, and requested the sage to turn to some other theme.

The Self-Ironical Tradition in Tagore

Every humorist writes his individual nonsense; and Bankim, Tagore, and Ray had their own individual nonsensical styles. But it is all the more remarkable that despite such difference they seem to be sketching the same collective portrait of the babu. It could be argued that nothing would reveal deep secret beliefs more than nonsense writing. When people are saying something on a subject as dear to ourselves as ourselves, it is easy to slip into pleasantly delusive things. In nonsense writing deeper structures of self-referring beliefs, the signature of an objective mind as it were, may find expression, precisely because the invigilation of reason is loose at the time.

Let us compare the hymns of the *Lok Rahasya* with another set of portraits of the babu from Tagore's early satirical poems. In a group of poems in *Manasi* (1890), Tagore sketches a very similar picture, with the difference that the condensation of adjectives of the *vyajastuti* form has disappeared. In *Duranta Asha* he writes

we are very civil, intensely peaceable, our souls thoroughly tamed;
always prone in contentment under our buttoned clothes;
the model of civility when we meet others,
our faces composed in an unperturbable sweetness,
idle bodies heaving with the effort of motion,
perpetually gravitating towards our homes,
short in height, generous in breadth, the children of Bengal.
we smile with the pleasure of servility
with hands folded in obeisance;
wagging their bodies with the proud delight
of being at the feet of their masters;
you lie under their shoes,
pick the rice mixed with contempt in eager fistfuls,
and return home to express pride

in your Aryan ancestors
whose very name sent shivers down the spine of the whole
   wide world.[33]

Little has changed apparently from Bankim's picture of the babu except the noticeable addition of an impressive ancestry to his name. Since Bankim's time, the babu has evidently compiled a history for himself of sufficiently uplifting character.

The education prescribed solicitously by Macaulay's Anglicist reform gave the babu an opportunity of knowing about the history of the wide world, as opposed to the narrow parochialism which made his ancestors worship their own past. It also teaches the babu the great principle of choice. The educated Bengali now *chooses* the history he wishes to revere, and through that, more subtly, selects his own intellectual ancestry. He has an option, in this expansive age of colonial reason, to choose between Indian or European history as his own past. And there is hardly any doubt or indecision about the babu's decisive choice.

In another poem in *Manasi*, two studious brothers celebrate the great deeds of mankind: a list in which the battles of Marathon and Thermopylae, Cromwell's exploits in the English civil war, the battle of Nasby, and the lives of Washington, Mazzini, and Garibaldi hold pride of place. Clearly, this is a narrative of world history in which the luminous events, forever recurring for remembrance, are successful wars of liberation from foreign oppression and tyranny. The conclusions they draw from their reading of history seem perfectly rational:

> Who can say we are a lesser people than the English? The only differences lie in physical proportion and manners. For we learn whatever they write: indeed, we translate them into Bengali and write commentaries which surpass our masters [*gurumara tike*,[34] a phrase we must note, because we shall encounter it again] . . . Look at me: I spread my bed in my room; I roam the libraries for books on history; I write volumes making things up

[33] Tagore 1967: 126–30.

[34] *Gurumara* literally means murdering the teacher; *tike* is a commentary. *Gurumara* is standardly used to describe a student, *gurumara chela*. Here this clearly means commentaries which exceed/destroy the texts. 'Bangavi', in Tagore 1967: 140–5.

(giving free rein to my imagination), in a carefully sharpened language. As a result, my heart catches fire; I have to control it by fanning myself; I still feel giddy with enthusiasm. There is still some hope for my country, I feel . . . I listen to great things; I speak great words, I gather and read great books, a sure way of achieving gradual greatness. Who could ever stop us?

Entirely in accord with this education that extends the mental horizon of Bengali youth, there are some particular passages of history which move these citizens of the republic of letters to tears of joy. Predictably, the blood runs faster in their veins when they recount what occurred at Marathon and Thermopylae. They cannot imagine what incalculable effects would have followed 'had their countrymen really read Garibaldi's biography in full.' They feel ashamed at the amazing illiteracy of a country whose people do not know by heart Washington's date of birth, and conclude 'Oh Cromwell, you indeed are immortal.' It is typical that the erudite adolescent is unable to read the account of Cromwell's exploits to the end; because an acquaintance comes in proposing a hand at cards, and the youthful babu abandons his historical quest unfinished.

Tagore's poems are important because they show the logic of the babu's quest for historical belonging. Each group after all makes its own construction of human history, and belongs to a mankind after its own heart, in which its preferred characteristics are accentuated and what it dislikes suffers narrative exclusion. The humanity that the babu would like to belong to, the humanity whose history he assiduously constructs because he believes that that forms his proper theatre of existence, is the humanity shaped by Western history. It is this history which he wishes to sneak into, in which he so desperately, cravenly, wishes to have a place. He is an illegal immigrant of narratives. We shall see later that there is also a complementary logic of belonging which is set in motion in these critiques of the babu. This would be a logic of belonging to the 'others', to those who have been conquered, disenfranchised, dispossessed.

Let us compare another story from Tagore's next work, *Sonar Tari* (1893).[35] This poem, too, is fundamentally similar to Bankim's original travestic writing in two respects: it is a nonsense story and its subject is the babu. The ruler of a mythical kingdom was once

[35] Hing Ting Chhat, in Tagore 1972: 118.

troubled by incomprehensible dreams. Along with his ministers and subjects, he lives in a meaningful, not a causal, world. Dreams therefore must be taken seriously, not laughed off as illusions. They must also be decoded correctly. In the king's dreams three monkeys pick lice lovingly from his royal hair, but they slap him if he stirs. At intervals the nitpickers utter a mysterious slogan: 'hing ting chhat'. In his bewilderment, the king, like modern governments, turns to scholarly consultants. Savants from several countries and continents are called in, including several from Europe. They try in their different ways, but fail, and some of them are given punishments that must appear somewhat disproportional to what is after all an intellectual failure. A humorous Frenchman is left to be devoured alive by dogs for suggesting that the complex of sounds was devoid of meaning but not of a certain aural melody.

The riddle, as one can expect, remains unsolved until a scholar arrives from Gaud, trained by Europeans, but already surpassing his masters, *jaban panditder gurumara chela*.[36] The relevant sequence then follows:

At this hour arrived the scholar from Gaud,
trained by foreign masters, only to surpass them.
Bareheaded, shabbily dressed to the point of being shameless
his clothes threatened to slip off him at times.
So thin was he that people could doubt his existence
which was of course decisively dispelled
as soon as the words began to emerge.
Indeed, the world wondered at how so much sound
could be produced by so slight a machine.
Arrogantly he asked:
What is the subject of dispute?
I could say a few words on the subject
if I knew what it was.
In fact, I can turn things upside down by elucidation.
Everyone shouted: *hing ting chhat.*
On being told of the matter
the Gaudiya' master made a somewhat solemn face
and took about an hour to explain what it meant.

[36] The phrase literally means a pupil of foreign scholars who has destroyed (i.e. surpassed) his instructors.

The meaning is in fact quite simple, he said,
indeed in one sense quite clear;
it is an ancient idea newly discovered:
the three-eyed god had three eyes, three times, and three qualities;
different forces lead to individual differentiation
redoubled in contrary cases.
Forces like attraction, repulsion, propulsion
are usually opposed to the forces of good;
in the kaleidoscope of life the three forces
are revealed in three forms.[37]
To put all this quite succinctly,
one could say *hing ting chhat.*
The court thundered to applause:
it is clear, absolutely lucid, said everyone . . .
whatever was incomprehensible was dissolved
and made absolutely limpid
like the empty sky.[38]

We discern some changes in the scene now. The babu is no longer the interested and imitative pupil of European learning, but a *gurumara chela*: he has decisively excelled his preceptors. The poem makes clear in what ways exactly the babu has taken rationalism beyond the point where Europeans left it.[39] Tagore emphasizes the intellectual presumption of the babu, a feature not shared by Europeans, not at

[37] It is impossible to convey the combination of lucidity and nonsensicality of the combination of phrases the Gaudiya scholar uses in his elucidation. Most of the individual concepts are meaningful terms used in Indian philosophy or theology. It is also true that sometimes explanations of phenomena in terms of traditional theological or astrological scholarship would sound very similar to this to lay ears, although they might be perfectly legitimate according to their internal systems of references and conceptual coherence. But this particular amalgam is of course wholly nonsensical. What should be noted is the mixing of concepts from traditional thought, like *tryamvaka, trinayana, trikala, prapancha*, etc., with modern scientific terminology, *akarshan, vikarshan*, etc.

[38] Hing Ting Chhat, in Tagore 1972: 118–19.

[39] This pointedly satirizes trends among contemporary Bengalis which sought to defend traditional metaphysical ideas by illegitimate and specious uses of modern science. For an interesting and detailed analysis of such trends, see Prakash 1993.

least in equal measure. There is another decisive change. His critics have disappeared; the literary world is now populated only with his admirers. The babu's 'others'—women, the subaltern, all those who could make fun of him in an earlier age—have disappeared, historically transformed into moulds of subalternity fashioned by his own hands. He now seems to have gained the unopposed right that belongs to dominant groups, in rare periods of uncontested glory, of making fun of others, without reply.

In the structure of the joking relationships common in Bengali bhadralok society, some of the historical transformations of that period were enduringly inscribed. Earlier the babu was often the object of ridicule, as Bankim's world showed; now the world is the object of his banter. Unfortunately, little systematic work has been done on such matters, but common babu jokes gradually turned outwards and showed the confident disdain of the Bengali middle class for the whole non-babu world. It included not merely non-Bengalis, but also Bengalis from other classes. Unlike jokes about Sikhs, which are often charmingly and generously self-referring, the babu jokes of middle-class Bengal display a strong parochial aggressiveness. Although he considers himself an inheritor of the classifactory fastidiousness of Western rationalism, he does not have the patience to catalogue the surrounding world minutely, or with any degree of precision. Anyone coming from the west of the hallowed land is a *khotta*, from the general vicinity of Rajasthan a *medo* (slang for Marwari), and from the general direction of the South a *madraji*.[40]

The chauvinistic Bengali is quite content to live with this indistinct map of nationalities of those he now considers his natural inferiors. Nothing is so revealing of the babu mind as the astounding geography of his contempt. Remarkably, the babu replicates in the world he dominates the inattentive and perfunctory classification of others so characteristic of European cultures. It blurs the other, the unfamiliar, just as the Europeans treated people as Slavs, Africans, Far Easterners and in such other broad, misleading, confidently ignorant nomenclatures. The common jokes among babus are directed against the people middle-class Bengalis lived with and depended on, those whose labour formed the things he used parasitically, a typically

[40] Literally, a resident of Madras.

uncharitable recompense for their work at his service. The culture
of the Calcutta Bengali is replete with jokes about the *ude*,[41] *medo,
khotta*, and closer home, the *bangal*.[42]

Tagore's poem on the Bengali intellect offers a list of its own
ennobling effects on its audience.[43]

> Whoever listens to this hallowed story of dream
> will be rid of all errors and delusions.
> He will never be deceived into believing
> that this world is indeed this world.
> He will never be led to take the true as true.
> He will realize in a moment that the true is false.
> Come, then, yawn and lie on your back
> in this uncertain world the only certain truth
> is that everything in the world is
> made of delusions, except the dreams themselves
> which are the only things one can call really true.

The structure of this travesty is exactly the same as *Kamalakanta*.
Its tone is of the same intense self-irony; it uses the same logic of
inversion. In Tagore's artistic evolution this tone was rather short-lived;
he would diverge from this self-ironical tradition in which the babu
constantly searched for the limits of his being.[44] Bengali literature
becomes more sombre and sanctimonious, until in modern times it
loses all taste for this cleansing, purifying laughter. But in Tagore's early

---

[41] Pejorative form for Oriya.

[42] *Bangal* was used to refer pejoratively to residents of East Bengal; but this
insult was heartily returned. West Bengal people were similarly called *ghati*.

[43] Again, in a perfectly traditional style. Religious texts were not content
with describing the extraordinary events of their divine and mortal protagonists.
Usually, they recited the this-worldly and otherwordly benefits to be gained
by hearing the narratives—an entirely understandable move in a culture with
such a teeming and competitive market for ennobling stories. Tagore's poem
accordingly spoofs this declaration at the end of Hing Ting Chhat. See Tagore
1972: 120.

[44] Though that does not mean that he abandoned the project of criticizing
the pretensions of middle-class Bengali culture. His novel, *Gora,* for instance,
is a complex extension of this critique; but the literary, *formal*, mode had
changed: he would make much less use of ironical banter.

writings the babu displays the same features, mentally and physically. His physical scantiness is dramatized: the world could doubt his existence until he burst into speech. What still constitutes his identity is the irrepressible, vacuous verbalism. This fatal gift is not an ability to produce arguments, or sense, but sounds (*shabda hai*). We are left in no doubt that we are dealing with a direct descendant of the animal whose special gift was the multiplication of words.

The lapse of time has done nothing to improve his arrogant incivility, though his skill lies in a derivative, unproductive art. He is adept not at producing ideas but at the parasitic function of interpreting; he is so confident before he knows what it is about that he can improve on what is being said. What impresses his audience is stilted nonsense, but interestingly the elements in that great colligation of senseless concepts are all individually significant ideas of classical Indian philosophy. Put together properly, it could produce a sensible if uncompelling argument, but by the depraving touch of the babu it degenerates into unmitigated drivel. The babu does not achieve the coherence of either traditional Indian discourse or the scientific reliability of modern rationalist ideas. In this tradition of self-irony thus the babu reflected on the contingency of his own historical emergence, with a mixture of admiration and secret anxiety.

The Meaning of Nonsense: Sukumar Ray's
Aboltabol

The last point at which I wish to analyse this tradition, where it is already becoming too light, is in Sukumar Ray's *Aboltabol* (1923).[45] This is a highly idiosyncratic work and its nonsense is so pure, its pleasure at defying expectations of normalcy so intense, that it is odd to expect social comment in its delightful pages. Yet, miraculously, the figure which recurs in its verses, often in an identical form, is the babu. Ray has a poem directly titled 'The Babu'.[46] He has now turned into a butt of general criticism, and it is worthy of note that Ray's babu, in his brief life within this short verse too, meets his denouement at the

[45] *Aboltabol* was translated twice, once by Satyajit Ray, and more recently by Sukanta Chaudhuri. Cf. 'The Blighty Cow', in Chaudhuri 1987.
[46] *Babu*, in *Khai Khai:* Ray 1985: 33.

hands of an uncomprehending lady. But the most direct description of the babu comes, I think, in the famous poem *Tansgaru*, 'the Westernised Cow'. Here the babu makes his appearance even in the animal world—the logic of babuness has spread so far—naturally with appropriately startling consequences.

Hybridization with a low imitative westernism and the surrender of cultural identity proceeds relentlessly after Bankim's time. It captures the Bengali social world, redefining everything from styles of speech to habits of food. This spread from idle adults, whom Bankim derided, to college-going adolescents in Tagore. In Ray, particularly through his vivid, inverting imagination, this logic of westernization has spread from the social world to the world of neighbouring animals. After all, they could not live under colonialism for so long and remain entirely unaffected. Animals too can become decisively and determinedly westernized. In this poem, accordingly, Ray speaks of a cultured cow, a pioneer of westernization among its species. And the poem clearly implies that although there is something seemingly appropriate in our wonder at his general demeanour, there is also something deeply inappropriate and unjust. For, after all, the Tansgaru merely re-enacts what every babu does every day without causing the slightest surprise. From the cow's point of view, we see his ways as ridiculous only because of our inexcusable anthropocentrism, our failure to treat all beings equally, our tendency groundlessly to discriminate between human and animal babus. If cows had a theoretical apparatus comparable to that of modern cultural critics, they would undoubtedly have produced something compelling about the invidious ideology of humanism.

All the characteristics Bankim had detected earlier reappear in the enlightened cow, who, notably, is male. Like human babus, he is a victim of misrecognized identity: in fact, he is not a cow but belongs to a species of bird. But the world, with characteristic injustice, denies him that title, just as the Bengali babu is unjustly classified by people as a mere Indian on purely racial grounds, though in terms of his ideas he has everything in common with the European rationalist. The cow's residence, like the babu's, is a sign of his identity: with unmistakable symbolism, he has an office—the space of colonial reason—not a stable, as his residence. Like babus in Bankim and Tagore, his obvious preference in positions is for lying down, symbolically renouncing action, as befits all animals of unusual intellect. Even his physical characteristics are middle class—he sports a neat parting in his dark and immaculate hair (*phitphat kala chul, terikata chosta*), evidently an attempt to imitate the common Bengali officegoer's toilet. Inconstancy is the special mark of his character, but what decisively marks his identity is his choice of food:

He does not eat fodder, grass, leaves or hay;
nor gram, flour, or sweets made of these;
he is indifferent to the delicacies of meat and *payes*
he lives, as rule, on candles and soapy soup.

Clearly, this list of rejected food contains a subtle hierarchy. The enlightened cow finds unacceptable the list of food that unwesternized and indigenist cows would presumably enjoy, the standard menu of grass, hay, and corn. He rejects even the usual food of indigenous human beings: but here we must not ignore the sharp culinary slope. *Chhola* and *chhatu* are edibles of lower orders of people from North India, especially migrant labourers from neighbouring Bihar. The list then rises through ordinary flour and sweets to the great high points of Bengali cuisine, preparations of fish and meat (*amish*) and *payes,* the ultimate in Bengali desserts. But such subrational food fails to tempt him. Only a Western regimen of soup made of soap and candles—both of Western provenance—appeals to his cultivated taste. Evidently, to the Tansgaru, the point of eating is not gastronomic but ideological. We are led to suspect that he chose his food on grounds of rationalism. As in the case of Vaishampayana's babus, who could not converse in Bengali, he once tried a piece of ordinary bovine food, a piece of rag, and was laid up in bed with indigestion for three months.

At first sight the behaviour of this cow might seem strange; but to Bankim's *Kamalakanta*, it would not. He admitted in his famous conversation with the socialist cat that human beings systematically discriminate against animals in matters of political theory, and found objectionable in animals what they took for granted in their own species.[47] The only thing wrong with this cow was that he had learnt to imitate his superiors: he had simply, driven by the spirit of the age, become a babu. Meanwhile, the babu had reached a sort of

[47] Bidal, in Chattopadhyay 1968: vol. II, 85–8.

natural limit in his historical career. The Tansgaru showed the extent, the limits, and the ironical consequences of the babu's conquest of society and history.

Dreams of an Other Self

But this discussion of the ironical tradition will not be complete if we do not look at another set of signs, markers of a very different move in the consciousness of the Bengali middle class. Bankim is the founder of this very different line of thought about the historical self. The discourse of both the *Kamalakanta* pieces in Bankim and the early poems of Tagore show a duality of thinking in this reflection about the Bengali self. The primary discourse in both is powerfully ironical; but, on occasion, another type of belief—of a very different tone and temper—crosses it, resounds through it. This voice is a natural end of this ironic lament, but very different from it in tone. Even the individual self, despite our conceits, is not beyond correction. The collective self appears even more eligible for such correction. The tone of lament, the recitation of qualities that are absent in the character of the modern Bengali, can lead to fantasies about another self, a self that could be, a self that is very different from what it is. In *Kamalakanta*, often in the midst of ironical discourse there is a sudden change into a language of inspiration and dreaming.[48]

Tagore's poems reveal with graphic clarity another crucial move of early patriotism. The ironical babu is out to invent a different self. He wishes to be and dreams that he is another. I have shown elsewhere that this process of making a new self involves the Bengali intellectual in appropriating the history of others, of Rajputs, Marathas, and others not equally renowned for their command of European rationalism.[49] But in Tagore's youthful poems, in his search for ingredients to make his new self, he goes even to the Bedouins in the Arab deserts.

After recounting the ordinary Bengali's enjoyment of the pleasures of colonial servility, one poem comes to an immediate counterpoint. Of course the earlier description is a slander on Bengalis in general;

[48] The best example of this is the essay Chattopadhyay 1968: vol. II, 79–81.

[49] In Kaviraj 1995.

what was described there would constitute a portrait of all Bengalis only if all Bengalis were babus. But it was typical of the babu to ignore such small errors of computation. This is counterpointed immediately by the free life in the desert of the alleged Bedouins (in point of fact, alas, equally vulnerable to the forces of British imperialism). But facts can hardly stand in way of such a rush of feelings.

> Would I were an Arab Bedouin
> with the great desert under my feet
> stretching to the horizon,
> on a galloping horse, in a cloud of dust
> pouring my life on to the sky, with a fire kindled in my soul,
> moving endlessly day and night,
> a spear in hand and hope in my heart,
> never lying still, just as a desert storm
> irresistible, moves through all that comes in its way.

This poem can help us understand the curious connection between the two apparently irreconcilable moods. The poem is called *Duranta Asha*, an irrepressible wish, something intensely desired yet known to be unattainable. This is precisely what gives rise to humour, because all the contradictory aspects of this mentality cannot be captured in any other mode of discourse. But this humour is not an end in itself, or the end or destination of this humorous discourse. A movement towards a cancellation of humour is contained within the humour itself. Tagore's poetic utterer sets out the theme with admirable clarity at the start of the poem: 'when you are being ripped apart by desire' (obsessive or drunken desire, literally), or by an irrepressible wish, 'when you lose yourself in anger' at the encumbrances that fate has placed around you, then, even then, you have to acquiesce, because 'Bengalis are professional mammals' unfit for more strenuous exertion. The depiction of the Bengali that follows replicates Bankim's list of adjectives meticulously: civil (*bhadra*), peaceable (*shanta*), with a domesticated soul (*poshamana e pran*), lying prone and contented under his buttoned shirt, decorous in manner, his face always composed, an idle body, a slow walk, responding to the gravitation of his home, well groomed, his body filled with the juices of sleep, short in intelligence, large in width. Notice that even the style is similar, deploying the same stream of adjectives of contempt.

To be other than what he is, the Bengali must have the opposite attributes. The transformed babu would like to live a life of heroic action as opposed to the routines of his office—'on the horseback', 'in a cloud of dust', 'with fire in his heart'. He is no longer enclosed in the familiar space: 'like the storm of the desert that does not brook any bonds', and 'with a spear in his hand and hope in his heart'. Obviously the entire imagery of the poem develops a countertype to what the Bengali is. This search has now transcended the Bengali heroes of earlier, more martial times, even the Rajputs—their unattainable heroic selves, the permanent inhabitants of his dreams, reaching a figure even more exotic. This is not arbitrary, because it follows the same generative principle. The familiar geography of the mango grove and the enclosed space of the middle class home is now contrasted to the unfamiliar geography of the endless burning desert. It accentuates the central contrast of the verbalizing inefficacy of the Bengali and the imagined decisiveness of the Arab. 'With a spear in hand and hope in my heart' is I think the crucial trope, part dream, part suggestion, part argument, for the ascending of passive resentment into militancy, and militancy into arms. These are typically dreams that suffuse Bankim's novels and his alternative history of India. The opposite of this dream are the crucial lines which indicate the failure of defiance, the impossibility of the babu's feeling rebellious at the indignity of political servitude.

> Can you ever feel beside yourself with rage?
> are you ever maddened by insults?
> does the blood boil in your veins?
> does the perpetual smile of contempt, the sharp point of insult
> pierce your heart like lightning?[50]

It is his ability to rationalize subjection through the delusive idea that wins the respect of the British, his collaboration that makes the babu so contemptible. Unlike others, the Bengali does not merely submit to foreign rule; he justifies and rationalizes it: 'the prisoner boasts of the length of his chain'.

The poem, *Duranta Asha*, shares another feature with Bankim's *Kamalakanta*. It wavers constantly, and I think significantly, between two verb forms. Part of it is in the first person singular, part in third

[50] *Duranta Asha.*

person plural, capturing with great sensitivity the tensions of an individual self implicated in a large collective which it can neither own nor disown. It wavers between the single, critical rebellious self and others composing the community of the Bengali middle class, contented in their enjoyment of colonial rule. Technically, this captures the tension between the individual and the collective self. This is particularly apt, because the self that speaks here, exactly like *Kamalakanta*, includes itself without self-delusion in the larger collectivity it criticizes. Like *Kamalakanta*, this creates a laughter in which, tragically, the self is the victim.

Within all this irony, there is of course a great silence. In search of this other and possible self, the babu, armed with his mastery of world history, ranges far and wide, from his own early Bengali annals, to the folklore of Rajasthan, to the imaginary defiance of the Bedouins for a model of non-verbal defiance. Ironically, he could have found nearer home, had he looked hard, examples of people, not so long ago, who 'had felt maddened by insults', some who thought as long as the spear was in hand there was hope. The events of 1857 were not even thirty years past, but they never come in for even the most oblique mention—they are wrapped in a strange forgetfulness, a vast silence at the heart of all this eloquence about the melancholy of servitude. Neither Tagore, nor even Bankim, usually refer to that event even with metaphorical indirectness. These dreams were irrevocably of the nature of dreams; if they threatened to become reality, in the history that immediately surrounded him the babu tended to recoil and erase it from his long and eloquent memory.

Yet in spite of this Bankim's feeling of indignity yields a sentiment that is truly and deeply political. It permeates his entire creative life, while Tagore passes through this in a moment of his artistic development. In Bankim, this irony simply shapes a question to which his later novels try to provide an answer. Evidently, these ironic poems do not have such significance in Tagore's intellectual biography: they do not indicate a high point, or crisis, or a new departure. On the contrary, this manner of irony would gradually decline in his poetic work. In his autobiographical fragment he would treat these sentiments as 'warming ourselves in the comfortable fire of excitement',[51] and dismiss them as less than serious. His art, accordingly, would enter,

---

[51] Tagore 1968: 78–9.

and indeed flourish inside, the 'enclosed space' of upper middle class
life.

Of course this is not true of Tagore alone, but represents a general
historic turn in Bengali literature. The ironical alternative that hints
at political militancy is given up as fanciful, unrealistic. Bengali fiction
returns from the desert to the mango grove, from the smoke of the
battlefields, in which signs of a lost and bitter war can be hazily seen, to
the security of domestic space, from the joys and sufferings of collective
action to personal heartbreaks. Its sense of historical tragedy shrinks
and retreats. The literature of the babu, in successive periods of its
development, has moved from the world, to the home, to the bed, his
ultimate theatre and stage.[52] Irony was also to change form, and assume
a more tortured, melancholy direction. *Kamalakanta*'s irony, despite
its sense of indignity ineradicably mixed with the historical present,
had not lost its touch entirely with laughter in the ordinary sense.
The predominant type of irony in Bengali literature after the 1940s
would appear in the deliberate contradiction between the utterance
and the form, like the famous poem by Sukanta Bhattacharyya
announcing in poetry the end of poetry, the birth of a world of utter
disillusionment, where all enchantment is torn to shreds. In a world of
hunger, the only language, he said with an irony dripping with a very
different anger, was prose, and in a wonderful rhetorical desecration,
the full moon, in an inverted metaphor, becomes a half burnt piece
of bread.[53] This is also irony, but emerging from a very different order
of disenchantment.

In my longer study of Bankimchandra I have attributed this self-
ironical laughter to a peculiar, almost miraculous, configuration of
artistic and political circumstances in Bengali history.[54] It created a
sense that two different ways of being in the world, coming from two
civilizations, were available to the cultivated Bengali, and a person
of real refinement found it hard to make a wholly one-sided choice.
The two civilizations had been brought into contact by history, each
providing entirely sensible grounds for criticizing the other. European

[52] The last stage reached in more recent novels imitative of European
existentialist literature.
[53] Bhattacharyya BS 1382: 87.
[54] Kaviraj 1995: ch. 2.

culture offered arguments undermining superstitions of traditional Indian social norms. But Indian culture, equally, offered reasonable grounds for being sceptical about the immodest claims of Western, especially colonial, rationalism. This kept the 'Bengali' character, his collective personality, in a state of tension, of unfinishedness and search. By the 1940s the Bengali babu, along with political groups all over India, had overcome his historical anxiety and found an answer to the uncertainty about the collective self. Consequently, there is a decline in this form of humour and selfirony; but with that is renounced a great principle of intellectual creativity. Eventually, Bengalis would allow their intellectualism to sink to a level where even the most obvious decline in their society and culture would not be described for fear of betraying cultural uncertainty. By turning a communist, the babu has not overcome his historical imperfections, but simply given them a left-wing form. His verbalizing excesses, as anyone conversant with Bengali politics knows, has not diminished. Left politics has provided him with a more appropriate theatre for kindling more fearsome verbal fires. But he has lost the rare ability to turn the humour against himself and get rid of his pretensions.

References

Bhattacharyya, Sukanta. BS 1382. He Mahajivan. In *Chhadpatra*. Calcutta: Saraswat Library (Bengali).

Chatterjee, Partha. 1986. *Nationalist Thought and the Colonial World: A Derivative Discourse?* Delhi: Oxford University Press.

Chattopadhyay, Bankimchandra. 1968. *Bankim Rachanavali*. Calcutta: Sahitya Samsad.

Chaudhuri, Sukanta. 1987. *The Select Nonsense of Sukumar Ray*. Delhi: Oxford University Press.

Giddens, Anthony. 1992. *Modernity and SelfIdentity*. Cambridge: Polity.

Kaviraj, Sudipta. 1990. Signs of Madness. In *Journal of Arts and Ideas*, Special Number on Representations.

———. 1992. Marxism and the Darkness of History. In Jan Nederveen Pieterse, ed., *Emancipations: Modern and Postmodern*. London: Sage.

———. 1994. The Poetry of Interiority: The Creation of a Language of Modern Subjectivity in Tagore's Poetry. Paper for a Conference on Identity in South Asian History, University of Calcutta, Department of History, 28–30 March.

———. 1995. *The Unhappy Consciousness: Bamkimchandra Chattopadhyay and the Formation of Nationalist Discourse in India.* Delhi: Oxford University Press.

Prakash, Gyan. 1993. Science between the Lines. In Shahid Amin and Dipesh Chakrabarti, eds, *Subaltern Studies IX.* Delhi: Oxford University Press.

Ray, Sukumar. 1985. *Sukumar Rachanavali.* Calcutta: Patra's Publications.

Raychaudhuri, Tapan. 1990. *Europe Reconsidered.* Delhi: Oxford University Press.

Shastri, K.S. Ramaswamy. Ed. 1956. *Natyashastra.* Baroda: Oriental Institute.

Sinha, Kaliprasanna. 1862/1991. *Hutom Penchar Naksha.* Kolkata: Subarnarekha.

Tagore, Rabindranath. 1967. *Manasi.* Calcutta: Visvabharati.

———. 1968. *Jivansmriti.* Calcutta: Visvabharati.

———. 1972. *Sonar Tari. Sanchayita.* Calcutta: Visvabharati.

Taylor, Charles. 1992. *Sources of the Self.* Cambridge: Cambridge University Press.

Vidyasagar, Ishwarchandra. 1869/1962. *Bhrantivilas.* Kolkata: Tuli-Kalam,.

8

Reading a Song of the City

Images of the City in Literature and Films

I n this essay I shall take an autobiographical line. As my experience of viewing Hindi films is very limited, the only sensible contri-bution I can make to this discussion is by comparing the filmic representation of the city with literary ones. Second, even the limited filmic evidence that I can draw upon, episodically and anecdotally, from personal experience, is limited to a few Bengali films. Though why people like me saw so few Hindi films is itself an interesting cultural question.

I shall here continue a line of argument made in an earlier paper,[1] presenting that view now in a fuller form. When speaking earlier on the culture of democracy I had begun by analysing a song from a film about Bombay showing that in the 1950s there was a clear, very widespread, *spatial* translation of the rupture between the modern and the traditional. The villages constituted the space of tradition—of caste oppression, of stagnant customs, of poor and undeveloping lives, of religious superstitions. The city, by contrast, was the space of the modern. And since democracy, or rather the democratic principle, was distinctively modern in this view of history, democracy lived in the city.

I used the example of a song taken from a film called *CID* (Criminal Investigation Department) which I had not seen, delivered in the film, I am authoritatively told, by a very popular comedian, Johny

This essay was first published in Preben Kaarsholm, ed., *City Flicks*, Calcutta: Seagull 2004.
[1] See Kaviraj 1998.

Walker, who held a typical city dweller's image to his audience. It was sung by Mohammad Rafi, the most popular playback singer of Hindi films of the Nehru era, in an enunciative style that took great pains to communicate in its lightness of utterance a typical urban knowingness. In spite of using it often in my social science arguments, I have not seen that particular film on the screen. Yet the song is one I have heard since my childhood, my schooldays, in a small religious town, Nabadwip, about sixty miles north of Calcutta.

Since I have chosen an autobiographical line, the circumstances in which I heard the song ought to be analysed in some detail. Significantly, Nabadwip was a historic religious centre for Bengali Vaishnavas as the place of birth of the fifteenth-century *bhakti* saint Chaitanya. Nabadwip in the 1960s was a strange but lively mixture of the traditional and the modern. The town's main reputation came from its association with Chaitanya's birth. Though others with deeper knowledge of Bengali cultural history would have known that it was the great centre of Sanskrit knowledge—particularly in Navyanyaya logic and in Smriti. It was a major centre of Vaishnava pilgrimage, particularly on significant occasions of the Vaishnava calendar—like the ceremonies of the *jhulan purnima*, the *raslila*, or *janmashtami*. Like other great religious centres, it was a centre for thriving commerce, and the modern railway made it more accessible to pilgrims.

Its second claim to fame as the traditional centre for esoteric Sanskrit learning, and the seat of a highly specialized system of ritual legality, was by then completely dwarfed, almost forgotten by its ordinary people. Few inhabitants of the city felt any pride in great logical schools. Also unnoticed by its pilgrims, and behind the spectacular religious aspect, it was by this time a considerable centre for the production of cotton sarees. The commercialization of its religious life fed directly into modern developments like cinemas, and a booming business in speakers and tannoys, which local shops and businesses used for advertising their wares, or announcements of upcoming films by cinemas, of public meetings by political parties, and municipal announcements by the local authorities. Aurally at least these tannoys and their blaring sounds were, in a literal sense, an inescapable part of our existence.

This sociological structure produced a very specific economy of sounds in the town—of various, different, often conflicting parts—and in this the tannoys played an indispensable role. That was the ubiquitous technological link between the blandishments of commercial advertisements, the enticement of the romantic films, and the exertions of the police to control the vast crowds streaming through the narrow streets at times of festivals. But this sound was distinctively modern, demonstrating the power and vulgarity of modern things. In a crowd of other sounds, they always pushed their way through. Because there were many other sounds in the town, Nabadwip was among other things a city of unceasing music. The Vaishnava sect around Chaitanya had developed a new communal form of worship, which took two unusual forms. On festival days there were religious processions in which devotees sang, played a drum called the *khol*, and collectively danced on the streets, which set this sect apart from most other Hindu worshippers. When Chaitanya first initiated this form of collective dancing and singing, it created a scandal among the orthodox brahmins of Nabadwip, who complained to the Qazi and implored him to suppress the uproar. But more routinely, in hundreds of small local temples, round the year lower-level performances called *palakirtan* went on. In these, a small troupe of *kathaks* (literally, tellers of tales) or performers enacted segments of the stories of the love of Krishna and Radha through a fascinating combination of simple narration, mimed enactment, sung passages recounting their famous trysts or verbal exchanges, and dancing.

It was an immensely powerful aesthetic economy—a combination of various narrative and interpretative media, held together tightly by a single theme, animated by a *rasa* aesthetic that the audience knew intimately and enjoyed in endless re-enactments. The average Vaishnava was strongly urged by his religious sensibility to use aesthetics—visual images, narrative forms, music and dance—to enliven and ennoble his quotidian existence; in other words, to have a fundamental attitude towards life that was aesthetic.

A part of this aesthetic reception of everyday life was a simple custom of singing a standard tune early in the morning. Except in the rainy season, despite its transcendent connections, the town experienced an acute shortage of municipal water supply; but that was offset by the 'divine' supply of water from the Ganga. Most people, for most of the year, went for a bath in the river early in the morning, as later in the day, especially in summer, the sand on the wide banks of the river became unbearably hot. One interesting technique of communal worship in the Vaishnava religion was that most of the songs sung in the morning had identical or very similar tunes, generically called *prabhati* (from *prabhat*, early morning). Early in the morning, from sunrise to mid-morning, the town hummed with this general melody of morning worship—gentle, pastoral, expressing a sense of restrained and elegant joyfulness.

Those were Nehruvian times, and the ability of authorities to enforce legal rules had not crumbled. Apparently, the municipality had a rule that banned the use of tannoys before eight in the morning. (I might be wrong about the exact hour; it may have been half past eight or nine. But in that town eight in the morning was quite late in the working day); at that exact hour, all the 'mike shops' (*maiker dokan*) on the main street started their tannoys, which usually carried the currently fashionable Bengali and Hindi popular music, instantly reordering the aural economy. This immediately introduced a different music with a very different reading of the nature of human existence.

Hindi film songs used to be vastly popular, despite the widespread belief among older family members that they were corrupting. In some ways this was rather strange. The Radha-Krishna stories were often deeply erotic; compared to them, the Bengali *adhunik* (literally, modern) songs and the Hindi film lyrics simply expressed a vague sense of romantic longing, in most cases narratively frustrated by immovable and unforgiving family obstacles.

Yet these songs were considered dangerous precisely because they were romantic. Eroticism of a kind was a recognized part of traditional culture. Romantic love was a modern moral ideal. Against the iron laws of arranged marriages, these songs advocated, however vaguely, the individualistic principle of the romantic choice of partners, and described this as a state of divine emotional fulfilment. Family elders might be faulted for their moral principles, but they acted on a highly accurate perception of the sociological implications of this relatively pedestrian poetry. Our family did not even own a radio through which such moral enticements might infiltrate the home. Listening to songs from Hindi films was disapproved of even more strongly, because the disapproval of romantic behaviour was compounded by the Bengali disdain for the general lowness of North Indian culture. They came under three degrees of prohibition—they were romantic, they were from films, and they were in Hindi. I first heard this song in that context.

Ironically, just as the religious music had a compelling repetitiveness, coming back to your hearing every morning and making it impossible to forget that that was the proper way to start the day (in a gentle and subtle attitude of thankfulness), this film music also had its own answering repetitiveness. Since the songs were immensely popular among the young, the shops played them often, many times a day, often during festivals when individual marquees would hire an individual tannoy with a supply of gramophone records. They were additionally often carried by popular music channels of the Delhi-based AIR (All India Radio), and for some curious reason by Radio Ceylon. Thus these songs were not an episodic musical experience; they had their own structures of repetition, which made it impossible to forget them. In a sense, they also came back every mid-morning or afternoon to remind you how to face life in the city. Long before I encountered sociological theories of modernity and tradition or heard of Max Weber, I learnt, vaguely but vividly, through this undeniable line across the musical experience of my everyday, that these two types of tunes represented two immense principles of organizing experience, or the life-world.

There are some other peculiarities to this hearing. The first interesting fact was that I heard these songs, and this one in particular, hundreds of times, without watching the film in which it figured. This indicates two important things. First, songs like these had a strangely dual character: they were both contextual, and freestanding. Of course, in the context of the narrative of a specific film, the song enhanced a situation, carried and amplified a mood, inserted a twist, or did something of immediate narrative import: within the film it was inextricably connected to the story. Indeed, in extension of an argument Mukund Lath makes, the underlying aesthetic of popular Hindi films had some distinct similarities to the aesthetic of the classical *Natyashastra*, and he argued that in the *natya*, i.e. a play/film, several primary modes came together to form a more complex form of aesthetic enjoyment, in which each mode enhanced the other.[2]

But apart from the contextual meaning in this immediate narrative structure, many of the most popular songs were capable of achieving a

[2] See Lath 1998.

freestanding meaningfulness as a literary, musical object, as a rhetorical comment on life. They were also part of a story, but in a different sense, not the story of this particular love, but the essential story of love in general. They had an ability to transcend the narrative frame in which they were conceived. There could be several reasons for this. A simple reason could be that some of the most popular songs from the better Hindi films were composed by Urdu poets of considerable standing who were slowly drawn into the capacious network of the film industry in Bombay. Composing for films probably gave them a highly remunerative but relatively undemanding occupation, leaving them free thereafter to be poets rather than overworked office drudges.

In many cases, I can believe that the creative urges of these writers went into the composition of even rather mundane film songs. In many cases, these songs survived after they performed their more limited, contextual purpose of advancing a particular story. Afterwards, they achieved something like cult status as free-standing cultural items, only slightly humbler than Urdu ghazals or Tagore songs—but vastly more popular. In part, this was helped by the loose structure of the average popular Bombay film. Although the various parts formed an interconnected whole as a film, some of these parts could also be enjoyed as independent artefacts unlinked from the film. The need for an aesthetic of the crowded, teeming, fast-moving city was deeply rooted in the circumstances of Indian modernity. Such songs gave to people who lived rather impoverished lives a lilting language that achieved a miraculous 'transfiguration of the commonplace'.

There is a second, related, point, which is linked to larger questions. The fact that items like this song could subsist as freestanding cultural objects—like poems, or songs in a superior artistic culture—was precisely because through these aesthetic processes a new aesthetic structure was being formed. This was an aesthetic structure in a narrower, technically structuralist theoretical sense—a stock of resources which were like elements for improvising acts of recombination—a cultural combinatory of the modern sensibility which managed to find a strangely joyous description of the grim city while recognizing its sordidness.

Thus the song could be said to have two entirely different contexts of meaningfulness. It emerged from a more immediate, closed context of the film narrative, which imparted to it its meaning, and in which the song in turn contributed to the total structure of meaningfulness of the film's signifying success as a complex structural form.

But it was also part of a second structure of meaningfulness—more relevant for our present discussion—about the aesthetic perception of the city in films. This song formed part of an entire repertoire of popular songs, mostly taken from the films, in which each song with its idiosyncratic sequencing of words, internal economy of images, and mood became a supporting neighbour to others of a similar kind. This poetry and these songs were not from the same films, or from identical narratives, or composed by the same poets. But taken together each of them advanced by slow and peculiar steps an aesthetic description and elaboration of the experience of modernity, and, at its centre, of the taste of city life. They were linked—not as parts of a single narrative, but rather of a single aesthetic.

I shall now turn to the song in greater detail to substantiate my point, and then go on to argue that this aesthetic interpretation of the city has important points of distinctiveness, and that its collective 'sense' of the city is vastly different from the more self-consciously artistic aesthetic of modern poetry. It is through these songs, forming an aesthetic series or combinatory, that the inhabitant of the modern city formed an expressive language of his emotions and moods, and his ultimate reception of this life-world. Most significantly, as I shall argue later, they made it possible to view the modern city as a place of joy—limited, contradictory, yet in an ultimate sense pleasurable.

The text of the lyric runs as follows:

Yeh hai Bombay meri jaan
Ay dil hai mushkil jina yahan (refrain)
Zara hathke zara bachke
Yeh hai Bombay meri jaan.
Kahin building kahin tramen kahin motor kahin mill
Milta hai yahan sabkuch ik milta nahi dil.
Insan ko nahin naam o nishan,
Zara hatke zara bachke
Yeh hai Bombay meri jaan.
CHORUS: Ay dil hai mushkil jina yahan . . .
Kahin satta kahin patta kahin chori kahin race,
Kahin daka kahin faka kahin thokar kahin thes.
Bekaron ke hain kayi kaam yahan,

Zara hatke zara bachke
Yeh hai Bombay meri jaan,
CHORUS: Ay dil hai mushkil jina yahan . . .
Beghar ko awara yahan kahte hans hans,
Khud katen gale sabke kahe isko bisnes [business].
Ik chiz ke hai kayi naam yahan,
Zara hatke zara bachke yeh hai Bombay meri jaan,
CHORUS: Ay dil hai mushkil jina yahan . . .

(female voice)

Bura duniya woh hai kehta aisa bhola tu na ban,
Jo hai karta voh hi bharta, yeh yahan ka hai chalan.
Dadagiri nahin chalne ki yahan
Yeh hai Bombay, yeh hai Bombay,
Yeh hai Bombay meri jaan.

(male voice)

Ay dil hai mushkil jina yahan,
Zara hatke zara bachke
Yeh hai Bombay meri jaan.

(female voice)

Ay dil hai asan jina yahan
Suno bandhu, suno Mister,
Yeh hai Bombay meri jaan.

CHORUS: My heart, it is difficult to live in this place,
Move aside, watch out, this is Bombay, my love.
Buildings, trams, motors and mills—
Everything's here but a human heart.
Not a trace of a human being
Move aside, watch out, this is Bombay, my love.
CHORUS:
Speculation, gambling, thieving, racing
Robberies, skipping meals, kicks, blows.
The jobless have a lot to do here,
Move aside, watch out, this is Bombay, my love.
CHORUS:
People laugh at the homeless as at madmen
They themselves cut everyone's throat, that's called business.
Every single thing here bears many names . . .
Move aside, watch out, this is Bombay, my love.

CHORUS:
(female voice)
He calls the world bad, don't be so childish
Here the law is: you reap what you sow.
Bullying will not do here
This is Bombay, this is Bombay, this is Bombay, my love.

(male voice)
My heart, it is difficult to live in this place,
Move aside, watch out, this is Bombay, my love.

(female voice)
It is easy to live here
Listen friend, listen Mister, this is Bombay, my love.

The two most striking aspects of the song are its lyrics and its tune. Since I am not qualified to comment on it musically, my analysis will remain restricted mainly to its poetic elements. As pointed out in my earlier essay,[3] there is considerable poetic artifice in the lyric. Even for a song, it starts with a pleasing abruptness, and its first sense of the city is almost a tactile feeling for its bustling, crowded dynamism. It instantly communicates the bodily rhythms of a person walking through a crowded Indian city—full of unruly, jostling crowds on the pavements and traffic on the streets.

Yet its crowdedness is unthreatening: it creates an atmosphere of anonymity within which the romantic couple can enjoy the strange seclusion of a romantic exchange. The singer says you have to twist, turn, stop, give way—because this is no ordinary town: *yeh hai Bombay meri jaan* (this is Bombay, my love), instantly creating a sense of the incomparability of Bombay, the paradigmatic metropolis. And Bombay's incomparability is constantly followed by the refrain: my heart, it is hard/difficult to live here (*ay dil hai mushkil jina yahan*).

The life-world of modernity turns into a struggle—not to live well, just to live—'un-adjectived' living, which should be the simplest activity of all. The song goes on immediately to set up a deliberate contrast between the modern and the natural. In the city there are buildings, trams, cars, and mills, and it is hardly an accident that these are all referred to by their English names—*kahin building,*

[3] Kaviraj 1998.

kahin tramen, kahin motor, kahin mill. Evidently, these are things not available outside the magic world of Bombay—they are absent in the countryside.

This is followed instantly by a sharp comment on the heartlessness of the city—*milta hai yahan sab kuch, ik milta nahi dil.* Everything is available here except the human heart. And this heartlessness is matched by the city's general deceptiveness—*ik chiz ke hai kayi naam yahan*—every single thing goes by several names. The city's defining characteristic is the difference, in paradigmatically Marxist terms, between appearance and reality, and its deep deceptiveness. Here people deceive each other smiling all the while, merchants cut throats and 'call it business', and those without homes or shelter are accused of being feckless tramps. In some Hindi films, particularly those by Raj Kapoor, the figure of the tramp in Chaplin is taken up with modifications as the 'natural' carrier of such an outsider's vision.

There is also a subtle exchange between the two figures in the song, though in the dialogical structure the presence of the female voice is asymmetric. She says very little; but brevity is compensated by the enormous power of her interjections. She cuts into the dolorous recitation of the city's lack of faith only twice. The first occasion is a triumph of composing technique: when we expect her to simply repeat the refrain 'it is difficult to live in this place', she says with unexpected, wonderful, sparkling irony, a sense of luminously optimistic surprise—*ay dil, hai asan jina yahan* (my heart, it is easy to live here). When we expect her to confirm the repetitive theme that it is hard to live here, she unexpectedly says the opposite. The sharp and brief sentence is not amplified. We are left to surmise: is this precisely because of the thousand excuses and occasions for deception? Is the city a great unbounded space of a lowly form of freedom, but freedom all the same, for a de Certeuesque game of disappearance from social invigilation and political control, the sordid pleasure of 'tactics'? Does the city allow people to hide—to fall in love in its vast and comforting anonymity? Does it make it possible to find a living, using its many opportunities? The second time, the same voice cuts into the song, taking the element of levity even further. I am sure the intended meaning here is to convey a certain streetwise intimacy: the woman calls her man *suno Mister, suno bandhu* (pal/buddy), *yeh hai Bombay meri jaan.*

What is remarkable in the lyric is a kind of critical sensibility of the city which sympathizes with the downtrodden, the fallen, the destitute. One suspects that this is the view of no common poor man, but the highly educated, high-cultured, lower-middle-class protagonist of modern Indian literature, the central, dominating figure of its poetry and novels. He is a strange and potent mixture of achievement and misfortune—educated, cultured, highly sophisticated in his social and aesthetic sensibility, yet always short of money, and acutely sensitive to the constant threat of indignity. He does not face the city with the numbness, despair, and deceit associated with the ordinary poor. He faces the city with indignation and a highly refined sense of cultural violation. Both these features—moral indignation and aesthetic distaste—are conditional on the possession of standards by which to judge the world; only a possessor of clearly defined moral principles, and equally clear aesthetic standards would feel these emotions against the modern city. Therefore, he uses a strange set of 'weapons of the weak': not foot-dragging, stealth, shortchanging; his weapons are high principle, irony, aesthetics. He has the great rare gift of turning his humiliation into poetry. He has the unmatched weapon, as long as the conflict is in the arena of culture, of middle-class eloquence.

Purely textually too we find an interesting structure of consciousness in the lyric. Remarkably, the lyric does not counterpose the city—the space of deprivation, deceit, and defilement—with an idealized space of the pastoral idyll of the village unspoilt by history.[4] The subtler current of thought running through the song is closer to a kind of humanist Marxism. Its imagic economy is very similar to Marx's analyses in the *Economic Philosophical Manuscripts*, in the famous sections on alienated labour and the power of money in bourgeois society. The 'badness' of the city is contrasted not to the 'goodness' of the village, which Marxists would have found reactionary and nostalgic, but with a 'natural' condition of man. Interestingly, from this natural condition of fulness and un-alienation both the poor and the rich are estranged: the poor are ground into degradation, the rich are mired in deceit.

Accordingly, the song demonstrates a suitably popular version of

---

[4] For a similar discussion about the pastoral idyll of the village in Bengali partition literature, see Chakrabarty 2002.

what Marxists would have called a Feuerbachian general humanism. What it misses in the city is not a rural, traditional ethic, but a general humanistic sympathy: there is no sign of the general sign of 'man' (*insan ka nahin naam o nishan*); and man in this naturalist sense is marked by the heart, which is the only thing that Bombay cannot offer (*milta hai yahan sabkuch, ik milta nahi dil*). The reason I associate this critical sensibility with the wide genealogy of Marxist thought is due precisely to its absence of a nostalgic relation with a rural past—it spurns that route as sentimentality, and firmly contrasts the degrading present of rising capitalism with a natural condition of humanity.

There is also a startling presence of the voice, which, if not directly radical, carries a suspicion of subalternity, all the more surprising because it is a feminine voice, which turns the usual expectation of roles upside down. Literary studies have shown conclusively that in the artistic literary reflection of the colonial world the voice of rational control, or of rational understanding of the external—particularly city—world, is a male voice. Rationalistic figures are primarily male figures. Women are generally associated with sentimentality and sustenance, occasionally with an invincible instinct for survival or protection of their children. But women are usually not the carriers of a sly knowledge of the city and its vast world of power and opportunities. They are never at home in the modern.

Here the feminine voice in the film song is refreshingly different—not merely from the standard enunciations of the literary values of femininity, but also from the disillusion expressed by the primary male voice about Bombay itself. Her four lines therefore deserve more careful analysis. The city produces a new, soiled kind of intelligence: and in some strikingly exceptional instances, at least in literature, this sly street wisdom is carried by women characters.

This stanza expresses some fairly complex judgements: unfortunately, the world we are thrown into is a bad world. But its ways, at least in the fallen city of Bombay, lays down that those who do the work reap the benefits, and fate does not rule people's lives. In the startling concluding turn, the woman declares a great and paradoxical truth about the city—*hai asan jina yahan*—this makes it easy to live here. And the two words 'Mister' and *bandhu* are also characteristic urban words of address. So the woman's lines in a sense agree with what the main voice of the song says about Bombay, but also asks the man to see the city as a space of contradiction, and to get reconciled to its other side—learning to live in this city, not by compromising his principles. To my sensibility, shaped no doubt by the tastes of Bengali *bhadralok* high literature, the two words of address appear a bit odd; but their meaning is unmistakable.

I now wish to take this reading in a more general direction. My reading of the lines has been frankly excessively literary: in fact, literary in two senses. First, I read it outside the narrative frame of the film, which I never saw. Second, I also read merely the words, in effect analysing what I convened from a song into a poem. But even as a lay listener, I find some features of its musical composition interesting. First, the tune contains a subtle parodic element. If we listen carefully, we begin to hear the familiar Western song, 'O my darling Clementine'. This opens up a potentially vast and interesting subject—of imitation, mimicry, modification, and appropriation, and the meanings of all these different cultural acts. Is this an act of borrowing, stealing, imitating? Does this signify exaggerated respect, an inability to produce one's own art? Or does this demonstrate a strange assurance which can deftly pick up a well-known piece of artistic creation and displace its meaning by highly deliberate modification? Does this demonstrate dependence of the cultural imagination, or a playful and confident creative subjectivity?

The composer has employed a technique that is not rare in Hindi film music. He has quickened the tempo and changed the tune ever so slightly to yield a very different *rasa*—a structure of feeling. Despite obvious similarities, users of *rasa* theory will not find it hard to demonstrate that the *rasa*-sensibility is different. The mood of the song is quick, witty, there is a sense of joyous enjoyment of the city's crowds and the rapid rhythms of its street life. By the change of pace, he has miraculously changed the meaning and the predominant colour of feeling. I call this relation 'parodic' in the sense that it picks up a very well-known cultural object, takes it out of its settled, familiar context, and by making it do something unusual changes its meaning completely. Yet the fresh meaning is not an unsuccessful pretence: it is a successful creation of a new meaning which is grasped, as the vast popularity of the tune showed, by the ordinary filmgoer across the entire country.

There is an equally impish and daring example of similar parodic appropriation of a famous European tune in Salil Chowdhury's composition of another film song: *itna na mujhse tu pyar badha* which is taken from Mozart's Symphony no. 40 in G Minor and altered in tempo. Anyone familiar with the original tune cannot escape a sense of wondrous enjoyment of the displacement of meaning.[5]

However, I am not an ideal listener of the song; let us bring the appreciation of the song closer to a more standard understanding of its ideal audience, made up of people who are habitual Hindi filmgoers, who know the actors, and the playback singers. What would they make of this song? How would they receive its various aspects? The reception of the song is a fairly complex affair. The narrative characters in the films performed their task of artistic enchantment by a deft combination of the familiar and the unfamiliar. Narrative characters are evidently recognized as belonging to types. Their power of aesthetic signification is at least in part drawn from this fact. Yet every story, however conventional and following narrative formulae, in the modern literary context, must have a quality of unrepeatedness, of being told for the first time, and contain a sense of surprise. The surprise operates within a general structure of recognition. We may have seen many films of revenge, but a particular story is different in particulars, though we can, from the structure of the plot, from the way the actions are arranged in its narrative composition, deduce fairly accurately what the resolution at the end is likely to be.

The enjoyment of narrative is a strange combination of the reassurance of such iterative patterns and surprise of the particular. In addition to these literary-narrative features of reassurance, or what can be called aspects of recognition, there are in films other techniques of recognition. The specific characters of the story are new to the audience, but they fall into recognition by the casting of the actors. Acclaimed heroes and heroines in Hindi popular films perform this function very strongly and very often. Even before the spectators have come into the film theatre, the simple association of an actress with a particular role creates a structure of fore-meanings and narrative expectations, which the actual unfolding of the film plot hermeneutically changes and confirms at the same time. The actress's association with a certain

---

[5] Salil Chowdhury's song occurs in a film called *Chhaya* and was sung by a very popular singer, Talat Mahmood.

standard type of role is created by a long and repetitive association with roles whose characteristic attributes she is acknowledged to bring out particularly well. Thus the complex narrative experience of the filmgoer is not the sensation of being open to an unfamiliar, entirely unpredictable run of events, convolution of plots, forming of characters. It is a more complex sensation of enjoyment in which along with these elements of unpredictability and surprise, there are equally strong elements of recognition or aesthetic repetition—seeing the same face, meeting one's favourite actor or actress—and above all a confirmation in the coloured, charged, heightened universe of imagination of the moral structure of the social world.

A second element of recognition occurs in film songs. The lyrics and their narrative frame of course are new—which offer the element of surprise. But the fact that a well-known playback singer like Mohammed Rafi or Mukesh sings it balances it with recognition—producing the peculiar work of aesthetic enchantment in the song itself.

Finally, I would make a large and speculative suggestion about this entire series of elements of recognition in the cultural universe of Nehruvian India. The films in their generally recognized and well-understood interconnection with supporting structures like the narrative economy of the world of novels, the poetic universe of lyrics, the imagic economy from assorted visual sources, produced a whole structure that acts as a complex but single aesthetic unity. I shall call it loosely an aesthetic of the city—the general sense of what 'the city' is.

This aesthetic sense is produced in various ways: first, it is produced by this combination of the single narrative, specific song, individual actors, etc. inside the single film. Each single film sends a message to the audience about what life in the city is as a possibility. But I am concerned with making a larger structuralist point. It is not merely the signifying relations between its dissimilar elements—the story, the acting, the songs, the stream of images inside the film—which constitute a unity. Each song forms a link, a part of a syntagmatic chain with other songs that speak about the joys and frustrations of urban love, forming a musical aesthetic of the city. Equally, this is done by the lyrics and the images. Eventually, since the spectator or the recipient is a repetitive consumer of separate but linked aesthetic discourse, the collective, iterative, total impact creates a general, overarching common aesthetic.

I wish now to briefly compare this aesthetic of the city in popular Hindi films with the aesthetic in high literature. My comparison has obvious difficulties. The Hindi film has a particular cultural habitus—a combination of the cultural styles from North Indian poetry and theatre combined with an experiential perception of the city drawn primarily from the bustling commercial metropolis of Bombay. The poetic aesthetic I am comparing it with is from Bengali literature, produced by poets of the generation after Tagore, a poetry of a deep moral scepticism and disillusionment. But there is some justification for this contrast, as both groups of people are artists engaged in thinking aesthetically about India's modernity, and they are living at roughly the same historical time.

From its inception, Bengali high literature developed a contradictory relationship with the city. In some ways, the modern life of the mind required the environment of the city as its condition of production. Most of the great literary writers—Bankimchandra Chattopadhyay, Rabindranath Tagore, Saratchandra Chattopadhyay—were city dwellers. It was clearly the new kind of social and intellectual life of their city, Calcutta, which gave them the intellectual, moral, and social sustenance from which their literary work emerged.

Yet, dwelling in the city did not always convince them that the colonial form of modernity offered by the city was above criticism. Bankimchandra did not write disparagingly of Calcutta in his novelistic writings, but in one of his long and influential humorous pieces, *Muchiram Guder Jibancharit*—the satirical life of a scoundrel who rose irresistibly to eminence in colonial society—Calcutta and other towns figure prominently. The satire is primarily about the inversion of values in colonial public life and institutions, but as these institutions—the courts and government offices—are mainly located in cities, they get an indirect lashing of the sarcasm in Bankim's humorous writing.

And although indirect, and secondary, the narrative establishes a central theme of Bengali writing about the city. The city is a space of travesty. It is the space in which modern principles, values, institutions, modes of life, unfold, but always in a travestied form. They are never true to their abstract principles, or even the institutional or practical form these values acquire in Europe's modernity. The forms these principles, values, and the characters embodying them have in Calcutta are in some ways a caricature of the original—just as Bengali modernity is a caricature of the modernity of the West.

In doing this, Bankim was in one sense continuing an earlier satirical tradition in Bengali writing, and in other ways transforming it. From the rise of the modern city of Calcutta, the social and moral conduct of the modern elites and middle classes who resided in the city—referred to by the collective appellation 'babu'—was a target of traditional farcical forms. In early Bengali literature, some highly talented authors like Kaliprasanna Sinha extended this tradition of satirical sketches and comments into a literary tradition of acerbic comment on the imitative excesses of the new parasitic urban elite.

Although this kind of comment always implies social criticism, the early writing on the city was mainly marked by its sense of fun at the expense of the babus and its general tone of light-heartedness. In Bankim's hands, the lightheartedness is continued, and the babu remains a butt of fun; but underlying that surface sparkle of gaiety, a new highly serious historical judgement is subtly introduced. This judgement indicates that it is wrong to repose great faith in the future achievements of Bengali modernity, because the relation between its European exemplars and their Bengali re-enactment is one of travesty. Evidently, this already forms a sufficiently dark background out of which the deeper and melancholic critiques of the modern city could emerge.

Tagore's relation with the city was predominantly one of aesthetic rejection. In his mature works, on many occasions, writing about the city in his poetry, he tries to show that the city cannot find a poetry of its own, because the city in its sordidness does not deserve poetry. His poems are therefore written with their back turned on the city they are talking about: their dominant urge is one of escape into nature, into the countryside, less frequently into a highly coloured romantic past. He is capable of writing wonderful poetry about the hazy cities of the past in which Kalidasa's heroines lived their lives, of a wonderfully mythical Ujjaini; but Calcutta was undeserving and incapable of a lyrical celebration of itself.

In poetry after Tagore, several highly talented poets continued this tone of negative reflection on the city, but with one highly significant difference. In Tagore, escapes from this city were primarily of three types—into imagination and dreams, into the unspoilt nature of the countryside, and into nostalgia. The new poets of the 1940s cut off all these routes of escape. They consequently forced the reading public to face the dirt and meaninglessness of the city quite squarely—not as a passing phase, not as a small part of a larger green, beautiful world, but as the undeniable, inescapable present, as the only world there is.

This sense of a claustrophobic space gradually finds two types of poetic enunciation. The more aesthetically sophisticated presentation of this new aesthetic of the city came in the wonderfully colourful imagery of despair in Jibanananda Das, whose visual sensibility constantly prowls the city, specially at night when it is deserted and exhausted, when the crowds have disappeared, when the city gives up, in a sense, its vast, dark, despairing truth. Das's poetry is an aesthetic wonder, because his weaving of words makes this despondent nightmare as beautiful as dreams. But despite everything, despite the immensely exciting craft, the amazing surprise of his imagery, the subtle, tired cadence of the understated meter, the city remains a space of despair.

To take a single typical example, which raises a complicated question about love and fulfilment, one of Das's best known poems, 'Banalata Sen', is about a woman once met in the past, now lost. In painting her face, Das wrote the unforgettable lines: '*chul tar kabekar andhakar bidishar nisha, mukh tar avantir karukarya*'—'her hair the ancient darkness of the night in Bidisha city, her face the sculpture of the past city of Avanti.' She is eventually lost, and constantly returns in memory—not, like a similar figure in Tagore ('Kshanika') to comfort but to hurt.

The present, the immediate, is entirely enclosed in the claustrophobic space of Calcutta with its subtle and ineradicable curse, where everything beautiful is transient, awaiting decomposition and death. Death, decay, the corpse eaten by birds of prey, is a constant theme in Jibanananda, as in the other famous image in his poetry—deer playing in a forest clearing in the improbably bright light of stars; but these deer are destined for slaughter; what eventually ends the idyll is the sharp, final, snap of a rifle shot ringing through that enchanted night.

In Das's poetry, love is constantly present, constantly stalked by a stealthy, confident, unavoidable death. In the themes we found in

Tagore, images of love are always linked in a great tenderness of words to the past, to memory, to nature which lives serenely outside the city, and to dreams. But clearly, all these things—the past, the unspoilt countryside, nature—are transient, threatened, ultimately brought to submission by the city.

A second strand of poetic reflection on the city developed alongside this one, animated by a powerful induction of communist ideology into Bengali culture. But the communist poets' sense of the city is not very different from the gloomy despair of Jibanananda. To take a characteristic example, Samar Sen, an acclaimed young leftist poet in the 1950s, saw the city very similarly—as a space of inevitable unfulfilment. And since love is such a shining emblem of fulfilment in earlier poetic aesthetics, this poetry shows a strangely perverse delight in soiling these traditional themes, images, and at times even well-known lines taken straight out of Tagore, continuing the tradition of parody, but with a further twist. The parody does not remain a vehicle of laughter as in Bankim, it turns vicious and primarily bears the imprint of melancholy. Women, still carriers of a remembered beauty in Jibanananda, become simply objects of lust; in Sen's poetry the space of Calcutta is surprisingly teeming with prostitutes. Some of Sen's lines show the working of the social sensibility behind this aesthetic with exceptional clarity: the figure of the *ganika*, the woman who can be bought, returns endlessly to haunt the poetic imagination, in the final travesty of love—she 'loves' him for the precise minutes for which the price has been paid. Samar Sen's poetry is also admirably explicit about the subject of this poetic enunciation and this sense of the city: this is the *madhyabitta*, the highly educated lower-middle-class male who is equipped with a cultural sensibility which can never find fulfilment in Calcutta's economic and social world.

By the 1940s this educated lower middle class had grown to a considerable size; and they were in any case the primary audience, the aesthetic consumers, of this poetic discourse. By the 1950s both the sociological and cultural developments conspired to ensure the utter dominance of this 'sense of the city' in Bengali literature to the exclusion of others. However, this connection between the sociological structure of the city and the enjoyment of its poetic aesthetics also restricted the frontiers of this sensibility. The city may have been culturally dominated by the lower middle class, but city experience was obviously more diverse. Ironically, the poor in the city did not necessarily share this gloomy sense of the city and its place in history. In economic terms, the income of different classes is a dominant consideration; but in the sociology of economic life it is the direction of movement of economic fortunes that is more important in creating a certain kind of collective sensibility. Other classes in the city did not necessarily share the historical melancholy of the educated lower middle class. The city for most people was a far more mixed and complex arena of experience. It certainly produced hopelessness and despair, but it was also a space in which anonymity gave a sense of freedom from restrictive village customs; it was enjoyed by most characters in the films as a context in which genuine love could be experienced against the deterrents of deprivation, and social and cultural taboos.

It is interesting to contrast these two sharply different rhetorical pictures of the city, and reflect about their different social and aesthetic associations. Descriptively, some of the associations are obvious. First, there is the contrast between a self-consciously 'high artistic' language and comportment of literary poetic writing. Writers like Jibanananda were engaging in a highly reflexive artistic enterprise in which the attention to form, the crafting of language and mood, were paramount; whether the poetry was generally intelligible was a far less important consideration. Some of the poets, engaging in self-interpretation, pointed out, quite rightly, that the intelligibility of poetry was a matter of the familiarity of conventions. Complaints of unintelligibility against modern, post-Tagore poetry often stemmed from the fact that the new poetic form or diction was unfamiliar rather than inherently obscure. Once used to the new diction (in Bengali often they used the term *uccharan*), the audience would begin to enjoy the new poetry and its unconventional linguistic surprises.

The rhetoric of the popular Hindi films, precisely because they were a constituent part of popular culture, entirely dependent on commercial success, could not take such high risks in terms of formal characteristics. That does not mean that there was not considerable craft in the making of the different aspects of these films. The literary elements of the films, in particular, though less visible and subordinated to commercial-popular elements, retained an aspiration to relative autonomy. Poets contributing to them wrote serious poetry independent of the films, and sedulously cultivated their literary reputations. It is not surprising that their general poetic reflection on subjects close to their heart often found expression in these compositions as well.

A second contrast between the two images of the city is probably of greater significance. Both poetry and popular films gave rise to specific aesthetic structures with very different readings of the meanings of city life. For the high artistic poetic discourse the image of the city is a dark one, where lives are unfulfilled and people go through the subtle defilement of their everyday existence. This is reflected in the strange delight that some poets have in the defilement of earlier objects of high art. Samar Sen, for instance, constantly brings up celebrated lines and images from Tagore to mock, to parody, and to defile. This sense of the city could not be a general, universal rhetoric precisely because of its narrow, partial focus on the city's deprivations. It could only be a poetic sense which was appreciated by a relatively highly-educated, middle-class minority which had the cultural skills to understand its subtleties and the social position to experience the nearness of this particular despair.

By contrast, the cinematic image of the city is more complex; it contains the dark image, but this is constantly relieved by an opposite image of hope and optimism—as in the counterpoint of the feminine statement that it is easy to live in the city, in the lilt of the pleasurable, optimistic tune of the song, in the general narrative structures of urban love. The filmic representation might be less self-consciously artistic, prone to a melodramatic simplification of emotions, but, from a different point of view, its image of the city was of a space of contradictions—where different things took place—not just of constant, unremitting despair. Unlike the high artistic portrayal of Calcutta, the Bombay of the films was, in this respect, in subtle and important ways, a city of joy.

References

Chakrabarty, Dipesh. 2002. *Habitations of Modernity*. Chicago: University of Chicago Press.

Kaviraj, Sudipta. 1998. The Culture of Representative Democracy. In Partha Chatterjee, ed., *Wages of Freedom: Fifty Years of the Indian Nation-State*. Delhi: Oxford University Press.

Lath, Mukund. 1998. *Transformation as Creation*. New Delhi: Aditya Prakashan.

9

The Art of Despair

The Sense of the City in Modern Bengali Poetry

I t is commonly acknowledged in historical literature that modernity, along with many other new things—in politics, economic life, social behaviour—brings a distinct aesthetic sensibility. Usually, modernity introduces a far-ranging and fundamental artistic transvaluation of objects. Things, images, attitudes, feelings which were valued earlier are forgotten or treated with indifference, new objects and orientations emerge to occupy the centre of artistic attention. This change of aesthetic sensibility is shown most graphically in thinking aesthetically about the city. I shall attempt a brief historical analysis of how the embarrassment about the city, the place which was the theatre of the most immediate and intense experience of modernity, but which seemed to defy aestheticization, captures this more general process in a microcosm.

Although I hope this illustrates a more general trend in aesthetic reflection, this is a study of a particular case. First, it is only about Bengali literature, not other varieties: secondly, it is about only one problem which troubled Bengali literatures among many other kinds of problems. But a discussion of this theme, and comparison with other regional literatures may show us whether we can make some general points about the aesthetic challenges of modernity. My discussion will focus only on poetry, which introduces a further peculiarity, as the specificities of the modern poetic form allow the aesthetic problems to

First published in Harsha V. Dehejia and Makarand Paranjape, eds, *Saundarya*, New Delhi: Samvad India Foundation, 2003.

be framed in peculiar ways. Literary forms other than poetry, like the short story, but particularly the novel, also engaged in sustained and intricate aesthetic explorations of city life. Some formal peculiarities of the novel made it a particularly good instrument for this purpose—its detailed descriptive accounts of space and dense networks of social relations into which characters were inserted. Poetry did not have that formal advantage of the descriptive, and its sense of the city had to be communicated through more abstract, indirect and condensed imagery. Yet, in terms of its different formal language, modern poetry engaged with the city as an aesthetic problem. After a short account of the description of the city in traditional literature, I shall focus on some well-known works of two utterly different poetic voices: Tagore and Jibanananda Das, because the point I wish to make comes out most sharply through this contrast. What remained a problem with Tagore was given a kind of solution by Jibanananda. That is why the fame of the latter has steadily increased in poetry after his rather neglected life, and his death.

To link this particular subject with the general theme of *saundarya*, I would like to make a few general points. To frame the general question around the relation of *saundarya* and modernity is to presuppose a modern aesthetic point of view. The general aesthetic transformation in modern times centres on two fundamental shifts of principle. The most fundamental and comprehensive change in aesthetic thinking was the general shift from an aesthetics centred on the organizing concept of *rasa* to one of *saundarya*. This change also altered some of the most fundamental orientations that audiences and consumers of art had towards artistic creation. The *rasa* theory offered an aesthetics of mediation/distanciation, based on the essential distinction in that theory between *bhava* and *rasa*, the emotions felt by actual subjects in the actual world, and the emotional life of those subjects, drawn from the fictional-artistic world, in which even the artistic depiction of something fearful produces in the audience, not an emotion of fear, but of a complex enjoyment. The influence of modern aesthetic thinking replaced this basic attitude with one in which identification—the replication and communication of states of mind from the artist to the receiver becomes central. One of the further implications of this change was the relative emphasis placed in these two aesthetics on the aspect of creation: the state of the author's mind, his artistic intentionality, the nature of the text and its inherent craft, and the aspect of reception; the historically shifting meanings of words through which readers could try to grasp the textual meaning, their emotional cultivation, their relation to the text. Broadly, the shift from the *rasa* aesthetics to *saundarya* aesthetics altered how aestheticians and artists regarded these two essential components of the relations of meaning in art—the authorial production, the textuality of the text itself, and the receivers' meaning.

In the context of Bengali literary aesthetics, this historical change also meant a sharp narrowing down of the boundaries of what was considered 'literary', and the shift resulted in a constriction of the far more expansive literary definitions of *rasa* literature. Historically, this meant, at least for a time, that only those things which could be regarded as beautiful by a fairly strict definition could be considered a fit subject for literary writing; and this meant that a whole range of themes which were traditionally considered essential elements of the literary imagination were disqualified from entry into literature's new and more sacral territory. I believe that this equation of literary art with beauty in the narrow sense produced a crisis of sorts in writing about the city. To put it schematically, if literature could speak only about beauty, and the city, especially the teeming, disorderly, ungainly modern city of Calcutta, was not by any definition a beautiful theme, it became nearly impossible to include that in the ambit of modern literature. As the new writers and, increasingly, the new readers experienced the city as their most immediate and powerful life world, this meant that literature, at least poetry—the part of literature most exclusively deicated to the celebration of the beautiful—could not speak about a most essential modern experience, at least without great embarrassment. I wish to show through the examples of Tagore and Jibanananda Das how this 'problem' was first created, and then resolved.

It must be mentioned however that the *rasa* aesthetics that was discarded by modern writers in favour of *saundarya* had become degraded. The magnificent edifice of traditional *rasa* theory had become, by the eighteenth century, only an arcanely scholastic subject. The actual literary productions of medieval Bengali, from the rise of the *mangalkavyas* to the eclectic literary tastes of the eighteenth century, did not demonstrate either great complexity or aesthetic sophistication: their basis was a vulgar and degraded aesthetics which a modern Western-derived literary taste could undermine with comparative case. Second, the Bengali reception of European aesthetics was peculiar in one respect. The great tradition of European aesthetics, drawn from its Aristotelian source, was not a limited and restrictive theory focused entirely on beauty in the narrow sense. European aesthetic thought had from its very early stages supplemented the idea of beauty with 'the sublime'.[1] In modern aesthetic thinking, in Burke, Kant, and Stendhal, the reflection on the place of the sublime in art and its representations of suffering avoided a narrow and impoverishing aestheticization. Curiously, in the Bengali reception of European aesthetics, it was only beauty that was emphasized, which made the problems of the artistic depiction of suffering, or the abundance of evil in the modern world, an especially acute problem.

To follow the historical movement of beauty as an aesthetic concept, let me start with a brief discussion of an eighteenth-century text. Bharatchandra's *Vidyasundar*, because the scene of the narrative action is the medieval city of Barddhaman, and this will give us a clear example of how an historically existing city is portrayed in a work of poetic fiction. In fact, the temporal distance of this text from the modern Bengali poetry of Tagore is of little more than a century. Yet within these hundred years a whole new social world of colonial modernity had emerged, reflected in a wholly new aesthetic language of literary art *Vidyasundar* is unmistakably a text of the pre-modern *literary* world,[2] linked in its literary memory, its compositional skills, its conception of what makes for literary enchantment, to the great traditions of Sanskrit poetry and the medieval Bengali *mangalkavyas*.

---

[1] This is true of the Islamic ingestion of Aristotelian aesthetics as well. Ibn Sina's writing on pleasure and wonder retains this wider definition of the aesthetic.

[2] I am emphasizing literary for a purely technical reason. In recent historical research revisionist historians have argued compellingly that the eighteenth century was a period of distinct protomodernity, that 'modern' processes like commercialization had already started apace in India before the colonial impact of Western institutions. But that changing socio-economic world could still be depicted in a pre-modern aesthetic style—which is what we find in Bharatchandra's *Vidyasundar*.

This can be seen clearly through an analysis of three themes in the text which we can then replay in the cases of Tagore and Jibananda: the treatment of the city, the treatment of love, and the treatment of literature as well as its central question—what does it offer to people who read it?

The Pre-modern City: Despair and Transcendence in *Vidyasundar*

How does the *Vidyasundar* answer these three questions? The text, generally acknowledged as Bharatchandra's masterpiece, uses a narrative widely known in various regional literatures of India, north and south, straddling the divide between the Sanskrit and the vernacular. Even a Persian version apparently existed. Hundreds of other accounts of *Vidyasundar* were composed, embellishing the story in various ways. But Bharatchandra's retelling contains some strikingly significant features which could not appear without deliberate authorial artifice. The story is about the vow taken by Vidya, the beautiful princess of Barddhaman, that she will only consent to marry a man who gets the better of her in a literary contest. Princes were generally not known for intellectual subtlety, and, not surprisingly, a long line of hopeful suitors failed. This led to dark forebodings that the most beautiful woman of the kingdom, cursed by her intelligence, might because of her rash resolve remain unwed and sexually unfulfilled. Interestingly, there is a polyvalence in the depiction of Vidya's character. It can be read as the view that only the acquisition of intellect makes a woman perfect; but it is equally plausible to see this craving for knowledge in a woman—a rare occurrence in that society—as a curse which can be overcome only by divine intervention.

Happily, in the muscular military world of princely life, a rare exception is Sundar, the prince of Kanchi, who travels to Barddhaman to woo Vidya. Briefly, he searches out Vidya through an intermediary, overcomes her in a private contest of literary excellence, is accepted as her lover, makes a tunnel into the royal palace, and starts seeing her. Vidya becomes pregnant, and after a search by a frantic *kotwal*, Sundar is caught in Vidya's apartments and sentenced to death. On his way to the cremation ground for execution, Sundar recites verses composed in Sanskrit, apparently recalling Vidya's beauty and their raptures in love. Bharatchandra exhibits great ingenuity at this point.

The verses that Sundar recites are not original; he simply appropriates conventionally well-known verses of a famous Sanskrit text of *shringar* poetry, the *Caurapancasat* or *Caurapancasika*. What saves this audacious move from the charge of plagiarism was an astonishing demonstration of technical virtuosity as a semanticist. Bharatchandra enjoyed a great, and on this evidence a deserved, reputation for his skill in the *alamkara* of *vyajastuti* (false or double-entendre praise). By clever use of semantic resolution (*anvyaya*) of the sentences he demonstrates that each verse can be interpreted in two ways. One meaning of the verse, the conventional reading, refers to Vidya and only contains erotic remembrance; the other refers to the goddess Kali and is a devotee's call of distress. Bharatchandra does not compose new verses, but utterly new meanings, supporting his reputation for the semantic-poetic virtuosity so highly valued by one strand of the Sanskrit *kavya* tradition. Moved by the intensity of his devotion (and his semantic erudition), the goddess acts entirely according to the conventions of *mangalkavya*, delivers the hero, and the lovers are reunited, now not in a furtive or transgressive enjoyment of their love but in a restful and sanctioned state.

This is an instance of narrative of reversal very common in both Sanskrit and Bengali poetry. For the purposes of our discussion, I am interested in three aspects of the text that provide us with a contrast to the treatment of similar themes in the modern period. These are: the images of the city as a social space; the thinking about love and intimacy; and the underlying sense of the literary—what makes for literary enjoyment or *rasa-nishpattih*.

Schematically, in medieval literature too, the city is differentiated from the countryside, but not by any distinctive *social* principle. Historians have pointed out that there were mainly two types of pre-modern cities—cities centred around the seats of deities, or of administration. Both were crowded, full of people, particularly of a transiting flow of populations. The crowding of the space offered opportunities to lovers for furtive signs of recognition, fleeting contacts, opportunities exploited by Sundar in his initial acquaintance with Vidya. Similar opportunities for charm and recognition are encountered in Urdu or Persian poetry as well, where the city, despite its many prohibitions and denials, precisely because of its size, offers opportunities of recognition. But these are mere breaks in the routine of a repressive, hierarchical, strictly controlled life. The traditional city is not marked by either of its two major characteristics in modern times: its democracy and its anonymity. It is not a space of equality because it is not a space of anonymity. In fact, as modern novels and narratives show, there is something insubstantial and fragile even about the equality of the early modern Indian city. People do treat each other with a kind of formal equality, the elementary principle of democracy. Usually, this equality is narratively short-lived: it crumbles very quickly as people get to know each other more fully as social subjects, and recognize that they are divided by caste, class, community, gender, the accidental animosities between families, etc. Still, in early modern narratives the city is an equalizing space: it regularly transforms individual characters in both high artistic Bengali novels and popular films. It can be a threatening space to those who fear its equalizing power, and liberating for those who welcome and enjoy its freedom, and at least a formal equality.

Bharatchandra's city is nothing like this. In terms of love and intimacy, again, Bharatchandra's literary aesthetics are firmly anchored in traditional designs. Here is an obvious process of literary individuation without which no narrative can function—the two main subjects of the narrative are differentiated from others in the background by their eminence in beauty and intellect, and their extraordinary attraction towards each other. But they are not individuated as ordinary but peculiar individuals, typical of the modern novel and poetry. Finally, their intimacy is, despite their initial games of intellect, essentially a sexual rapture.

The space of the city in *Vidyasundar* remains pre-modern because it is not disenchanted. It is a space where all kinds of extraordinary and supernatural events take place. The affection that develops between Vidya and Sundar is extraordinary, just as are the devices used in the narrative. It is as if these are quite common and credible occurrences— Sundar getting access to the royal household, his digging the tunnel, and finally and climactically his deliverance in the cremation ground by a miracle worked by the goddess. Bharatchandra's text does not give us an impression that townspeople are different kinds of individuals, with a distinct form of life and sociality, or that their lives produce different sorts of crises and require special solutions in literary art.

Within a century of the composition of *Vidyasundar*, Bengali society began an extraordinarily rapid transformation through the entry of colonial power. By the end of the eighteenth century the colonial city of Calcutta had emerged as a central theme in the spatial *imaginaire* of Bengali literature. From early on, two strands of literary and metaphorical thinking about space are clearly discernible. One strand sees the city as being increasingly central to the new social experience of modernity. But the early literary probings of this new social space are understandably cautious. The literary sense of this new city is deeply ambivalent, for obvious reasons. The Calcutta of the early nineteenth century is a place of new ambitions and dreams; but even these dreams are disorienting, because they are not historically familiar dreams, or conventionally cherished through the social grammar of desires. Opportunities of an utterly new type open up, with attendant risks, to people who combine the characteristics of economic opportunists and moral adventurers. It is hardly surprising that literature first approaches this new social space and its unfamiliar sociability through a form peculiarly suited to express this ambivalence. This strange combination of curiosity and reproach, an emerging sense that there might be possibilities of unforeseen liberation, is mixed with the apprehension that in its search deeply cherished social values might be sacrificed. The moral ambivalence towards Calcutta is appropriately expressed in the formal ambivalence of humour.

Kaliprasanna Sinha, who organized a full translation of the *Mahabharata*, was, alongside this high serious engagement with Sanskritic tradition, probing Calcutta's ambiguous morality through a series of sketches. *Hutom Pencar Naksa*, a series of fiercely critical sketches of the successful, enterprising, avaricious, profligate, and degenerate Calcutta elite became one of the first triumphs of modern Bengali literature. I believe this was primarily because it captured with perfection this duality of attitude of the modern Bengali towards Calcutta and its excesses. The sketches make fun of the new elite's taste for exaggeration, entirely useless consumption, formation of pointless cliques around landowning magnates, and their sexual profligacy from an interestingly complex point of view. In one sense, it is the view of those who were excluded from this unexpected, unaccountable prosperity of a group of people who appeared to be entirely accidental beneficiaries of colonial rule. No particular achievement, except a fortuitous proximity to powerful British officials, entitled them to this entirely undeserving eminence. This line of thought was carried on relentlessly and powerfully in Bankim's famous satire about the irresistible rise of mediocrity in the colonial society of Calcutta, *Muchiram Guder Jivancharit.* However, the writers of humorous sketches, in the case of both Kaliprasanna and Bankim, show nothing of the literary awkwardness of the lower orders: they make fluent use of the high Sanskritic techniques of *vyanga* and *vyajastuti*; they are among the foremost authors who are experimenting with a new, powerful, racy, Bengali idiom.

A second strand of writing about Calcutta is less positive about its promise. It looks at Calcutta as a space of degeneration, as a city which spoils the lives of both those with wealth and those without. The excessively rich, who benefited from their connection with the rising colonial power, but who cannot as yet claim any particular distinction, are usually spoiled precisely by their gift of fortune. Unearned wealth made them prone to conspicuous consumption, and an undirected aimlessness in their lives, leading often to a life of complete idleness and degeneracy. On the other side of the divide, Calcutta showed the despairing existence of the poor and an unusually large class of dependants who lived a life of unspecified employment as unctuous, servile assistants of this newly opulent elite. A second strand of early modern Bengali literature thus views Calcutta through eyes of unrelieved moral darkness, as a space in which society seems to be sliding into a relentless logic of modernist degeneration.

After the rise of colonialism, an additional element came into this literary reflection on Calcutta. As the colonial capital of India, Calcutta always connects the Indian/Bengali elite's power with its subservience to British rule. Calcutta's glory as a city thus remains not the glory of the Bengalis, but of someone else, a strangely heteronomous eminence. Thus, celebrations of Calcutta have a strangely dual character, sometimes not deliberately portrayed with satirical intent. It was a celebration of both the glory of the Bengalis and, as Bankim's Kamalakanta would immediately add, of their unrelieved servility to their colonial masters.[3] The sense of power, of unworried sovereignty over a spatial and material world that comes with the assurance of unchallenged political and commercial power, is never found in early modern writings about Calcutta as a city. It is always a space in which

---

[3] I have discussed some instances of this literary strand, in particular in Bankim, Rabindranath, and Sukumar Ray, in Kaviraj 2000.

the Bengali upper class lacks sovereignty; even when it parades its unrestricted supremacy over the surrounding world, this is marred or threatened by reminders of its subservience. There never was a literature showing a straightforward celebration of Calcutta and the human existence of it.

Calcutta as a Space of Freedom

However, sociological and cultural changes were undeniably taking place which, despite the reluctance of the more artistic writers, found their way into literary descriptions of the common world. However much writers might deplore the degeneration of morals in the colonial city, their narratives illustrate some sociological truisms. Characters in the narratives seek and find both adventure and freedom in Calcutta, away from the monotonous and repressive routines of everyday life in the countryside. Bankim's novels already reveal this trend, in which the lawyers and modern professionals live in Calcutta, in ways that are socially different from the conventions of the countryside. Some of these sociological changes are reflected more graphically in relatively pedestrian narrativisation. Authors of elevated artistic texts like Bankim naturally work with highly deliberate narrative intent, and their fictional art, instead of passively reflecting ordinary social life, is deeply driven by those artistic interests. 'Little texts' of literature—the relatively commonplace narratives by less celebrated and talented writers—constitute a much better mirror of social change, precisely because of the lack of an overriding high artistic design. In such narratives, over time, Calcutta comes to achieve a different kind of status as a space of freedom and anonymity. Certainly, it contained the surprising disorientation of anonymity in a big city of people used to the dense intimacy of rural life. Characters, of course, routinely complain about the city's heartlessness, especially when they are newcomers. They feel lost and baffled. But they usually recover from these difficulties fairly quickly by making new contacts in the city, which, in novelistic stories, they often turn into new relations of pretended kinship.[4] Recurrently, their attitude towards the city

---

[4] Bhudev Mukhopadhyay, in his social analysis of Bengali domesticity, *Parivarik Prabandha*, uses an interesting phrase to capture this: *kritrim svajanata*, artificial kinship.

changes when they meet someone they can love, usually someone they could not have in principle met in the restrictive social order of village life. Through these endless romances in early Bengali novels and stories, a slow rise to self-awareness is the most repetitive theme; these characters fall in love, enter into unexpected social conflict, and are forced to consider the relations around themselves with a new kind of critical intelligence. This leads to the process of their 'finding themselves', realizing who they are, or, more significantly, they see the importance of finding an ideal which they then wish to realise in their lives: finding themselves not in the sense of discovering an immanent self, but fashioning their selves through the transformative conflict of experience.[5]

This way of looking at Calcutta gradually became routine in novels, precisely because novels always contain a more expanded sociology of societies than other forms of literature. Eventually, this rhetoric of Calcutta spread from novels into films, as films depended initially very heavily for their narrative material and dialogue on novels and stories. It became conventional in Bengali story-telling in the novelistic or filmic form for main characters, usually male, to leave an idyllic village and find their way to Calcutta's mixture of bafflement and allure. Heroes regularly make their homes in the crowded city, unaccountably disregarding greater social position and the comforts of the life of a rural gentry, losing their hearts to pert city girls. They accept life in disorderly, cramped rooms, in a world of strangers, which their more innocent rural relatives find impossible to understand. The general line in this kind of narrative is that Calcutta, and the modern city in general, corrupts people by its freedom. The lure of a life free from restraints keeps people tied to the city. Grudgingly, the novelistic genres nevertheless acknowledge the status of Calcutta as a space of freedom.

My main argument, however, deals with a different branch of literary writing—modern poetry. While novels and stories, which

[5] An excellent example of this pattern of narrative structure can be found in Tagore's famous novel *Gora*. But this structural form of narrative acquaintance with the city is repeated in thousands of stories—from Bankimchandra's social novels to contemporary fiction. An example from relatively recent fiction is Samares Majumdar's highly acclaimed novel of a Naxalite rite of passage, *Uttarpurush*.

have to offer sketchy but credible sociologies, celebrated Calcutta as a space of freedom, this was not reflected in the parallel development of the poetic reflection on the city. The growth of modern poetry can be sub-periodized into several stages; and although the poetry written by Michael Madhusudan Dutt or Hemchandra Bandyopadhyay or Navinchandra Sen represents modern poetry in comparison to Bharatchandra, they still constitute an early modern phase. There is clearly a further break with that tradition of modern poetic mentality in the work of later writers like Biharilal Chakrabarty, culminating in Tagore. The new modern poetry dispenses with the earlier generations' fascination with narrative or dramatic poetry, which rely for their interest on an underlying mythical or historical story.[6] The exploration and expression of emotions and their ever-changing shades, the principal task of modern lyrical poetry, is in its infancy. Early Bengali poetry is still troubled by an embarrassment about emotions. In the hands of more talented poets, as with Madhusudan, the exploration of emotions occurs through the exposition of character of the major protagonists. Still, the entirely free-standing elaboration of emotional states is relatively rare. By the time we reach Tagore's early poetry, this characteristically modern theme is firmly established in Bengali writing, and the task of modern poetry is seen to be the exploration and adequate expression of emotional life. Since city life was universally acknowledged to be new and different from conventional rural existence, and gave rise to a new structure of emotions, literary audiences naturally looked to poetry for an interpretation of urban emotions.

I do not wish here to enter the tricky problem of the strange and enigmatic character of the modernity of Tagore's writing. It is a vast and complex question. Only a few points are relevant for our discussion of poetic representation of city life.

Tagore lived an urban life. His literary triumphs required an educated, literarily sophisticated audience which was mainly resident in Calcutta. The religious context of his life was furnished by an upper-class Brahmo community which was also primarily based in

---

[6] The work of these three poets will fall into that category, though in the case of Hemchandra's *Vrtrasamhar* and Madhusudan's *Meghanadvadh* and *Tilottama* the themes are mythological and in Navinchandra's *Palasir Yuddha* the narrative is historical.

the city. At the same time, he spent a great deal of time and enterprise in building up his idyllic rural enclave at Santiniketan—an ideal, almost utopian combination of the moral values of modernity and closeness to nature in the unspoilt countryside of Birbhum. It is also amply recorded that he felt suffocated in Calcutta, both by its material environment and its institutional entanglements, and at the first opportunity went to live in his boat in Shilaidaha, in the green riverine world of eastern Bengal.

Not surprisingly, this ambivalence is deeply reflected in his art. All his life, he struggled with Calcutta as an aesthetic problem. He wrote repeatedly on Calcutta, in a great variety of literary forms; and in this variety of I find an indecision of forms, as if he is constantly experimenting with forms and moods to make new poetic approaches to the subject of Calcutta, trying to capture the poetic essence of the city but never quite finding it. Since his novels generally explore modern lives and its emotional complexities, they are almost invariably set in Calcutta, and dominated by the inner lives of urban characters. But his poetry, universally admitted to be the centre of his art, shows a very different relation to Calcutta. A comprehensive analysis of his poetic sense of the city would have to treat not merely poems which are formally directed at the city, but also the teeming, ubiquitous references to an urban world in poetry which looks inattentively at the city. That cannot be attempted here: I shall refer only to those poems which are directly about Calcutta as a subject.

Some of his poems make slightly humorous essays into the subject, like the famous dream of a child in which Calcutta, like an impossibly lugubrious train, is moving forward in a great comic confusion of collisions and displacements.[7] I wish to draw attention mainly to two poems, of more serious intent, written at widely different points of his life. The first is called 'Nagarsangit', literally a song of the city. The tone of the song is primarily one of lament—for the loss of that green sward of nature with the deep blue borders of a horizon, an earth which is called *sundar* and *shubha*, an earth marked by beauty and an auspicious wholeness.

Kotha gela sei mahan santa nava nirmal syamalkanta
Ujjavalanil vasanpranta sundar subha dharani! (241)

[7] '*Ekdin rate ami svapna dekhinu, Chhadar Chhabi*'. Tagore 1972: 759.

This quiet blue earth has been replaced by a world of inauspicious, unnatural greed and acquisition marked by its physical semiosis.[8]

kata na artha kata anartha avil karichhe svarga martya
tapta-tapan dhuli avarta uthhichhe sunya akuli.

The heated eddies of dust soiling the sky and the earth.[9]

Tagore's lines play wonderfully on the meanings of *artha* (money) and *anartha* (generally bad things; meaningless, evil deeds), etymological antonyms, subtly suggesting a connection between the abundance/excess of wealth and the corresponding abundance of evil in the modern city. All the figures of choking, depression, dying out, and enervation occur with a deadening repetitiveness. An astonishing analysis of human effort at the heart of the modern city follows: everything is momentary, fragmented, disconnected, leaving no trace behind, coming together a moment, at the next going asunder. Such a life of enterprise and instability produces a world of strong and contradictory emotions: pitiful weeping, hard unfeeling laughter, unlimited arrogance, obsequious servility, desperate effort, a cruel commentary on what it has achieved—all running in vast crowds. At the centre of this constantly shifting, unstable, dynamic world, Tagore has no doubt, lies the enticement of vast wealth.[10] This vast enterprise of commerce is seen by him—in a characteristic

[8] In many instances, it seems, Tagore's poetic phrasing carries an unfaded memory of Kalidasa's famous description of the distant earth in the *Raghuvamsam*:

durat ayascakranibhasya tanvi vanarajinila
abhati vela lavanmburaser dhara nivaddheva kalankarekha.

In Tagore's writing there are recurrent references to the earth as '*vanarajinila*'.

[9] However, *avil* in Bengali suggests not just dusty or dirty, but also morally impure. And modernity's power to soil not just the earthly world, but also *svarga* (not just the sky, but also heaven, the transcending foil for the fallen earth), is a new powerfully unconventional trope.

[10] *Kon mayamrga kothai nitya/ svarna/ halake karichhe nrtya/ tahare bandhite lolupcitta chhitichhe vrddha-balake* (Where some golden hind is carrying out its uneasing dance; and old and young are running maddened by the desire to catch it: 242).

transposition of an ancient trope into a modern context—as a vast sacrificial fire-bowl (*vipul yagnakunda*); but this is the magic bowl of fire which attracts creatures from the world around to run towards it and seek cremation. Men and women break up the urns of their own life, decanting their life-blood into it. All it's devotees circle around it, addicted to this golden-coloured death, bringing their bones and their blood to its great sacrifice. The sacrifice itself, the rapacious enterprise of commerce, 'is growing into leaping uncontainable tongues of flame, blackening every corner of the sky with a terrible noise, obscures the sun and the moon with a burning enveloping the earth. The vast legions of the wind circle those flames and roam uncontented breathing its fiery breath' (242).

To Tagore its destructive consequences are clear, but its strange attraction for its victims is morbidly fascinating: 'As if desperate insects watch this vast conflagration, they wish to sever their own limbs and cut their own veins [for sacrifice]' (242). The creation of the vast commercial world, with the modern city at its centre, is obviously influenced by both romantic and socialist visions, and is similar to descriptions of the European city in the young Marx and Engels, and indeed Tocqueville. What is remarkable is the persistence with which the poem, despite the constrictions of verse form, elaborates the central strangeness of the spectacle: it is not its likeness to a vast conflagration of destroyed lives that is remarkable in his eyes, but the attraction it exerts on human beings. They come to the conflagration of their own, compelled by an irresistible desire for wealth and a debased utopia.

At the mid-point of the poem, there is suddenly a turn of the poetic voice: 'O city, today I shall drink the overflowing draught of your foaming wine, and I shall forget myself' (242). In what follows, Tagore presents an astonishingly precise portrayal of the joys of modern life symbolized by the city. A careful and detailed reading of his images reveals a characteristic way of thinking about the city and its attractions. The city is called the stony-hearted nurse of humanity who offers the joys of sleepless intoxicated nights.

Ghurnacakra janatasamgha bandhanhin maha-asanga
Tari majhe ami kariba bhanga apan gopan svapane
Ksudra santi kariba tuccha padiba nimne cadiba ucca
Dhariba dhumraketur puccha bahu badaiba tapane . . .
Hate tuli laba vijaybadya ami asanta, ami abadhya

Jaha kichhe acche ati asadhya tahare dhariba sabale
Ami nirmam, ami nrsamsa sabete basaba nijer amsa
Paramukh hate kariya bhramsa tuliba apan kabale
Manate janiba sakal prthvi amari caran-asan-bhitti
Rajar rajya dasyuvrtti kono bhed nai ubhaye . . .
Naba naba ksudha natun trsna, nitya nutan karmanistha
Jibangranthe nutan prstha ultiya jaba tvarite . . .
Tabe dhali dao kebalmatra ducari divas, ducari ratra,
Purna kariya jivanparta janasamghatmadira.

I shall break into pieces my secret dream of wholeness and peace in this whirlwind of humanity, this great gathering of men without ties. I shall disdain the small life of peace, ride high and fall down, I shall grasp the comet's tail, stretch my arm toward the sun itself. I'll pick up the drums of victory, I shall be unquiet, insubordinate, I will grasp with all my strength whatever is unattainable. I'll learn to be pitiless, cruel, I'll take a share in everything, I will snatch things from others' mouths and bring them in my grasp. I'll know in my heart of hearts that the entire world is merely the pedestal of my self; there is no difference between the rule of kings and the profession of robbers. I'll feel constantly new thirsts, constantly new aspirations; I'll turn the pages of my life as fast as I can . . . Then pour, for just a few days and nights, filling the cup of my life with this wine of human conflict.

There has been comparatively little research on the detailed traces of intellectual influence which can be gleaned from Tagore's writing; but the sources of this critique are, in broad terms, quite apparent. The Romantic rejection of a thrusting and incessant industrial enterprise which vandalizes nature and its sustenance is combined with a nearly socialist distaste for extractive greed—what he was to characterize in his drama, *Raktakarabi*, as the deplorable shift from an agricultural to an extractive civilization (*karsnajivilakarsanjivi sabhyata*), but these are interlaced with ideas drawn from a pastoralist interpretation of Upanishadic advice on a life of restraint and non-acquisitiveness. But some of the characterizations are startlingly close to the concerns of early modern social theory: *bandhanhin maha-asanga* is a strange phrase that comes very close to 'unsocial sociability'—a great conglomeration of people who have no feeling of attachment and relate to each other only instrumentally. It shatters and leaves behind his secret dreams of happiness and contentment; but the images solve the mystery of modernity's powerful enchantment. It is in his powerful image, a firestorm of unrestrained desire for power and acquisition, an extension of the self by relentlessly attaching everything within its grasp. The conquest of things is its only insatiable happiness.

This worship of success through conflict comes close to another celebrated description of human nature from early modern European theory: 'to constantly outgo the next before is felicity, to be outgone by others is misery, to forsake the course is to die.' But Tagore realizes with wonder that there is something deeply attractive in this world of frenetic effort, that the swarms of human insects fly, driven by a strange fatal desire towards this great fire, though in his view it leads to an addiction, a 'death the colour of gold'. The poem also captures the contradiction at the heart of modern life—it is based on a pitiless search for what we desire, with all the means within our grasp, but it is also a life that is transformed by the enchantment of the new—it forces human beings not merely to satisfy their desires but to invent a new hunger, a new thirst ('*nava nava ksudha, nutan trsna*'). The final resolution of the poem is the decision to take part in this life only partially (just for a few days and nights—'*kevalmatra duchari divas ratra*'), to drink its frothy brew for only a few days because it is, ultimately, an unfulfilling form of life.

It is the first section of the poem, which expresses surprise at arriving at the scene of modern existence from a rural idyll, that states a deep conviction of Tagore's artistic vision. The poem is significant because it presents an essential connection, in Tagore's aesthetic thinking, of the link between *sundar* and *shubha* (or *mangal*)—between the beautiful and the good.[11] This of course is not a peculiar or idiosyncratic view. It constitutes a fundamental question of many types of aesthetic thinking, and figures prominently in Kant's analysis of aesthetic disinterestedness in the *Third Critique*. Beauty, for Kant, must be free from all interest—not merely the more mundane interests of gain, but also from a purely moral interest in the good. Interestingly, after arguing powerfully for this distinction throughout the text, at

---

[11] I have discussed the question of modernity and the problem of evil in my essay on Bengali literature in Pollock 2003. It is particularly instructive to look at the complex arguments in defence of Tagore by the distinguished literary critic, Abu Saiyad Ayub. See Ayub 1968.

the end Kant endorses a position that is partially similar to Tagore's. He acknowledges that there is a fundamental, and to him entirely understandable, proclivity in human minds to connect what is beautiful with what is morally good, at least as a legitimate metaphor (157-60, 223). Although he was not a systematic aesthetician, Tagore gave reasoned presentations of his aesthetic beliefs, not leaving them entirely to unreliable inferences from his poetic work. Several of his essays on aesthetics make serious theoretical approaches to the problem of *saundarya*, two in particular, 'Saundaryabodh' (A Sense of Beauty) and 'Saundarya O Sahitya' (Beauty and Literature). In a fairly elaborate reflection on the place of literature in human life, Tagore suggests there are three ways in which human beings relate to the world—through knowledge (*jnana*), through action (*karma*), and through enjoyment (*ananda*). These are separate and distinctly valuable 'means of understanding' the world. He continues:

> Let alone the Himalayas, if an ordinary pond overgrown with algae is presented before our mind's eye we experience delight. We have seen this pond many times through our eyes. But to see it through language makes it a new seeing. What the mind can see using the sense of the eyes, if it can see through language, the mind can experience a new kind of *rasa*. Thus literature becomes something like a new sense [*indriya*] and presents the world to us anew. Not just making it new. Language has a special quality. It is something that is our own, in part created by our mind. Therefore, when it brings anything from the outside to us, it is made human in a special way (87).

A second feature of literary seeing, according to Tagore, is that 'when we see through beauty, we see not only that particular object, but through that, everything else' (79). In another essay explaining his theory of aesthetics, he presented an idea of cultivation which sought to bring together the capacity for knowledge and a sense of beauty: his particular concern was to guard against an argument which, using the idea that beauty is disinterested, not driven by *prayojan* (need), treated it as less significant for human life. Fulfilment in a human life consists in relating to as much of the world as possible:

> My extension, my expanse depends on whatever of this world I acquire through knowledge and receive through my heart . . . [w]hat does our sense of beauty contribute to our self-development? Does it illuminate

to our heart only that part of the truth which we call beautiful, and thus turn the rest into the dull and the derided? If that had been the case, then our sense of beauty would have been an obstacle in our development, a hurdle in the path of stretching our heart into the expanse of the truth as a whole . . . I tried to say that this was not true . . . Just as knowledge (science) seeks slowly to bring everything into the grasp of our intelligence, our sense of beauty must gradually bring the whole world into the grasp of our delight: this is the only way it can be meaningful. Everything that exists is true, and therefore objects of our knowledge; everything that exists is beautiful, and therefore objects of our sense of beauty.

The City and the Problem of Transcendence

The trouble with this theoretical argument is that it does not fit very easily with Tagore's artistic distillation of modernity, his actual artistic practice. The argument that all that is part of life is a legitimate part of art, and therefore evil, and the despair it causes must find a representation in artistic creation, remains merely formal. In a narrower sense, this aesthetic only made his artistic practice appear contradictory. He found the city persistently difficult to turn into an aesthetic object. Individual things, a flower, a ray of sunlight, a figure of shadows could be seen and celebrated as beautiful, not the city as a whole, and these could evoke a tragic beauty precisely because they were small things of beauty imperilled by a vast threatening city, small intimations of beauty fated to succumb to the march of an enveloping ugliness. So the city as a whole was impossible to celebrate in literary art.

   This becomes even more poignant because Tagore's art is full of a delighted imaginary inhabitance of past cities, particularly sketches of city-life reworked from Kalidasa's poetry—with Ujjayini recurring as a trope of nostalgic fulfilment. In a humorous sketch on Kalidasa he gives us a nostalgic account of what his life would have been like had he been born in Kalidasa's time (which is incidentally the title of the poem). It is a pleasurable life of urban delights, unattainable in the history of the present. But even their pretended memory causes pleasure. In the second part of the poem he says there are substantial consolations in present times, in the unaltered continuity of the undiminished beauty of nature and women. But the humour I think conceals the underlying problem of his fundamental evaluation of modern city life as unfulfilling. Then there is a last poem of Tagore, which shows his ambivalence about the city with the greatest clarity.

It is well known that, in the last part of Tagore's long life, his work came to dominate the literary scene to such an extent that this became a crisis of sorts. Other poets found it impossible to move out of the shadow of the poetic idiom he had created, yet many felt deeply that a simple continuation of his art by less talented imitators was stultifying. Younger poets tried, from the 1940s, to experiment with other styles, and in the bitter discussions around this theme the most recurrent criticism against Tagore was his restrictive aesthetics: one which did not have a language for expressing some of the most important experiences of city life—the degradation and frustration that were the common fate of the lower middle class. By the early twentieth century the expansion of education was starting to show poisonous effects: it produced a much larger educated class *vis-à-vis* the opportunities available in the modern professions. Educated middle-class people, who formed the major part of the audience of modern Bengali literature, faced a life of new frustrations. Sociological and economic facts enhanced the more metaphysical sense of despair that war and other failures of modernity increasingly brought to people's consciousness. Not only did the younger poets of this class face urban educated misery, but they turned that increasingly into a central critical criterion for literary meaningfulness. Tagore's art, defined by its high moral tone, its literary sense of restraint, its artistic ideal of beauty, was assailed by this criticism as escapist and remote, already fatally antiquated during the later life of its creator.

In a late poem called 'Bansi' (642–5), Tagore tried to respond to the criticism of younger modernist poets that the city and the life of unfulfilment that the ordinary lower-middle-class office-goer eked out in Calcutta was a part of truth and therefore must have, on his own theory, a place of honour in poetry. In his later life Tagore faced this strange dilemma of modern temporality—its unmerciful, quickened obsolescence—with great seriousness. Instead of dismissing this criticism he sought to respond to its central charge by showing that he could, if he chose, produce an art of this redefined modernity of degradation. Among other things, this poem is a major effort in such a direction. It is a poem of considerable artistic skill, and it has the sort of fluent grace that Tagore could command so easily. It also tries, which is rare in his work, to look unrelentingly at the spectacle of an unfulfilled, wasted life—the life of a *kerani* (the office clerk). Remarkably, the protagonist is introduced without a formal, caste surname, but only as Haripada Kerani. Besides his personal first name, the only encompassing attribute of his life is being a *kerani*, a word that conveys a sense of pointless slaving in an office which the English word 'clerk' does not capture.

Structurally, the poem is divided into three segments. The first depicts the rooms which provide the context to the life of its protagonist, Haripada Kerani, his degrading castle of privacy, with plaster peeling off the walls, and subtle, infinitely sad intimations of even his longing for love. The plaster has fallen off in places, at others there are large patches of rising damp. But the depiction is not without some dark humour: the only adornment is a print of Ganesha, the giver of success, on a cheap sheet of cloth; his only companion is a lizard which lives without paying extra rent— and its distinct advantage over the clerk is that it faces no shortage of food. But the clerk's life is not without some preparation for love. He was meant to marry a girl from his aunt's village, and indeed went to the ceremony. The girl wore a Dhaka sari, with a vermilion mark on her forehead. The time (*lagna*) must have been truly auspicious, for Haripada's nerve failed at the last moment, and he fled, leaving the girl unwed, narrowly escaping a life of unrelieved drudgery. In a beautiful wistful line, he confesses: she could not come into his home, but she constantly came into his dreams/mind: '*Gharete elona se to, mane tar nitya asa jaoya.*'

In the second segment the despair becomes more intense, reflected in the material surroundings of the grimy street:

Things pile up, things putrefy
The skin and stone of mangoes, leavings from jackfruits,
Fish—, a dead kitten,
And assorted garbage . . .
The dark shadows of the rain clouds
Enter the damp room
And lies unconscious, limp
Like an animal caught in a trap.
I feel day and night bound tight to the back of some half-dead world.

It appears that the despair in this damp, rain-sodden, loveless world is entirely unrelievable. But in the third part, finally, Tagore finds a transcendence which seems more like an excuse. A resident at the corner of the filthy street plays the clarinet on some evenings. This leads to an instant transformation of the world:

In that moment reveals the utter unreality/falsity of this narrow street
Like the unbearable delirious ravings of a drunk
Suddenly the news reaches me
That there is no difference between Emperor Akbar and the clerk
  Haripada
The torn umbrella and the royal canopy
Are carried along the tunes of the flute
To an identical paradise.

Tagore's poetic powers are instantly kindled in this part, and the poem of the city can come to a suitably beauteous end. This effort, like his famous novel *Seser Kabita*, written very late in his life, sought to address the problem of modernity seriously—at least as he understood it—partly as a matter of using modernist forms like unrhymed lines, and partly as an engagement with the subject of 'evil' (as one of his best critical interpreters put it, a sense of the inauspicious: *amangalabodh*).[12]

In his later life Tagore worked out a different solution to this problem: by acknowledging that all aspects of life's truth were not reflected in his writing but would find a place in literature in general. A late poem, 'Aikatan' (Orchestra), directly acknowledged that he had on a few occasions reached the edge of the courtyard of the next neighborhood of poverty, but entirely lacked 'the strength' to step inside. He reprimanded those who practised a literature of fashionable plebeianism, because that was, in his view, 'stealing the fame of literature without paying its true price' in experience (821–4). This acknowledgement of the limitations of his own poetic imagination produced a satisfying solution at the personal level, and Tagore was much admired for his admission of something faintly suggestive of guilt. But it did not solve the larger aesthetic question: is it possible to write about Calcutta in its realist ugliness as an aesthetic object? And what could be a proper aesthetic language for this task?

In part, this problem was historical. The modern city in India is a bad copy of cities in modern Europe. In the European context the modern city expressed by its vast, organized, material configuration of space, several forces that were intrinsic to the magnificence of modern civilization: the spectacular power of the state, the luxurious opulence of the bourgeoisie, and the imaginative power of intellectuals.

[12] Ibid. I have discussed this more fully in Kaviraj 2003.

The power of the bourgeoisie and its state were expressed through the spatial imagination of the engineers and architects of Paris and London. In India, the city lacks the rationalistic order and pleasured expansiveness of Western cities. Cities here present a spectacle of wretchedness rather than splendour. *Saundarya*, accordingly, is a peculiarly difficult concept to apply to an aesthetics dealing with it as a special subject. There was also a more specific problem with the city of Calcutta. After a century of subimperialist expansion with colonial power, by the 1940s the Bengali middle class faced the unprecedented prospect of a sharp downturn in their prosperity. It remained a numerically large part of Bengali society, and particularly dominated Calcutta, but its prospects of economic prosperity shrank drastically. A life like Jibanananda Das's, in which a highly sensitive and educated man, endowed with an expansive and generous culture drawn from the whole world, was crushed into a life of misery, economic stringency, and humiliation, where the society which encouraged this cultivation lacked the means to reward it, became increasingly common. High literature after Tagore had also passed a kind of class barrier. By the 1940s most literary writers came from the disillusioned, embittered lower middle class, precariously balanced on the borders of real poverty and trying increasingly, unavailingly, to protect their sense of gentility against a hostile, contracting world. Though Tagore's art was an indispensable part of this obligatory Bengali *bildung*, for the more sensitive and thinking members of this petty bourgeoisie, it constituted a form of betrayal. It was impossible to see this art and its ideals realized in the real world of Calcutta's lower-middle-class life. It lacked, from the very start, almost by definition, the hopeful expansiveness it contained, and some of its vital aspects—its urban poise, its access to nature, its sense of peace, its confidence in finding love. The desolation of middle-class consciousness demanded a literary language of a different kind. It could not be worked out by writing imitations of Tagore.

The intensifying dissatisfaction with Tagore, a poet who had in a way given Bengalis their language for an aesthetic transaction with the world, left a huge emptiness and led naturally to a search for alternative models. Readers of English literature were drawn towards Eliot and some other modern poets; but the solution came unexpectedly through a rather untidy discussion about what modern poetry was. Buddhadev Basu, a leading post-Tagore poet and one of the finest critics of his time, began the transformation with a translation of Baudelaire. He recommended Baudelaire's seeing of Paris, the city of 'steeples and chimneys', and the darkly pessimistic emotions of his 'flowers of evil', as a model of modern poetic sensibility. This instantly set up a powerful contrast between Tagore's aesthetic world and Baudelaire's, mainly their utterly different principles of selection of themes in modern poetic art. Some of the most searching discussions of the meaning of poetic modernity took place in response to Basu's programmatic preface to his book of translations, particularly his claim that Tagore's poetry, though deservingly famous and indispensable, had undergone a strangely rapid obsolescence; and though the poet was still alive and writing significant work, he was already a part of the past. Bengalis needed modernity in their poetry, a poetry closer in spirit to Baudelaire, with loss, melancholy, a soiled romance, and degradation as its primary themes. This went directly against Tagore's aesthetic doctrine that it was only those things that evoked *mangal* which deserved a place in art, particularly poetic art. Abu Sayed Ayub, one of the foremost literary critics of that generation and an admirer of Tagore's poetry, wrote a spirited rejoinder—a series of interlinked essays published as a single text, *Rabindranath and Modernity*.

Younger poets began frantic experimentation with ways of getting out of a world dominated by Tagore. The finest response to the city as an aesthetic problem in Bengali poetry came from the 'poet of loneliness' Jibanananda Das.[13] Jibanananda was a loner, not much involved in the social circles of patrician or middle-class intelligentsia—unlike Sudhin Datta, Buddhadev Basu, or Bishnu De. Like several other Bengali poets, he was a teacher of English literature in suburban colleges in Calcutta, and, for a short while, in an unsatisfactory stint in Delhi. He published a first book of poems, which was not substantial in either its content or style, staying within the safe boundaries of post-Tagore Bengali poetry. But his second collection discovered a startlingly different poetic language for an artistic imagery

---

[13] Das has been given various sobriquets. The most commonly repeated is the apt description by Buddhadev Bose in introducing his poetry to readers unfamiliar with his style: *nirjanatama kavi* (the loneliest of poets), which gestured towards his ability to listen to an inner silence, as also his difference from others in style and his personal aloofness. Clinton Seely's excellent study, *A Poet Apart*, plays on Bose's phrase. Abdul Mannan Saiyad has a set of interesting essays with the title *Shuddhatama Kavi* (The Purest of Poets).

that was exactly at the opposite pole from Tagore's—decay in nature, degradation in human beings, and the recurrent theme of death. Death, of course, was not a new theme in Bengali poetry; but poetic death was always meaningful—fantasies of death in unrequited love, normal death transcended by remembrance, at times a reconciliation with death as a natural end which brought a conclusion and a meaning to a life. Jibanananda's deaths were very different: death as a natural condition of things, the violent death of deer playing in the forest at the hand of a hunter, the death of an apparently successful middle-class man by suicide sleeping at last on the dissecting table in the morgue, the death of innocence, desires, and loves. In one sense Das worked out a simple solution to the poetic problems of the city by simply radicalizing Tagore's distinction. For Das too, there was no poetry which could find a single language to cover the lives of the city and the countryside. As a consequence, he simply divided his poetic world into two radically dissimilar parts. In one part he began to write about rural Bengal, especially its natural world, with an astonishing, almost Keatsian sensibility—observing dewdrops on leaves, the fragrances of nature, the night of birds, green light under deep foliage, the murmur of running water—and crafted a language of infinitely loving sensuousness.

His poetry of the city was an entirely different matter. I shall discuss two examples. It is possible and tempting to compose an artificial poem out of fragments of his poems. His artistic style invites this by its sameness of metre and subject of vision and reflection. Poems seem to end only provisionally: the unconcluded themes are taken up again in subsequent compositions. In one of his well-known poems, 'Ratri' (Night), the city is seen at midnight, after the ceaseless activity, crowding, and traffic of daytime in Calcutta have ended. There is a subtle suggestion that the night is in a sense the real time of the city, when it can be seen for what it really is. After daytime's frenzy is taken away, what is left are the irreducible elements of modern life, and these are captured in unforgettable figures of emptiness and degradation. The most renowned lines run:

> *Hydrant khule diye kushtharogi chete ney jal*
> *Athaba se hydrant haitoba giyechhila phense*
> *Ekhan dupto rat magarite dalbendhe name*
> *Ekti motorcar gadoler mata gelo keshe*

A leper drags himself to a hydrant and licks water
Or perhaps that hydrant had sprung a leak
Now the deep night descend on this city in droves
A motorcar goes past coughing like a lout.[14]

The distance from Tagore's evocation of *sundar* and *mangal* could not be greater.[15] The poem does not give us time to prepare for its images: it begins like some forms of modern music with an image of great shocking power: the leper licking water from the hydrant—our first acquaintance with both nature and culture, with night and the city. The iconic figure is the leper; a common sight in cities in Das's time, they were symbols in which several layers of degradation could be condensed—begging, friendless, helpless, socially degraded, physically decaying, the utmost sign of fallenness. The leper is depicted in his most abject state—dragging himself to a hydrant, not to drink water as ordinary people do, but to lick it from its filthy drip.

Another famous poem captures, better than anything else in modern Bengali poetry, the despair and pointlessness of lower-middle-class Bengali life. It describes a corpse lying on a table in the morgue: initially titled, 'One day eight years back' (*At bacchar ager ekdin*) it was later changed to the more deliberate 'In the morgue' (but in Bengali '*lashkata ghare*'—the image is more gruesome; it translates literally as 'in the room for cutting corpses'). The poem, as appropriate, wonders why a man apparently happily married, with a stable family, unaccountably committed suicide: because of what indefinable sorrow seeping out of his apparently settled life, out of what ineradicable tiredness?

Last night, when the five-day old moon
Had drowned in the darkness of night
He felt an urge to die [*maribar sadh halo tar*]
His wife was lying next to him, and his child
There was love, was hope—still in that wash of moonlight

---

[14] Das 1988: 97.

[15] Sunil Gangopadhyay wrote an excellent essay on the poetic contrast between Tagore and Jibanananda Das, '*Prajjvalanta surya ebam satti tarar timir*' (The Effulgent Sun and a Darkness Made by Seven Stars), in his *Amar Jibanananda Aviskar O Anyanya* (My Discovery of Jibanananda and Other Essays).

What ghost came to his sight?
Why did he wake from his sleep?
Or he had not slept for a long, long time
And now in the morgue he finds some sleep.
Maybe he wanted precisely this sleep:
Like a pestilential rat, with blood foaming from his mouth,
In a dark corner, he sleeps now.
Never to wake again.[16]

There is something interesting in this poem that goes beyond the merely sociological point made earlier. The emptiness in it is not linked to material restrictions but to a metaphysical taste of modernity. In some of its lines Das makes it clear that this man was not condemned to a poor life in the ordinary sense: he was not frustrated in unrequited love: there was no dross in his marital life; he had tasted the sweetness of intellection (*mananer madhu*); he never knew the withering cold of the winter of poverty and hunger. The poem, however, finds a reason for his choosing this socially unaccountable death:

I know, I know despite this
A woman's heart, love, child, home—these are not all:
Not wealth, not success, not affluence—
There is another fearful, wounding wonder
That plays inside our inmost blood.
That makes us tired, tired, tired.
The morgue does not have that tiredness.[17]

The sense of desolation of modern life is dissociated from material loss; it becomes a fearful sense of wonder that plays inside our blood. Clearly, this desolation does not admit of the sense of good that brings transcendence through music in Tagore's poems. It is an untranscended sense of despair. Tagore's aesthetic would find inhabitance in this dark world impossible. Jibanananda wrote comparatively little explanatory or selfinterpretive prose: but his poetry constantly attempts intellectual clarification of itself, constantly painting emotions and giving reasons for them. In another poem we find a statement that in a way addresses our aesthetic question. 'Bodh', which in Bengali bears a

[16] Das 1988: 77.
[17] Ibid.

complex connotation that mixes the meanings of sense, intelligence, awareness:

Alo-andhakare jai—mathar bhitare
Svapna nai, kon ek bodh kaj kare,
Svapna nai, santi nai, bhalobasa nai,
hrdayer majhe ek bodh janma lay (Bodh)[18]

Jibanananda is notoriously difficult to translate, but a rough literal rendering is:

I walk through light and darkness—inside my head/mind
Not a dream, but an intelligence starts its work
Not dreams, not quiet, not love.
In my heart an intelligence takes birth.

The third line, I think, is his poetic answer to Tagore's aesthetic doctrine, a rejection of transcendence in every form. A poetry of modernity cannot retreat inside dreams into an untroubled tranquillity, even into love which, in most troubled poetry, still reveals poetry's untroubled centre. What modern art achieves is not a sense of beauty but an intelligence. Jibanananda's world is most fatally disenchanted, without god, and bereft of the three consolations of dream, peace, and love which helped man to ward off bitterness. However, in this world in which god has been murdered, man's search for meaning does not cease:

Manush kauke chaye, tar sei nihata ujjval
Isvarer parivarte anya kono sadhanar phal

Man desires someone—instead of his murdered luminous God, some fulfilment which stand at the end of a different search.[19]

In my reading, Jibanananda's poetry displaces the ideal of the beautiful, in particular, the ideal of beauty affiliated to the good, in its search for an aesthetic of the modern. The world of modernity contains, ineradicably, too much evil, degradation, and an unspectacular desolation of uncomplaining everyday lives filled

---

[18] Ibid.: Bodh.
[19] Ibid.: 'Suranjana', 56.

with meaninglessless, rendering obsolete the earlier aesthetic of beauty. Tagore, the creator of Bengali's modern idiom, despite his inexhaustible genius, struggled with it in vain. Jibanananda Das, in his shorter, intenser oeuvre, succeeded at least in capturing this aspect of a modern sensibility by fashioning an unmistakably beautiful language for the expression of bitterness. Ironically, traditional Indian aesthetics, with its clear conception that artistic *rasas* can include the *adbhuta* and the *bibhatsa*, may have found it easier to understand this aspect of modern sensibility. Tagore's replacement of this more flexible, capacious aeshethic doctrine by a stricter, narrower and purer ideal of beauty made the aesthetic distillation of modernity's dark side more difficult.

References

Ayub, Abu Saiyad. 1968. *Adhunikata O Rabindranath*. Calcutta: Dey's Publishing.

Das, Jibanananda. 1988. *Jibanananda Daser Sreshtha Kabita*. Calcutta: Bharavi.

Gangopadhyay, Sunil. 1999. *Amar Jibanananda Aviskar O Anyanya*. Calcutta: Ananda Publishers.

Kant, Immanuel. 1988. *Critique of Judgement*. Trans. James Creed Meredith. Oxford: Oxford University Press.

Kaviraj, Sudipta. 2000. Laughter and Subjectivity: The Self-ironical Tradition in Bengali Literature. In *Modern Asian Studies*. December.

———. 2003. Two Histories of Bangla Literary Culture. In *Literary Cultures in South Asia*. Ed. Sheldon Pollock. Berkeley: University of California Press.

Majumdar, Samares. n.d. *Uttarpurush*. Calcutta: Ananda Publishers.

Tagore, Rabindranath. 1972. *Sanchayita*. Calcutta: Visva Bharati.

———. 2000a. Saundaryabodh. *Sahitya*. Calcutta: Visva Bharati.

———. 2000b. Saundarya o Sahitya. *Sahitya*. Calcutta: Visva Bharati.

10

The Invention of Private Life

A Reading of Sibnath Sastri's *Autobiography*

This essay offers an analysis of a single text by a single individual in nineteenth-century Bengal, but it seeks to make a more general point about how concepts and practices travel through history and between societies. It is sometimes stated that all societies share certain common values and that distinctions between public and private (because they centre on the universal question of sexual life and how people should relate to their own and others' sexuality) are correspondingly universal. All societies, in this view, have some idea of what is public and what is private. This point of view is well intentioned, but historically lazy and inaccurate.

My general point can be made by an analogy with the phenomena of marriage and kinship. Sexual relations are a biological universal, but kinship is a social construction and its universality is rather like that of human language. All societies have language, but each society has a language of its own. Kinship always centers on relations between the sexes, but *social* relations are configured in startlingly different ways. I wish to argue, similarly, that a distinction between what is accessible—seen, heard, communicated—to others, and what is not, is common to most societies; but exactly where the lines of distinction fall, and where conceptual distinctions are inflected, differs widely between societies. Accordingly, although the sense that the individual

First published in David Arnold and Stuart Blackburn, eds, *Telling Lives in India* (Delhi: Permanent Black, 2005).

has some properties or mental features which cannot be shared by others (and should therefore be socially protected) occurs in many cultures, especially through religious reflections on interiority, the idea of a 'private life' is a historical construction of Western modernity.

When this idea travels to other societies, and is accepted by certain social groups, it has to be translated into the different context of that society through two parallel processes. Firstly, the incorporation of these practices requires experimentation with their lives by adventurous individuals. But, secondly, these experiments cannot affect social practice without a discursive accompaniment. Additionally, as many pre-modern cultures possess pre-existing concepts and arguments about interiority, affability of emotions, and associated states of consciousness, the reception of modern Western concepts is inevitably mediated through these intellectual habits.

In the Bengali context, this discursive accompaniment, or a constant reflexive commentary on this mode of social being, is provided by new forms of writing, primarily novels, lyric poetry, and autobiography. Novels provide both description and evaluative commentary on the fictive lives of characters. But in the nineteenth century the literary canon of modernity is composed primarily of realistic novels. The central characters in these must be socially credible and act like ordinary individuals in society, which means that interior reflections and commentaries can apply to actual social life. Lyric poetry, in its characteristically universal, unindexed mode of enunciation of the abstract self, explores the emotional universe associated with a new kind of conjugal relationship. It is striking that, almost universally, the romantic novel is interested in the period in which a relationship is negotiated between two individuals, when their romantic encounter is in its formative stage, and requires a re-education of sentiments and its moral justification. The autobiography, the third distinctively modern literary form, holds a peculiarly significant place in this inauguration of new forms of social life. It describes and reflexively comments on real—not fictive—lives. Novels assert the possibility of modern lives in the abstract; autobiographies have the ineradicable advantage of describing the real. Every autobiography is thus a vindication that such a new kind of life for the individual is not merely desirable, but actually possible.

Sastri's *Atmacarit*

The text taken up here for analysis is an early Bengali autobiography (Sastri 1918), written by Sibnath Sastri, a major Brahmo intellectual in late-nineteenth-century Calcutta. Besides being a major religious reformer, Sastri was a literary writer of considerable repute who composed poetry and wrote social novels, though not of such stature as to be included in the highest canon of modern Bengali. Bengali school students are likely to learn about him in histories of literature as a second-level figure rather than to read his texts. However, much of modern intellectual history has stressed the importance of the 'little texts' which surround the great texts and constitute their language and fields of signification. Seeking to understand social history only through great literature can be misleading: individuals who are not leading writers often play a determining role in shaping social norms and in the creation of a modern consciousness. Sastri belonged to the latter type. His reputation rested on his fame as a man of 'high character' (*unnata caritra*), as a reformer, an eloquent preacher of the Brahmo religion, and as a person who lived a new kind of intensely moral life. For Bengalis cautiously intending to be modern, his life thus had a double, slightly contradictory, attraction: it was both 'saintly' and rationalistically modern. Its central theme was that it was possible to remain religious while acting in impeccably rationalistic ways.

In studying the 'translation' of ideas from the West, or just the historical inauguration of modernity, performances in the purely intellectual field are not the only relevant measure. Performances in the translation or transformations in practice are of equal, often greater, significance.[1] Sastri was, in many ways, a heroic figure—not merely in articulating intellectual ideas and arguments, but in his character (his *caritra*), in 'leading a life' that was exemplary in a modern way. What people admired were not the texts he wrote, but the life he authored, the events that constituted it, the principles that structured

---

[1] A similar change, or shift of emphasis, can be seen in recent Western studies of modernity. See Wagner 1994; but this tendency toward a revisionist understanding of modernity can be seen in several essays in the collection 'Multiple Modernities', in *Daedalus*, February 2000, which is not confined to the West.

it, gave it its peculiar form and direction, and its historic meaning. The *Atmacarit* is his own chronicle of his life. It is called simply *Atmacarit* (*Atmacharit* in the more usual Bengali transliteration), a compound of two well-known words. *Atma* means the self. *Carita* contains the fertile ambiguity of reference to both the character displayed in the events of the life and a recounting of that story. Thus the title and its presentation are as simple and intentionally humble as possible, and there is an almost deliberate gesture of conspicuous humility in the plainness of the title and the invitation it offers to the reader.

This plainness is deceptive, however, not because the humility is insincere, as in many traditional saints who often turn such gestures into a conventionalized excess of inconspicuousness.[2] Nor is it a conventional hyperbole. Yet there is a peculiar irony in the emotion and the gesture itself. The traditional gesture of moral debasement worked through a simple technique. By asserting the extraordinary sinfulness of the devotee, it indirectly enhanced the glory of the redeemer: for the more fallen the sinner, the greater the glory of God who purified him. But Sastri's autobiography follows a modern moral path, which considered such self-abasement unworthy of human dignity. In his ability to shape a moral life for himself, the modern individual moral subject took a much more upright stance. The entire life narrated in Sastri's book continues this ironic relation to ordinariness: because, clearly, to be successful with its intended audience, it must appear as both ordinary and extraordinary. It is a kind of life that Sastri, through the story of his life, and its example, attempts to appear reasonable and socially possible to everybody. But, in his historical context, that required extraordinary effort, dramatic conflict, and social tension. The story of his life is a contest between two models of ordinariness, two contrasting, if not conflicting, forms of what an ordinary life should be. This conflict of two 'common senses' spread to every level—one's self-identity, childhood, youth, conjugality, parenthood, friendship,

---

[2] In the Bengali tradition of religious thought the most famous enunciation of the practice of humility comes from Caitanya in his famous *sloka*: *trnadapi sunicena taroriva sahisnuna/ amanina manadena kirtaniya sada harih/*. But there is a highly conventionalized form of moral abjection which makes the saint-devotee describe himself as a sinner ineligible even for God's redemptive grace.

religiosity, rationalism, cosmopolitanism. All these themes, ideas, and practices had their given, ordinary, meanings in customary Hindu life. For nearly all of them Sastri wanted a new definition to make them 'ordinary.' But that required the substitution of one discourse of 'common sense' by another. Thus the title is deceptive in its plainness. By trying hard not to embellish the title or the literary performance in the narrating, the author seeks to convey a sense of commonness. But it is not in any sense a common life. It is a life of great moral achievement, and it is lived with extraordinary deliberateness in a historical world, a language, and a changing sensibility.

The Awkwardness of the Autobiography

The autobiography is a highly specific literary form, and at Sastri's time it was not commonplace, as it would become within fifty years. In *Atmacarit*, the two words which are compounded are both common; but their conjunction is not. *Carita* or *caritra* is a common religious biographical genre. It may appear, anachronistically, that writing an *Atmacarit* is simply transferring the skills from that convention to just another object—one's self. Instead of another person of extraordinary merit, the object of narration is the person who happens to be the writer. But it is not that simple. In fact, some of the well-understood rules of this convention of biographical composition have to be abandoned, at times inverted, when a person starts to write a *carita* about himself. This involves not merely writing about a different subject; the subject forces the writer to engage in a very different kind of writing.

Conventional biographies were written about persons of great religious merit or sometimes about military conquerors, both of whom were clearly claimants to extraordinary lives. Ordinary people do not live the excessively religious, or morally unimpeachable, lives of saints; nor do they have the power and authority to embark on military conquests and glory. It is precisely the extraordinariness of those other lives which made them deserving of the distinction of a narrative. But the connection between ordinary people and this kind of exemplary or extraordinary life is significant. Most people in traditional society would be expected to live their lives according to strict routines of occupation and conduct, which set out their social roles, the criteria for their exemplary performance, and the norms of moral behavior according to the station to which they belonged. Some individuals' lives would be 'extraordinary' because they would conform to these standards to an extent not normally achieved by others. Exemplary lives would be exemplary in the literal sense, their devotion to their roles and their internal criteria of excellence would be of such a high degree of perfection as to serve as examples to others. By following these life-story models, ordinary lives would become firmer in their conception of their own roles and modes of meritorious conduct; ordinary lives would tend toward those high ideals without ever reaching their levels of perfection of moral performance. Thus these stories could contribute to the building of 'character'. Interestingly, there is a necessary relation of non-identity in this narrative arrangement. The saint never recites his own life, his moral achievements: someone less capable of such excellence does. To put it another way, there is a necessary separation between the protagonist and the narrator. This is the concept of *caritrapuja* (character-worship).

Why should there be an implicit rule of disjunction between the character and the narrator? First, the character has a perfection of personality that does not need models of this kind. He is also usually bound by rules of reticence,[3] so that it would become immodest on his part to narrate what he has achieved. His life is seen by a separate, different, lesser eye, which can, precisely because of this difference in the scale of achievement, grasp and admire its greatness. Saints, in any case, are heroes of moral action; they lack the leisure to be writers. Their lives are spent in creating bold acts, showing that such perfect acts are possible, not by preaching them, but by enacting them. In great acts, whether of kindness, compassion, sacrifice, or conquest, it is the doing that convinces, not mere saying. By definition, therefore, they do not have the time to narrate what they have accomplished. It requires a different role—that of the disciple, author, narrator, and litterateur. So every Caitanya has a Krishnadas, every Rama a Valmiki,

---

[3] One can compare Sibnath Sastri's unwillingness to talk about the sexual side of his conjugality with a similar kind of reticence in the poet Mahadevi Varma: see Francesca Orsini's essay in Arnold and Blackburn 2005, and compare Jawaharlal Nehru's silence about his private life in his celebrated *Autobiography* (1936).

every Krishna a Vyasa.[4] The author of acts and the author of stories must be different.

It is that combination—the undeniability of the ideal and its simultaneous unattainability—which induces ordinary individuals to a life of virtue. This 'building' has two connotations. It connotes the act of combining elements from different sources and giving them a crafted and fashioned coherence, and also of putting things together to make something strong. A true human character needs both: it needs to search for and select elements—dispositions, skills, and capacities—that can be culled from the most wide-ranging and diverse sources to make it rich, complex, and interesting; but it must also be a combination of some fundamental dispositions in which the person would have an immovable faith.

There are dangers in unifying the subject and the narrator. Human beings are naturally prone to self-indulgence; it is too easy and pleasant to be deluded about oneself, and fatally easy to be self-righteous about the course of one's life. Stories told by the self cannot have completeness, because they are not told at the completion of a well-lived life, impartiality—because we tend to rationalize our acts, and because of the utter impossibility of achieving the detachment required in a moral tale. Thus, it is possible to make a strong case for the separation of the liver of the life and its narration, to devise a powerful pre-emptive argument against the autobiographic impulse. An autobiography written by an Indian in this cultural habitus must surmount some of these traditional concerns.

This set of concerns about narratives of the self, which barred their writing,[5] could, however, be dramatically undermined by a new kind of moral thinking framing the individual and his God. Following Weber, it is possible to sketch the most important ideas of this framework of moral life. Individuals always live in the unblinking

[4] Though it would be wrong to believe that the relationship between the great figure, such as Rama or Krishna, and the great narrator, such as Valmiki or Vyasa, is a straightforward one of recording, it is a far more complex relationship.

[5] There are some well-known autobiographical narratives from medieval India: the best known of these, precisely because it tells the life of an ordinary individual, is *Ardhakathanaka* ('Half a Tale') by the merchant Banarasi Das, written in Hindi during the reign of Jahangir in the seventeenth century.

gaze of God. There might be some escape from human criticism, but none from the ever-present scrutiny of God, particularly because he is not an external witness, but an internal one. He lives *inside* the human heart, inside the Rousseauian moral sentiments instilled in human beings by nature (Taylor 1989). In the Brahmo literature, it is interesting to see how *isvara* (God) is slowly turned into somebody who is *hrdayavasi*, one who resides inside the heart. Thus there is a constant need to be honest and examine one's own actions and the events constituting one's life unceasingly, and to face the challenge, often the mortification, of making them public. This is also why there is such a constant need for penitence: the need to open oneself to God and to his rebukes. The self is thus divided into two parts: it is both the vehicle of the person's experience and its judge. Moral judgment cannot be avoided because the agent of this judgement lives inside, not outside.

There is also another interesting transformation in the nature of God. It is his suspiciously Christian-looking pity and kindness for erring human souls that is constantly evoked in the Brahmo literature, rather than his more Hindu characteristics of infinite power or infinite knowledge. Sometimes, there is a sense of a deep intimacy with one's God, but the quality of this intimacy is vastly different from the *vatsalya* intimacy of the Hindu devotee of Krishna. There is a strange ring to constantly repeated phrases like 'God's infinite kindness'. The traditional God was also infinitely kind, but not in quite this sense.

Schematically, Sastri's text begins with a brief genealogy, indicating where his family came from—both in the sense of their physical origins in South India and the values it passed on. The original, unreconstructed answer to the question of who they were came in the splendidly rhetorical exaggeration of a verse his grandfather taught him in his childhood:

Yavay merau sthita deva
yavat ganga mahitale/
candrarkau gagane yavat/
tavat viprakule vayam

['as long as the Ganga flows on this earth, and the sun and the moon are in the heavens, have we been Brahmins.']

Note here the intended ambiguity of the indescribable tense. There is no way of telling whether it is a reference to antiquity or to unendingness, to the past or the future. Sastri later decided that he was what he was not because of birth but by choice. He moves from the repetitiveness of the village community and its unchosen vocations to a city where lives are elected by a series of willed decisions. One of his main concerns is about domesticity and conjugality, which creates one of the greatest tensions in his life, and so also in the narrative. Marriage, which was the most passive event in the life of the Hindu adolescent, becomes a matter of the most wide-ranging experiments—of marriage among grown adults, marriage of widows, turning an arranged marriage into something utterly unlike itself, a companionate marriage of love. The autobiography is also tormented by his attempts to produce a defensible code for his two marriages, of doing right in a situation that is inherently wrong—having two wives. The movements and agitations of his life do not cease: he is forced into the upheavals and transformations of the Brahmo Samaj. The conflict between the two principles of kinship and friendship, between given and chosen relationships, is never resolved. The commonness of collective interest or intellectually shared enthusiasm never produces a thick enough sociality. It constantly, achingly, seeks something like a family; in being different from the ties of kinship it constantly mimics it, looks for the warmth, the comfort, the unthinking, assumed trustworthiness and availability of kin, parent, brother or sister. His physical movement into differently signified spaces also never ceases: he comes out of his village to Calcutta, to India, and literally to the world, to distant England. Everywhere his cultivated nature is put to the test—of being collected, civilized, never lost for words, or for acts of grace and kindness in a different milieu. That is the test of character. So, in a sense, what he is writing about is not a single person, but a type, the modern individual, of whom he is an example.

An Outline of Sastri's Life

Sibnath Sastri was born in 1847 in a small village in the southern part of modern West Bengal, close to the Sundarban forests. But in this desolate region the kingdom of the Bengali ruler Pratapaditya had flourished a century earlier and Sastri's ancestors, who came from an unspecified region of South India, were invited to settle there by the king. Sastri gave up the practice of caste as repugnant, but was not entirely above a certain sense of pride in his line of *daksinatya* (southern) Brahmins. He was born into a family of renowned pandits. His grandfather enjoyed a great reputation for his erudition in the *sastras*, which he passed on to Sastri's father. The latter received a modern education, but could not acquire a sufficiently advanced English education to be able to enter the wholly modern teaching sector. He led a strangely mixed existence, teaching Sanskrit in the school system run by the government, a situation of some irony and considerable discomfort. Sastri's maternal ancestors were also illustrious. His eldest maternal uncle, Dwarkanath Tarkabhushan, taught at the Calcutta Sanskrit College. He was the editor of *Somprakash*, a leading journal in which Sastri had his writing apprenticeship. Dwarkanath was a close friend of the reformer Iswarchandra Vidyasagar, whom Sastri knew intimately from his childhood. He recounts how, as a child, he avoided meeting Vidyasagar: he had a pot belly, and Vidyasagar had a strange way of showing his affection by pinching his tummy.

Sastri's father lacked the means to send him to the most progressive English-medium schools in Calcutta, and sent him, somewhat regretfully, to the Sanskrit College, which was going through its glorious phase with Vidyasagar as its principal. As was common among *daksinatya* Brahmins, he was married at the age of sixteen to a girl, Prasannamayi, from a family of similarly high descent, though of distinctly less erudite reputation. This caused the most significant revolution in his life. His family, particularly his father, looked down on the background of the new daughter-in-law, and afterward, following a trifling incident, decided to send her back to her parental home. Sastri, as we shall see, ineffectually protested to his father about this, but was forced to marry a second time. He kept regretting his second marriage, apparently on two different grounds. Firstly, by this time he had joined the modern-educated progressive intelligentsia in Calcutta who rejected the polygamous ways of traditional Brahmins; and, secondly, he obviously felt keenly the injustice in the treatment of his first wife. This conflict, he asserts, made him increasingly critical of traditional religious customs and drew him toward the progressivism of Brahmo culture. After joining the Brahmo Samaj, he called his first wife back to live with him in Calcutta, but was irretrievably saddled with his second wife. He had wild and impractical ideas about practicing a form of monogamy within this compulsorily bigamous life, without eventually working out a wholly immaculate solution. Apparently he lived ever after in moderate happiness in this morally messy relationship with his two wives.

Sastri's autobiography is a report on a religious life. He soon gained prominence in the Brahmo Samaj and came close to two of its major figures: Devendranath Tagore, the poet Rabindranath's father, who led the Samaj for some time, and the mercurial Kesabchandra Sen. Sen constantly experimented with both the emotional and philosophical content of the Brahmo religion and its institutional form. This caused him to lead a life of exhausting religious enthusiasm and institutional turbulence. A substantial part of Sastri's autobiography deals with these upheavals. It faithfully chronicles his initial attraction to Kesabchandra, joining him in his experiment with a modern ashram, and his gradual disillusionment with Sen's arbitrary and tyrannical style. Eventually, he became one of the major *pracaraks* (itinerant preachers) of the Sadharan Brahmo Samaj. He gave up his comfortable employment as a head teacher for the uncertainty of the itinerant life of a preacher and organizer, living primarily on charity. In the second part of his active life he traveled widely—first in the immediate Bengali sub-empire of the presidency, but later more widely in northern, western and southern India. A significant part of the autobiography is devoted to his six-month sojourn in England and his exchanges with British religious figures. He spent the rest of his life in the service of the Brahmo Samaj, which was by that time fast losing its radical and revolutionary character and turning into one unremarkable sect among the various strands of modern Hinduism.

Sastri was a writer of considerable range and versatility. His writing career began in his early student days, composing satirical verses on the foibles of anglicized Bengalis. In his maturity, much of his writing was devoted to internal disputes among the Brahmo sects. His sermons to Brahmo meetings were collected in a volume, *Dharmajivan* (A Life in Religion), published by the Samaj. He also wrote *Mejobau*, an early social novel, and volumes of poetry, often meant to be set as Brahmo hymns. However, his long-term reputation rests on his *Atmacarit* and his masterful sociological account of Bengal in *Ramtanu Lahiri O Tatkalin Bangasamaj* (Ramtanu Lahiri and the Bengali Society of His Times). As often happens, there is a certain inextricability between the two works: the concerns of one work spill over into the other, or themes abandoned in one are taken up and resumed for reflection in the other. One can see a simple division of principle between the two works: *Atmacarit* is more the story of an individual life, and the tone is somewhat more personal, while *Ramtanu Lahiri* is a more general account of society; but the two are also obviously connected. The assumption behind the telling of the life story was not that such a life was incredible, extraordinary, and unrepeatable, but that it was possible and ordinary. If the story was remarkable, it was because it was witness to a society which was equally noteworthy. Even fifty years earlier, a life of this kind would have been unthinkable.

As a result, the autobiography narrates the life of the person and also of the community of which he is a significant part: it tells the story of Sastri's life by telling the story of the Brahmo Samaj, and beyond that of Bengali society. All these conceptions of sociability of different scale and qualities are contained in the altering semantics of the term *samaj*. In the early parts of the story, when Sastri decides to join the Brahmos and reject orthodox brahminical conduct, his father disowns him. This was for two reasons: his father was a sufficiently enlightened modern person to acknowledge the right of the individual to his religious conscience, a right recognized by Hindu polytheism. He disagreed with the Brahmos and disapproved of his son's heterodoxy; but at least in part this was also because he had to lose face in his community, his samaj in the oldest, entirely traditional sense. 'Samaj' here invokes the idea of a circle of people joined by birth and kinship, and those to whom one should rightly feel the greatest obligations of sociability. However, the Brahmos also constitute a samaj. In so doing, however, they wish to obliterate the principle that birth and kinship impose the most significant obligations. They emphatically retain the idea of a community, or samaj, infused with obligations, but based, unlike the earlier brahminical community, on choice and intellectual fellowship. Finally, when Sastri wrote about the state of *Bangasamaj* at the time of Ramtanu Lahiri, his friend and contemporary, this signified society in the abstract modern sense.

Formal Aspects of Sastri's Autobiography

Autobiographies clearly exhibit many different styles of writing. In the Western autobiography this is clearly reflected in various ways of presenting the self. Obviously, there is a strong connection between the tone or style of writing and the type of self the author wants to present to his audience. Take the most obvious examples: St Augustine and Rousseau. Taking these two is not entirely irrelevant, because Sastri's Brahmo religious experiences were in deep contact with various strands of Christian thought. Evidently, the tone of personal relationship with God, divested of brahminical ritualism and priestcraft, had an equal measure of debt to Christian, particularly Protestant, examples and rationalist thinking. Though there are no explicit references to St Augustine in his work, the attitude of devotion to God is striking. Rousseau's thought was widely known and deeply influential among his generation, though there are no significant direct references to him in the text. However, I am using these two examples as forms of writing, and wish to contrast Sastri's writing with them because of its striking difference on some points.

European autobiographies are often personal in two radically different ways. Augustine's confessions are deeply personal, written in a tone which is a mixture of introspective soliloquy and formal writing. Despite the perfection of its formal execution, the tone is of one speaking to himself, or in his case to the self of his self, someone sitting deep inside him. Although this image of God as seated in an inner self is not strictly part of traditional Hinduism (which commonly regarded God as *antaryami*, one who can go inside persons, which is different from residing inside them), by the time Tagore was writing his deeply introspective poetry he could refer to his God as '*ke go antaratara se*,' that is, one more inside than the inside. Christian autobiographies often put the inner content of religious life—with its doctrines, emotions, doubts, and states of mind—into the act of writing. Thus, Augustine's *Confessions* turns the recounting of the events of his life into a long prayer. Accounts of even apparently insignificant incidents are turned into an invocation and celebration of God—from his first breaking into inarticulate sociability through a smile, to his being led astray through theft in his boyhood. Augustine's confessions have an unrivaled intensity of introspective attention. It is almost as if, during the laborious composition of this highly literary masterpiece, he does not take his eyes off his inner self. The world exists and comes in only in reports of his unbroken continuous conversation with his self and God sitting inside this self. Augustine's autobiography constantly reports the states of his mind, and of his religious emotion, and in the latter task, naturally, there is a detailed analysis of Christian religious doctrines and their adversaries.

There is a second kind of personal writing in Rousseau, whose *Confessions* is equally intent on his internal emotions: Rousseau is a painter of emotions for himself as much as for others. In addition, in this entirely secular recounting of emotional life, there is a subtle gratification of daring, to be able to talk about personal things and to bring them to public view. There is a combination of both confessional moral courage of a certain kind and the very different courage of causing outrage.

On the formal side, Sastri's autobiography differs sharply from both Augustine and Rousseau. It is written artlessly, without any attempt to bring in literary skills or subtlety. Religious issues and crises are reported, but Sastri never adopts the tone of introspective intimacy, never reports the states of his consciousness psychologically. His text is strikingly unemotional and unpsychological. And, although he often touches on subjects which could be intimate or embarrassing, there is hardly any of the confessional daring of the personal autobiography. The personal is simply hinted at, intimacies are implied, but everything is reported in a tone of unemotional calm and matter-of-fact detachment, as if he is writing about someone else's life. I feel this is because the embarrassment of the autobiography in the Indian context has been overwhelming. It is often the story of a person, but mostly of the public side of his life and of emotions which can be shared in public. Only Gandhi's autobiography, *The Story of My Experiments with Truth*, is able to overcome this reticence about the private. Yet there is something remarkably accomplished in Sastri's book. Without detail about his relations with his wives, or his dealings with his friends, or much psychological reporting of his thinking about God, Sastri records an astonishing phase of change in Bengali social life: the subject of this story, told so unemotionally, is precisely the invention of something called the private life of the individual, an essential part of the invention of a modern self.

The Idea of a Private Life

Family life, surprisingly, was the theatre of some of the greatest changes in early modern Bengal, and this was reflected in contests in the practice of family life and an intense intellectual disputation about the nature of the institution of the family and the role of the family in the structure of social life. To put it simply, there were two sides to the family debate or theoretical disputes about private life. Both thought that the family was at the center of the arrangement of various layers of sociability and their specific structuring in Hindu society. But the two sides' conceptions of the family and its underlying principles were radically different.

Without going into the details of this complex literature, I shall discuss the arguments of two most remarkable participants in this contest over the hearts and minds of modern Bengalis, both exceptionally gifted in intellectual debate, exceptionally convinced of the justice of their views, and interestingly, both equally convinced that what they experienced in their own lives showed, unproblematically, the justifiability of much larger social forms. These two figures are Bhudev Mukhopadhyay and Sibnath Sastri. It is not entirely accidental that they wrote about very similar things, though from opposing (or at least very distinct) points of view. Both of them spent much of their lives searching for answers to some of the central moral questions of their age: what was *dharma* (an ethical life)? What was the place of the family in it? What was the form of a good society in the Indian context? And what was to be learnt from the modern West? Bhudev's answers to these questions about the family are contained in his famous tract, *Parivarik Prabandha*. Sastri's book, *Grhadharma*, was equally central to Brahmo domesticity and is a strikingly coherent and reasoned discourse on the ethics of domestic life.

Parivarik Prabandha is a text of astonishing complexity. What is most remarkable about the book is not what it says, but what is left unsaid. Bhudev's conservatism is utterly different from the conservatism of other Hindu orthodox writers: it gives up an appeal to habitualism and replaces it with rationalist arguments. But in the end Bhudev's treatise on the family was disappointing: it provides, on most matters, a total intellectual justification of conventional Hindu families. Sastri's highly influential *Grhadharma* argues the opposite case. There is no direct reference to Bhudev; but the subjects are common. Both Bhudev and Sastri write about marriage and the nature of conjugality, parents' relation with children, the circle of friends (*bandhu*), the maintenance of the household, cleanliness, and domestic order. What Sastri omits from his discussion of the family is also symptomatic: he does not discuss obligations to various types of kinship—*gnati* and *kutumba*—which loom very large in Bhudev's picture of domesticity. This is a long and intricate argument in itself. Let me show an example of their differences by taking their views on child marriage. Bhudev writes:

The two who are united in their childhood by parents grow together like two creepers intertwining each other. The kind of permanent affection that is possible among them, how can that affection grow among adults? . . . [Among young people] the senses are irresistible, imagination is powerful, and affection/attraction is intense. The intelligence and patience that is required in testing each other's character is usually entirely disabled at that stage. Just one arch look, one sweet smile, one peculiarity of movement captures the fortress of the heart at once. It does not allow time for examination of character, disposition or taste. (Mukhopadhyay 1884: 2–4)

And Bhudev concludes correctly that in all societies where marriage is based on individual choice there are arrangements for divorce.

Sastri's arguments are entirely hostile to child marriage:

At the root of marriage is love, at the root of love is respect, and at the root of respect lies knowledge of each other. Therefore, the custom of arranging marriage through *ghataks* [marriage brokers] that exists in this country is not the correct path. Young men and women would mix with a lot of others, and from them would nominate one person—this should be the main principle of marriage. Where marriage is based on love it brings an amazing education to the hearts of men and women. First, it binds individuals to the community (*janasamaj*); second it binds them with religion (*dharma*), third it binds them to God (*isvar*). (Sastri 1963: 28)

What did Sastri see as being narratable in his life, so that he could overcome reticence about the self? I think it was his sense that his life showed the transformation of some of the most fundamental definitions of social conduct, the meanings of religion, leading a religious life, and of the everyday activities of living in a marriage, raising children and passing one's life with friends. All these had changed historically, and he thought, correctly, that his life was an excellent example of how it had changed, and what people had to go through to make that change happen.

Before individuals can have and defend private lives, the concept of a private life has to become common in society, a matter of social decision which can give rise to intense public debate because these changes signify a fundamental reorientation of the most inescapable province of conduct and experience for all individuals. Sastri's autobiography is fascinating precisely because it is a chronicle of the unremitting struggles of a man trying to live a private life in a society which still refuses to recognize such an idea, and to take, unmolested by others, what appear to us to be the most inoffensively ordinary decisions. His questions were about how to practice his religion, how to think of God and best to serve him, how to decide about his own career, how to marry, to bring up his children. I shall analyze his story now in terms of three forms of *intimacy*—conjugality, the relation between parents and children, and friendship. But I shall follow the sequences of an ideal biography, starting with relations with parents, because they come first, followed by marriage and the setting up of his own *separate* family, and developing relations of friendship with acquaintances through work and intellectual fellowship rather than kinship and family (Bhudev's *gnati-kutumba*).

The Relation of Parent and Child

One of the most significant strands of his autobiography concerns Sastri's relations with his elders, in particular the very different inflections of intimacy with his father and mother. Sastri receives a classical and exacting traditional education in being a good child. His father is unable to stay with his family and has to teach in government schools, but his values and personality traits determine some of the outlines of their domestic life. He is obviously a man of learning and great honesty; but despite his straitened financial circumstances he defies the power of the local landlords in sending his daughters to the village girls' school. There is, also, an interesting distinction at the heart of Hindu Brahmin domesticity: several incidents clearly demonstrate that inner religious life is considered both sacred and, in the traditional way, personal. A son wishing to follow the Shakta form of worship might cause a Vaishnava father some displeasure, but he would not normally interfere in these matters of belief. Turning Brahmo was, in one sense, simply changing religious conviction within the broad Hindu fold. Yet clearly becoming a Brahmo was treated as an act of a different kind. In traditional Hindu conduct, the liberty of inner attachment to God in any of his usual Hindu forms is counterbalanced by a strong emphasis on orthopraxy, the acceptance and performance of suitable conduct for a caste and associated occupation. If Brahmo doctrine had been associated with religious beliefs or doxa, it would not have been different from earlier Hindu sects; but its revolutionary heteropraxy was intolerable to traditional Brahmins.

In the traditional system of beliefs, childhood implied two things: only the first and evident part of it is the inability of the child to perform grown-up activities, his inability to feed or look after himself. Far more important, theoretically, was the principle of hierarchy, the son giving way to the father's wishes, whatever their age. Children outgrew the first kind of dependence, but never the second. In extreme cases, when the father might become senile and wish something clearly unreasonable, the son might uphold the appearance of accepting his father's wish while in fact doing what is socially reasonable. But this external appearance of obedience, even when it is utterly formal and unreasonable, was considered an act of great merit. Sastri's conflict with his father centered on these principles of heteronomy and unreasonable hierarchy, the idea that whatever the case, and whatever their age, the son must always submit to the will of his father.

His childhood and early youth did not see any conflict with his father: in many respects, Sibnath was an ideal child—obedient, gifted, highly successful in education. He also looked on his father's character with considerable filial pride. But the first and vital clash concerned the question of family life. Sastri was married very early to Prasannamayi, and she came to stay in their household, although Sastri was still mainly in Calcutta at the Sanskrit College. Sastri's own account of the critical incident gives us some significant pointers:

> When I was immersed in the enjoyment of the pleasures of poetry, an unfortunate family incident took place. For some particular reason, my father became angry with my first wife, Prasannamayi, and her family, and sent her back to her father's house. He said she would never be welcomed back. When it was decided to reject her finally, the question arose how, since I was an only son, the family line could be maintained. Thus it was decided that I was to be married again. By that time, I had grown up enough to know that polygamy was reprehensible. It was not that I had a particular affection for Prasannamayi. However, I felt that she and her

family were being given a severe punishment entirely disproportional to their lapse. My mind became agitated thinking about how I could possibly assist in such a ruthless [heartless] act. However, from childhood I was in such fear of my father that it was impossible for me to oppose his resolve. Still, I let him know myself, and through my mother, that I did not consent to such a [second] marriage. (Sastri 1918: 67)

Sastri recalls that, on a journey to the village, he took courage in both hands and told his father, to his face, that he objected to these plans. His father, with characteristic vehemence, which he consistently confused with the legendary brahminical force of character (*tejas*), threatened to beat him with his slippers and told him to return to Calcutta. Sibnath persisted in accompanying him to the village, complained to his mother, but his mother pleaded inability to dissuade his father. Sibnath was duly married for the second time to Virajmohini; but he was so little involved he was unsure if it happened in 1865 or 1866. Sastri thought in retrospect that this was the most significant event of his life: and the two sections in the *Atmacarit* are tellingly entitled 'consequences of the second marriage' and 'the beginnings of religious life.' His own record is highly suggestive:

Immediately following this marriage, my mind was ravaged by a terrible sense of guilt [*anutap*: regret felt after a wrong act]. A punishment was wrongly inflicted on an innocent woman, and despite my unwillingness, I became the central figure in that wrongful act; at this thought I was overwhelmed by shame and sorrow. Before going out to marry at my father's command, I had prepared my mind by thinking that Ramachandra had gone through fourteen years of exile in a forest to obey his father's command; I might have to undergo suffering throughout my life. But at this moment of crisis, that thought failed to give me [moral] strength. I began to think, individuals are responsible for their own actions; even with a thousand parental commands, no one takes a share of one's guilt [*pap*]. My mind was tormented by self-condemnation. When I think of that intense self-hatred, I tremble even today. I used to be a happy, humoros, friendly character; my sense of humor and happiness disappeared. I was drowned in deep gloom. While stepping forward, it seemed I was stepping into an abyss. When night arrived, it seemed better if morning never came. (Sastri 1918: 68)

'In this state', Sastri says, 'I took refuge in, and sought succor, from God' (1918: 68). His father, in an apparent attempt to help him solve his moral dilemmas, engaged him in discussions of atheistic doctrines from Hindu philosophy and sometimes indicated that Vidyasagar was an atheist. But Sastri had never liked atheism. Previously, he had never thought deeply about the relation between God and the individual soul; he did not have a habit of serious prayer. One of his friends sent him Theodore Parker's *Ten Sermons and Prayers*, and these prayers gave him 'a new life.' 'While praying, I observed two changes in my mind. First I got strength in place of weakness: I decided 'I shall fearlessly act on what I would see as my duty, even if it led to sacrifice of wealth, prestige or life.' I prepared myself to follow the commands of dharma [moral truth], and of God who lives inside our heart' (1918: 69). The external manifestation of this resolve was to attend the prayer congregations of the Bhawanipore Brahmo Samaj, in which he was initially somewhat shamefaced, but slowly acquired conviction.

His immediate worry, as he recalls decades afterwards, was his slow but decisive alienation from his father. Sastri explains: 'I had said before that prayers gave me strength, which meant that my mind gradually became free of the fear of other human beings, and the inclination to act according to my own beliefs became stronger.' His father heard of his visits to the Brahmo congregations and asked him to stop:

> I said calmly, 'Father, you know I have never disobeyed your commands. I am willing to obey all your wishes. But do not interfere with my religious life. I cannot give up joining the worship at the Brahmo Samaj.' My father said nothing in the rented house I shared with others, but he found this answer so novel and terrible that I heard he wept inconsolably that day. (Sastri 1918: 70)

When his father returned to his village, as his mother asked for news of their son the cryptic answer came back 'He is dead.' It took his mother some time before she realized this 'death' was metaphorical. Sastri took recourse to prayers at this point of moral crisis, greatly aided by Parker's humorous and optimistic devotion. He faced 'severe struggles' now. Earlier, when he returned home during his holidays, he used to perform the domestic worship, *puja*, in place of his father. That summer, Sastri went home and told his mother of his resolve not to perform the household worship ceremony. His father was initially furious, and took up a wooden plank to beat him with. But when Sastri, once again 'calmly' refused, he did not insist and performed it himself. Even in his village, Sastri began to join a few Brahmo friends for daily prayers. His conversion to the Brahmo faith could not now remain an internal family secret and became a scandal for the joint family. When he returned to Calcutta he joined the Brahmo social reform movement with enthusiasm and played a leading role in negotiating one of the first widow remarriages in Calcutta. His father was eventually so enraged that he engaged a gang of thugs to beat his son. After many years he relented slightly and simply left home when his son came back to meet his mother; still later he contented himself with being around but not speaking to him. Sastri's father apparently kept his vow of never speaking to his son until the very end. There were only two exceptions: once when Sastri was seriously ill in Calcutta, he took his mother to nurse him back to health—but as a man of honor, accomplishing this rather complex task without exchanging words. At the time of his death, when Sastri went to Benaras to see his father, there was a brief final reconciliation.

Sastri's account shows with great clarity that it was possible to respond to the new ideas of the Brahmo faith in two radically different ways. His parents responded to his conversion very differently. His father's sense of brahminical piety was strongly intellectual, with a deep pride in devotion to knowledge and acceptance of a life of high-minded poverty; but it was, in consequence, utterly inflexible. When Sastri gave up idolatry, abandoned his sacred thread, and joined Brahmoism (entailing non-observance of caste practices), his father resolved never to speak to him again, i.e. never to take up a rational dialogical stance. Throughout his life he stuck to this high-minded, peculiarly principled inflexibility as a mark of his brahminical 'character'. From his point of view, it would have been cheating if he disapproved of his son's conduct and carried on as usual in their father–son relationship. Sastri himself expresses admiration for this devotion to principles and claims he learnt his sense of moral rectitude from his father, though he used it in the service of different religious principles.

Yet, inside the family, his mother's response to his conversion was radically different. She did not express consternation when he joined the Brahmos, and her only concern on his announcement that he would not do the household worship was that her advice would have no weight with his father. She did not respond in this way because her religious conviction was less intense. When his father debated *nastika darsana* (atheistic schools) with his son, she strongly disapproved and feared this would lead to his moral ruin. She regarded her relationship as a mother as morally more important than her duties as a Hindu, and worked out a rational trade-off between the two. She often also performed the role of a highly sensitive and skilled intermediary between childishly and insensitively inflexible intellectual men—a common theme in Bengali novels.

Sastri's autobiography moves on at a fast, hurried pace, without pausing to reflect on the principles involved in the social changes he was enacting in his personal life. He gives us little information about his relations with his children, and whether in his own life he worked out fundamentally different moral relations with the next generation. But the conflict with his father can be analyzed to yield some points on which his sense of correct relationships was 'new and terrible.' His father, despite a modern education and proximity to people like Vidyasagar and Dwarkanath Vidyabhusan, clung to the traditional principles of hierarchy and an unreasoning continuity of religious conduct. In all such cases, continuity of conduct involves the added Hindu principle of submission to authority. In these moral systems, acting on one's own views, however considered, is regarded as willfullness and a kind of ethical egotism. Ability to submit to the will of 'elders' is similar to selflessness. In that moral world, too, there was a difference between 'being a Brahmin' well or badly; but 'being a Brahmin' was not itself subject to rational choice. More importantly, Sastri thought it right to give children a right to choose their own religious orientation. Given that freedom of choice, the relation between parents and children could continue to be intense and intimate. But the most important principle, to which others were subordinate, was the one of individuality and autonomy. For Sastri, religion was nothing without autonomy; it was a dull, repetitious routine, without the thrill of acting well. For his father religion was nothing if autonomy was brought into it. Yet, in the way Sastri paints his mother's reactions to his religious crisis, it is clear he believed that there was a possible solution of this problem from within the traditional repertoire of moral conduct. His mother's response was not due to a weaker sense of religious conviction, but a different kind.

Relationships of Conjugality

Sociologically, parent–child relationships are intrinsically related to alterations in the central notions about conjugal life. Modern occupational life disrupts the structural form of the joint family based on common agricultural labor, and the replication of occupation across generations which gives individuals a fund of skills they absorb easily through their close family context. Training for an occupation was internal to the traditional caste-based family system, rather than externally arranged through schools or academies. In early modern Bengal conjugality changed fundamentally through a combination of intellectual and social influences. Sibnath Sastri's family was typical of the first wave of social groups who benefited from, and were deeply affected by, institutional changes brought in by early modernity. His grandfather had lived a life of the traditional pandit in the local context of the village; but his father received an education that was modern in spirit, though his specific qualification was in the traditional discipline of Sanskrit. Harananda Bhattacharyya, Sibnath's father, was placed in a strangely mixed position: his learning was traditional but his occupational position was drastically different from his ancestors'. He did his teaching in government-funded schools, for a regular salary, independent of the earlier system of village support, usually supplemented by some ownership of land. Sastri does not tell us very much about his family's finances, but it is clear that his father's family survived mainly on his small salary, and the smooth running of the household depended on his mother's intelligent ability to manage on such meager means.

Despite the insufficiency of the pay, the *structural* difference was enormous. In a single generation, Sastri's family had exchanged the older, village-bound, caste-based, localized occupational system for the life of the salaried professional. Since salaried people often had to move from place to place on government jobs, this had an immediate impact on the way the family ran. Harananda arranged his family in the traditional manner: he did not leave his ancestral seat in the village, the spatial center of his existence. He kept his wife and young children in the ancestral home, and moved himself to his places of work. The distances were manageable, and he was able to spend time with his family over weekends or holidays. But this made life difficult for his wife. She had to run the household entirely on her own, as well as fending off unwelcome attention from amorous males, like her son's primary schoolteacher. For his entire life, Harananda maintained this dual existence—of the family seat as the principal home (*badi*) and an insubstantial, rented residence at the place of work for the single male (*basa*). In fact, both in everyday thinking and in high literary discourse, there was much play on these two forms of residence. For Harananda, Calcutta was the place of learning, with occasional visits to family members or valued friends, but nothing more.

In Sastri's generation successful people commonly took up government employment, which immediately altered all the circumstances of intimacy in their lives and the kinds of people with whom they spent most of their time, in the closest emotional relationships. Usually, these jobs came with high salaries and associated perks. These salaried individuals had to leave their ancestral homes, take up residence in often large, luxurious government accommodation; but the most significant change in their lives was sociological. They had to live permanently away from their circles of intimate relatives in the village or towns; thus a traditional existence surrounded by close kin—siblings, cousins, in-laws, etc.—was impossible. Increasingly, however, both their salaries and their mental orientation allowed them to take their wives to live with them—a structure of conjugal life radically different from the village-centered world of Sibnath's father. In many of these cases, particularly for the financially fortunate ones, this left a couple of relatively young people of comfortable income in the unaccustomed intimacy of each other's unobstructed company. They lived in large, spacious, fashionable homes, which invited decoration as their intimate living space. Decoration accorded to this space a special individuality and marks of intimacy. It marked the space off as 'their space', separated from others'. The private character of this space was marked by objects of personal taste, conjugal photographs, even the double bed. Till fairly recently, traditional people regarded these as a vulgar display of sexuality: as a shameless display of selfish indulgence.[6] The private space could be filled with furniture and household things which not merely declared their relative level of opulence, but also a space for the display of taste and a material

[6] Compare how, in Jonathan Parry's essay in Arnold and Blackburn 2005, a man who had led a fairly adventurous sexual life regarded the double bed in his daughter's house as an almost pornographic object.

culture of owning things of sophistication and delicacy. Material objects came to have a role that was different from, and beyond, the dry functionality of objects in the rural household.

Traditional conjugality had to develop in the context of the joint family, and from both novelistic and biographic evidence it can be clearly seen that those circumstances produced a peculiar ethic of good conjugal behaviour. Young couples felt shame at being together in the presence of others: for both males and females there was a peculiar ethic of demonstrative attention toward others, to show to members of the joint family that they were not given to a selfish, and probably carnal, attentiveness to their spouses. For women, especially, this ethic of inattentiveness encompassed a demonstration of love for children other than one's own. The internal ethic of the joint family enjoined a rule of equality with respect to children, and a good mother was the woman who treated all the other children as her own.

Spatial relocation away from the ancestral seat of the joint family altered this sociological context radically. There were no relatives, particularly elders, to enforce the ethic of conjugal shame. More substantially, since elders and other close kin were not around for constant influence and consultation, the husband's main ally and adviser became his wife. This resulted in a tendency toward greater equality in their relationship, not in terms of power, but because they were subjected to the same experiences and had to find their joint way through problems, opportunities, and decisions. Excessively unequal relationships became unhelpful for men. It was a seriously inconvenient situation if the wife did not have the education to share the husband's tastes and concerns. Evidently, this did not lead to a sudden era of women's empowerment; but husbands found it in their own interest to give education to their wives and make them culturally more their equals. As couples went through their lives in situations of mutual dependence, and as no one in their joint family could share this joint memory and experience of life, this tended to cement the bond between the spouses and mark them off from others. Thus a new form of intimacy developed between married men and women living a modern life, driven by material circumstances of sharing occupational experience and ideological power of rationalistic doctrines of autonomy, assisted by the moral imagination of romantic novels. Many marriages did not start as romantic, but were made so retrospectively.

Sibnath initially regarded his village home as the spatial center of his existence, the central point from which all spatial relations radiated outward toward his increasingly expanding universe of experience; and whenever he had the chance, on short or long holidays, he went back to the village. His life with Prasannamayi began in highly fraught circumstances. He was married very young, and when his father decided to send her away he confesses he did not feel great attachment to her. He began to think seriously about her out of a sense of moral responsibility rather than emotional attachment, and only when he was driven into his second marriage. He requested his uncle to call Prasannamayi to his house and went there to meet her and apologize to her. She stayed in his uncle's house, and he went there every Saturday—to set up a new, partially autonomous relationship with her. His father was initially furious at this disobedient action but subsequently accepted it and even relented, accepting her back into his own family. Eventually, when his father threw him out for becoming a Brahmo, Sastri had to set up home in Calcutta. He brought Prasannamayi to Calcutta to set up his own nuclear family. This, however, left the question of his second wife very unsatisfactorily unresolved. When he set up a base in Calcutta with a friend whom he supported in marrying a widow, he had some 'wild designs' (Sastri 1918: 79). 'At this time, all kinds of absurd projects entered my mind, all kind of projects for the deliverance of India', among which, he retrospectively recognized, were his designs about his second wife.

He was sharing a house in Calcutta with his friend Yogendra, who had lost his wife and married a widow. Sastri used to teach her English and Bengali, while 'at this time, reading John Stuart Mill's works, Yogendra temporarily turned into an atheist' (1918: 79).

> We three people had become such great 'reformers' that we decided that we would bring my second wife Virajmohini and marry her off a second time. I had not yet taken Virajmohini as a wife. In the year 1868 I once went to bring her. She was a girl of 11 or 12 years. Probably, they [Virajmohini's family] refused to send her down with me because I had gone without my parents' permission. I did not treat her as my wife because it would have been wrong to live with someone I was intending to marry off a second time (1918: 79).

On this occasion the problem passed, as her parents did not allow her to accompany him, and he could not put his reforming ideas of marrying his wife to a second husband into practice. By 1872, however, her parents and siblings had died in a cholera epidemic. Her uncles accepted her unwillingly and asked Sibnath to take responsibility for her. He accepted his responsibility to look after her, but his Brahmo friends pointed out: 'A Brahmo living with two wives is a detestable idea. One of our major principles is to protest against the practice of polygamy. If you live with two wives, how would you protest against polygamy?' (1918: 112). Sastri replied: 'But I am not going to fetch her with the intention of living with two wives. What is her guilt that I shall not offer her refuge after her parents passed away? The guilt of this bigamy rests with me, not her. I am going to bring her here because I will educate her; if she agrees, I will give her in marriage a second time' (1918: 112). Sastri and his friends had obviously over-looked some problems in their state of moral enthusiasm: it would mean bigamy for his second wife, a far more problematic status for Hindu women, and also the small matter—for ideological supporters of moral autonomy—of the choice of the woman herself. Faced with this moral conflict, Sastri sought advice from Kesabchandra Sen, his religious leader at the time. Sen gave him the practical advice of bringing in his second wife, saying to Sastri: 'In a society that practices child marriage, how can women be held guilty in cases of bigamy? If a man marries ten women and then becomes a Brahmo, it is his moral duty to give shelter to these ten women. In fact, if he refuses to take care of them, and any of these women goes astray, he is responsible for that' (1918: 112).

Sastri reports that he had some difficulty persuading Prasannamayi to accept this high-minded scheme of bringing in the second wife, and giving her an education until she could be remarried. But the greater oversight in this was that no one considered the possible views of the woman herself. When she was brought to Calcutta, Sastri explained to her two possible courses of action: the first was for her to grow up and marry someone else when she came of age; the second was for her to get an education, so that she could take care of herself. To both these high-minded proposals she responded, not surprisingly, with horror. 'She was startled by the first proposal [of remarriage], and exclaimed, 'My God, how many times can a woman marry?' On seeing her reaction, and her deep repugnance for the idea of a second marriage, the genie I had kept in my head for so long left at once. I realized that it was the second proposal that I had to turn to practice' (1918: 112).

Understandably, this led to a serious domestic crisis:

> From another angle, I faced a further severe test. When Prasannamayi and Virajmohini began to live under the same roof, I did not treat Virajmohini as my wife and I began to feel that it was morally right for that period to live apart, away from Prasannamayi. By then we had a long conjugal relationship, and Hemlata, Tarangini and Priyanath had been born. But inside the ashram there were no outside rooms except for the schoolroom and Kesabchandra's office. Where do I sleep at night, if not in Prasannamayi's room? To live apart became a great struggle for me. It was also very distressing for Prasannamayi. Eventually, I managed to convince Prasannamayi, and took her leave, and started sleeping wherever I could. By chance, an expedient came to light. On the verandah of the Hindu College, there was an empty table [that] . . . lay empty at night. After dinner at night I took a book with me, and placing my head on that book, I slept soundly on that table.

He added, somewhat incongruously, 'I spent my time wonderfully' (1918: 112–13).

However, both his wives got to know of this unorthodox arrangement and became disconsolate. Soon afterwards, Sastri was called by his uncle to take charge of his highly respected journal, *Somprakash*, and went to live in a small town, Harinabhi, leaving his two distressed wives in Kesabchandra's ashram in Calcutta. Again, not surprisingly, Kesabchandra expressed concern about the untenability of the arrangements, and said he feared Virajmohini might commit suicide. Eventually, Sastri decided on an ingenious plan which combined domestic peace with moral rectitude: 'When I found that Virajmohini did not want to be separated from me, I decided to take the following course: when she would be with Prasannamayi, I would live apart from both of them. When they would live in different houses, I would unite with them as their husband. We started acting accordingly. For a long time, as long as Prasannamayi lived, this is how it went on' (1918: 113).

By this strange device, Sastri saved his conscience and turned his bigamous life into discrete monogamies with two wives. Strange times need strangely imperfect moral solutions.

Apart from the peculiarity of this marital story, what is interesting is the unfolding of the principles of conjugality in Sastri's autobiography. Several types of conjugality figure in the social universe around him. Conventional orthodox relationships, of course, abounded: many Brahmos or progressive Hindus practiced their progressivism in strictly segmented spheres. They lived a life of friendship and work with male friends who shared their world, but retained a totally orthodox relation with their wives. But most of Sastri's intimate circle experimented with a different flavor of conjugal relationship. A few who married widows were fortunate to have as wives women who were comparatively older, more mature, usually educated, from cultivated, liberal families. These women shared the interests of their husbands' lives more fully, and apparently controlled the domestic sphere, which included considerable freedom of financial expenditure. Others married wives who were too young, and usually less educated than themselves, but they quite often spent considerable effort in getting such wives educated, and often succeeded.

In most cases the huge moral ideal of the romantic novel, of a companionate relationship with one's wife, based on love, could not be translated into reality easily or entirely. The women were rarely independent, nor free to choose their partners at the time of their marriage; nor did the circumstances favor pre-marital courtship. But after marriage, when the wives came to maturity, progressive men often tried very hard to graft a quasi-romantic relation on that heteronomous arrangement. And although women never enjoyed complete equality within those relationships, they often earned a great deal of autonomy of action and respect. Sastri's own short sketch of Prasannamayi is a wonderful example of such respect, expressed with great dignity and restraint. But the moral imaginary of the novel is of great significance: it was always one step ahead of social practice, drawing social conduct toward that ideal by the most intangible and powerful enticement. Novelistic plots painted, as it were, a picture of a completely ideal conjugal relationship, and although reality usually fell far short of such exhilarating and ennobling emotion, they constantly stretched the margins of possibility, legitimizing in the sacred language of literature a mode of conduct which real life could not sustain.

Relationships with Friends

Another significant new development was the emergence of a new sociability of friendship. This should not be taken to mean that before the arrival of modern influences Indians did not know what friendship was. But with the advent of modernity, the recasting of social norms leads to two kinds of changes in patterns of friendship. First, the range of people from whom friends can be selected is vastly widened, though we should be careful in recognizing its limits as well. Second, the place of friendship among other types of sociability changed fundamentally in a general reorganization of relationships of intimacy. It would be grotesque not to observe the existence of mythological and literary models of friendship in the traditional literature, not least because, even after the new form of friendship flourished, traditional literary examples remained powerful models. Friends were made traditionally either in the pursuit of a common caste profession or within the circle of kinship. Caste made friendship outside of common professions improbable and difficult to sustain, and it was usually disapproved of by society. The functional interdependence so central to the operation of the caste system disallowed intimacy and friendships across the boundaries of caste and kin, which were related in any case.

This order was decisively broken with the arrival of the forms of modern sociability. Some economic and structural changes played a central role in this transformation. Evidently, these changes affected only the more upper-class elements in Bengali society, residing in urban centers, and living their lives on the plane of a new kind of professional space spanning the whole of the British imperial domain. Bengalis monopolized administrative posts, and a doctor or an inspector of schools—such as Bhudev Mukhopadhyay—could be posted to distant reaches of the empire. This process of constant relocation affected the structure of sociability of such people deeply. As it loosened the ties with the paternal family and kin, it compelled people to seek out others who could provide them with a social life in unfamiliar areas. Modern professionals therefore developed strong friendships with people from similar stations and professions in life, and who had similar ideas about social norms. Groups like the Brahmos provided a much-needed structure of social sustenance in this sense, apart from their more explicit doctrinal norms. Among the Brahmos, precisely because they rejected conventional Hindu customs, there was a strong urge to codify the rules of a new domesticity, and Sastri's *Grhadharma* played an important role in the standardization of domestic conduct. In his own life the importance of friendships of the new kind was inestimable. As his family refused to give him sustenance, he depended increasingly on his friends.

At an early stage, his friends come primarily from college mates, or students studying in Calcutta and forced to mess together in rented houses with common living space and servants. There are also touching examples of Sastri providing support to others in need, such as his attempt to support a friend who married a widow at his instigation. As they advance in life, these examples of youthful frenzies of idealistic enthusiasm abate somewhat, but the close relations with friends continue. Friends made in early life, at college or through common enthusiasm for Brahmo reform, mostly grow into successful professional men, because, in the colonial dispensation, once a person became part of the modern education system, he could hardly fail. This imparts a certain homogeneity to the social group—financially and ideologically—among whom this was practised. But evidently, prosperous friends tended to support less fortunate ones, as evident from the life of the poet Michael Madhusudan Dutt, who led a peculiarly difficult life. In Sastri's case, the relationship with friends was slightly different: although prosperous friends sometimes paid for his needs, he was in the morally superior station of the religious preacher.

What is remarkable in his autobiography is the total absence of intimacy with his kin, and the complete dominance of relationships with friends. This demonstrates the social possibility of a new kind of life for the reformed Hindu of intense sociability without the kinship circle. There is always an underlying theoretical argument. Influenced by some contemporary Western theories, the new individuals in effect assert that traditional friendship and sociability limited to kin becomes morally unjustifiable if they accept a process of individual differentiation. Even close kin, like brothers or sisters, might not share an individual's temperament or intellectual enthusiasms and,

as economic modernity unfolded, his occupational culture. Relations
with friends are based, by contrast, on similarity of temperament and
intellectual inclination: these are, therefore, more intense and reliable.
In any case, it seems clear that, in the life of socially mobile upper-
class Bengalis, relationships of friendships became more important
over time than kin-based intimacies. In literary writing, particularly
in the novels of Tagore and Saratchandra Chattopadhyay, there is a
constant and searching reflection of the nature of friendship—its
various possible forms and intricate structures. Instances of strong
friendship are very central to novelistic narratives, and, in some
striking cases, intellectual bonds survive serious misunderstandings.
In some instances there is also a suggestion of complementarity, as in
the case of Binoy and Gora, both in terms of character and intellectual
arguments in Tagore's novel, *Gora*. Literary narratives also speculate
about the possibility of a 'friendship' between men and women which
is distinct from (and does not constitute simply) the early stages of
romance.

The Self and Intimacy with God

The autobiography is, after all, the story of a self. What kind of sense
of self is portrayed in Sastri's work? Is this sense of self different from
more traditional ones? Is there a connection between these redefined
intimacies and the exact nature of religious life Sastri valued? I think
there is a strong connection between the redefinition of intimacies
and the particular conception of the moral self that was central to
Brahmo doctrine. Although these doctrinal arguments are oddly
absent from the *Atmacarit*, Sastri presented them with great theoretical
clarity in some of his regular Brahmo sermons. In a sermon entitled
'God resides in the heart', he first rejects several conventional Hindu
conceptions—of a God declaring moral rules through the infallible
verbality of the Vedas, a God available to men as *avatara*, and a God
of idolaters.

The common fault with all these conceptions of religious life is that
it makes moral rules into something to be laid down from outside,
and therefore experienced as constraining, rather than discovered
from inside, and thus experienced as fulfilling. In all these pictures of
moral life, God appears intermittently and suddenly to light up the

true path. True religiosity yearns for an intimate and incessant contact with God. Unlike the Hindu belief in God's externality, God resides inside the human heart, and his commands are not written in external tablets of religious instruction but are whispered by the utterings of our conscience. In the deeper self, human beings are in contact with the divine. In accordance with this view, Brahmo temples have to reject the noisy chaos of Hindu worship, and, most important of all, every Bengali home must replicate the peace and domestic order Sastri had found in the homes of the English middle class. What he admired most in English homes was the designation of a private space, however small, for each individual, where every person could enjoy undisturbed solitude, where he could develop an intimacy with himself, and listen to God speaking through his heart. In the usual distractions and clatter of everyday life, these whispers are stilled (Sastri 1933, 2: 73–84). It requires peace and silence to listen to the God sitting inside us and speaking through the untrammeled language of conscience. Sastri develops a theory of a particular relationship with one's self which is also couched, in a sense, in a language of intimacy.

In the intense debates about the nature of religious life, and the two crucial concepts at its very center—God and the self—essential social practices were being redefined. But it is characteristic that these social themes figure in a religious debate. Sastri's religion is radically different from Bhudev's. It rejects and disconnects itself from the Hinduism which values external manifestations and ritualism. It is radically critical of caste and its dual commitment to predestination and hierarchy. And it reorders the picture of the universe by placing God inside men rather than in an inaccessible part of the world—creating a deep moral impulse toward an intellectual and religious individualism. Intense religious and intellectual individualism was a precondition for individualist social practices. Precisely because these reorientations of practical conduct touched some of the fundamental moral values of Hindu society, they needed not just the force of economic change to secure them but a language of moral legitimation to impart to them something close to sacrality. The creation of privacy was not just an arrangement of convenience, but part of a moral order.

Just as Weber saw in Protestant loneliness in the world the sanctifying language for capitalist conduct, Sastri produces through his religious ideas the essential moral arguments for the new institution of the Bengali individual's privacy. The Bengali individual could from now on become different from his father in his profession, keep his deepest thoughts from his family, value his friends more than his kin, seek from his wife companionship rather than subjection, use his affection for children to let them develop as individuals—all unthinkable infringements of traditional Hindu conduct. This is the historical invention of a private sphere, of a private life for individuals, a conceptual space in which they are sovereign, subject to some rules of sociability. Sastri's religious teaching seeks to make this private sphere more than just intellectually acceptable. He wants to make it sacred. The modern individual, he believes, needs this space, literal and metaphorical, not just to escape from everyday aggravation, but to meet himself, and his 'more than inner' (*antaratara*) God.

References

Arnold, David, and Stuart Blackburn. Eds. 2005. *Telling Lives in India*. Delhi: Permanent Black
Eisenstadt, S.N. Ed. 2000. Multiple Modernities. *Daedalus*, Winter.
Mukhopadhyay, Bhudev. 1884. *Parivarik Prabandha*. Calcutta.
Sastri, Sibnath. 1918. *Atmacarit*. Calcutta: Prabasi Karyalaya.
———. 1933. *Dharmajivan*. 3 vols. Calcutta: Sadharan Brahmo Samaj.
———. 1963. *Grhadharma*. Calcutta: Sadharan Brahmo Samaj.
Tagore, Rabindranath. 1970. *Gitabitan*. Calcutta: Visvabharati.
Taylor, Charles. 1989. *The Sources of the Self*. Cambridge: Cambridge University Press.
Wagner, Peter. 1994. *A Sociology of Modernity: Liberty and Discipline*. London: Routledge.

11

The Second Mahabharata

This essay is about reading the Mahabharata, but it is also partly about the innate complexities of reading. Theories about aesthetics can be read in two ways: historically and structurally/ theoretically. In one sense, it is more appropriate, while reading texts from the past, to treat them historically—in terms of the intellectual context in which they appeared; and, if the theory is a contribution to a tradition of theoretical debates, to look at the precise emendations and additions that one theory makes to the stock of concepts and arguments it had received from earlier ones.

To follow that procedure, we should look at Abhinavagupta's views about *rasanispatti*, and compare them with the preceding doctrines against which he developed his own precise concepts and arguments. This will involve looking at earlier theorists' attempts to solve the problem of conceptual underdetermination—in the crucial term *rasa-nispatti*—by the concepts of irruption (*utpatti*), inference (*pratiti*), expression (*vyanjana*), or universalization (*sadharanikarana*).[1] Such analysis will closely examine which concepts he rejects, on what grounds; and which, like *sadharanikarana*, he continues to use; and

[1] These arguments are discussed and serially rejected in the first section of the Abhinavagupta (hereafter AB) commentary on the *rasasutra*. See Abhinavagupta 1992: ch. 6. The idea of *utpatti*—origin or irruption—is associated with Lollata; *pratiti*—inference—with Sankuka; *vyanjana*— coming into expression—with Anandavardhana; and the crucial concept of *sadharanikarana* (generalization/universalization) which Abhinava accepts, but uses somewhat differently, from the provocative Bhattanayaka who said with brilliant provocation '*rasa na utpadyate, na pratiyate, nabhibyanjate*' (*rasa* neither erupts, nor becomes an object of inference, nor comes into expression). Ibid.: AB commentary, 278.

if he uses concepts in the same sense or not, or extends them; and whether the exact arrangement in which he places them is the same or not: in other words, it would explore the conceptual structure in an Althusserian sense.[2] The other way is to deliberately abstract from the historical genealogies of concepts, arguments, and theories, and to compare them, without regard to historical specificity, with other theories which might have a structural, not family resemblance to them. This essay offers an exercise of the second, more structural kind.

The Mahabharata (hereafter MB) is a text that inevitably produces bafflement at various levels, by its very scale. All kinds of usual activity regarding a text—writing, reading, understanding—are exceeded by its scale, both by the scale of its simple extent, and the scale of its complexity. Faced with a text of this kind, the appropriate response is bafflement. Before we read the text, we have to read the myths which surround it, and which assist in understanding the kind of text we face. The legends then usefully split the activity of 'writing' into two—writing in the sense of composing the meanings, and the more external sense of actually inscribing those thoughts on pages. Nor surprisingly, these required the inhuman powers of Vyasa, and Ganesa, and miraculously, the legend goes, Vyasa avoided a burn-out and went on to compose other serious stuff—like the Harivamsa and the Brahmasutra. Hearing the MB is also meant to produce effects unobtainable by the reading of more mundane texts: even the hearing of this story is meant to cleanse us of sins. But the MB does nothing in a straightforward or conventional fashion. On some philosophic readings, the MB's ability to cleanse us is not through some mysterious powers of chanting these verses, but by the fact that understanding them enhances our ability to grasp the meaning of a moral life, and to lead it. It produces in us a *pratyavigna*, an anamnetic effect on our powers of moral insight and recognition.

Are these legends, in the guise of asserting some things about the writing end of the text, really telling us something about the reading

---

[2] Althusser 1970: see the chapter 'On the Materialist Dialectic'. For instance, there is Althusser's insistence that a concept like alienation may be used by the theories of both the young and the mature Marx, but their theoretical significance might be different, depending on exactly where the concept is placed in the general structure of the conceptual architecture.

end? Are these ideas not really about Vyasa and Ganesa, but about us, those who have embarked on an equally vast, equally improbable enterprise? Is it the suggestion that the text was dictated by a divinely inspired sage to a divine scribe really a warning to its undivine readers that they are undertaking to grasp a meaning of improbable vastness, difficulty, and complexity? This presents to us the enormous single problem: how does one make some meaning of a text like the MB? It is not surprising that the extraordinary scale and complexity of the text has elicited equally extraordinary attempts to deal with it. I shall be concerned with one of these efforts in the ninth-tenth century which has left one of the most lasting and fruitful interpretative legacies regarding the aesthetics of the MB.

It is a tribute to the philosophic fecundity of the MB that the question of its meaningfulness could be viewed in two radically different ways. I shall present both arguments: for, although I wish to develop the second, I am not entirely immune to the powerful intellectual allure of the first line of reasoning. It is commonly said that the MB mirrors life itself. This is a remark of colossal ambiguity, and it can be read in two entirely different ways. One reading could be that it is pointless to search for a meaning in the vast, disorderly, fascinating complexity of the MB for something singular like a meaning: it mirrors life precisely because it is as vast, endless, formless as life itself. Therefore there are many ways in which we can learn from it—by reading single episodes, reflecting on its vast narrative expanse, its gallery of characters, its astonishing construction of situations: but that is not a search for a meaning. The MB does not have a meaning, just as life does not: there are episodes, events, experiences, both in life and in MB, in which meaning can be found.

This is a powerful and sophisticated form of cognitive pessimism, but I wish to develop an argument from the opposite side—that, despite its scale and complexity, it is possible to find a meaning in the MB. The argument I want to offer can be made in two distinct forms. It can be presented as an historical argument in the strict sense, trying to situate a new understanding of the meaning of the MB in the aesthetic and philosophic discussions of the ninth-tenth-century

Sanskrit culture. I lack the historical and technical scholarship to make the argument in that form with any rigour. But I believe the same argument can be made more theoretically, and inevitably more speculatively, by simply contrasting the two most probable and compelling conceptions of what the story could mean to its readers. I also believe that for anyone who has spent time with the MB, which must mean that he has been reading different versions and different parts of the text at different points and intervals of his life, this is likely to be a personal evolution as well: we move, if we engage with it for a long time, from the first meaning of the story to the second.

Interpretative Conditions for the
Second Epic Addition of the Santa Rasa

The standard understanding of the MB narrative regards it as a *virarasa* text, a narrative of great heroism, although it is immediately apparent to any reader that it strives to present a picture of heroism—the life of *vira* in all its complexity and extremity, two qualities which constantly dominate the narrative imagination of the epic. The fundamental relations of human life, which should have an ineffaceable simplicity—the relation between a mother and a son, between wife and her husband—are bent into unrecognizably bizarre shape, like Kunti's relation to Karna, or Draupadi's marriage to five husbands. Human conditions and experiences are constantly pushed narratively to points of amazing extremity: Draupadi suffers a degradation worse than rape, Bhima extracts a strangely fascinating combination of just retribution and inhumanity. Eighteen *aksauhini* of soldiers gather on the battlefield, with few survivors. But the standard interpretation is to view it as a story of disputes attendant on royal succession and the enjoyment of vast imperial power, of utter degradation and bravery, and eventually an end that declares the restoration of a just *dharmic* order in which truth triumphs (*satyameva jayate*) and order is eventually restored. The Gita promises a destruction of evil and *dharmasamsthapana*, the re-establishment of a just order. After the development of the distinctive aesthetic philosophy of the Kashmir Saivas, their interpreters claim that, contrary to these semblances, the MB is a text of the *santa rasa*. This involves a major innovation at two levels: the suggestion at the level of narrative interpretation that the MB should be seen as a *santa rasa* text; but that interpretative innovation is attendant on a more fundamental theoretical innovation in aesthetics. In previous thinking of *rasa* theory, commentators agreed with Bharata that eight *rasas* existed, corresponding to the eight *sthayibhavas* in human emotions. Kashmiri theorists, since the time of Udbhata, speculate about *santa rasa* as a separate theme, and following this tradition of reflection Abhinavagupta adds a ninth *rasa*, the *santa* (tranquil) to this register—astonishingly through a commentarial operation on the *Natyasastra's* original text. This was a fundamental revision of aesthetic theory; and its success can be measured from the subsequent dominance of the idea of *navarasa* in Indian artistic reflection.

Bharata's text prosaically states there are eight *rasas*:

Srngara-hasya-karuna-raudro-viro-bhayanaka
Vibhatsadbhuta cetasca astah sastre rasah smrtah[3]

The *Abhinavabharati* maintains the pretense of a commentary, and offers an ostensible gesture of assuming the subordinate relation that the commentary bears to the principal text. Yet, in a remarkable instance of intellectual daring, where the actual innovation defies the formal stance of subservience, Abhinava makes the really '*abhinava*' (new/unprecedented) claim that Bharata's intention is to present nine *rasas*, including the *santa* as the ninth. But he does not state it openly, because he expresses his ideas through aesthetic suggestion—*dhvani*. Explicit suggestion of an idea by its own name—*svasabda*—is inferior to indirect suggestiveness. By a long and dazzlingly arcane demonstration of reading virtuosity, he suggests that the apparent absence of the *santa* is subtly permeated with its suggested presence.

Historically, the time and place of this innovation is intriguing. V. Raghavan, the distinguished Sanskrit scholar, suggests in one

---

[3] This is probably the most celebrated line in Indian aesthetics: Abhinavagupta 1992: ch. 6, the *rasadhyaya*. But by the fourteenth century, in Visvanatha Kaviraja's systematizing treatise *Sahityadarpana*, the ninth is equally authoritatively established by a deft displacement of words:
srngarahasyakarunaraudravirabhayanakah
vibhatasodbhuta etyastau rasa santastatha matah
Visvanatha 2004: ch. 3, 182, 106.

of his essays that Abhinava derived the ninth *rasa* from Buddhist philosophical reflection regarding the moral complexities of human life.[4] Since the predominant attitude that Buddhists recommended towards the sufferings of life was an attitude that could be called *santa*, or imperturbable tranquillity, even if the Buddhists did not have a pronounced and properly elaborated philosophical aesthetics it is a credible hypothesis that the philosophical idea or the moral ideal of the *santa* was taken through an aesthetic translation by the foremost Saiva commentator on aesthetic matters. The *Abhinavabharati* simply enumerated the *rasas* as nine, in simple, utter, and undeniable defiance of the primary text. Abhinava does not offer any expostulation for this startling emendation of the text he is supposed to be merely elucidating. He simply goes on to offer a rather unconvincingly recondite argument that it is clear from some embedded signals in textual Bharata's text that the santa is both implied and dominant.

What is the Commentarial Function?

This raises an obvious question: how was the commentarial function viewed by these philosophers? Of course, commentaries were of many different types. Those on Kalidasa's poetic works could be said to enhance readers' understanding of the narrative complexities, or the subtle aesthetic points of individual turns of phrase, but not alter the contents of the text itself. Commentaries were also required for philosophical texts, for a different reason. Works of speculation regarding major issues required both elucidation and a different activity which started with philosophic evaluation of the text's claims. They could go on to either *elaboration of arguments* which were ambiguous, unclear, or undeveloped; or go into *an argument with* the textual propositions if they were questionable. Abhinava could thus go on to elaborate what was undeveloped in the *sutras* of the *Natyasastra* (hereafter NS), and add elements which were absent earlier, but without contradicting its major ideas or produce incoherence.[5]

---

[4] Raghavan 1967.

[5] This is a serious question for Abhinavagupta, shown by the fact that he returns to this at several places: for instance, another famous passage in the commentary on the *rasasutra*, where he introduces the metaphor of the *vivekasopanaparamapara* (Abhinavagupta 1992: 280), the ladder of reasoning.

Abhinava does not stop with just an insertion, an addition of another *rasa* to the palette of elementary emotions. Partly because he has to claim that it is implied, he is forced to enlarge the claim and make it much broader. *Santa* cannot be a *rasa* which sits laterally with all the other eight *rasas*; it must have a different kind of relation to this basic taxonomy. In Abhinava's hands, it becomes a superordinate *rasa* which can encompass, embrace, and override all the rest.[6] Once this extension of the rasa repertoire is complete, it becomes possible to turn to the revision of specific aesthetic judgements. Clearly, one of the most startling revisionist suggestions about classical literature is the one that, to a truly philosophic reading, the great epic reveals itself as a work of the *santa rasa*.[7]

Gary Tubb's Analysis of the *Dhvanyaloka*

Numerous technical problem come in the way of establishing *santa* as the predominant *rasa* of a vast and complicated text like the MB. I am not trying to argue against Gary Tubb's excellent, scrupulously detailed consideration of technical issues with Anandavardhana's *santa* interpretation of the MB.[8] Tubb demonstrates convincingly the difficulties of accepting the MB as a text in which *santa* is the dominant *rasa* if we follow the technical requirements of *rasa* theory. First, there are serious difficulties in inserting the *santa* inside the textual intentionalities of the NS, to assert, as the Kashmiri *dhvanikaras* do, that the *santa* is stated precisely through its absence. The idea that the *sthayin* of the *santa*—the *bhava* of *nirveda*—is suggested in the NS by its first place in the list of the *vyabhicaris* is too far-fetched a reading. But the obvious objection to this gloss is that the concept of *dhvani* is appropriate to literary texts. NS is a text *about* literature, but not a literary text. Ambiguity and indirectness are enhancements of a

---

I have discussed this passage briefly in 'The Sudden Death of Sanskrit Knowledge' (reproduced within the present volume).

[6] For details of the argument, see Raghavan 1967.

[7] This suggestion is advanced, with typical economy and audacity, in the final sections of Anandavardhana's *Dhvanyaloka*, and taken up by Abhinava's interlinked commentary, the *Locana*. See Anandvardhana 1990: 696.

[8] Tubb 1985: 141–67.

poetic language, but major deficiencies in a philosophical reasoning. We can have as much of *dhvani* as possible in literature, but it causes confusion if philosophical texts start working through *dhvani*.

The narrative difficulties are also numerous. There are obstacles in the way of regarding Yudhisthira as the main protagonist of the epic, as Tubb shows through his ingenious comparison of the role of Yudhisthira in the MB with the figure of the Buddha in Asvaghosa's *Buddhacarita*. Kashmiri theorists try to get round this by repeated observations in the last section of the *Dhvanyaloka* that the main protagonist of the MB is neither Arjuna nor Yudhisthira but Vasudeva, whichever way you gloss the meaning of that name.[9] We are left eventually with the powerful suggestion, again at the end of the *Dhvanyoaloka*, that 'the miserable end of the Vrsnis and the Pandavas' indicates that the overriding narrative purpose of the epic is to point to the futility of all worldly enthusiasm—for power, wealth, love, loyalty, victory. Since all these states are marked by fulfilled desire, the lesson of the MB is to teach the value of what Abhinava terms *trsnaksayasukha*: the happiness that arises from a cessation of desire. The *Dhvanyaloka* uses a sloka from the *Anukramanika* to gloss it, rather distantly: 'For the meaning intended to be hereby suggested is as follows. The adventures of the Pandavas and others which are recounted, since they come to a miserable conclusion, represent the elaboration of worldly illusion, whereas it is the blessed Vasudeva, representing ultimate truth, who is here glorified.'[10]

Dhvanyaloka's major reinterpretative statement is not based on signals embedded in textual fragments like the *Anukramanika* phrases; it lies in a general observation about the narrative concatenation itself: 'in the MB, which has the form of a didactic work although it contains poetic beauty, the great sage who was its author, *by his furnishing a conclusion* that dismays our hearts by the miserable ends of the Vrsnis and the Pandavas, shows that the primary aim of his work has been to produce a disenchantment with the world, and he has intended his primary subject to be liberation from worldly life and the rasa of peace.'[11]

[9] Anandavardhana 1990: 691.
[10] Ibid.
[11] Ibid.: 690–1. Emphasis added.

I wish to suggest a reconstruction of this claim by means of arguments that are obviously modern, using the readings of the *dhvani* theorists as our materials, rather than our methodological guide. I select elements from their analyses but recompose them in other ways, and, of course, we are free to add arguments of our own from the intellectual culture we inhabit. I wish to offer mainly two suggestions: the first is about the historical direction of change in Sanskrit literary hermeneutics, and the second is a reading of the signification of the narrative ending. This will, I hope, yield two sets of interesting implications: the first set about narrative intentionalities, or the play of intentions in narrative texts, which need to be brought to 're-presentation' in Gadamer's sense;[12] and second, about the process of moral knowledge in the MB narrative.

Texts as a Field of Intentionalities/ Textual Intentionalities

To a lay modern observer,[13] it appears that the revision in aesthetic theory attempts to shift the emphasis in interpretative theory to the readers' side—to the *sahrdaya*—although most theories make a further distinction between the aesthetic address of the reader and the spectator, because the general category of *kavya* is subdivided into *drsya* (visual) and *sravya* (aural) *kavyas*. Against earlier theories, which are content with a vague and unclear notion of aesthetic pleasure, new theories require a rigorous conception of the exact psychological event occurring in the process of aesthetic enjoyment. Through successive philosophic elaborations on what exactly happens in the case of *rasanispatti*,[14] the *dhvani* theorists aquire a clearer picture of the reading-event as a complex happening on what could be termed an interpretative field stretching from author to character to actor to

[12] I am referring to the well-known passages in *Truth and Method*, regarding the meaning of an act of representation. See Gadamer 1981: 97ff.

[13] I wish to stress that I am not a scholar of Sanskrit or of ancient Indian aesthetics, and therefore the following discussion depends exclusively on modern, primarily Western, cultural theory.

[14] The first section of the commentary on the rasasutra concisely present these successive attempts at elucidation of that event as *upaciti, pratiti, vyanjana* and *sadharanikarana*. Abhinavagupta 1992: ch. 6.

reader.[15] As the theory evolves and gets more elaborate, it gives more detailed attention to what is happening between the actor on the stage and the spectator in the theatre, or to the poetic-literary text and its reader. From the angle I want to develop, the fact that the discussion has to deal with the slightly awkward distinction between theatrical and poetic texts, between *natya* and *kavya*, really serves to bring out an essential feature of aesthetic interpretation. *Natya* brings out the act of mediation in the process of representation more clearly than *kavya*. Thus, there is some advantage in thinking about the literary text by way of a detour through drama. The argument appears similar to Gadamer's analysis of textuality.[16] Minimally, a text stands between an author and a reader/recipient. It is misleading, in Gadamer's view, to think of understanding the meaning of a text exclusively as an imaginative recapture of the authorial meaning, because reading is also, if not equally, a meaning-creating activity. To recapture meanings readers have to work through language, and because of the ineradicable historicity of the lingual, the means of the capture—the language of the reader's time—is partly a means of help, partly an obstacle. A reader creates the meaning of a text by working through resources available in the historicized formation of his culture, which includes the aesthetic language, historically specific intellectual formations, and cultural sensibilities.[17]

Interestingly, Gadamer too illustrates his point about the literary intention of the receiver by an example from drama. Without an act of representational mediation—by a complex function of an actor/director—the text cannot exist as drama: only when it is enacted is it

[15] It is interesting to compare the pictures of the act of interpretation in modern theories like Ricouer's and the Kashmiri one. Ricoeur's *Interpretation Theory* places the text, as in Gadamer, between the author and the reader:
author...........[_text_]..............reader
The Kashmiri theorists view the field of interpretation/signification as
author..........character..............actor/reciter..............reader/hearer/
spectator
See Ricoeur 1976.
[16] Gadamer 1981: pt II, 91ff.
[17] We are dealing with the narrowly aesthetic considerations of historicity, but Gadamer also advances much broader ontological arguments regarding obstacles to a perfect re-imagination of authorial meanings.

truly a play, not the printed text. The text, in other words, contains the *possibility* of meaning, but not, in a fundamentally literal sense, meaning itself. In another evocative example, we cannot have music until it begins to sound: a musical score is a text which contains the potential of musical meaning, but not meaning in the real sense. There is a direction in Gadamer's theory of textual meaning: it seeks to shift the emphasis in the analytics of interpretation from an excessively author-sided conception of texts into a more reader-sided one.

Although the earlier stratum of *rasa* theory was not author-sided in the same sense, the *dhvani* elaboration appears to move in the same direction as Gadamer's. It elaborates a theory which assigns a proper and specific function to each of these figures in the field of literary meaning. Each of these functions—the author's composition (A), the character's function as the 'vessel' of the emotion (B),[18] the actor's evocation(C),[19] and the spectator's/reader's reception/appreciation (D).[20] In the AB, in the long commentary on the *rasasutra* involving debates with Bhattalollata, Sankuka, and Bhattanayaka, theoretical attention is almost exclusively focused on relations between C and D, and secondarily on B and C. Particularly in some phases of the debates, for instance in Sankuka's argument that the spectator goes through a process of inference starting from a necessary false cognition,

---

[18] The term for actor *patra*—a vessel—captures this inflection perfectly.

[19] The *dhvani* tradition produces the most elaborate, intricate, and subtle analysis of the relation between the actor and the spectator, through its argument, developed particularly in Abhinavagupta, that true understanding must avoid the errors of *svagatatva* and *paragatatva*. Abhinavagupta 1992: 281–3. It also offers astonishing subtle reflections on even apparently mundane things like our understanding of the idea that Krsna was a beautiful person through the suggestive presence of a handsome actor. We must not believe that Rama was handsome literally like actor X, who is also handsome; we, in any case, have no means of knowing how handsome Krsna really was; we must submit ourselves to a free-floating conception of 'handsomeness' which is *generalised*. Abhinavagupta 1992: 281–3.

[20] Appreciation is probably a better translation, because although there is a trend towards *sadharanikarana* or universalization, the offer of the text is not indiscriminate; there is an opposite tendency at work when it specifies that appreciation can be achieved only by those who are *vimalapratibhanasali* receivers of art.

the entire philosophical enterprise is to understand the conditions of possibility of spectatorial rapture.[21] There can be two types of theories: theories of *communication*, which ask how the author communicates to the actor, and the actor to the spectator; or theories of *reception*, which ask how the spectator understands? What exactly does he see or feel? The NS, which constitutes the primary level of this theory, does not offer a theory of communication,[22] and therefore it would be wrong to suggest that here, as in the case of the tradition running from Schleiermacher to Gadamer, a heavily author-sided theory is slowly balanced by a reader-sided correction. Rather, the NS states the whole point with such self-defeating terseness that the issue, which is central to an understanding of the *rasa* process, is left deeply obscure. The subsequent process of the *dhvanikaras'* glossing produces a conception of the aesthetic field; but the distinctive form of its elaboration is from the side of the reader.

Two aspects of the theory appear remarkable: its specification of the series of relations of reception/communication in the aesthetic-textual field, and its close attention to the exact nature of the intentional acts performed by the different figures. It is not content by simply stating that these are intentional acts, or states. As intentional acts are directional (Searle),[23] the theory is trying to ascertain the exact direction, and the exact nature of the intentional act or state in each case, particularly B, C, and D.[24] The theory suggests that the idea

[21] Rapture, although awkward in other respects, is appropriate because the theory emphasizes the spectators' absorption (raptness) which the *Sahityadarpana* puts beautifully as '*vedyantara-sparsa-sunya*', untouched by any other perception. Visvanatha 2004: chs. 3, 2, 48.

[22] It is remarkable how little the *rasasutra* commits itself to: '*vibhava-anubhava-vyabhicari-samyogat rasa-nispattih*'—the sentence is interpretatively primitive.

[23] Searle 1970.

[24] Paradaoxically, the *Dhvanyaloka* discussion on the MB, after spending a great deal of effort to disentangle the intentional stances of A, B, and D, which opens up the possibility of developing a theory which protects us from using authorial intention as the final court of appeal, relapses into an argument which critically depends on authorial intent. By 'the miserable end of the Vrsnis and the Pandavas', they maintain, the author wishes to show us that the cognitive purpose of the epic is a cessation of desire.

of textual intention needs to be revised, and in fact there is a play of intentionalities, in the plural, on each text. There is an intentional node at each of these points. The fundamental structure of an aesthetic text is such that it allows the intervention of intentionalities at these vital points of the text coming into meaning—through the different kinds of intentionalities exercised by the author, the actor, musician, and the receiver. We are then saved from the need to appeal to the intention of the author in that narrow and absolute sense.

Another significant advantage of this revision is that this can accommodate the effects of history much more easily,[25] to deal with the ironic fate of all classic works—which float 'in the waters of time',[26] from their moorings in one age down to transient resting places in very different ages possessing radically different sensibilities. This leads to an 'historical' form of the 'death of the author'—the original context of meaning becomes so distant that the methodological demand for a reconstruction of authorial intention becomes practically meaningless. Frequent legends of divine authorship rhetorically endorse this sense that the author and the mundane world of his intentions are irrecoverable. The reader has to find a strategy to deal with a text without an author.

If we decide not to accept their exact move to attribute the *santa rasa* intention to the author, but to work with the textual field of complex intentionalities—in which the actor's intentionality plays upon the author's, and the receiver's upon the actor's, it becomes possible to maintain that there can be various readings of the text, which are all simultaneously on offer. In case of the MB, the two contenders for interpretative primacy would be a conventional *vira rasa* reading and a *santa rasa* one.

Reading a Narrative Structure: 'The Last of Life for which the First was Made'

To partially justify the *santa rasa* reading, we could use a modern technique: look at the narrative meaning of the epic's 'miserable end'.

---

[25] Again remarkably similar to Gadamer's ideas about effective historicity. Gadamer 1981: 305–41.

[26] The persistent Sanskrit metaphor of *kalasrotah*—the river of time.

Endings are particularly significant in a narrative structure, if we take the meaning of the term narrative in a strict sense. Arthur Danto argued in his *Narration and Knowledge* that there is a peculiar structure of temporal relations which define a 'narrative sentence'.[27] Two events which happened at different points in time but are linked by a peculiar relation are captured by a narrative sentence; but its *narrative* character, as opposed to other qualities, lies in the fact that *the later event governs the understanding of the earlier one*.[28] To state that the first prime minister of India was born in 1889 is to use a sentence with a narrative structure: because in 1889 the conditions for the existence of a prime minister were not there. A mere child was born to Motilal Nehru, who was of course, a successful barrister and leading figure of the Indian National Congress. Only after Independence in 1947 are the conditions for the existence of a prime minister of India in place. Statements about Nehru which seek some historical understanding of his life after 1947 must recognize this unavoidably significant fact. In a sense, the second event affects indelibly our understanding of the first one.

This can be easily generalized for historical and narrative series. A history of the Russian revolution written in the 1950s would be quite different from one written today: the events of that phase of Russian history have not changed, what has changed is the significance of those events by the emergent relation with new events like the fall of communism. Remarkably, this change is not due to an evaluative change in the observer, but to the occurrence of a subsequent set of events, which make it impossible to write the history of the earlier event without taking into account the latter ones. This is made evident in the autobiography, because in that form the writing of the text and the temporality of the last segment coincide. What happens in a narrative of fiction is identical to what happens in a real human life, and in autobiographic retelling: in a sense, narrative unfolding shows that it is for everybody, not Rabbi Ben Ezra alone, that it is the last of life for which the first was made: and we should trust the author, read all, not be afraid.[29]

---

[27] Danto 1985.
[28] Ibid.: ch. VIII.
[29] Browning's poem, 'Rabbi Ben Ezra', Stanza 1.

If we characterize this as the invariant structure of *narrative judgement*, we can see something similar occurring in the process of fictional unfolding. It is common knowledge that the meaning of a story is determined by not merely what happens inside the series of events constituting the story, but by how it ends. A story about a mutiny which ends at the moment of the mutineers' triumph is a story that tells a very different story from one that ends with their eventual defeat. In fact, the idea that literature/poetry is *niyatikrtaniyamarahita* and *ananyaparatantra* stresses precisely this truth. Literary narrative is *not conditional on* historical truth, it is *ananyaparatantra*. A literary sequence of events is not obliged to follow on an historical sequence: it is unconditional in two senses: it is not conditioned by any sequence of events because of its facticity; it is also not constrained to follow the syntax of natural things. Within the universe of aesthetics, the rebellion is successful, however much and however finally it might be defeated in the universe of history. This is the sense in which the language of the poet (*bharati kaverjayati*) triumphs over the language of the chronicler tied to the rules and conditions of historical happenings. By shifting the end of the story to a point chronologically before the defeat of a rebellion the poet can help the rebels win—*in a different universe.*

Following this view of a narrative statement, we could offer a similar argument about the narrative structure in a story. A narrative structure can exist in both factual and fictional accounts, connecting these two by their common narrativity, which consists in a movement over time in which events that happen later add significant consequents to the earlier processes and modify their character. The overall meaning of the existing earlier series is modified by a significant later event, because the earlier series then becomes a 'preparation' or a series leading to the last segment in the chain. What the meaning of the chain of events is, is determined by the nature of the last segment. This will also throw some light on a commonly observed but analytically neglected process. The narratives of the Ramayana and the MB of course exist in hundreds of versions, and one of the major differentiating features between these stories is precisely the matter of their ending segment. As a child, I read some versions of the MB and the Ramayana which end with the conclusion of the Kuruksetra battle and with Rama's coronation in Ayodhya. Often, dramatic enactments in the Ramlila use the same narrative device. It is inexact to view these recensions as a *shorter* form of the story; they are a *different* version. These do not stop the narrative series at a slightly earlier stage; by making a different segment the last one, they offer us a story with a different structure which then bears a seriously different meaning. In fact, fiction is teleological in a way that history is not.

Meanings of the Mahabharata

What is the meaning of the MB? Can we turn this question, given the two readings, into meaning*s* of the two MBs? Modern literary theory often claims that narratives in modern literary cultures entertain a more pronounced aspiration towards cognitive understanding of the world and the characters' place in it. Sanskrit aesthetic texts routinely assume that literary narratives contain a strong cognitive element: but they refine the exact tone of this cognitive function. Stories offer *upadesa* to their readers, but in the way of a *prabhu*, of a *suhrt* or of a *kanta*.[30] The *Dhvanyaloka* directly admits that the MB speaks to us in two styles: as *sastra* (as doctrine) and as *kavya* (as art). Literary cultures bear a close relation with interconnected cultures of religious and moral beliefs, but the MB has its own peculiar way of connecting these two spheres.

Ostensibly, the most effective way of teaching moral rules is to enunciate them clearly, and to offer arguments in favour. But such assertoric and argumentative presentation of ethical rules is not always effective, because by stating the rule blandly this teaching does not prepare us for the constant surprises of real moral life. For, in actual life the situations of ethical choice arise in complex, unpredictable, unrecognizable ways. To take an example from the MB, it is simple and easy to command the telling of truth; but this can work in case of a relatively simple choice between telling the truth and lying. The MB carefully constructs the tale of the hermit facing a band of robbers who ask him to tell the truth about a man they have pursued and who is hiding in his ashram.[31] Simple *sastric* (assertoric) command does

[30] See Mammata's *Kavyaprakasa*, Ist Ullasa, 2.

[31] Arjuna's demeanour of untroubled confidence in his unequal battle with the Kuru army during the *uttaragograha* (the capture of Virata's cattle from

not take into account the situational complexity in which pursuing a good act has to occur; the complementary function of narrative is to warn readers about it. The narrative does not merely add a diverting *example* of a rule that is already clear; rather, it adds an indispensable cognitive dimension to our knowledge of moral life by suggesting that although the rule in its assertoric form is clear, it is misleading in its contextual bareness. The MB teaches ethical rules by a combination of these two functions: of enunciating principles, as in the Santiparva, and of narrative complication.

To understand the sastric uptake of the MB, we should caution ourselves that we are dealing with a pre-modern culture which does not presuppose the typically modern enunciation of moral rules as universal injunctions. These are not rules meant for 'individuals' who are all alike, living in a shared ethical universe.[32] Characters live in a social world deeply segmented along *varna* lines. The story gives a narrative exposition of social ideals, particularly the norms of warrior courage, brahminic wisdom, and an aspect the epics never neglect— the corresponding virtues of women in these statuses. In elaborating both the norms and the attendant dangers of high status, the quite different feminine encounter with the world is elaborated with equal vividness: Sita and Draupadi are as indispensable to the narratives' putative norms as Rama or the Pandavas. The virtues of heroism and contemplation do not exist separately, they belong together in a social world in which these two groups are dominant: therefore the 'complete' story of their society must be *their* story.

The First Mahabharata and its Inadequacies

On the conventional view, if we accept there are eight *rasas*, it is hard to avoid a conclusion that the predominant *rasa* of the MB must be the *vira*, if a text of that size and complexity can be said to have a dominant *rasa* at all. The narrative illustrates the virtues required by

---

the northern side) at the end of the '*goharanaparvadhyaya*', in Virataparva, Mahabharata.

[32] See Bakhtin's argument that epic characters come from a social universe which are segmented between groups, but homogeneous within them. See Bakhtin 1990.

a social world of this character, especially three kinds of virtues—the intellectual ideals required by brahmanical life; the warrior ideals demanded by the truly Ksatriya life served in fearless service of a just order; and not least the life of a woman who has to pass through the uncertainties of such a life with undiminished dignity. They have to make their way in a world in which they do not take decisions, yet are most affected by them. According to this reading, the lives of the warriors are marked by uncertainties which are nonetheless faced with courage—dangers like facing a numerically larger army,[33] the unavoidable temptations of using unjust means.[34] The lives of the Pandavas show how true Ksatriyas can emerge out of such trials with honour. Even in this reading, the MB has much narrative complexity, but the global meaning of the expanse of narrative incidents consists in an eventual assurance that, although the proper order of the universe is sometimes seriously challenged, it is eventually restored: and Ksatriya glory lies in not pointless victories in mundane battles, but a great defining battle which has this restorative character. A conventional *vira rasa* reading would confirm a confidence in the unshakable 'truth' of this social order. The narrative is one that ends in triumph—not of the characters, the Pandavas, but of the principle (of *satyameva jayate*).[35]

The MB has, however, strangely disturbing episodes, too numerous to recount, which put these virtues and the order which they reinforce into radical questioning. Kunti's curiosity about her boon leads to the birth of her first, secret child, who is abandoned, but he is destined for glory and returns to trouble her peace and the lives of her other children. Or consider the little episode of the Vanaparva where the heroism of the four martially more accomplished brothers are mocked: they are brought back to life by a martially feeble, intellectual elder

[33] Arjuna's demeanour of untroubled confidence in his unequal battle with the Kuru army during the *uttaragograha* (the capture of Virata's cattle from the northern side) at the end of the 'goharanaparvadhyaya', in Virataparva, MB.

[34] A celebrated example is Yudhisthira's eventual agreement to use a partial lie in the death of Drona, his teacher. Dronaparva, MB.

[35] In various parts of the narrative this is indicated directly. For instance, when Yudhisthira asks for Drona's blessings before the commencement of the battle, Drona states 'yato Ksrna stato dharmah yato dharma stato jayah'. Bhismavadhaparvadhyaya, Bhismaparva, MB.

brother. Think of the beautiful description of Draupadi's delight at Arjuna's success,[36] and her dismay at Kunti's thoughtless order which determines the rest of her life. This is revealed right at the end when Yudhisthira explains to Bhima the reason for Draupadi's fall on the *mahaprasthana*.[37] Instead of confirming the central rules of the moral and social order, the story seems to take pleasure in constructing situations of transgression. There are of course the last incidents of their 'miserable end'—not just the end of the Vrsnis in a drunken catastrophe which Krsna was powerless to stop, but the strange inability of Arjuna, the victor of Kuruksetra, to lift his bow when attacked by common thieves while escorting Vrsni women to safety.[38] There are two ways of looking for the dark end of the narrative. One is to follow the explicit instruction from the *Dhvanyaloka* where the dark reminder of catastrophe is contained at the end, narratively governing the meaning of the whole preceding sequence. An alternative way is to be sensitive to the signals of imminent failure, of small disasters that accompany overt victories, of the recurrent signals of moral unmaking constantly shadowing the march of heroic events.

The Second Mahabharata

The addition of the ninth *rasa* makes it possible to register, reflect, and imaginatively expand on these signs embedded in the interstices, almost the underside, of the narrative structure. Read through the theory of the nine *rasas*, we get a second MB, fundamentally different from the first in its moral flavour, and perhaps its historical import. Commentaries are of two kinds: in some, meanings which are condensed or inexplicit are elaborated by expounding on the meanings of words, their syntactical connections, and their interpretative

---

[36] *Viddhantu laksyam prasamiksya krsna*
parthantu sakrapratimam niriksya
svabhyastarupapi naveva nityam
vinapi hasam hasativa kanya
madadretehpi skhalativa bhavair
baca-byaharativa drastya. Svayamvaraparvadhyaya, Adiparva MB 1.179.22

[37] Mahaprasthanikaparva, MB.

[38] Mausalaparva, MB.

connotation; but in this case the *Dhvanyaloka* makes a profound but exceptionally concise gesture towards the epic's meaning, without further elaboration. The task of the elaboration is left to the reader. The interpretative act leaves the reader free to follow its direction creatively. The 'miserable ending' is not a formula to think through, which absolves readers of the responsibility of reflection, but a trigger to think, an incitement to our own interpretative imagination.

In this reading, the MB is a text of the *santa rasa*, a tragic sense of the world,[39] which reveals the insubstantiality of every single component of the Brahman-Ksatriya social-ethical ideal. It shows the political order built around kingship as desperately fallible, starting from the impossibility of determination of the rights of succession. The rule of primogeniture seeks to provide a clear, unquestionable line of royal succession. But the story leads us to a situation where both sides of a clan can lay claim to rightful kingship, and can have a complaint that they lost it by an unjust turn of fate.[40] It shows the futility of valour which rarely achieves justice, particularly because sometimes the most important injustices happen not on the battlefield but inside the secure and ordered space of the court. The greatest iniquity of the MB occurs not in the blind and desperate moments of battles but in the public space of the court.

This space marked for the announcement and enforcement of justice is turned into the space for the gravest iniquity. Renowned warriors allow themselves to become parts the most inhuman degradation of a woman. In its totality, the story shows that justice is rarely achieved in the mundane world. Beauty is only rewarded by lust, vulnerability, and indignity. From the moment she enters the

[39] The use of the term tragic is both helpful and misleading: that is the closest term of technical aesthetics by which we can partly elucidate what the *santa* means; but it is, in the strict sense, quite different from the tragic sense. It is a form of tranquillity that is achieved after going through the experience of suffering, when its intensity is stilled and the immediate suffering is distanced. In Tagore's poem, Karna describes the end of the war in similar terms: *heritechhi santimay sunya parinam* (I can see the end—empty, and tranquil), and he asks Kunti: *'je pakser parajay, se paksa tyajite more koro na ahvan'* (Do not ask me to leave the side of those destined for defeat). Tagore 1972: 403.

[40] Dhrtarastra was blind, but should this disability cause the royal line of pass to Pandu's lineage, or is it a disability which is personal and should not affect his line?

world, Draupadi is an object of desire and contention.[41] Detachment is often indistinguishable from moral failure. There can be endless dispute on whether Bhishma and Drona were at that fateful moment detached or simply morally feeble. Revenge is peculiarly unsatisfying: because though at the end of the battle the Pandavas have extracted revenge, it is a catastrophe for the winners as much as for the losers. In the night of the *tarpana*, when dead warriors are reunited with their loved ones for a few hours of revival, they join in an indistinguishably common mourning.[42]

Other signs in the text are equally profound and intriguing. If we accept that the *sastric* element is very significant in the MB, the manner in which this is delivered is astonishingly unusual. The great philosophical peroration in the text is delivered not by a Brahman whose socially designated function is contemplation, but by a warrior. Krishna is, however, a warrior who has given up war, and decided through a subterfuge of common kinship not to fight at Kuruksetra. Is there an 'event' in this apparent anomaly? Should we read this narrative fact? At the end one might wonder if this story points to any *sukha* at all, even *trsna-ksay-asukha*, which, according to this theory, only the *vimalapartibhanasali* readers will be able to grasp. If the purpose of the text is to produce moral knowledge—not in the sense of teaching individual moral principles, but showing what leading a moral life involves—then the darker version of the story throws a clearer light upon the world. It does not show us how to lead a moral life; it suggests, rather, that to lead a moral life is something that cannot be shown. The goodness of acts has to be invented at every significant step: and individuals should live in humility at the contingency, fallibility, and imperfection of their effort at being good.

Aesthetic and Social Ideals

Other questions, of radically non-aesthetic kinds, could be raised about the two readings of the epic. It is fascinating to ask how this

[41] It is doubtful if any modern narrative can rival the MB in its demonstration of the terrible effects of regarding women as objects of desire, and as tokens of the indirect exchanges of male malevolence.
[42] Putradarsanaparvadhyaya, Asramavasikaparva, MB. It is interesting to reflect on the nature of this narrative element. It is for the men to destroy, and for women to try to heal, for men to kill, and for the women to mourn.

aesthetic reflection might be related to the moral universe of this
historical epoch.[43] Where did this suggestion of adding the *santa* to
the existing *rasa* register come from? As noticed earlier, V. Raghavan
suggests, intriguingly, that the idea of the *santa* did not come an
internal elaboration of conventional brahminical religious thought,
but is an original invention of the Buddhist tradition.[44] Buddhist
philosophical reflection is much concerned with the meaning of
tranquillity in conduct, and the *santa* is the predominant *rasa* of
the Buddhist play *Naganada*.[45] Kashmiri Saiva philosophers were
engaged in a fierce doctrinal battle against the Buddhists and played
a significant role in the eventual decline in Buddhist religious
influence. Despite this overt doctrinal conflict, on Raghavan's view
Abhinavagupta acted in a manner not uncommon in great philosophic
debates: one side absorbs what it considers the most valuable, and
therefore the less controvertible, elements from the adversarial theory.
This strengthens the theory which can effect this subsumption; and
it also ensures, for the surrounding intellectual culture, that, despite
the decline of a school, the valuable elements of its thinking are
never lost.[46] Saiva thinking, while refuting Buddhist arguments,
enriched its aesthetic thought by incorporating the most valuable
contribution of the Buddhists, probably by converting a philosophical

[43] For a magisterial survey of the history of Sanskrit literature, see Pollock
2006, and the central question of the work is the connection between culture
and power.

[44] Raghavan 1967. 'Udbhata recognizes the santa as can be seen from his
Kavyalamkarasarasamgraha. He is thus the first commentator on the NS and
the first alankarika now known to have definitely begun to speak of Rasas as
nine in number. He may therefore have made the necessary alteration in the
text of the NS as shown above and pointed out by Abhinavagupta.' (p. 13).
The revised text is:

srngarahasyakarunah raudravirabhayanakah
vibhastadbhutasantasca nava natye rasah smrtah (p.13).

[45] Sri Harsa 1992.

[46] It is possible to find examples of this kind from contemporary social and
political theory. Rawls's theory of liberalism could be viewed as one which
subsumes elements from socialist thought—like its concern for justice and
egalitarianism—to construct a version of liberalism that is much harder to
argue against.

thesis into an aesthetic theory. Historians have noted that Kashmir in Abhinavagupta's time seems to be going through serious social and ideological transformation.[47] Buddhism, after all, presented the most fundamental challenge to the moral ideal of classical brahminical society. It is always problematic to connect the changes in aesthetic thinking with contextual social change too directly. But it is an interesting, if speculative, question to ask: does the revision of aesthetic theory and the resultant re-reading of the *rasa* of the epic text bear any relation to a transformation of intellectual culture in response to a fundamental social crisis?

Alexis Sanderson has suggested that Saivas were elaborating a new model of religiosity that 'tried to transcend the disjunctions and oppositions of the brahmanical social order' by finding through their doctrine of *pratyabhijna* a wider base for Hindu religious life.[48] In the absence of more accurate sociological knowledge, it is possible only to speculate about what the social and historical roots of such momentous revisions were in patterns of intellectual life. But the aesthetic revision is undeniable. Kashmiri theorists deserve our eternal gratitude for their amazing gift to all future readers—without changing a single word of the text, they managed to give us a second Mahabharata.

References

Abhinavagupta. 1956. *Abhinavabharati*, in M. Ramakrishna Kavi, ed., *Natyasastra of Bharatamuni with the Commentary Abhinavabharati of Abhinavaguptacarya*, Gaekwad Oriental Series, No. 36 [NS]. Baroda: Sadhana Press.

Althusser, Louis. 1970. *For Marx*. London: Allen Lane, Penguin.

Anandavardhana. 1990. *Dhvanyaloka*. Cambridge, Mass.: Harvard University Press.

Bakhtin, Mikhail. 1990. Epic and Novel. In Mikhail Bakhtin, *The Dialogic Imagination*. Austin: The University of Texas Press.

Danto, Arthur. 1985. *Narration and Knowledge*. New York: Columbia University Press.

Gadamer, H.G. 1981. *Truth and Method*. London: Sheed and Ward.

Kavyaprakasa of Mammata. 1965. Ed. Vamanacharya Jhalkikar, 7th edition. Poona: Bhandarkar Oriental Research Institute.

[47] Pollock 2006.
[48] Sanderson 2006: 5.

Mahabharata. 1927–66. Ed. V.S. Sukhthankar, *et al.* Poona: Bhandarkar Oriental Institute.

Pollock, Sheldon. 2006. *The Language of the Gods in the World of Men.* Berkeley: The University of California Press.

Raghavan, V. 1967. *The Number of Rasas.* Madras: Adyar Research Centre and Library.

Ricoeur, Paul. 1976. *Interpretation Theory.* Fort Worth: Texas Christian University Press.

Sanderson, Alexis. 2006 *Saivism and Brahamanism in the Early Medieval Period.* Gonda Lectures. Amsterdam: The Royal Netherlands Academy of Arts and Sciences.

Searle, John. 1970. *Speech Acts.* Cambridge: Cambridge University Press.

Sri Harsa. 1992. *Naganada.* Delhi: Motilal Banarasidass.

Tagore, Rabindranath. 1972. Karna-kunti-samvad. In *Katha o Kahini. Sancayita.* Kolkata: Visvabharati.

Tubb, Gary. 1985. The Santarasa in the Mahabharata. In Arvind Sharma, ed., *Essays on the Mahabharata. Journal of South Asian Literature.* Winter-Spring.

Visvanatha. 2004. *Sahityadarpana.* Delhi: Motilal Banarasidass.

Index

past as history, 45
saundarya, 273
self-transformation of structures, 3
moral
autonomy of individuals, 37
life, 6, 26–7, 37, 303–4, 307, 332, 336, 350–1, 355
Mother India (Bharatmata), 146, 149n27
Muchiram Guder Jibancharit, 266
Müller, Max, 219
Mukhopadhyay, Bhudev, 50, 73, 92n61, 184, 212n24, 281n4, 315–17, 330
Mukhopadhyay, Subhas, 104
Muslims, 44, 75, 86, 136, 138, 140

Nabadwip, 252
Nandy, Ashis, 154
narrative(s)
celebration of ordinary, 31
of modern novels, 32
reading, 347–50
temporality, 135
nationalism, Indian, 11, 13–14, 118, 156
natural science, 199–200
nature, 142–5
Natyasastra (NS), 228–9, 255, 339–40, 346, 356n44
Navyanyaya, 252
Nehru, Jawaharlal, 141, 155, 252, 254, 265, 306n3, 348
Nehru, Motilal, 348
nonsense, 97, 147, 226, 234, 237, 241–4. See also *Aboltabol*
novels, 5–6, 29, 34, 36
of Bankim, 171–2

formal peculiarities of, 273
of Tagore, 34

Olson, Mancur, 121n2
ordinariness, 29–30, 36, 173–5, 183–5
celebration of moral, 30
meaning of, 29
orientalist knowledge, 13, 14–15

padavali kirtan, 99
palakirtans, 66, 253
Palasir Yuddha, 283n6
Pali language, 54
pancalis, poets and composers of, 74
Paradise Lost, 79, 224n15
Paricay, 101–2
Parishesh, 203, 207
Parisodh/Shyama (Repayment), 175–8
Parivarik Prabandha, 281n4, 315
Parker, Theodore, 320
Parry, Jonathan, 324
Parvati, 165–6, 170, 174
patriotism, 119, 123–4, 137–8, 140, 148, 151
Bankim and, 145
of disenchantment, 154–7
political
correctness, 12–15
nationalism, 146, 149
study of history, 15–17
theory, 2, 12
Pollock, Sheldon, 5, 9, 47, 81n48, 288n11
post-colonial theory, 20–1
prakrti, 142
Prasannamayi, 310, 318–19, 326–9
pratyabhijna doctrine, 336, 357
prem, 161–4, 167, 176–7, 181